HAMAS

HAMAS

politics, charity, and terrorism
in the service of jihad

matthew levitt

foreword by ambassador dennis ross,

u.s. envoy to the middle east, 1988–2000

yale university press / new haven and london

Published in cooperation with the Washington Institute for Near East Policy

Set in Minion and Franklin Gothic by Integrated Publishing Solutions.
Printed in the United States of America by R.R. Donnelley, Harrisonburg, Virginia.

Library of Congress Cataloging-in-Publication Data

Levitt, Matthew, 1970–
    Hamas : politics, charity, and terrorism in the service of jihad / Matthew Levitt;
foreword by Dennis Ross.
        p.   cm.
    Includes bibliographical references and index.
    ISBN-13: 978-0-300-11053-1 (alk. paper)
    ISBN-10: 0-300-11053-7 (alk. paper)
    1. Ḥarakat al-Muqāwamah al-Islāmīyah.   2. Daʻwah (Islam)   3. Suicide
bombings—Israel.   I. Title
JQ1830.A98H3756   2006
956.95'3044—dc22   2006004381

A catalogue record for this book is available from the British Library.

The paper in this book meets the guidelines for permanence and durability of the
Committee on Production Guidelines for Book Longevity of the Council on Library
Resources.

10   9   8   7   6   5   4   3   2   1

In honor of all victims of terrorism

Dedicated to Dina, my guiding light

CONTENTS

FOREWORD

Ambassador Dennis Ross
U.S. Envoy to the Middle East, 1988–2000

Who is Hamas? Where did they come from? How do they fund their activities? Why do they seem to have roots in Palestinian society? Can they accept anything but struggle and conflict with Israel? And, will they ever lash out at the United States or will they always restrict their terror to Israel?

Matthew Levitt addresses these and other questions in his very timely book on the Hamas. In Arabic, Hamas is an abbreviation for the Islamic Resistance Movement. The word literally means "zeal," and that certainly describes those who have led this group.

As an organization, Hamas is much talked about, but poorly understood. Given its stunning victory in the Palestinian Legislative Council elections in early 2006, Hamas is no longer a fringe player in the Palestinian political scene. While the champion of suicide bombing against Israelis, Hamas has developed an appeal among Palestinians for several reasons: It is not corrupt in the sea of corruption that has so characterized the Palestinian Authority. It provides services—clinics, after-school programs, food distribution centers—that the Palestinian Authority fails to offer. It has demonstrated that it can hurt Israelis when, in the eyes of Palestinians, the Israelis have been hurting them.

Notwithstanding the reasons for Hamas having a following among Palestinians, its popularity throughout the 1990s never exceeded 30 percent of the Palestinian population. And even that figure greatly exaggerated its standing for most of the period when Palestinians were more hopeful about the future. Support for Hamas has grown out of frustration and anger and the ability of the organization to fill a vacuum of leadership.

If there is a secular alternative that is credible, most Palestinians would support it, particularly because Palestinian society remains far more secular than religiously devout. If there was hope and belief again in the possibility of peace, Hamas would again be reduced in terms of its political potential. In reality, most Palestinians would like to have a normal life, and, as long as Hamas is defined by its commitment to confrontation with Israel, Hamas will not be able to deliver what most Palestinians seek. For that, Hamas would have to change its credo and objectives.

This book spells out in persuasive detail why Hamas is unlikely to undergo such a transformation. Dr. Levitt shows that Hamas emerged from the Muslim Brotherhood, founded in Egypt. He outlines the connection and, indeed, dependency of Hamas on the *dawa*, the social support structure and services of the organization. He demonstrates clearly that there is no separation between the so-called political and military wings of Hamas—both being tied together in an organic whole, with the political wing providing the guidance and the religious justification for the suicidal attacks against Israelis in buses, restaurants, and shops.

Dr. Levitt also exposes the use of charities to fund Hamas. While some of the funds from charities certainly have gone to finance the services of the dawa, they have also gone to support terror attacks. And, of course, even the services are shaped to recruit and socialize new suicide bombers.

Finally, this book reveals the extent to which Hamas uses funding from foreign sources to pursue its aims. Support has come from fronts in the United States, Europe, and Saudi Arabia and the Gulf states.

This book would be of great value if it only provided this explanation of Hamas, its roots, its character, its funding, and its operations. But it does more, spelling out how the Palestinian Authority should have competed with Hamas by replacing the dawa and by providing the critical social services in its place.

Ultimately, it has been the corruption of the Palestinian Authority, the failures within Palestinian society, and the loss of hope that have fueled Hamas and its purposes. To be sure, Hamas is not passive in this regard. It has consistently carried out acts of terror whenever there has been even a hint of progress toward peace—not only because it does not believe in it, but also because it is unlikely to be able to survive in circumstances where peace, prosperity, and a sense of possibility characterize the Palestinian reality and its future.

With Hamas having now catapulted itself into a position of potential power, the prospects for peace between Israelis and Palestinians have never been lower. Nonetheless, Hamas for its own reasons may seek a continuing period of calm with Israel. Hamas in power needs to deliver reform and change—the banner it ran under—and that gives it a strong reason to avoid confrontation for the time being. After all, it can hardly remake Palestinian society, end corruption, lawlessness, and chaos on the one hand and produce economic renewal on the other if it is at war with Israel. Hamas is bound to seek help from the international community to produce societal renewal even while it resists all efforts to get it to give up its principles of rejection of Israel and promotion of violence. The international community should neither let it off the hook nor allow it to escape the dilemmas of actually having to govern. Hamas must be put in a position of having to choose: govern successfully by transforming itself or fail and be discredited.

Will it transform itself? Unlikely, but if one wants to understand what makes Hamas and its leaders tick and what may be the best ways to exert leverage on it, a good place to start is with Matthew Levitt's book. Policy makers would be well advised to shape their strategy with his prescriptions in mind.

introduction: hamas' muddied waters

How does Hamas, a militant Islamist group in a relatively secular society fatigued by conflict, attract and retain its base of operatives and supporters? How does it radicalize, recruit, and dispatch Palestinian suicide bombers and still woo Palestinian voters to vote it into power as the ruling political party? While it may be the case that Hamas' victory in Palestinian parliamentary elections in January 2006 was in large part a protest vote against the septuagenarian kleptocrats of Yasser Arafat's Fatah party, the vote undeniably demonstrated that under the right conditions a majority of Palestinians was willing to accept and support Hamas. But is this support a result of the group's bold suicide bombings targeting Israelis, of its campaign to Islamize Palestinian society, of its reputation for honesty in a sea of political corruption, of its grassroots social activism, or of some or all of the above? How are the political, charitable, and terrorist activities of Hamas to be understood and reconciled? Are these disparate activities carried out by separate and unconnected wings of a larger movement, or is Hamas a unitary organization that sees good works and murder as equally legitimate means to achieve its non-negotiable ends?

Hamas leaders, for their part, are keen to stress that Hamas is "one body." The day before Hamas' electoral victory, Hamas leader Mahmoud al-Zahar vowed that the group's military wing would never be disbanded. Miriam Farhat, a Hamas candidate who won a seat in the Palestinian Legislative Council, stressed that the group's participation in politics would not moderate its stance on continued terror attacks: "Those who say we have changed our methods, we will never change." Farhat entered the electoral race with a measure of name recognition as the mother who appeared on

1

her son's martyrdom video blessing his decision to participate in a Hamas suicide attack. Indeed, Hamas relies on its political and social activists and organizations to build grassroots support for the movement, to spot and recruit future operatives, to provide day jobs and cover to current operatives, and to serve as the logistical and financial support network for the group's terror cells. Often the Hamas operatives running the group's political and charitable offices are closely tied to the group's terror cells, or are themselves current or former terror-cell members. Muddying the waters between its political activism, good works, and terrorist attacks, Hamas is able to use its overt political and charitable organizations as a financial and logistical support network for its terrorist operations.[1]

Some of the ways these institutions support Hamas terrorism are by glorifying acts of violence, Islamizing Palestinian society, and providing a social welfare safety net for Hamas activists and their families. As an Arab commentator noted in the online edition of the Egyptian weekly *al-Ahram*, "In Palestine, when young men and women who carry out suicide attacks are known to the entire public [sic]. Their pictures adorn homes, their stories are told, and their families get financial help." In the Palestinian context, the commentator continued, "a young man or woman undergoes a process of psychological preparation, a process captured on film which [is] later released to the public. The bomber is promised paradise in the afterlife and glory in this one. Only God knows what goes on in paradise, but in the life the bomber's achievement is recorded and glorified." The financial assistance provided to martyrs' families also comes through Hamas *dawa* organizations under the banner of humanitarian aid.[2]

Little attention, however, is paid to the support Hamas terrorists receive through a network of political leaders and charitable organizations one, two, or several steps removed from terrorist attacks and operating under the guise of legitimate political, humanitarian, social, and communal activities. Understandably, analysts and pundits commenting on Hamas focus either on the group's surprise electoral victory in January 2006 or on its indiscriminate suicide bombings and other attacks. But what these commentators miss by overlooking this network of political and charitable support is the how and why behind Hamas' dramatic electoral and operational success.

THE MYTH OF DISPARATE WINGS

As a result of the heightened focus on exposing terrorist networks in the post-9/11 global environment, investigators have revealed how terrorist groups systematically conceal their activities behind charitable, social, and political fronts. Indeed, many of these fronts have seen their officials arrested, their assets seized, and their offices shut down by authorities. Still, Hamas benefits from an ostensible distinction drawn by some analysts between its "military" and "political" or "social" wings. Analysts who make such a distinction regularly dwell on the good works of Hamas, rarely looking at the connections between these activities and the attacks on civilians and the suicide bombings that are the organization's trademark. Because of the notion that Hamas has independent "wings," its political and charitable fronts are allowed to operate openly in many Western and Middle Eastern capitals. In these cities, Islamic social welfare groups tied to Hamas are often tolerated when their logistical and financial support for Hamas is conducted under the rubric of charitable or humanitarian assistance.

While convenient for Hamas and its supporters, this distinction is contradicted by the consistent if scattered findings of investigators, journalists, and analysts. A review of the evidence regarding the integration of Hamas' political activism, social services, and terrorism demonstrates the centrality of the group's overt activities to the organization's ability to recruit, indoctrinate, train, fund, and dispatch suicide bombers to attack civilian targets.

The social welfare organizations of Hamas answer to the same political leaders who play hands-on roles in Hamas terrorist attacks. In some cases, the mere existence of these institutions is invoked to classify Hamas as a social welfare rather than a terrorist organization. To debunk these specious assumptions, it is necessary to fully expose what Hamas calls the dawa (its social welfare and proselytization network). This is sometimes difficult because, as one U.S. official explained, "Hamas is loosely structured, with some elements working clandestinely and others working openly through mosques and social service institutions to recruit members, raise money, organize activities, and distribute propaganda."[3]

Nevertheless, there is ample evidence of the role Hamas social institutions and political leaders play in the terror activities directed and authorized by Hamas leaders and commanders. Consider, for example, the case of the Hamas suicide bombing at the Park Hotel in Netanya on Passover Eve, March 27, 2002.[4]

ANATOMY OF A SUICIDE BOMBING

Holocaust survivor Clara Rosenberger wanted to feel safe after a shooting attack in Netanya a few weeks earlier, so she decided to celebrate the Passover Seder in a communal setting at the Park Hotel. It was a decision she and 154 other wounded victims would live to regret; 29 less fortunate victims died when Hamas suicide bomber Abdel Aziz Basset Odeh, disguised as a woman to hide the explosives-laden vest strapped to his torso, entered the hotel dining hall and detonated the bomb sewn into his clothes in the midst of some 250—mostly elderly—people.[5]

The attack, perpetrated on a major Jewish holiday and targeting elderly civilians, was the most devastating one since the outbreak of the Intifada in September 2000. Despite early setbacks like the capture or killing of two bomb makers and the loss of one of two planned suicide bombers to the common cold, the Nablus-Tulkarm cell responsible for the attack successfully executed the most severe in a string of suicide bombings. Coming on the heels of this surge in Palestinian suicide bombings, the Park Hotel attack led to the reinvasion of much of the West Bank by Israeli forces in Operation Defensive Shield in March and April 2002. At the time of the attack Arab leaders were meeting in Beirut at an Arab League summit where Saudi officials proposed that Arab states agree to recognize Israel and establish normal relations in the event of a just two-state solution to the Israeli-Palestinian conflict. Hamas leader Sheikh Ahmed Yassin told Palestinian television that the attack was a message rejecting the Arab League proposal, adding, "the Palestinians will not surrender."[6]

Beyond its timing and deadly effect, the attack also stands out as a paradigmatic example of how Hamas political and social activists play hands-on roles in the group's terror attacks. The mastermind of the attack, Abbas al-Sayyid, served simultaneously as both the overt political Hamas leader in Tulkarm and the covert head of the Qassam Brigades terrorist cell there. Wearing these two hats, al-Sayyid gave public speeches and represented Hamas at public functions even as he secretly recruited military operatives and suicide bombers, received orders and funds from Hamas leaders in Lebanon and Syria, and personally planned and oversaw the cell's operations. Al-Sayyid openly acknowledged his contacts with Hamas leaders abroad, but maintained these were purely political in nature. In fact, al-Sayyid took active measures to hide the military nature of these contacts. For example, while funds for Hamas political activity—$10,000—$13,000 a month—were overtly transferred from Hamas leaders abroad into al-Sayyid's personal bank account, Hamas leaders in Syria transferred funds for Hamas terrorist operations to an account al-Sayyid opened under a fictitious American-sounding name.[7] At the operational level, almost all the Hamas terrorists involved in the attack rose through the ranks of Hamas through the group's Islamic Bloc student movement. Al-Sayyid himself began drifting toward Hamas while in high school after hearing the lectures of

Sheikh Jamal Mansour, a prominent Hamas political and dawa leader. Three of the operatives, including both intended suicide bombers, were members of a singing troupe called al-Ansar that lauded Hamas and its suicide bombers. Hamas dawa activists and institutions performed a variety of key functions like helping fugitive cell members hide from authorities. In one case female Hamas activists helped a cell member move around Tulkarm disguised as a woman. Covert operatives also used mosques tied to Hamas as meeting places and as dead-drops where messages and matériel—including the suicide bombing vests—were left and retrieved by parties unknown to one another. Long after the attack, the Hamas dawa would use the Park Hotel bombing as a means to radicalize and recruit future operatives by printing posters glorifying the attack and naming community events like a soccer tournament after Abdel Aziz Basset Odeh, the suicide bomber.[8]

MUDDYING THE WATERS

Inside the Palestinian territories, the battery of mosques, schools, orphanages, summer camps, and sports leagues sponsored by Hamas are integral parts of an overarching apparatus of terror. These Hamas entities engage in incitement and radicalize society, and undertake recruitment efforts to socialize even the youngest children to aspire to die as martyrs. They provide logistical and operational support for weapons smuggling, reconnaissance, and suicide bombings. They provide day jobs for field commanders and shelter fugitive operatives.

So why did Hamas surprise everyone, including itself, when it won 44.5 percent of the vote and became the majority party in the election of January 2006? Because Hamas also provides desperately needed social services to needy Palestinians and—until Hamas' stunning electoral victory—served as a de facto Islamist opposition to the secular Palestinian Authority (PA).[9]

It is a painful reality that Palestinians living in the West Bank and Gaza have endured a deplorably low standard of living for years. Palestinians suffer not only from living under occupation, but from the neglect of a corrupt Palestinian leadership as well. As a result, the economic, social, and health conditions in the West Bank and Gaza Strip are truly miserable, leaving a void that groups like Hamas are all too eager to fill.

Palestinians suffer from extensive economic hardship. The West Bank and Gaza economies are in crisis, as evidenced by an unemployment rate as high as 33.5 percent in 2003. With a struggling economy and limited employment opportunities, it is not surprising that by 2004 approximately three-fourths of the Palestinian population living in the West Bank and Gaza survived below the poverty line of $2 per day. Health conditions in the West Bank, and especially Gaza, are very poor. As of 2003, 30 percent of Palestinian children under age five suffered from chronic malnutrition and 21 percent from acute malnutrition. In 2001, Palestinian Ministry of Health officials estimated that the infant mortality rate in Gaza was at 40 deaths per 1,000 live births.[10]

Clearly, the vast majority of Palestinians are in desperate need of assistance, ranging from unemployment compensation to food, childcare, and access to proper medical care. Both the Israeli government and Palestinian leadership have consistently failed to provide these essential services to the Palestinian community. The situation is further complicated by Hamas' efforts to capitalize on this humanitarian crisis to further its own agenda.

Hamas has successfully blurred the lines between political and charitable activities and terrorism in large part because many governments, experts, and academics continue to subscribe to the shallow argument that terrorist groups maintain distinct social, political, and militant wings. In fact, Hamas political leaders are intimately involved in the group's terrorist activities, as are the group's charities and social welfare organizations. Hamas uses the mosques and hospitals it maintains as meeting places; buries caches of arms and explosives under its own kindergarten playgrounds; uses social-welfare operatives' cars and homes to ferry and hide fugitives; and transfers and launders funds for terrorist activity through local charity committees.

The Hamas dawa serves several distinct functions in support of the group's objectives and through which it facilitates Hamas attacks. In many cases, dawa operatives and organizations fund and participate in Hamas attacks. Far more frequently, however, the dawa functions as Hamas' logistical support network and provides day jobs to Hamas leaders and operatives. Hamas dawa charities and social organizations radicalize Palestinian society, and their activities are targeted to building grassroots support for Hamas at the expense of more moderate Palestinian groups.

Hamas political offices, dawa organizations, and Qassam Brigades terror cells are funded through a combination of means. These include charitable giving, via both genuine Islamist charities and Hamas organizations fronting as legitimate charities, by states like Iran and Saudi Arabia, by individual wealthy donors, through front companies and criminal enterprises, and in cooperative relationships with other terrorist groups. Shutting off the flow of funds from such sources to Hamas is absolutely critical, but must be accompanied by an international humanitarian aid effort—one with strict oversight components at both the donor and recipient ends of the aid spectrum—to fill the gap in desperately needed social services that shutting Hamas fronts would create. The international support necessary to crack down on Hamas, however, can be achieved only when governments, experts, and academics develop a fuller understanding of the role the Hamas dawa plays in the group's suicide and other terror attacks.

Moreover, while Hamas is not an al-Qaeda affiliate, the repercussions of Hamas terror echo far beyond the borders of the West Bank and Gaza. Not only does Hamas threaten peace and regional security in the Middle East, but by fanning the flames of the Israeli-Palestinian conflict and laboring to undermine peace initiatives, the group directly contributes to the rabid anti-Americanism spreading throughout the region. To counter such a multilayered threat, one must first expose the veil of legitimacy behind which it hides. This book is the first open-source effort to do just that, and employs evidence that is qualitatively and quantitatively unmatched on the subject. It details the intimate ties between the political, social, and military "wings" of Hamas, catalogues the means by which Hamas political leaders and dawa organizations support Hamas terror, and offers concrete and detailed examples of such support. To do so as comprehensively as possible, and to offer the most concrete examples, the study makes use of previously undisclosed intelligence material, including declassified reports from the Central Intelligence Agency (CIA), Federal Bureau of Investigation (FBI), Department of Homeland Security (DHS), Canadian Secret Intelligence Service (CSIS), Israel Security Agency (ISA, or Shin Bet), Israel police, and more. These sources are supplemented by open-source material, including U.S. government affidavits and other court documents, seized Palestinian intelligence documents, congressional testimonies, official press releases, government and academic studies, press reports, and extensive personal interviews in Israel, the West Bank and Gaza, Jordan, Europe, and the United States. The book was in the final stages of completion when the elections of 2006 occurred, and minor revisions have been made to reflect the outcome for the sake of clarification.

1

origins of the hamas dawa

A BRIEF HISTORY OF HAMAS

Hamas, both an acronym for *Harakat al-Muqawama al-Islamiya* (Islamic Resistance Movement) and an Arabic word meaning "zeal," is a Palestinian Islamist group that emerged in 1987 as an outgrowth of the Palestinian branch of the Egypt-based Muslim Brotherhood. Hamas was founded in December of that year with the goal of eliminating the State of Israel and establishing in its place an Islamist state in all of what was once British Mandatory Palestine—a territory that today comprises Israel, the West Bank, and the Gaza Strip. Hamas employs a three-pronged strategy to achieve this goal: (1) social welfare activity that builds grassroots support for the organization, (2) political activity that competes with the secular Palestine Liberation Organization (PLO) and the Palestinian Authority (PA), and (3) guerilla and terrorist attacks that target Israeli soldiers and civilians. Hamas also seeks to counter what it perceives as the secularization and westernization of Arab society, and to become internationally recognized as the sole representative of the Palestinian people, a distinction held by the PLO since the 1974 Arab League conference in Rabat, Morocco. Hamas' slogan, as declared in Article 8 of the group's charter, reflects the centrality of violent *jihad*—religiously sanctioned resistance against perceived enemies of Islam—to these strategies: "Allah is its target, the Prophet is its model, the Koran its constitution: Jihad is its path and death for the sake of Allah is the loftiest of its wishes."[1]

The term *jihad* literally translates as "struggle," and has two meanings—only one of which is violent. The non-violent meaning of jihad refers to the personal struggle for virtue and morality, the striving to follow God's will. According to John Esposito, a leading scholar on Islam, jihad can also refer to "fighting injustice and oppression, spreading and defending Islam, and creating a just society through preaching, teaching, and, if necessary, armed struggle or holy war." The two broad meanings of jihad, non-violent and violent, are exemplified in a well-known Prophetic tradition: after returning from a military expedition, the Prophet Mohammad said, "We have returned from the lesser jihad (*jihad al-asghar*) to the greater jihad (*jihad al-akbar*)." When asked, "O, Messenger of Allah, what is the greater jihad?" Mohammad answered, "It is the jihad against one's soul." In the context of Hamas' calls for suicide bombings and other terrorist attacks, the term *jihad* clearly refers to the violent struggle against perceived enemies of Islam.[2]

While the immediate goal of replacing Israel with an Islamist Palestinian state is Hamas' overarching priority, the group also sees itself as leading a broader, pan-Islamist international movement. "Hamas is not a local organization," explains Khaled Mishal, the head of the Hamas political bureau, "but the spearhead of a national project, which has Arab, Islamic and international ambitions as well." It is for this reason, Mishal says, that the group "must attain positions of control by 'legal' means, which will grant it political legitimacy." But even as it participates in the Palestinian political system, insists Dr. Osama al-Mahmoudi, a Hamas ideologue, "the Palestinian people have a right to have the opposition [i.e., Hamas] fulfill its role in defending them, politically, socially, financially and in terms of security, as it did in the conflict with the Zionist enemy." In other words, Hamas sees simultaneous participation in civil politics and acts of violence against civilians as complementary, not mutually exclusive, concepts.[3]

Hamas is composed of three interrelated wings. The social welfare and political wings are the public faces of the group's social, administrative, political, and propaganda activities. The military wing is principally engaged in covert activities such as executing suspected collaborators, surveilling potential targets, procuring weapons, and carrying out guerilla and terrorist attacks. Overseeing all Hamas activities is a *Majlis al-Shura,* or consultative council, which is the group's overarching political and decision-making body in Damascus. Under this Shura council are committees responsible for supervising a wide array of activities, from media relations to military operations. At the grassroots level in the West Bank and Gaza sit corresponding local Hamas committees that answer to the Shura council and its committees and carry out the decisions on the ground. According to Sheikh

Hassan Yusef, a Hamas founder and senior political leader in the West Bank, the Shura council "includes representatives from the movement's four centers—the Gaza Strip, the West Bank, abroad and representatives of the 300 Hamas members in Israeli jails." Though it was founded as an underground movement, Hamas' public wings—its political and social branches—were for many years able to operate openly in Gaza under license from Israeli authorities. From the start, however, the military wing was divided into regional networks and local cells which communicated covertly through coded messages passed through internal communications channels, especially couriers.[4]

The so-called external leadership of Hamas—located outside the West Bank and Gaza Strip—has traditionally played a more dominant decision-making role than the group's internal or local leaders. This management trend began when the first head of the Hamas political bureau, Mousa Abu Marzook, ran the organization from his home in the United States, and continued as the group later established political headquarters in Amman, Jordan, and then Damascus, Syria. The external leadership is divided into two main groups, one of Gazans led by Marzook, and one composed mostly of Hamas members from the West Bank who have studied or worked in Kuwait. The so-called *Kuwaidia*, or Kuwaiti group, is led by Khaled Mishal. The two factions work closely together, but there is some resentment of the Kuwaiti group by Marzook's faction, because Mishal's Kuwaidia tend to dominate key positions within the Hamas political bureau.[5]

The structure of Hamas was static for its first few years, largely because Yasser Arafat's secular Palestine Liberation Organization was still weak and headquartered hundreds of miles away in Tunis. Israel was not yet a regular target of Hamas attacks, and was not therefore focusing on the group at the time. Hamas activities were distributed into functional branches whose operations were further broken down by region. These included:

- A social welfare and administrative branch (the *dawa*), responsible for recruitment, funding, and social services;
- *Al-Mujahideen al-Filastinun*, an entity responsible for arms procurement and military activities, containing a subgroup charged with overseeing and coordinating demonstrations and other popular resistance, as well as organized violence in the framework of the first Intifada (uprising);
- A security branch (the *Jehaz Aman*) responsible for collecting information on suspected collaborators, and then apprehending, interrogating, and killing them; and,

- A publications or media branch (the *A'alam*) responsible for producing and distributing leaflets, staffing press offices, and addressing propaganda issues.[6]

Then and now it is the group's political wing that oversees the activities of the rest of the movement's various component parts. Over time, however, the structure and responsibilities of Hamas' overt and covert wings developed to accommodate the changing environment in which the group found itself. In 1987, Hamas military cells began to carry out their first attacks targeting Israelis. At this point, Israeli collaborators within Palestinian society became a primary obstacle to Hamas' operations, so the *Majd* (an acronym for *Majmouath Jihad u-Dawa*, or the Holy War and Sermonizing Group) was created to serve as the strike force of the one-year-old Jehaz Aman security branch. Its role was to discover and deal with Palestinians suspected of helping Israel. Founded in 1982, five years before the official founding of Hamas, the al-Mujahideen al-Filastinun was entrusted with the responsibility of procuring weapons. After the uprising broke out, this group was in charge of executing shooting and bombing attacks as well.[7]

By 1991, both the Majd and the Mujahideen al-Filastinun were incorporated into a reorganized Hamas military wing under the name *Izz al-Din al-Qassam Brigades*. The first Qassam Brigades cell—named for a Muslim Brotherhood leader killed in action against British forces in 1935—was established by Zaccaria Walid Akel, then the head of the Hamas military wing in Gaza. The Qassam Brigades continued the Majd duties of kidnapping and murdering suspected collaborators, but soon branched out into targeting Israeli civilians. In December 1991, it carried out the first terrorist attack against an Israeli civilian, murdering Doron Shorshan, an Israeli resident of the Kfar Darom settlement in Gaza. This attack marked a turning point in the modus operandi of Hamas and set the group on the road toward the spectacular and indiscriminate suicide bombings and other attacks for which it is now well known.[8]

Despite having rounded the terrorist corner and established a full-fledged terrorist wing, it still took time for the group to develop capabilities equal to its intent. The evolutionary development of Hamas' terrorist tactics led to the group's first suicide car bomb attack on April 16, 1993, when the Qassam Brigades claimed responsibility for a blast outside a roadside cafeteria near the Mehola settlement in the West Bank. Though the car bomb killed only the driver and an Arab worker, the bomber had pulled up alongside two Egged buses, specifically targeting Israeli civilians. Luckily for them, most of the fifty or so passengers had left the buses and were mingling around the service counter when the explosion detonated, ripping through the two buses and setting them on fire. A year later, on April 6, 1994, Hamas carried out its first successful suicide car bomb attack in Israel proper when a car packed with nearly 400 pounds of explosives detonated beside a bus picking up students in the Israeli town of Afula, forty miles northwest of Jerusalem. Eight people, mostly teenagers, were killed and over forty others were wounded in the attack, which was perpetrated by a Palestinian from the West Bank.[9]

Since its founding in 1987, Hamas has committed countless acts of violence against both military and civilian targets, including suicide and other bombings and Qassam rocket, mortar fire, and shooting attacks. In its early years Hamas conducted small-scale attacks, like the 1989 abductions and murders of Israeli soldiers Avi Sasportas and Ilan Sa'adon. But the group is best known for its suicide bombing attacks. Between February 1989 and March 2000 Hamas carried out at least twenty-seven attacks, including twelve suicide bombings and three failed bombings. These attacks caused approximately 185 deaths and left over 1,200 people wounded.[10]

With the onset of the second Intifada in September 2000, the pace of Hamas attacks increased dramatically. From September 29, 2000, through March 24, 2004, Hamas executed 52 suicide attacks, killing 288 people and wounding 1,646 more. In total, Hamas conducted 425 terrorist attacks during this period, killing 377 people and wounding 2,076.[11]

Hamas attacks increased throughout this period. In 2003 alone, Hamas was responsible for 218 acts of violence. That figure more than doubled in 2004, in which Hamas carried out 555 terrorist attacks. Also in 2004, Hamas mortar attacks increased by 500 percent and its Qassam rocket attacks increased by 40 percent compared to the previous year.[12]

Intended to terrorize not only the targeted individuals but the general Israeli population, Hamas attacks are indiscriminate in nature. Hamas suicide bombings may not target Westerners but the group's shrapnel-studded suicide vests do not discriminate among passengers on Israeli buses or patrons at Israeli cafes. As such, innocent civilians from around the world have been killed in Hamas attacks, including civilians from the United States, the United Kingdom, Ukraine, Romania, China, the Philippines, and Sweden, among other nations. For example, on June 7, 2005, a Qassam rocket fired by Hamas killed a Chinese laborer working in the Ganei Tal settlement in the Gaza Strip. Goldie Taubenfeld, an American mother of thirteen, was killed in a Hamas suicide bus bombing in Jerusalem on August 19, 2003, along with her three-month-old son. On September 19, 2002, Jonathan Jesner, a Scottish medical student, was also murdered on a Tel Aviv bus when a Hamas suicide bomber detonated the explosive device he was wearing. Hamas has purposely targeted many busy civilian venues including, buses, bus stops, discotheques, restaurants, markets, and universities.[13]

In early 2003, Hamas military commanders began recruiting supporters and forming them into a popular army, or standing militia, in Gaza. By March 2004, Hamas' new popular army (the *Murabitun*) had recruited and trained members, and amassed weapons. According to Israeli intelligence, the several hundred new recruits came from the pool of Hamas supporters, not from within Hamas' Qassam Brigades. Indeed, Salah Shehadah, one of the founders of the Qassam Brigades, envisioned the popular army as something that was to be distinct from the Qassam Brigades. As Sheikh Yassin put it, "The popular defense operates within the Gaza Strip and is responsible for resistance, defense and rescue operations. The al-Qassam brigades act against the Zionist enemy, wherever it may be."[14]

Israeli political analyst Ehud Ya'ari has emphasized the potential threat such a military force poses to regional security, in light of Israeli withdrawal from the Gaza Strip in August 2005. "If the popular army is allowed to develop it will turn into a parallel, highly-motivated armed force to rival the puny security apparatuses of the Palestinian Authority," says Ya'ari. "From the moment that Hamas achieves its goal of a militia of thousands of fighters, there will be no hope of stopping it from turning the Gaza Strip into 'Hamas-stan,' like the 'Hizballahstan' that rose up in the wake of the Israeli withdrawal from southern Lebanon." In a sign of the importance Hamas leaders accord the establishment of the group's new militia, the popular army is said by Israeli intelligence to be headed by seasoned Hamas operatives Ahmed Jabr and Mohammad Deif.[15]

JOINT OPERATIONS WITH OTHER GROUPS

While Hamas remains the foremost Palestinian militant group conducting attacks against Israel, it is by no means the only such group. For many years, secular—primarily Marxist—Palestinian groups operating under the umbrella of the Palestine Liberation Organization (PLO) dominated the stage of Palestinian extremism. Known for hijacking airplanes and raiding Israeli border communities, groups like the Popular Front for the Liberation of Palestine (PFLP), the Popular Front for the Liberation of Palestine–General Command (PFLP-GC), the Democratic Front for the Liberation of Palestine (DFLP), the Palestine Liberation Front (PLF), the Abu Nidal Organization (ANO), and many others were household names in the 1970s and 1980s. In the wake of Israel's 1967 defeat of Arab armies and its occupation of the West Bank and Gaza, and then even more so following the Islamic awakening that came with the Iranian revolution in 1979, theologically based rejectionist groups like Islamic Jihad and Hamas began to develop greater footprints in the Palestinian territories. In the 1990s some of these groups—like the Abu Nidal Organization—fell apart while others—like the PFLP-GC—shed their socialist ideology and developed an Islamist identity more in line with the thinking of their Iranian patrons. Throughout the period of the Oslo peace process, generally speaking 1994 to 2000, these groups committed only sporadic and low-intensity attacks. In contrast, Islamic Jihad and, even more so, Hamas, executed increasingly lethal and frequent suicide bombings and other attacks.

The establishment of the al-Aqsa Martyrs Brigades, a recent addition to the collection of Palestinian paramilitary groups and an offshoot of Arafat's more mainstream Fatah party, was a factor of Fatah's perceived need to establish its own credentials as a resistance organization following the collapse of peace talks in 2000. Thus, West Bank Preventive Security Organization chief Jibril Rajoub described the group to the *al-Ayyam* newspaper as "the noblest phenomenon in the history of Fatah, because they restored the movement's honor and bolstered the political and security echelons of the Palestinian Authority." Within a short period of time the al-Aqsa Martyrs Brigades began carrying out numerous roadside shootings, ambushes of Israeli military personnel, attacks on civilian population centers, and suicide bombings both in the West Bank and across the Green Line in Israel proper.[16]

Palestinian groups would occasionally carry out joint attacks, but it was not until the collapse of peace negotiations and the eruption of the al-Aqsa Intifada in September 2000 that several of these groups, especially Hamas and Islamic Jihad, began to work together more regularly. Material found in Israeli raids of the West Bank carried out in 2002 revealed this cooperation was the product of Iranian prodding. For example, a seized Palestinian General Intelligence Services document dated June 1, 2000, describes a meeting between Iranian ambassador to Syria Sheikh al-Islam and Islamic Jihad secretary general Ramadan Abdullah Shallah, which took place on the eve of Israel's withdrawal from southern Lebanon. The Iranian ambassador requested "that the PIJ and Hamas carry out terrorist attacks 'inside Palestine,' without assuming responsibility for them."[17]

The following year, in a document dated October 2001, Palestinian Preventive Security chief Jibril Rajoub briefed Yasser Arafat on the activities of Palestinian terrorist groups in Syria, citing intelligence indicating that "intensive meetings are being held in Damascus, in which leaders of the Hamas, Islamic Jihad, the Popular Front [for the Liberation of Palestine] and Hizballah take part, in an attempt to increase the joint activities 'inside,' with financial support from Iran."[18]

Iran's coaxing—and consequent financial support—proved successful. As early as October 2000, within weeks of the failed peace summit at Camp David, Hamas leader Mahmoud Zahar announced that Hamas and Islamic Jihad leaders were meeting with Fatah and Palestinian Authority officials "at least once daily." Meanwhile, Abdullah Shami, an Islamic Jihad leader in Gaza, stated that "all are going to share in the clashes." Six months later, Hamas spokesman Ibrahim Ghosheh described the "harmony" that quickly developed between "the Islamic forces represented in the Hamas and [Islamic] Jihad movements and the national forces, especially the Fatah movement." Speaking at an April 2001 conference in Tehran in support of the Intifada, Palestine National Council speaker Salim al-Zanun declared: "Brothers, we are united with the national and Islamic forces. This means all factions, including the Hamas movement and Islamic Jihad."[19]

Documents seized in Israel's March 2002 raid of the Jenin refugee camp revealed that Islamic Jihad, Hamas, and Fatah operatives had established a joint framework for patrolling the camp, including a "combined force" and a "joint operations room." Internal Palestinian intelligence documents seized by Israel indicate senior Palestinian security officers "supplied PIJ and Hamas in the Jenin area with most of the weapons in their possession." With the help of Hamas, Islamic Jihad also gained technical expertise in the manufacture of rockets, developing a homemade rocket similar to Hamas' Qassam rocket. On May 25, 2002, Islamic Jihad's al-Quds Brigade fired three of these rockets from Gaza toward the Israeli town of Sderot and broadcast the attack on Hezbollah's al-Manar television station.[20]

According to West Bank Hamas leader Adnan Asfour, successful Israeli counterterrorism measures led Hamas and Islamic Jihad to coordinate operations not only at the local, cellular level but also at the level of more senior leadership. "With the expansion of Israel's circle of aggression, there must be an expansion of the circle of resistance," Asfour explained in an October 2003 interview. To this end, Hamas and Islamic Jihad negotiated a preliminary deal to merge their military wings in late 2003, reportedly agreed upon (but in the end never implemented) by Hamas leader Khaled

Mishal and Islamic Jihad leader Ramadan Shallah at a meeting of the group's leadership in Beirut.[21]

But while Hamas will engage in joint operations with other groups to achieve the common goal of attacking Israel, it jealously guards its grassroots network of dawa organizations. Among militant groups, only Hamas focuses so heavily on social and political activism, albeit parallel to and in support of its military activities. Hamas relies on its dawa organizations to recruit for, fund, and facilitate terrorism, but it should be noted that the Islamic principle of dawa is not intended to support violence.

DAWA IN ISLAM

According to Islamic tradition, all Muslims are obligated to submit themselves to God (*ibadah*) and preach or propagate (*dawa*, literally "a call to God") true Islam. The obligation to spread true Islam covers a wide spectrum of outreach activity, from outright proselytizing (which benefits the soul) to charitable giving and social welfare activities (which benefit the body). To fulfill these social welfare duties, the Islamic endowments (*waqf*, or *awqaf* in the plural) that are responsible for the upkeep of mosques and holy sites in contemporary Muslim societies also typically manage social service institutions. Throughout the Muslim world, revenue derived from the waqf's endowed properties and individual donations typically fund "a veritable network of welfare and charitable services (such as schools, orphanages, soup kitchens)." These not only provide for the temporal needs of the population but are also a means of drawing in the people to whom religious leaders want to preach.[22]

Within the more radical *Salafi* strain of Sunni Islam, dawa activities are seen as protecting the *umma* (Islamic community, or nation) from insufficiently Islamic rulers and other perceived enemies of Islam, such as non-Muslim infidels. *Salafiyya* is a school within Sunni Islam that spread throughout the Arab world in the twentieth century. Its name comes from the Arabic words *al-salaf al-salih*, "the venerable forefathers," which refers to the generation of the Prophet Mohammad and his companions. Salafis believed Islam had been corrupted by idolatry, and they sought to bring it back to the purity of its earliest days as it was practiced in the time of the Prophet. Accordingly, Salafis today reject modernizing tendencies, and believe that the Koran and Hadith (traditions of the Prophet) should be interpreted as they were during the first few generations after Mohammad's death. Salafis are sometimes considered extreme in belief; after 9/11 the term has been used to describe various groups within Sunni Islamic ideology that practice purist or reactionary interpretations of Islam—especially the militant expressions of these ideologies.[23]

To promote their particular version of Islam, many Salafis use dawa activities to promote a "pure" Islamic practice modeled after the lifestyle of the Prophet Mohammed, emphasizing individual piety and self-purification. When, as with Salafis, the goal is "the transformation of society through religious education, and moral and social reform," the wide array of social services that make up the dawa are ideally suited to complement religious goals of reviving and propagating the faith in a population. This Salafist ideological framework is common to the various modern militant Islamist organizations that, like Hamas, grew out of the Muslim Brotherhood. As the Congressional Research Service notes of the leader of another well-known terrorist organization, "Bin Laden has identified Salafist thinkers such as his former mentor Abdallah Azzam, Hamas founder Ahmed Yassin, World Trade Center bombing conspirator Omar Abdel Rahman, Saudi dissident clerics Salman al-Awdah and Safar al-Hawali, and thirteenth century Islamic scholar Ibn Taymiyah as prominent ideological influences."[24]

Dawa and Politics

The Islamist movement whose dawa tradition has most influenced Hamas, the Egyptian Muslim Brotherhood, is notable for having a politically activist nature. Academic scholars have noted that Brotherhood activists use communal activities at the grassroots level to "reshape the political consciousness of educated youth." By focusing on impressionable youth and in areas lacking social welfare services, the Brotherhood's Islamic institutions serve as "functional substitutes for the welfare apparatus of the state and constitute a natural and familiar setting in which young activists can reach out to uncommitted peers." In other words, social services institutions function as an ideal tool used by Islamists to radicalize and recruit Muslim youth.[25]

It should therefore not surprise that, in line with the Muslim Brotherhood's political tradition, the Hamas dawa was directly involved in promoting Hamas candidates in the round of municipal elections held in May 2005. In Bethlehem, Hamas won five of the seven council seats allocated to Muslims, and a sixth seat was won by Islamic Jihad. A Palestinian-Christian from Bethlehem suggested that Hamas attempted to "buy" votes in the election via dawa activity. "You'd wake up in the morning," the woman explained, "and find a box of staples like oil and sugar here on the sidewalk." Considering that according to an exit poll conducted during the second round of Palestinian local elections on May 5, 2005, the most important problem, as defined by 35 percent of the voters, was poverty and unemployment, it is not hard to understand why Hamas dawa donating of food in the period leading up to and during elections was an effective means of garnering support for Hamas political candidates.[26]

Dawa and Violence

One of the ideological principles developed by Muslim Brotherhood theoretician Sayyid Qutb is that "the duty of the faithful Muslim is to revive Islam to transform the *jahili* [immoral, pre-Islamic] society through proselytization (dawah) and militant jihad." Islam scholar Olivier Roy has noted that militant behavior in Islamist groups appears to be motivated more by a particularly aggressive style of religious preaching than by political training. For Roy, the word *dawa* is defined as "militant preaching" (he literally translates the word as "call" or "invitation") and is a more significant cause of militant behavior than is strictly political training. Indeed, Muslim Brotherhood founder Hassan al-Banna wrote a tract titled *Da'watuna* (Our Militant Preaching). Among Muslim militants, Roy points out, "Preaching (*da'wa*) is the instrument of the march to power." Thus, while the Israeli occupation contextualizes Hamas' success, the group's radical activists are also part of a larger phenomenon.[27]

Many open societies, particularly democratic ones, are concerned about the preaching and social welfare activities of groups with militant ties, particularly because the dawa culture often promotes anti-democratic and anti-Western undertones. The Dutch General Intelligence and Security Service (AIVD) outlined these concerns in a report entitled "From Dawa to Jihad: The Various Threats from Radical Islam to the Democratic Legal Order." Groups that focus on dawa activities, the report claimed, "follow a long-term strategy of continuous influencing based on extreme puritanical, intolerant and anti-Western ideas." The report warned that "the choice of [some] dawa-oriented groups for non-violent activities does not always imply that they are non-violent on principle. Often they simply do not yet consider armed Jihad expedient for practical reasons (Jihad can be counterproductive or impossible because of the other side's superiority) or for religious reasons (the Jihad against non-believers is only possible when all Muslims have returned to their 'pure' faith)."[28]

Tellingly, the Saudi-based Muslim World League (MWL), the largest organization engaged in dawa activities across the globe, is also the subject of several ongoing counterterrorism investigations in the United States and elsewhere related to Hamas, al-Qaeda, and other terrorist groups. The MWL lists as its main objectives: "to disseminate Islamic *Dawah* and expound the teachings of Islam. To defend Islamic causes in a manner that safeguards the interests and aspirations of Muslims, solves their problems, refutes false allegations against Islam, and repels inimical trends and dogma which the enemies of Islam seek to exploit in order to destroy the unity of Muslims and to sow seeds of doubt in our Muslim brethren." The nature of the MWL's ties to terrorism is extensive and includes both senior officials and branch offices. A senior MWL official in Pakistan, Wael Hamza al-Jlaidan, is listed as a Specially Designated Terrorist by the U.S. Treasury Department. And in March 2002, the northern Virginia offices of both the MWL and one of its subsidiaries, the International Islamic Relief Organization (IIRO), were raided by a Treasury Department task force searching for evidence that the groups were raising or laundering funds for al-Qaeda, Hamas, or Palestinian Islamic Jihad.[29]

Of course, there is nothing inherently violent or antisocial about dawa activities, per se. Indeed, the opposite is true: dawa organizations—frequently formed as local charities, non-governmental organizations, or private voluntary organizations—play an important communal role in Islamic history and culture. Like their Salafi cousins, however, Muslim Brotherhood organizations like Hamas take advantage of the otherwise laudable Islamic tradition of charity and good works not only to teach their particular version of Islam but also to actively support terrorist operations. Not surprisingly, many of the charities and NGOs tied to al-Qaeda in investigations spawned by the September 11th attacks have significant ties to the Muslim Brotherhood. By looking into this Brotherhood connection, investigators have found that many al-Qaeda fronts and cells have also funded Hamas.[30]

MUSLIM BROTHERHOOD: THE ROOTS OF HAMAS DAWA

Though it was officially founded on December 14, 1987, a semi-official history of Hamas establishes 1967 as the year of the group's genesis—as the Muslim Brotherhood's Palestinian wing. Hamas acknowledges its Brotherhood roots in its April 1988 charter: "The Islamic Resistance Movement is one of the wings of Moslem Brotherhood in Palestine." Hamas' roots actually extend further back than 1967. "The mother movement to which Hamas belongs," according to Jordanian Muslim Brotherhood leader Ziad Abu Ghanima, "is the Muslim Brotherhood Society which has been digging its roots into Palestinian soil for decades before the establishment of the occupying Zionist entity."[31]

The Muslim Brotherhood (*Jamiat al-Ikhwan al-Muslimeen*) is a religious and political organization founded in 1928 in the Suez Canal town of Ismailiya, Egypt, by an Egyptian schoolteacher named Hassan al-Banna. The organization opposed the drift toward secularism perceived to be taking place in Egypt and other Arab countries, and sought to counter foreign influence by encouraging a return to an Islamic society based on the original precepts of the Koran. The Brotherhood's activity in Palestinian areas dates back to 1935, when Hassan al-Banna's brother, Abdel Rahman al-Banna, visited the Mufti of Jerusalem, Hajj Amin al-Husseini. As a consequence of this meeting, Hassan al-Banna created and personally led the General Central Committee to Aid Palestine, which protested the British presence there and promoted the Palestinian national cause. In 1936, Muslim Brotherhood volunteers participated in attacks on British and Jewish interests, in what became known as the "1936 Revolt." Brotherhood activist Said Ramadan opened the first Muslim Brotherhood branch in Palestinian areas in Jerusalem in 1945; by 1947, the Brotherhood was running some 25 branches throughout the British Mandate, with a membership ranging from 12,000 to 20,000. After Israel won independence in 1948, Muslim Brotherhood volunteers, both acting on their own and organized into Muslim Brotherhood battalions, actively fought against the new state.[32] Hamas boasts of these deep anti-Zionist roots in its charter:

> The Islamic Resistance Movement is one of the links in the chain of the struggle against the Zionist invaders. It goes back to 1939, to the emergence of the martyr Izz al-Din al-Kissam and his brethren the fighters, members of Moslem Brotherhood. It goes on to reach out and become one with another chain that includes the struggle of the Palestinians and Moslem Brotherhood in the 1948 war and the Jihad operations of the Moslem Brotherhood in 1968 and after.[33]

After 1948, the Brotherhood branches in Gaza fell under Egyptian jurisdiction, while those in the West Bank were subject to Jordanian law. In Egypt, the group was suppressed, and in Jordan the Islamists were both tolerated and co-opted (to such an extent that, in the 1950s, the Brotherhood sided with the Jordanian regime against secular Palestinian groups). It was a fallow time for the Brotherhood, as one Israeli scholar notes: "Between 1948 and 1967 the Brothers were weak and kept a low profile. In the

Gaza Strip the movement was under systematic repression by the Nasserist regime, while in the West Bank it was effectively monitored by the Jordanian authorities."[34]

In the wake of the Israeli victory over Arab armies in the Six Day War—the 1967 conflict in which Israel occupied the West Bank and Gaza Strip, and which consequently bolstered Palestinian national and Islamic consciousness—the Brotherhood dropped its low profile and reorganized into a considerably more activist entity. According to Hamas leader Khaled Mishal, "This pushed the Muslim Brotherhood to restructure their organization." Following the war, Palestinian groups in the now-occupied West Bank and Gaza were cut off from Egypt and (to a lesser extent) Jordan and were thus forced to focus on their local communities and populations. While the Egyptian Muslim Brotherhood, which included Islamists in Gaza, evolved into a more openly oppositional movement, the Jordanian Muslim Brotherhood, including branches on both the West and East banks of the Jordan River, developed an equivocal relationship with the Hashemite monarchy that ruled Jordan.[35]

This evolution of the Brotherhood as an increasingly open opposition to secular Arab rulers, combined with Israeli tolerance of non-violent Islamist activities, enabled the Brotherhood to regroup. During this period, Israeli scholar Meir Hatina writes, "the movement [was able] to intensify its activities, centered on mosques, charitable organizations, schools, student councils and trade unions" which "operated [not only] as social and cultural centers, but also as powerful bases for political activity."[36] A 1988 article in the Kuwaiti newspaper al-Anba offered an Arab perception of the increasing importance of the Brotherhood's dawa activities during this period:

During the years 1967–1975 the role of the Islamic movement was characterized by the building of mosques, bringing the [younger] generation into the fold, providing them with guidance and strengthening their ideology. To this end, the movement utilized all means at its disposal. The mosque, therefore, did not serve solely as a place of worship, but also as school, kindergarten, or even library or venue for women's activities. Ideology and religion were preached at clubs, schools and universities, where mosques were often built, and politics discussed. In this fashion the [younger] generation opened its eyes and discovered the Jewish plots against the nation.[37]

According to Palestinian scholar Ziad Abu-Amr, the Brotherhood began to recognize the power of social and charitable organizations to spread its message and influence:

> The society founded Islamic charity associations, which supervised local schools. It also managed nursery schools and kindergartens, which were usually attached to mosques. The Brotherhood also established neighborhood libraries and sports clubs. In subsequent years, the Muslim Brotherhood and other Islamic elements formed several Islamic societies and organizations in Hebron, Nablus, Jenin, Jerusalem, the Gaza Strip, and other Palestinian towns.[38]

Such organizations, Abu-Amr notes, rallied support for the Islamic movement, especially by using "alms money *zakat* to help thousands of needy families. And thousands of students and children were enrolled in schools and kindergartens run by the Islamic movement."[39] The future founder and spiritual leader of Hamas was deeply involved in this period of dawa flowering, as its political bureau chief, Khaled Mishal, notes:

> In the 1970s, the organizational structure of the Muslim Brotherhood was rebuilt and the movement spread among young men and women students, in mosques, which are the essential pillars of educating the society and treating the defections the occupation caused. People were attracted to the mosques where they were religiously and nationally mobilized. Social institutions were established in order to develop youth sports and cultural activities and improved social services for poor people and orphans. One of the most important institutions is the Islamic Center founded by Sheikh Ahmed Yassin.[40]

According to its own semi-official history, Hamas evolved over time through four stages:

1. 1967–1976: Construction of the "hard core" of the Muslim Brotherhood in the Gaza Strip in the face of oppressive Israeli rule.
2. 1976–1981: Geographical expansion through participation in professional associations in the Gaza Strip and the West Bank, and institution-building, notably al-Mujama al-Islamiya, al-Jamiya al-Islamiya, and the Islamic University in Gaza.
3. 1981–1987: Political influence through establishment of the mechanisms of action and preparation for armed struggle.
4. 1987: Founding of Hamas as the combatant arm of the Muslim Brotherhood in Palestine and the launching of a continuing jihad.[41]

In a 1995 lecture, Sheikh Jamil Hamami, a party to the founding of Hamas and a senior member of its West Bank leadership, expounded on the importance of Hamas' dawa infrastructure as the soil from which militancy would flower: "During the time before the outbreak of the Intifada [i.e., before the official founding of Hamas in 1987]," he said, "we prepared ourselves and this rebellious generation." Having laid that groundwork, Hamami insisted, "yes, now is the time for the explosion, the stage of preparations is over . . . we will not sleep, Palestine is in our hearts always, we have not forgotten Jerusalem, Haifa, Gaza and Jericho, Zefad, Nazareth, Umm al-Fahem and all Palestine even for a day. This [pre-Intifada period] was the education and preparation stage."[42]

In a telling sign of Hamas's self-identification with the Muslim Brotherhood, the group's banners and posters often depict the Hamas leaders alongside Muslim Brotherhood founder Hassan al-Banna, or other Brotherhood dignitaries such as Sheikh Abdallah Azzam. For example, the Hamas student group at the American University in Jenin distributed posters of Hamas founder Sheikh Yassin, the group's Gaza leader Abdel Aziz al-Rantissi, bomb maker Yihye Ayash, and al-Banna, among others. By advertising its link to the Muslim Brotherhood, alongside claims of providing for needy Palestinians and disdain for personal or organizational corruption, Hamas leverages the appreciation (and indebtedness) it earns through social welfare activities to garner support—both political and logistical—for its terrorist activities. Indeed, the activities of the group's political, social, and military "wings" are so intertwined that Palestinian security officials themselves see them as one and the same. In the words of Palestinian Brigadier General Nizar Ammar, "the difference between the [political, social, and military] wings of Hamas is often a fiction."[43]

THE HAMAS DAWA

Hamas' original security branch, the Jehaz Aman, was founded by Sheikh Ahmed Yassin and several of his closest associates, who together also headed the group's main social welfare organization, Mujama al-Islamiya (Islamic Center) in Gaza. The Center remains one of the largest and most successful Hamas institutions today. Just as the security wing of Hamas developed into the Qassam Brigades, the social services infrastructure has blossomed into an efficient network of grassroots service organizations across the Gaza Strip and the West Bank. These institutions are crucial to Hamas' terrorist activity: they provide cover for raising, laundering, and transferring funds, facilitate the group's propaganda and recruitment efforts, provide employment to its operatives, and serve as a logistical support network for its terrorist operations.

Hamas spiritual leader and cofounder Sheikh Ahmed Yassin set up the Hamas dawa to mirror the structure he had helped perfect as a Muslim Brotherhood activist. According to a pair of Israeli scholars, Yassin's "focus on *da'wa* was the result of a major lesson the MB [Muslim Brotherhood] had learned from its experience in Egypt: as long as it confined its activity to education and preaching, the regime would leave it alone." Proceeding from this premise, Yassin "embarked on a systematic penetration of [Palestinian] society by creating cells of three members each through the [Gaza] Strip, reaching even the neighborhood level." On this point Arab analysts sympathetic to Hamas' ideological program agree with their Israeli counterparts, that the Hamas dawa infrastructure is a product of its parent organization, the Muslim Brotherhood. Scholars and historians on both sides also agree that from the late 1960s to the mid-1980s the Brotherhood benefited from the Israeli government's support of non-violent Islamist Palestinian factions, believing these groups would function as a useful counterweight to the secular nationalist Palestinian groups then hijacking airplanes and conducting commando raids into Israel from neighboring Arab states. As Israeli scholar Meir Hatina describes it, "the Israeli Civil Administration [in the West Bank and Gaza] displayed a relatively tolerant attitude toward religious activity, in part in order to undermine the influence of the PLO." For example, Israeli authorities permitted the number of mosques in the Gaza Strip to double from 1967 to 1986. The civil administration also officially sanctioned dawa organizations that would become central to the Hamas infrastructure, such as the Islamic Center (al-Mujama al-Islamiya) in Gaza. By 1987, al-Mujama controlled an estimated 40 percent of all mosques in the Gaza Strip.[44]

Hamas political leader Ismail Abu Shanab told Harvard scholar Jessica Stern that "even before Hamas came into being, in 1976, there were two organizations that were engaged in social welfare functions: al-Jamiya al-Islamiya and al-Mujama. In those days the priority was to work on social, education, and welfare programs. After 1980, there were three such organizations, including the Islamic Benevolence Society." But cognizant of the implications of admitting his involvement in organizations that spawned Hamas, Shanab hastened to downplay his involvement, saying these organizations "had no connection with politics, even during the occupation. I founded Jam'iya al-Islamiyah, but I cut my connection with them when Hamas was first established" in December 1987. Despite Shanab's disavowals, both al-Jamiya al-Islamiya and al-Mujama were founded by prominent Hamas personalities, including Ahmed Yassin, Abdel Aziz al-Rantissi, Ibrahim al-Yazuri, Mahmoud al-Zahar, Ahmed Ismail Bahr, and others.[45]

Both Israeli scholar Mair Hatina and Palestinian scholar Ziad Abu-Amr list the Islamic University in Gaza (IUG) as another Hamas precursor organization run and established by Brotherhood-cum-Hamas leaders. Hatina describes these as the three main institutions that "coordinated Brotherhood activities in the Gaza Strip and later constituted a springboard for Hamas"; Abu-Amr depicts al-Mujama as "a front organization for the Muslim Brotherhood Society in Gaza" and the IUG as "the principal Muslim Brotherhood stronghold. The university's administration, most of the employees who work there, and the majority of students are Brotherhood supporters." Salah Shehadah, founder of the Izz al-Din al-Qassam Brigades, features prominently among the many political, social, and military Hamas leaders that have been affiliated with IUG. In an indication of the depth of the relationship between Hamas and the university, Hamas' Khaled Mishal has boasted of his group's participation in the building of the campus in 1978.[46]

PALESTINIAN ISLAMIC JIHAD: VIOLENCE WITHOUT DAWA

Hamas' main rival (and sometimes partner) within the Palestinian rejectionist movement is the smaller but ruthlessly efficient Islamic Jihad. Islamic Jihad (*Al-Jihad Al-Islami fi Filastin*) originated in the 1970s among Palestinian students in Cairo, notably Fathi Shiqaqi, a former leftist who grew disillusioned with the secular Palestinian movements and joined the Egyptian Muslim Brotherhood. By the mid-1970s, he had rejected the teachings of the Brotherhood, which held that the destruction of Israel must await an "internal jihad" to reform and unify the Islamic world, and embraced the 1979 revolution in Iran as a model of action. Hamas, in contrast, remains committed to the Muslim Brotherhood and considers itself the Palestinian wing of the Brotherhood. Although a number of other radical Palestinian Islamists inspired by the Islamic Republic in Tehran adopted the name Islamic Jihad as a cover for terrorist activity, the faction started by Shiqaqi is the one that flourishes today.[47]

Following the assassination of Egyptian president Anwar Sadat in 1981, Shiqaqi was expelled from the country and returned to Gaza, where he formally established Islamic Jihad. Unlike Hamas, which grew out of the social welfare network it ran as the Palestinian Muslim Brotherhood even prior to its founding under the name Hamas, Islamic Jihad made little effort to develop a social and educational infrastructure or attract a mass following. Shiqaqi believed that a campaign of spectacular terrorist attacks against Israel in the name of revolutionary Islam would inspire a popular revolt. After securing funding from Iran's mullahs, who had ended their early flirtation with the PLO and were anxious to sponsor like-minded (if Sunni) Palestinian revolutionaries, Shiqaqi began developing the group's military apparatus, the Jerusalem Brigades (Saraya al-Quds), which started carrying out attacks against Israeli soldiers in the mid-1980s. The most notorious was the Gate of Moors operation in October 1986, when Islamic Jihad operatives threw hand grenades at military recruits attending an induction ceremony near the Wailing Wall in Jerusalem, wounding seventy and killing the father of a soldier.

In 1988, after spending two years in an Israeli prison for smuggling arms into Gaza, Shiqaqi was deported to Lebanon and the following year established a headquarters in Damascus, Syria. This transition brought Islamic Jihad leaders into direct contact with Iranian officials for the first time through the Islamic Republic's embassies in Beirut and Damascus. Unlike Hamas, which strove to spread its external political and military infrastructure across several different countries in the 1990s and came to depend primarily on Syria only after its activities were curtailed elsewhere, the Islamic Jihad presence abroad has always been concentrated in Syria and Syrian-occupied Lebanon. Islamic Jihad operatives soon began training at Hezbollah camps in Lebanon, under the supervision of Iranian Revolutionary Guards stationed in the country, and carried out some joint operations with Hezbollah against Israeli forces in south Lebanon during the 1990s.

Islamic Jihad and Hamas were fierce rivals in the late 1980s and early 1990s, largely a result of ideological differences relating to Islamic Jihad's affinity for—and Hamas' rejection of—Iranian Khomeinism and the principle of *waliyat al-faqih,* that is, rule by the jurisprudent (entrusting governance to clerics). Moreover, while both groups grew out of the Muslim Brotherhood, Islamic Jihad marginalized the role of social activity in favor of militant activity, while Hamas gave prominence to social welfare activity and proselytizing (dawa), even as it too engaged in a simultaneous terror campaign.

After the signing of the 1993 Oslo Accords, however, both Hamas and Islamic Jihad joined the Damascus-based Alliance of Palestinian Forces (APF) and—for the most part—set aside their differences. By 1995, Hamas joined Islamic Jihad in establishing its operational headquarters in Damascus (its political office was then still in Amman) and, at the behest of Iran and facilitation of Hezbollah, the two groups coordinated their terrorist activities.

Competition between the groups largely arose over issues such as Islamic Jihad's perceived infringement on Hamas' social welfare turf or on Hamas reaching out to radicalized Israeli-Arabs (which had traditionally been a constituency of Islamic Jihad). Periodically, Hamas' ideologues would take issue with the intimacy of Islamic Jihad's relationship with Shi'a Iran—especially during the rare cases when Islamic Jihad members converted to Shi'ism.

One of the most visible periods of tension between Hamas and Islamic Jihad occurred in 1994 and 1995 when, even as they continued to conduct joint operations, the groups engaged in a mild but public competition over Islamic Jihad leaders' short-lived decision to establish a dawa social welfare network of their own to compete with that of Hamas. Even then, however, Hamas and Islamic Jihad sought to work through their differences. For example, according to the indictment of several Islamic Jihad operatives in the United States, it was around this period that "the members of the conspiracy would and did work with PIJ and its leaders in coordinating its activities with Hamas, including the possibility of Hamas and PIJ reconciling their differences and engaging in joint terrorism operations." According to U.S. prosecutors, in early 1995 Islamic Jihad members "continued to discuss PIJ recruitment, the interrelationship between PIJ and Hamas, and the possibility of joining forces."[48]

While competition over dominance in the realm of social welfare activity was short-lived, Islamic Jihad does run a small number of dawa organizations that fill logistical and financial support functions and build grassroots support for the group. Most important among these are the al-Ansar Charity Association and the al-Ihsan Society (also known as the Birr Elehssan Society) in Gaza. However, Islamic Jihad no longer aspires to build the kind of widespread dawa infrastructure that would challenge the Hamas dawa apparatus, thus removing a key bone of contention between the two groups.[49]

Following the October 1995 assassination of Islamic Jihad leader Fathi Shiqaqi in Malta, the group managed to execute only a brief spate of attacks in early 1996 before its terror attacks dropped off so dramatically that in 1997 the *Jerusalem Post* reported "a void in the organization so deep that the group barely functions today."[50]

With the beginning of the Palestinian uprising in September 2000, however, Islamic Jihad sprang back to life. Since then, it has claimed responsibility for scores of terrorist attacks. In part, this has reflected the group's greater coordination with other Palestinian groups, especially

Hamas. But lacking a social network and political activism on which to fall back, Islamic Jihad shunned the idea of participating in Palestinian elections in late 2005 and early 2006 and rejected requests to honor a *tahdiya*, or period of calm, in the period leading up to those elections. A critical factor in the group's revival was a dramatic increase in Iranian funding. According to American officials, Tehran began paying Islamic Jihad millions of dollars in cash bonuses for each attack against Israel. This was necessary in large part because Islamic Jihad lacked the kind of grassroots institutions established by Hamas through which it could launder and transfer significant amounts of funds raised abroad to operatives in the West Bank and Gaza Strip. In contrast, Hamas fundraisers in North America, Europe, and the Persian Gulf have a large selection of Hamas-run charities, social service organizations, and communal institutions through which they can send funds to Hamas.[51]

THE ORIGINS OF HAMAS IN THE UNITED STATES

The development of Hamas in the United States sheds additional light on the metamorphosis of the Palestinian Muslim Brotherhood into the paramilitary-political terrorist group we know today as Hamas. Mohammad Salah is a self-confessed Hamas member and military commander from the Chicago suburb of Bridgeview, Illinois, who was indicted in August 2002 in U.S. federal court on terrorism charges based on his Hamas activities. In December of that year Salah and a group of co-defendants were found liable for Hamas activity—specifically, the 1996 murder of U.S.-Israeli dual national David Boim—in a civil case also tried in Chicago. Salah was reportedly first recruited into the Muslim Brotherhood by Sheikh Jamal Said, the imam of a mosque in Bridgeview and a leader of the Palestinian wing of the Muslim Brotherhood in the United States. Shortly after Salah joined the Brotherhood, Mousa Abu Marzook—who would later become the overall head of Hamas' political bureau—personally recruited Salah into a Hamas precursor group based in the United States called the "Palestine Organization."[52] An Israeli military indictment against Salah describes the Palestine Organization in more detail:

> The defendant joined an organization called "Palestine," which was an independent organization connected with the Muslim Brotherhood organization. The man in charge of this organization was Mussa Abu Marzuq. The organization's goal was the unification of all Palestinians

in the United States in support of the Muslim Brotherhood organization, particularly its military and political wings, for the escalation of the struggle against Israeli rule in the Judea-Samaria regions [i.e., West Bank].[53]

Akram Harubi, a former professor at George Washington University in Washington, D.C., would later serve as an official of the Holy Land Foundation for Relief and Development, exposed as a Hamas-fundraising front organization and shut by U.S. authorities in December 2001. Later still, Harubi served as a member of the Hamas coordinating committee in the West Bank. In a statement to Israeli police that would subsequently be admitted as evidence in a civil proceeding against Hamas activists in a U.S. court, Harubi told of being recruited by Marzook's personal secretary, Nasser al-Khatib:

> In the end of 1989 or beginning of 1990, while I was working at a university in the United States, I was approached by a man named Nasser, with whose details I am not familiar. He was about thirty years old, involved in commerce and was usually appear [sic] in the company of Mousa Abu Marzook. Nasser proposed to me to join the Moslem Brothers in the U.S. I accepted his proposal and officially joined. I asked Nasser what my job would be, and he said it would be to host people from the Moslem Brothers (Organization) who came from outside the U.S.[54]

When Hamas was officially founded in December 1987, the Palestinian Muslim Brotherhood faction in the United States changed its name accordingly—though the membership remained largely unchanged. Over time, they would build an extensive Hamas support network in the United States responsible for financial, logistical, propaganda, and even military activities. A key node in this network, Harubi returned to the West Bank from the United States, and couriered funds for Hamas from Jordan to the West Bank, maintaining direct contact with Hamas leaders abroad (including Khaled Mishal and Mousa Abu Marzook) and coordinating meetings—usually held in his own home—between regional Hamas committees across the West Bank. In October 1993, as Hamas came under increased scrutiny for its violent opposition to the peace process that was then gaining momentum, Hamas leaders in the United States met in Philadelphia to develop a coordinated strategy to undermine the Israeli-Palestinian peace process, and to streamline Hamas fundraising and other activities in the United States. To conceal their association with Hamas, the participants would refer to Hamas as "Samah" (Hamas spelled backwards) or simply as "The Movement."[55]

THE DISTINCTION BETWEEN HAMAS
AND THE MUSLIM BROTHERHOOD

Ideologically, the Muslim Brotherhood remains the primary self-identifying affiliation for most Palestinian Islamists. An academic study based on interviews of jailed terrorist operatives found that the "pre-recruitment" social environment for members of Islamist groups like Hamas "was dominated by the mosque, religious organizations and religious instruction." For the Islamist groups, the study found, "almost 50 percent [of members] cite the mosque, Moslem Brotherhood or other religious influence as central."[56]

But there is a critical philosophical distinction between Hamas and the Brotherhood. Hamas disputes the Brotherhood view that the Muslim nation (*umma*) must first be brought back to the true path of Islam before it can engage in a violent jihad against infidels, especially Israel. Indeed, it is this divergence of opinion that explains why the founders of a great many Sunni Muslim terrorist groups, including Egyptian Islamic Jihad, *Gama'ah al-Islamiyah* (Islamic Group), Palestinian Islamic Jihad, and Hamas, have separated from their shared Muslim Brotherhood roots.

Unlike the Gama'ah al-Islamiyah and the Egyptian and Palestinian variants of Islamic Jihad, however, Hamas never fully broke from the Brotherhood. Hamas is not a splinter group; rather, it *is* the Palestinian branch of the Muslim Brotherhood, but with an explicitly violent agenda. When Hamas was established, former Muslim Brotherhood activists were simply redirected from merely promoting Islamic observance to engaging in violent anti-Israel activities. Khaled Mishal acknowledges that "inside, we had several names: the Islamic Movement [Hamas]; Muslim Brotherhood, Islamic Front, the (Islamic) Youth Center and the Islamic Bloc. It was one organization with different names."[57]

With the invention of the name "Hamas" in the winter of 1987, Yassin and his associates created, as one scholar puts it, "a front group for the Muslim Brethren, participating as that group's proxy in the illegal and clandestine activities of the uprising." In so doing, Hamas sought to safeguard the legal status of the Muslim Brotherhood, its parent organization. Despite its divergence from the priorities of the Brotherhood, Hamas has always existed as a dependent of the Brotherhood hierarchy. Indeed, four years before Hamas was even established the Palestinian Muslim Brotherhood group was already plotting terrorist attacks. Khaled Mishal recounts that "in 1983, we carried out our first military experience under the leadership of Sheikh Ahmed Yassin; the 1983 organization that sought to gather weapons to prepare groups for military training and launch the jihad project." Mishal adds, "It is no secret that the 1983 arms deal was funded from abroad; Hamas was still forming." Hamas has always maintained a fluid relationship between its "internal" leadership in the Israel-occupied territories, and Brotherhood and Hamas leaders on the "outside." According to Mishal, "a number of Hamas leaders," including both "inside" and "outside" leaders, attended a 1983 meeting at which "the decision to found the Palestinian Islamic project for the cause and preparing the requirements for its success was taken." While the internal leadership recruits on campuses, in the mosques, and among social service organizations, the outside leadership plays, according to Mishal, "a political, media and financial role."[58]

This leadership rejects peace with Israel on religious, nationalist, and ideological grounds. As its covenant makes clear, "The Islamic Resistance Movement believes that the land of Palestine is an Islamic *Waqf* endowment consecrated for future Moslem generations until Judgment Day. It, or any part of it, should not be squandered: it, or any part of it, should not be given up." It follows logically, as the Hamas charter explains, that "there is no solution for the Palestinian question except through Jihad." In other words, while Hamas engages in military, social, and political activities alike, the strategic purpose of each of these tactics is the same jihadist principle of destroying Israel under the ideological framework of confronting the perceived enemies of Islam, and Islamizing Palestinian society. It should, therefore, not surprise that even after its sweeping electoral victory in Parliamentary elections Hamas leaders did not soften their rhetoric. Instead of allowing participation in the political process to co-opt them into moderation, Hamas leaders underlined their intention to continue attacking Israel and make Palestinian society more Islamic. Hamas leader Mahmoud Zahar insisted the group's Qassam Brigades "will remain, they will grow, they will be armed more and more until the complete liberation of all Palestine." Under Hamas, Zahar predicted, the new Palestinian government would promote "martyr tourism" to draw tourists interested in the history of armed Palestinian resistance and the ministry of culture would produce literature about jihad. If elected, a Hamas candidate from Rafah promised, Hamas would enact legislation consistent with Islamic *Shariah* (religious law). "We would present to the ummah [Muslim nation] and the Palestinian people the laws and legislation compatible with the Islamic Shariah and would do our best to nullify the non-Islamic ones." This would come hand in hand, the candidate promised, with enhanced social services courtesy of the Hamas dawa.[59]

THE CENTRALITY OF DAWA TO HAMAS PARAMILITARY ACTIVITIES

According to the statements of its own leadership, Hamas' dawa activities have always been its most important tool for furthering the organization's goals of destroying Israel, undermining the Palestinian Authority, and re-cruiting grassroots and operational support. It is no coincidence that the first security body established by Hamas was referred to as "jihad and dawa," and officially called "Majd." The dawa is the secret to Hamas' success, as it were. "We started getting involved in charity before Hezbollah did," says Ismail Abu Shanab. "Our obligation as Muslims is comprehensive. This is the meaning of the phrase 'Islam is the solution.' The PA doesn't understand this. They don't provide social welfare."[60]

2

terror and the hamas political leadership

Despite evidence to the contrary, there persists in the minds of many observers an ethical distinction between the social-political branches of Hamas, popularly known for opposing peacemaking with Israel and for welfare projects that aid needy Palestinians, and its military wing, known for suicide bombers that target Israeli civilians. In fact, the links between members of the Hamas political wing and terrorist activities are symbiotic and have been intertwined since the founding of Hamas in 1987. The goal of this chapter is to describe and provide evidence for links between Hamas' political and military activities, with the aim of debunking the myth that there are "good" and "bad" wings within Hamas. The relationship between the social and military wings is the subject of subsequent chapters.

The relationship between Hamas political leadership and terrorism takes many forms. Hamas political leaders—arrayed across the West Bank and Gaza Strip, Israel, Syria, Jordan, elsewhere in the Middle East, and in Europe and the United States—recruit terrorists, equip them with weapons, raise money for operations, and function as outright military commanders. In the following pages we will meet some of the Hamas political leadership and explore their intimate involvement in terrorist activities. This is by no means intended to be an exhaustive compendium of known Hamas political leaders and their explicit terrorist activities; rather, these personalities are chosen because, as a representative cross sample, they best illustrate the myriad ways in which virtually every Hamas political and social activity is inextricably bound up with its terrorist mission. We devote particular attention to Hamas founder Sheikh Ahmed Yassin, because his 2003 assassination by Israel aroused considerable sympathy for the spiritual leader and the organization he founded. While the killing of an aged, wheelchair-bound religious figure might naturally stimulate a compassionate or out-raged reaction, that reaction has also obscured Yassin's significant military role within Hamas.

The evidence presented here is gathered from a broad sample of intel-ligence sources, including those from countries and analysts generally con-sidered "anti-Israeli" and "pro-Palestinian." By the end of the chapter, we will have observed a broad consensus among Hamas-watchers of diverse stripes that there is no meaningful distinction between the group's politi-cal, social, and terrorist leadership. As Hamas founder Sheikh Ahmed Yassin himself said about making distinctions between the various wings of Hamas: "We can not separate the wing from the body. If we do so, the body will not be able to fly. Hamas is one body."[1]

SHEIKH AHMED YASSIN

Ahmed Yassin was born in 1936, the second youngest of nine children, to a middle-class farming family in the village of al-Jora near Ashqelon, just north of Gaza in what is today Israel but was then part of British Manda-tory Palestine. When Israel was founded in 1948, Yassin and his family moved to the Gaza Strip's refugee camps.[2]

His early life was marked by personal tragedy. In 1952, at age sixteen, Yassin was hurt while playing on the beach; the damage to his spinal col-umn left him paralyzed and confined to a wheelchair for the rest of his life.[3] During his grade school and high school years in Gaza, Yassin spent a lot of time at a mosque affiliated with the Muslim Brotherhood, where he was ex-posed to the teachings of Hassan al-Banna and others. Yassin also frequented a Muslim Brotherhood front organization called *Jamiyat al-Tawhid*. Dur-ing his early adult years, Yassin focused on Islamic studies, and moved to Cairo to study at al-Azhar University. It was there that Yassin first came into contact with the Egyptian branch of the Muslim Brotherhood. This associa-tion continued back in Gaza, where Yassin and other Brotherhood members were arrested by Egyptian authorities following an attempt by the Brother-hood to seize power in Egypt. Yassin soon became known for his work as a teacher and spiritual leader, and in 1973 he founded al-Mujama al-Islamiya, the Islamic Center, an umbrella organization for many religious organiza-tions in Gaza. When not under arrest, Yassin spent the remainder of his life in Gaza City, where he raised eleven children with his wife, Halima.[4]

How did this supposedly moderate political and spiritual leader—this blind, wizened, handicapped man who was wheeled to a mosque every morning—earn in 2003 the ignominious distinction of Specially Designated Global Terrorist (SDGT) by the United States? Why did Secretary of State Condoleeza Rice feel compelled to remind a television reporter, who had quite rationally questioned the political wisdom of assassinating a sixty-seven-year-old paraplegic sheikh by helicopter rocket, that viewing audiences ought to "remember that Hamas is a terrorist organization and that Sheikh Yassin has himself, personally, we believe, been involved in terrorist planning"?[5]

The answer emerges when we look beyond the sheikh's religious persona and examine the evidence of Ahmed Yassin's connection to terrorist activities. Before the Palestinian branch of the Muslim Brotherhood became known as Hamas, it was already plotting and carrying out terrorist attacks. And long before Sheikh Ahmed Yassin became a political threat to secular Palestinian leaders, he was leading those attacks. As Hamas leader Khaled Mishal recounted in a December 2003 media interview, "In 1983 we carried out our first military experience under the leadership of Sheikh Ahmed Yassin." After the group was reborn in 1987 as Hamas, Yassin led the establishment of the logistical and financial support network known as the dawa, the charitable infrastructure that also served his need of identifying and recruiting new members and military operatives. Once they were recruited, Yassin himself organized these Hamas cadres into small cells—often no more than three members each—throughout the Gaza Strip.[6]

Yassin's multiple arrests by Israel have yielded personal admissions of his own direct role in managing military operations, and of the ultimate subordination of the military branch of Hamas to the "non-military" political wing he headed. Following an abortive attempt by the Brotherhood to seize power in 1965, many Brotherhood members were arrested in Gaza, including Yassin. He spent forty-five days in jail and was then released. After his arrest in 1983, Yassin told Israeli authorities that the organization he had founded was intent on "fighting non-religious [Palestinian] factions in the territories and carrying out jihad operations against Israel." Then, following his release in a 1985 prisoner exchange, Yassin hatched a plot in 1989 to kidnap and murder Israeli soldiers with the plan of using their bodies to bargain for the release of Hamas prisoners in Israeli jails. For his role in the subsequent abduction and murder of Israeli soldiers Ilan Sa'adon and Avi Sasportas, Yassin was again arrested in 1989. After this arrest, Yassin told his interrogators that it was he who had personally tasked Salah Shehadah with establishing the Izz al-Din al-Qassam Brigades—a point confirmed by Shehadah in his own interrogation—and also that he, Yassin, personally "approved the drafting of terrorists as well as the carrying out of terrorist attacks." Yassin was again released from prison in 1997 as part of a deal with Jordan's King Hussein in the wake of Israel's botched attempt to assassinate Hamas leader Khaled Mishal in Jordan. The sheikh played an increasingly proactive role in coordinating and financing Hamas attacks until his assassination in March 2004.[7]

A U.S. Treasury Department assessment of Yassin in the months before his assassination described the cleric as "the head of Hamas in Gaza." According to the August 2003 report, "[Yassin] maintains a direct line of communication with other Hamas leaders on coordination of Hamas's military activities and openly admits that there is no distinguishing the political and military wings of Hamas." In addition to managing Hamas military operations, Yassin was also involved in coordinating military strategy with other Palestinian terrorist organizations. Yassin's primary means of issuing military directives was through Abdel Aziz al-Rantissi (see below), but the cleric also surrounded himself with a constant entourage of "bodyguards" and personal assistants. In addition to attending to his physical needs as a paraplegic, this entourage facilitated Yassin's hands-on leadership of Hamas' terrorist activities, composed as it was of militants and military operatives. Again, according to the U.S. report: "Surrounding Yassin is an entourage of personal 'bodyguards,' including many implicated in providing information and supplies to fugitives, recruiting personnel to undertake military operations, planning terrorist cells, attacking settlements, and manufacturing weapons and explosives."[8]

Indeed, of the four people killed with Yassin, two were his sons and two were bodyguards with long records as Hamas operatives involved in acts of terrorism. Several years earlier, in March 2000, Palestinian security officials arrested several people from Yassin's entourage, including two bodyguards who led PA authorities to explosives hidden in a Gaza kindergarten that were intended for an attack against Israelis. Those Palestinian arrests were carried out with information gathered in an Israeli raid on a Hamas safe house in the Israeli-Arab town of Taibeh—a raid that had foiled a major terrorist attack. Israeli authorities determined that one of Yassin's bodyguards, Nasser al-Bughdadi, had dispatched the would-be bombers and gave the go-ahead for the foiled attack.[9]

In addition to spearheading Hamas coordination with other Palestinian militant groups, Yassin was also directly involved in the one documented case of operational crossover between Hamas and al-Qaeda. In 1997 a group of five Hamas dawa activists traveled to Pakistan for religious training. One of them, Nabil Awqil, was recruited there by a Palestinian *jihadi* for military training, first in the Pakistani-controlled Kashmiri area and then in al-Qaeda camps in Afghanistan. After completing his training in April 1998, Awqil returned to Gaza, where he visited Sheikh Yassin and announced his plans to establish a terrorist cell in Gaza. Yassin appointed Iyad al-Beihk, a Hamas operative, to serve as an intermediary between himself and Awqil, and then provided Awqil with $5,000 seed money to finance his cell. Later, when Awqil and one of his recruits planned to travel back to Pakistan and Afghanistan for additional training and meetings, Yassin provided another $5,000 and prepared a cover story for the militants that would disguise their trip as a journey to Jordan for medical treatment. A month before his August 2001 arrest in Israel, Awqil played host in Gaza to al-Qaeda recruit Richard Reid. The following year, Reid would become known as the "shoe-bomber" for his attempt to detonate a bomb hidden in the sole of his shoe while flying from Paris to Miami.[10]

The "internal" leadership of Hamas in Gaza (and, to a lesser extent, the West Bank) often appears relatively moderate in tone when compared to the "external" leadership based primarily in Syria (see section on Mousa Abu Marzook, below). From the comfort of its Syrian safe haven, the Damascus-based leadership can give full voice to its extremist ideology, without fear of consequence. The internal leadership, however, must consider the crackdowns Israel (and, periodically, the PA) imposes in the wake of terrorist attacks, as well as the likely impact those attacks have on the grassroots support of Palestinians forced to deal with closures, roadblocks, and more. The relative moderation of Gaza-based leaders like Yassin, however, should not be interpreted as a disavowal of violence; rather it is prudent tactical planning based on a strategic commitment to violence. Until his death Yassin remained committed to the group's terrorist agenda as articulated in the Hamas charter, which declares, "There is no solution for the Palestinian question except through Jihad."[11]

ABDEL AZIZ AL-RANTISSI

Abdel Aziz al-Rantissi was born in 1947 in a village near the present-day Israeli city of Jaffa. A year later, after the establishment of Israel, al-Rantissi's family moved to a refugee camp in the Gaza Strip town of Khan Yunis. A gifted student, al-Rantissi was top of his class at Egypt's Alexandria University medical school, where he earned a medical degree. It was here that he first made contact with the Muslim Brotherhood, already banned by Egypt as a radical Islamist organization.[12]

Al-Rantissi returned to Gaza in 1973 and co-founded the Islamic Center—a mosque, social service center, and charity—together with Yassin and other Brotherhood leaders. He returned to Egypt to obtain an M.A. in pediatrics, settling back in Gaza in 1976. When the Islamic University in Gaza opened in 1978, al-Rantissi lectured there on general science, genetics, and parasitology (the science of parasites). He later worked as head of pediatrics at Nasser Hospital in Khan Yunis until 1983, when he was dismissed from his position by Israeli authorities for refusing to pay taxes—one of his first overt political gestures. Al-Rantissi helped establish Hamas during the first Intifada in 1987, but his name wasn't widely known until he became the spokesman for 418 suspected Hamas and other Palestinian militants deported to Lebanon in 1992. Al-Rantissi and his fellow militants were deported for supporting or participating in armed attacks on Israel. After his return from Lebanon in 1993, al-Rantissi was briefly held by Israel, and was subsequently arrested and detained multiple times by the Palestinian Authority for facilitating Hamas military activity. He rose to prominence after Sheikh Ahmed Yassin's release from an Israeli prison in 1997, when the two Hamas founders worked closely together to direct the organization's military and other activities. According to the U.S. government, Hamas leader al-Rantissi operated directly under Yassin and maintained "a direct line of communication for the coordination of military operations" with the Hamas leader. For this role, the U.S. Treasury Department designated al-Rantissi as a Specially Designated Global Terrorist entity. After Yassin's assassination by the Israeli Defense Forces in March 2004, al-Rantissi assumed the reins of Hamas, a position he held for four weeks, until he, too, was assassinated by the IDF on April 17, 2004. He was married, with two sons and four daughters.[13]

According to an Israeli report released in October 2003, al-Rantissi was more than a Hamas mouthpiece. During interrogations, Hamas operatives have said that al-Rantissi actually directed Hamas terrorist policy. His public statements, according to the captured militants, were sometimes coded "instructions for terrorists to carry out attacks."[14] Consider the following examples in light of this conclusion:

In the fall of 2001, al-Rantissi participated in an online question-and-answer session on an Islamist website, bahrainonline.org. A person using the online handle "Ismahan" asked al-Rantissi how a person from Bahrain might volunteer for a suicide mission in Palestine or otherwise contribute to the Palestinian jihad. Al-Rantissi answered by first praising the suicide operations. Then he wrote:

As to a person from outside of Palestine who wishes to carry out a suicide operation, there might be a need for that in the future. As to one who wishes to donate money for those who were harmed in this battle, here is the bank account—the Arab Bank in Gaza, account no. 36444, on the name of Sheikh Ahmad Yassin. As to the support by propaganda, this dialogue is part of it, in addition to the participation in the satellite channels in favor of the Mujahidin against the aggressive Jews, and to the writing of articles, managing festivals, etc.[15]

In an interview with BBC radio the following year, al-Rantissi announced that Hamas was planning new attacks. "The resistance is still strong," he said on the air. "We will hear about operations in the coming few weeks or days." Speaking about the group's decision not to sign a new ceasefire agreement after a lull in Hamas suicide attacks, al-Rantissi told Reuters in December 2003 that "martyrdom operations come as waves so there are gaps between the waves. We are just in the period of a gap between waves."[16]

Al-Rantissi didn't always use the press to communicate with Hamas militants; when he could, he would issue orders to them directly. In a 1993 interview with Israeli authorities, several Hamas operatives identified al-Rantissi "as the individual who they were in contact with in regard to Hamas activity, which included assistance for military activists, the transfer of letters and the coordination of nominating activists for different positions in the Movement." Also according to Israel, "Rantissi was in contact with central military Hamas activists in the Gaza Strip and served as the person responsible for the supervision and establishment of covert military squads for terror activity."[17]

Al-Rantissi was an articulate and effective spokesman for Hamas who usually remembered when speaking to the press to perpetuate the myth of a formal separation between the political and military branches of Hamas. But he occasionally slipped. In 2001, al-Rantissi told a Reuters reporter that the Hamas military wing operates at the pleasure of the political bureau, and is subordinate to it. "The Hamas political leadership has freed the hand of the [Izz al-Din al-Qassam] brigades to do whatever they want against the brothers of monkey and pigs," al-Rantissi said. The article concluded that "Hamas' political wing determines overall policy for the movement." Elsewhere, al-Rantissi conflated the fundamental nature of the political and military wings, eschewing the rhetorical distinction: "The political and military wings both are struggling," he told Harvard scholar Jessica Stern. "That is the meaning of jihad."[18]

On at least one occasion, al-Rantissi publicly acknowledged his own personal involvement in military activities. In October of 2002, the Egyptian newspaper *al-Hayat* reported that al-Rantissi claimed personal responsibility for the assassination of a Palestinian Authority police colonel.[19]

MOUSA ABU MARZOOK

The eighth of nine children, Mousa Mohammad Abu Marzook was born in 1951 in the Gaza Strip town of Rafah. After receiving his bachelor's degree in engineering from Cairo's Ein Shams University in 1976, Marzook moved to Abu Dhabi.[20] There he became an increasingly prominent political activist in the Muslim Brotherhood.

In 1982, Marzook arrived in the United States on a student visa to begin work on his doctorate in industrial engineering from Columbia State University in Louisiana. While he traveled to Jordan periodically, Marzook and his wife, Nadia, and their six children remained in the United States until 1995. Following his graduate studies, Marzook moved his family to northern Virginia and began working as political director of the United Association for Studies and Research (UASR), a Muslim think tank with close ties to Hamas. He also helped establish and endow the Islamic Association of Palestine (IAP) and the Holy Land Foundation for Relief and Development, two organizations accused of raising money for Hamas.[21] (These organizations and their ties to Hamas are considered in detail in Chapter 6.)

Following Sheikh Ahmed Yassin's arrest by Israel in 1989, Marzook, then in the United States, effectively took over the leadership of Hamas and oversaw the organization's growth in fundraising, military operations, and social services infrastructure. When the Hamas political bureau was established in the early 1990s Marzook was appointed as its head. In 1995 Marzook was deported from the United States and repaired to Jordan. Four years later, when Jordanian authorities shut the Hamas offices there and expelled Marzook and several other Hamas leaders, Marzook and his colleagues moved to Damascus, Syria.[22]

Much of what we know of Marzook came out during his 1995 extradition case in the United States. In July of 1995, Marzook and his family were held for questioning when they attempted to reenter the United States after a visit to Jordan. When security agents discovered he was listed in what was then the Immigration and Naturalization Service's (INS) Look-Out system, Marzook was deferred for a secondary inspection. He attempted to conceal a small suitcase and an attaché case from inspectors; when discovered, these were found to include financial and personal records, as well as an address book INS agents would later describe as "crucial." According to the affidavit of FBI Special Agent Joseph Hummel, who interviewed Marzook, "we asked Marzook several times during the course of the interview whether he possessed any telephone/address books. Marzook consistently denied possessing any telephone/address book." Marzook also insisted that his wife, Nadia, was carrying no address book. Nadia was escorted to a private room with two female immigration agents, for a search of her clothing. As she was removing her underwear, a small address book fell to the floor.[23] Among the names included in this book were:

- Hassan al-Turabi, then the radical leader of Sudan who provided safe haven to radical terrorists, including Hamas members;
- Ahmed Mohammad Yusef, a former member of the Sudanese mission in New York who had participated in plots to assassinate the president of Egypt and to bomb the United Nations;
- George Habash, head of the Popular Front for the Liberation of Palestine (PFLP), a secular Palestinian terrorist group;
- Ahmad Jibril, leader of the Popular Front for the Liberation of Palestine's General Command (PFLP-GC), another secular Palestinian terrorist group;
- The Islamic Call Society in Islamabad, Pakistan, an organization that the FBI believes is used to move money to terrorists.[24]

(In his interviews with law enforcement agents, Marzook also acknowledged knowing Yihye Ayash, a Hamas bomb-maker known as "the Engineer" who perfected the suicide-bombing belt. Marzook described Ayash as a "hero, a great man.") Though he insisted he was merely a "mid-level political activist" within the political wing of Hamas, the FBI recognized Marzook as "actually the head of the political arm of Hamas."[25]

The detention of Mousa Abu Marzook by INS agents in New York and consequent investigation would yield a trove of information about the connection between the Hamas political leadership and the organization's other activities. The evidence would lead an American court to concur with the previously held Israeli assessment that "the [political] bureau operates as the highest ranking leadership body in the Hamas organization, setting policies and guidelines respecting Hamas' activities. In addition to its other functions, this bureau has responsibility for directing and coordinating terrorist acts by Hamas against soldiers and civilians in Israel and the territories."[26]

During the first half of the 1990s, Marzook oversaw from his home in the United States the international funding effort for both the Hamas dawa and the terrorist operations of its Qassam Brigades, activities that are detailed in Marzook's personal correspondence. For example, in October 1992 Hamas activist Bassem Musa wrote to Marzook requesting financial assistance: "The truth is, Abu Ammar [Marzook], that we did not receive from you the allowance for the 'al-dawa' society, and what derives from it, but for the 'positive' [i.e., military, operational], the sum of 100,000 only [currency unstated]. While the actual budget we need to cover all our activities and plans for the three months is no less than 700,000." According to another letter asking Marzook for funds, Bassem Musa indicates that Marzook personally negotiated an arms deal for Hamas involving thousands of weapons: "I called Chicago several times, but have not received anything despite the promises that it will be soon," writes Musa. "I am ashamed to write to the mediator of the deal [of the ten thousand weapons] because I don't have the money except for what [I will receive] if I sell my car and my property and get organized." As recently as January 2004, Marzook himself confirmed that the Hamas political leadership oversees the compensation of families of Hamas suicide bombers and remains in touch with their families. Speaking of the many Palestinians who "choose freedom for their country and they sacrifice themselves for the sake of it," Marzook noted, "They are certainly taken care of and their families are compensated. Nobody could neglect those martyrs and their families, they are in our hearts, all of us: Hamas, Fatah and all the Palestinian factions. We all stand by their families and compensate them and take care of them and keep the memory of the martyrs."[27]

The extra-political activity of this leading Hamas politician was not limited to moving money and buying weapons but extended also into the hands-on realm of terrorist recruiting. Much of what we know about Marzook's recruiting and fundraising activity comes from Mohammad Salah, a Hamas agent arrested by Israel in 1993 whom Marzook personally recruited into a Hamas precursor paramilitary group based in the United States called the "Palestine Organization." Not only did Marzook oversee fundraising activity and Qassam Brigades operations from his Virginia home, but he also initiated the recruitment and training of Hamas operatives on U.S. soil. According to Salah, pursuant to the initiative and supervision of Abu Marzook, around 1990 Salah "hand selected ten people to serve on a military team and had them trained in the United States by Muslim instructors from the United States and Lebanon who had military expertise." As a result, Israeli intelligence concluded, "various operatives [in the United States] learned how to prepare explosive charges. These activists were planned to come to Israel and join the military activities of the Hamas there."[28]

According to Salah, Marzook dispatched him to the West Bank and Gaza four times between 1989 and 1993 to fund the Hamas military wing following major disruptions to its operational abilities, such as the 1988 arrest of 260 Hamas and other radical activists, and the 1992 deportation of 418 of Hamas and other radical Islamists to Lebanon. At Marzook's request, Salah went to Israel on two occasions in 1989 and 1990 to assess the situation in the territories. He then went on two later trips in August 1992 and January 1993 to organize and finance Hamas activities and to assess the military situation on the ground.[29]

Salah's role in financing Hamas terror cells on behalf of Marzook offers a critical window into how Hamas has managed its affairs from the United States. FBI analysis of bank and airline records, together with Salah's own statements to Israeli authorities, has led U.S. investigators to conclude that "between June 18, 1991, and December 30, 1992, Mohammad Salah expended in excess of $100,000 in direct support of Hamas military activities." Salah confirmed to Israeli officials that Marzook and Ismail Elbarrase, another Hamas activist in the United States, provided the money he funneled to Hamas. "It is true," Salah told his interrogators, "that the money was passed on by means of brother Musa Abu Marzuk and brother Ismail Al-Barusa [sic]." From his U.S. base, Marzook also weighed in on the planning of military operations in the occupied territories. For example, at one point Salah suggested to Abu Marzook that the former murder Sari Nusieba, a prominent Palestinian intellectual, for his role in the peace talks. In another case, Marzook instructed Salah to designate one of the new Hamas operatives Salah was training to replace the head of the Hamas military wing in Ramallah.[30]

KHALED MISHAL

Khaled Mishal was born May 28, 1956, in the conservative village of Selwad in the Ramallah district, then under Jordanian rule. His father moved to Kuwait in the 1960s for work, and Khaled and the rest of the family joined him after the 1967 war. Deeply influenced by his father's stories about resisting the British mandate, Mishal befriended several Muslim Brotherhood members while a student at Kuwait's Abdullah al-Salem High School and eventually joined the organization himself in 1971 at age fifteen. A strong student, Mishal went on to earn a B.S. in physics from Kuwait University in 1978. His interest in Palestinian national issues intensified at university, and he led the Palestinian Islamic group there and participated in founding the Islamic Bloc, which competed for control of the General Union for the Palestinian Students at Kuwait University. After graduation, Mishal started a teaching career and married in 1981. He became involved with Hamas during the early years of the organization's conception during the first half of the 1980s. Mishal and his family (he has seven children) stayed in Kuwait until 1990, when the monarchy expelled all Palestinians as retribution for the PLO's support of Saddam Hussein's invasion of Kuwait in 1990. During Mishal's formative years in Kuwait he forged relationships with like-minded students and fellow professionals there, many of whom would end up in key positions in Hamas' political bureaucracy. There is some resentment of these Mishal-led *Kuwaidia* (the Kuwaiti group) for their dominance of Hamas' political bureau, particularly by followers of Mousa Abu Marzook, whose own faction is largely populated by people whose seminal years, like his, were spent in Gaza. Despite simmering resentment, the two factions do work very closely together.[31]

Mishal relocated to Jordan in 1990, where he assumed responsibility for Hamas' international fundraising efforts out of the Amman office. Though he has been a member of the Hamas Political Bureau since its creation, it was not until after the 1995 arrest of Mousa Abu Marzook that Mishal was elected bureau chairman. From that point on Mishal has assumed responsibility for Marzook's organizational portfolio and for the terror activities undertaken by the Qassam Brigades. He splits his time between Damascus, Syria, and Doha, Qatar.[32]

Mishal was the target of a failed Israeli assassination attempt in 1997. On the morning of September 25 he was attacked in Amman by two Mossad agents, one of whom injected a toxic substance into Mishal's pores without actually penetrating his skin. Jordanian authorities apprehended the agents. Two hours later Mishal felt the impact of the poison and eventually lost consciousness; he was revived only when the Israeli prime minister, under intense diplomatic pressure, sent an antidote. The botched assassination was a catastrophe for Israel—both for its operational failure and the diplomatic row that followed—and resulted in the release of Sheikh Ahmed Yassin from an Israeli prison.[33]

Among the Hamas political leaders marked by the United States as Specially Designated Global Terrorist entities—including Sheikh Ahmed

Yassin, Imad al-Alami, Osama Hamdan, Khaled Mishal, Mousa Abu Mar-zook, and Abdel Aziz al-Rantissi—Mishal is noteworthy for heading up the Hamas Political Bureau. He is perhaps the most explicitly "political" of Hamas leaders, and his personal involvement in the group's terrorist opera-tions is evidence of the military wing's subordination to the political wing. From his office in Damascus, Mishal personally oversees Hamas terrorist cells and supervises their operations. According to U.S. authorities, not only are there "cells in the military wing based in the West Bank that are under Mishaal's control," these cells "have been implicated in efforts by Hamas to plan large attacks that would undermine the road map peace plan." Ac-cording to an August 2003 Treasury Department report, "Mishaal has been responsible for supervising assassination operations, bombings and the killing of Israeli settlers. To execute Hamas military activities, Mishaal maintains a direct link to Gaza-based Hamas leader Abdel Aziz al-Rantissi. He also provides instructions to other parts of the Hamas military wing."[34]

Mishal's office in Damascus is essentially a reincarnation of the Hamas political committee he and Mousa Abu Marzook ran in Amman for most of the 1990s. Jordanian documents related to Mishal and Marzook's expul-sion from Amman in 1999 shed light on the nature of "political" activity historically practiced by the Hamas Politburo. On September 22, 1999, Mishal was arrested at Jordan's Queen Alia International Airport along with Marzook, Hamas spokesman Ibrahim Ghosheh, and four other aides upon their arrival in Jordan from Iran. Marzook, a Yemeni national, was the only one of the seven who was not Jordanian and was immediately sent back to Iran on the same airplane that brought him to Jordan. Mishal and Ghosheh were taken into custody and charged with being members of a militant Palestinian group outlawed by Jordan. Mishal was also charged with possession of an unlicensed pistol.[35]

Several weeks later Mishal and Ghosheh were indicted on additional charges of possessing "three unlicensed Kalashnikov rifles, illegal posses-sion of a hand grenade, forging a public administration stamp, fraud, and raising funds for a non-authorized association," and pled not guilty. War-rants for the arrest of Marzook, Mishal, and Ghosheh had been issued by Jordan in late August 1999 after Jordanian police raided and shut down the Hamas offices there.[36]

The reason for Jordan's crackdown on Hamas offices in Amman ap-pears to be related to Hamas' increasingly brazen and public presence there following Israel's botched assassination attempt of Mishal in 1997. According to former Jordanian Prime Minister Abdul-Elah al-Khatib, Jordan's outrage over the assassination attempt—and consequent demand that Israel release Sheikh Ahmed Yassin from an Israeli prison—was misinterpreted by Hamas supporters as King Hussein's tacit approval of Hamas operations in Jordan. "Hamas misunderstood Jordan's reaction to the Mishal affair," said al-Khatib.[37]

As a chief spokesman for the group, Mishal continues al-Rantissi's tradition of exhorting militants and would-be militants to action at political rallies. "Great people of Palestine," Mishal told the crowd at a Hezbollah-organized rally in Beirut in 2000, "burn the ground under the feet of the invaders. Ramadan is a great month to escalate." More recently, he has spoken explicitly on behalf of Hamas' military wing, saying, "The Qassam Brigades swear that their retaliation will be 100 martyrdom attacks in the heart of your homes. We will burn the earth under your feet."[38]

Mishal's day-to-day contribution to Hamas' terrorist operations includes not only oversight of terrorist activity but also forging close relationships with political leaders sympathetic to Hamas' cause and managing fundraising operations that furnish money directly to Hamas operatives. For many years Mishal served as Hamas' official liaison to Muslim and Arab organizations. In December 1993 he participated in a conference in Sudan hosted by the government's radical Islamist government, which assembled an opposition front of Islamist radicals and Arab Marxists to oppose the 1993 Oslo Accords. Mishal also led several Hamas delegations to Muslim countries for fundraising efforts and has met regularly with Iranian leaders, including several meetings with then President Mohammad Khatami in Tehran in 1999. Mishal also met Khatami outside Iran. In May 1999 they met in Damascus at a high-level meeting at the Iranian Embassy at which leaders of several militant Palestinian factions were present.[39]

In April 2001, Mishal attended a two-day, pro-Intifada conference in Tehran, attended by Iranian leaders, Hezbollah's Sheikh Hassan Nasrallah, and Islamic Jihad's Ramadan Abdullah Shallah, among others. At the conference, Mishal explained that "what we want is: one, a political decision that accepts the responsibility of the Palestinian resistance; two, financial support; and three, armed support."[40]

Mishal also visited Baghdad in 1996 to meet with Taha Yassin Ramadan, the former vice president of Saddam Hussein's regime. After the 2004 assassinations of Ahmed Yassin and al-Rantissi, Mishal sought increased funding from Iran and a direct channel to Iranian Revolutionary Guards Corps (IRGC) in an effort to reinvigorate Hamas' operational cells.[41]

He was appointed the new overall leader of Hamas on March 24, 2004, following the assassination of Sheikh Yassin.

JAMAL TAWIL

Our previous examples have highlighted how well-known Hamas political leaders have also been managers, facilitators, and executors of military activities. The example of Jamal Tawil illuminates the opposite: a Hamas military commander from Ramallah who takes on political or dawa-related roles as a way to camouflage and enable the violent operations that are his primary duty.

Israeli security forces arrested Jamal Tawil during Operation Defensive Shield, a major Israeli operation in the West Bank in April 2002 that was precipitated by a string of Hamas suicide bombings. Then thirty-nine, Tawil was a senior Hamas military commander in the West Bank believed to have planned multiple suicide bombing attacks, including a car bombing in a Jerusalem pedestrian mall that killed twelve Israelis and wounded nearly two hundred. After this, his third arrest by Israel since 1996, investigators would learn that Tawil—under the guidance of more senior Hamas leaders—had adopted political and dawa roles in order to facilitate and conceal his military activities. Among the revelations was that the head of the Hamas propaganda bureau in Lebanon, whose nom de guerre is Abu Ahmad, had instructed Tawil to become the Hamas spokesman in Ramallah. Abu Ahmad taught Tawil how to use e-mail for publicity and communication purposes but also to maintain contact with Khaled Mishal and other senior Hamas political officials in Lebanon and Syria. Tawil told his interrogators that in March 1998 Abu Ahmad began to wire monthly bank transfers of $12,000 for Hamas activities—first into Tawil's personal account and later into the local account of the al-Islah Charitable Society—the Hamas charity Tawil was instructed to found in Ramallah. (Israeli authorities believe Abu Ahmad is really Ismael Srour, who oversees money transfers from Hamas leadership in Syria to operatives in the West Bank and Gaza.)[42]

Tawil was also told to head up a Hamas prisoners committee charged with supporting the families of Hamas prisoners and providing canteen money to the prisoners themselves. In this role, Tawil instructed Hamas inmates to have bank accounts opened for them into which Hamas could deposit funds. He also collected and forwarded information on prisoners to Hamas political leaders in Lebanon. When he failed to secure a PA license for his prisoners committee, Tawil was advised by other Hamas leaders to found a branch of the al-Islah charity in Ramallah, "to camouflage the activities of the prisoners committee and to enable it to expand and receive donations from Islamic charitable societies abroad."[43]

Tawil also received letters from Hamas leaders abroad, meeting an anonymous messenger at prearranged meeting places and using code words to identify each other. Fellow Hamas operative Mohammad Omar Hamdan told Tawil how this cover system of passing couriered messages would work:

> [Tawil was told] to wait near al-Bireh's municipal hall at a certain time to meet the messenger who would bring him the letters. He told him that the messenger had his (Tawil's) cellular phone number and that he would call and say he was from the Tahan family and interested in enrolling his children in al-Urduniyyah school (where al-Tawil was principal), and then he knew he was to go to the meeting place.

As of February 2005, he remains in an Israeli prison.[44]

THE INTERNATIONAL CONSENSUS ON THE LINK BETWEEN HAMAS POLITICIANS AND TERRORISM

Israel

Much of the available evidence linking Hamas political leaders to terrorist activity comes from Israeli sources, so it will come as no surprise that Israeli military intelligence has concluded that the Hamas political bureau "determines terrorism policy, draws conclusions from terrorist attacks already perpetrated and relays them to activists, assists Hamas fugitives, supports terrorist attacks, encourages additional terror and praises the movement for 'having advanced the Intifada from the stone age to suicide attacks.'" (These "political" functions, notably, not only are highlighted by Israeli authorities, they are also explicitly listed in the Hamas publication *al-Risala*.)[45]

Palestinian Authority

Perhaps more surprising is that the Israeli intelligence assessment is confirmed by Palestinian intelligence. A Palestinian report dated December 10, 2000, documents operational links between Damascus-based Hamas leaders such as Mousa Abu Marzook, Imad al-Alami, Osama Hamdan, and Khaled Mishal, with Hamas political leaders on the ground in the West Bank and Gaza such as Ismail Abu Shanab, Ismail Haniyeh, and Sheikh Jamal Salim. According to the report, "The Hamas movement in Syria published instructions for the [Izz al-Din] al-Qassam Battalions 'inside,' according to which they should immediately send a financial situation picture report and a situation assessment of the military squads 'inside.' [The Hamas leaders in Syria] gave a green light to the military arm headquarters to carry out military operations against Israeli military targets, without being committed to any decision of the Hamas' military arm 'inside.' [In fact], the Battalions were also told to distance themselves from the Hamas leaders who are coordinating their activity with the Palestinian Authority." Long before that report was published, Palestinian Brigadier General Nizar Ammar was highlighting the overlap between the Hamas political, social, and military wings. According to Ammar, "We learned from interrogations that some of the people involved in operations inside Israel had been in the political wing only forty-eight hours before the operation. This is a big problem for the PA interrogators because people jump between the political and military wings at a moment's notice."[46]

Jordan

The Jordanian General Intelligence Directorate (GID) shares the view that Hamas is a dangerous terrorist organization. In August 1999 a royal decree formally banned Hamas from operating in the kingdom and led to the closure of the Hamas political offices in Amman and the arrest of several Hamas leaders. Jordanian raids of Hamas political offices produced unlicensed personal weapons and documentary evidence that Hamas had been actively smuggling weapons to Hamas militants in the West Bank through Jordan. Prime Minister Abdel Rauef al-Rawabdeh said Hamas' presence in the country appeared to be "threatening the kingdom's stability." Other Jordanian officials said at the time that Hamas had been "conducting paramilitary training, raising funds for subversive purposes, using forged Jordanian passports, and recruiting in Jordan's Palestinian refugee camps and universities." According to Jordanian counterterrorism officials, "Hamas officials in Jordan were involved in weapons smuggling plots and infiltration efforts through northern Jordan and they were cooperating with Hizballah to send weapons and recruits to the West Bank from Syria via Jordan." In addition, evidence was found that the four political Hamas leaders had authorized the collection of intelligence on Jordan and Jordanian officials.[47]

North America

U.S. officials, too, concur with the Israeli assessment. Not only have the FBI and Department of Homeland Security (DHS) both included the Israeli affidavits cited above in court documents filed in support of criminal terrorism cases and deportation proceedings, but information collected by U.S. intelligence and law enforcement agencies also corroborates the Israeli information. Thus, in its August 2003 announcement designating five charities and six senior Hamas political leaders as terrorist entities, the U.S. Treasury Department asserted that "the political leadership of Hamas directs its terrorist networks just as they oversee their other activities." Noting the active role Hamas political leaders play in funding and overseeing Hamas terror attacks, the U.S. Treasury Department has designated Hamas political leaders Sheikh Ahmed Yassin, Imad al-Alami, Osama Hamdan, Khaled Mishal, Mousa Abu Marzook, and Abdel Aziz al-Rantissi as Specially Designated Global Terrorist entities.[48]

Likewise, Canadian intelligence has determined that Hamas political offices in Damascus also serve as militant recruitment centers. A Canadian intelligence report notes that along with Iran, Lebanon, and Sudan, where Hamas maintains training camps, "Syria also contributes with the provision of safe houses and offices used for recruitment." The Canadian and U.S. information appears to corroborate Israeli claims that terrorist elements in Damascus, where the political leadership of groups like Hamas operate, are "conveying clear and precise instructions to perpetrate terror attacks in the West Bank and Gaza" and are "transferring cash to banks in Nablus to fund these operations."[49]

Europe

The military wing of Hamas has been identified by the European Union as a terrorist organization since 2001, but European countries have been historically reluctant to issue blanket condemnations of all Hamas-related groups—preferring instead to distinguish between ostensibly "charitable" and "political" Hamas factions and explicitly military ones. In 2003, there emerged a European consensus that such distinctions are no longer tenable given available evidence of the interdependence between such groups. In that year, British Foreign Secretary Jack Straw led a campaign to convince EU member nations to include the political wing on the terrorist blacklist as well. "I think the case against Hamas—its so-called political wing as well as its military wing—is now overwhelming," Straw told reporters. After public endorsements of the British position by Italy and the Czech Republic, France dropped its long-standing opposition to the ban, and the EU banned all Hamas wings, including charitable and political factions. EU foreign policy chief Javier Solana has said that a precondition for European recognition of Hamas as a legitimate political player in the Mideast peace process is total rejection of terrorism. "Everyone would very much like, we've said many times, to have Hamas as a political organization, breaking . . . ties with terrorist activities and at the same time becoming a political party," said Solana. In the summer of 2005, following Hamas victories in several rounds of municipal elections, Straw again stressed that "the fact that a terror organization stands in elections doesn't mean it ceases to be a terror organization. Hamas will stay on the [British] list of terror groups until it has renounced terrorist violence in action as well as in words."[50] A month later, French president Jacques Chirac concurred, asserting that "Hamas is a terrorist organization that cannot be an interlocutor of the international community as long as it does not renounce violence and does not recognize Israel's right to exist. This is the unambiguous position of the EU and it will not change."[51]

Academics and NGOs

The general consensus of agreement on the role Hamas political leaders play in the group's terror activity extends beyond international intelligence services. Terrorism scholars also generally recognize that, as Harvard's Jessica Stern has noted, the Hamas political leadership, notably people like Khaled Mishal and Mousa Abu Marzook in Damascus, "send the funding and provide overall direction from their safe houses elsewhere in the Middle East."[52] Human Rights Watch, an international human rights non-governmental organization, also agrees with this assessment. A Human Rights Watch report concluded that Hamas functions as a unified entity, with the military operatives subservient to the political leadership:

> In the case of Hamas, there is abundant evidence that the military wing is accountable to a political steering committee that includes Shaikh Ahmad Yassin, the group's acknowledged "spiritual leader," as well as spokespersons such as Ismail Abu Shanab, 'Abd al-'Aziz al-Rantissi, and Mahmud Zahar. Yassin himself, as well as Salah Shehadah, the late founder and commander of the 'Izz al-Din al-Qassam Brigades, have confirmed in public remarks that the military wing implements the policies that are set by the political wing.[53]

3

economic jihad: how hamas finances terror

Behind every successful suicide bombing lies a network of recruiters, trainers, bomb makers, facilitators, and financiers. Providing these and other means of logistical support are functions of the Hamas dawa.

The next three chapters, then, focus in detail on how the dawa supports (indeed, makes possible) the paramilitary terrorist activity for which the group is infamous. We will present evidence showing that the dawa—though ostensibly a charitable, non-political, non-military network of social service organizations—facilitates terrorism in five primary ways:

- Raising the massive budgets required to fund terrorist operations;
- Laundering and transferring funds to terrorists via charitable and religious fronts;
- Recruiting, employing, and hiding Hamas militants;
- Providing essential administrative support to terrorist cells;
- Engendering popular Palestinian (and broader Muslim) support for terrorism.

This chapter focuses on the first two items, those relating to the financial contribution to terrorism made by the dawa. The cost of running a paramilitary terrorist operation like Hamas' is enormous. Without leveraging the charitable instincts deeply ingrained in Muslim cultures—and the veil of legitimacy these cultural institutions afford their malefactors—Hamas as we know it today would be unthinkable.[1]

THE COST OF RUNNING HAMAS

The cost of running Hamas encompasses interdependent but separate operational, political, and dawa expenses. Operational costs include expenses for weapons and ammunition, explosive precursors, chemicals for bombs and poisoning, safe houses, communications, travel, transportation, bribes, intelligence payments, and training. They are contingent on political and dawa costs. These expenditures comprise propaganda, print collateral, and political campaigns in the political realm, and salaries, overhead, payments to orphans and widows, education, health, and food in the social welfare service domain. These dawa costs are far more expensive than purely operational costs, accounting for large-scale and long-term infrastructure investments. This infrastructure forms the foundation not only for Hamas' social welfare but its political, guerilla, and terrorist activities as well. And, money being fungible, the funds raised by and for this dawa infrastructure benefit individuals, organizations, and activities throughout Hamas and its component parts.

Speaking before a gathering of G-7 finance ministers in February 2005, U.S. Treasury Undersecretary John Taylor highlighted the critical role that combating terror-financing plays in undermining terrorist groups' long-term capabilities. "By breaking the financial backbone of terrorist groups and insurgents," he said, "we can encumber and thwart their short-term ambitions while rupturing their long-term agendas. Choking off funds that aid terrorists can lead to the ultimate ruin of terrorist organizations."[2]

Still, some experts maintain that terrorism costs little money. An Ivy League professor made this misleading conclusion in her October 2003 testimony before the U.S. Senate Committee on Banking, Housing, and Urban Affairs. Terrorism is "cheap," she testified, arguing that although the spectacular September 11 attacks are estimated to have cost half a million dollars, it takes "a great deal less to buy some fertilizer, rent a truck, and bring down a building." Moreover, terrorists do not need generous state sponsors, such as Iran, to fund their operations, the professor said. The tactical appeal of terrorism is that "one can get so much bang for one's buck. It is cheap and easy and lends itself to dramatic impact."[3]

While it is true that any given terrorist attack may be relatively inexpensive, the actual funding of discrete operations accounts for a small fraction of a terrorist group's expenses. Bullets and bombs are cheap, and a suicide bombing can cost as little as a few thousand or even a few hundred dollars. But this manner of accounting neglects to account for the high cost of maintaining the financial and logistical support network that terrorists carrying out such attacks must draw upon time and again. Terrorist organizations incur many long-term costs, including renting safe houses, buying loyalties, maintaining the physical infrastructure of their networks, paying member salaries, printing posters and banners, and other costs. As a U.S. General Accounting Office report found, the cost of funding an actual operation accounts for "a small portion of the assets that terrorist organizations require for their support infrastructure such as indoctrination, recruitment, training, logistical support, the dissemination of propaganda, and other material support." When we fail to account for more than just bullets and explosives, we may well come to the mistaken conclusion that terrorism is an inexpensive business. Such an assumption may lead even concerned observers to conclude that most of the massive funding raised by Hamas goes toward its political and public-service projects; in fact the social and political wings of Hamas play essential—and expensive—roles in maintaining the group's operational terrorist capacity.[4]

So how much money does it take to run Hamas? Obviously, it's impossible to say with certainty. Hamas is not a publicly held corporation subject to transparent accounting obligations, independent audits, and government oversight. It is an organization that engages in covert activity designed to thwart precisely such an analysis. What information we have about Hamas' finances is the result of investigations that necessarily rely sometimes on uncooperative sources. Nevertheless, Hamas' nefarious activities have made it a subject of intense examination by intelligence and criminal justice experts around the world, yielding troves of useful and dependable data. The following analysis is an attempt to summarize what we do know—and make logical and reasonable extrapolations from that knowledge—with the ultimate aim of debunking the myth that terrorism is inexpensive.

The Cost of an Attack

Estimates of Hamas' total annual budget range from $30 million to $90 million a year. According to FBI testimony before Congress in 2003, the U.S. government believes that Hamas' annual budget is at least $50 million. Hamas receives an estimated $25 million to $30 million of foreign funding through its charitable dawa network each year. This money goes to terror activities, social welfare, and ambiguously overlapping areas such as money paid to the families of suicide bombers. According to the Jordanian General Intelligence Directorate, it costs $2.8 million per month, or $33.6 million a year, just to run Hamas activities in the Palestinian territories. Israeli Shin Bet experts believe that this figure accounts merely for the money passing through Jordan, and that the total figure from all sources is much higher.[5]

There is a range of opinion regarding what constitutes the cost of a Palestinian terror attack. In a 2002 interview, Salah Shehada, the founder of the Izz al-Din al-Qassam Brigades, claimed an operation could cost from $3,500 to $50,000. A Hezbollah member has put the figure of a terror attack at $665–$1,105 (3,000–5,000 NIS). Another terrorist from Palestinian Islamic Jihad, Ahmad Sari Hussein, received $2,210 (10,000 NIS) for his terrorist activity, while Wael Ghanam, a Tanzim activist from the Tulkarem refugee camp, said he received $7,000 to manufacture explosive charges. Others have claimed that a suicide bombing mission could be set up for as little as $150, consisting essentially of a bomb of chemicals (sugar or fertilizer), a battery, a light switch, wire, and a belt. Still others figure the cost of each bomb belt at $1,500 to $4,300.[6]

Operation Defensive Shield, a large-scale military operation carried out by the IDF in April 2002 against Palestinian targets in the West Bank, uncovered useful information about the cost of a representative attack. On November 27, 2001, a joint Palestinian Islamic Jihad–Fatah/al-Aqsa Martyrs Brigades shooting attack was carried out at the central bus station in Afula, a city in northern Israel. Two Israeli civilians were killed and forty-eight wounded. According to a letter from one Islamic Jihad operative to another that was seized by Israeli soldiers, money earmarked for this attack was transferred from the Islamic Jihad headquarters in Damascus. The document states that "the remainder of the action's expenses" was a sum of $31,000. Another example revealing the broader costs of a terrorist attack comes from a bombing on July 31, 2002, at Jerusalem's Hebrew University, an attack that murdered seven civilians, including five Americans, and wounded eighty-six others. At a mall rally in Amman, Jordan, leaders of the Jordanian Islamic Action Front (IAF) honored the suicide bombing and asserted that the attack cost $50,000.[7]

While some terrorism experts claim that suicide bombers are the most cost-effective weapons available to terrorists, maintaining an infrastructure with the ability to deliver an unremitting campaign of such suicide attacks remains costly. While suicide bombers do make ultimate "smart bombs"— able to make calculated decisions and make undercover corrections en route to their targets—they are not inexpensive to deploy. To be accurate, financial estimates of terrorist attacks should also account for the costs of establishing and maintaining logistical support networks, such as recruitment and bomb making. The more money you have, the smoother your particular terrorism machinery operates. Moreover, Hamas and other Palestinian groups invest money in aggressive intelligence collection—primarily bribing officials—in an effort to penetrate the Palestinian Authority or other targets. For example, a Palestinian intelligence document dated February

2002 details the activities of Hamas and Islamic Jihad cells in the Jenin area and openly concedes that both groups "have penetrated into the security apparatuses in Jenin, including the General Intelligence, through money payments." In one instance, for the sum of $1,500 to $3,000, Hamas and Islamic Jihad obtained intelligence from officers affiliated with the Palestinian General and Preventive Intelligence services, including advance warning of pending arrests.[8]

Here is how one Hezbollah member itemized the expenses for a typical Palestinian terrorist operation:

- M-16 A2 assault rifle: $6,642 (30,000 NIS)
- M-16 A1 assault rifle: $4,428–$5,313 (20,000–24,000 NIS)
- AK-47 assault rifle: $1,550–$2,210 (7,000–10,000 NIS)
- Sanobal (locally made) rifle: $1,105 (5,000 NIS)
- Handgun: $1,439–$1,771 (6,500–8,000 NIS)
- Bullets for AK-47: $2.20 (10 NIS) each
- Bullets for Sanobal gun or rifle: $0.55 (2.5 NIS) each
- Bullets for M-16: $0.44 (2 NIS) each
- Stolen vehicle or a vehicle without licenses: $656–$1,550 (3,000–7,000 NIS)
- A cellular phone chip: $11 (50 NIS)[9]

The Cost of Maintaining the Dawa

The general deprivation of the Palestinian people in the Israeli-occupied territories predisposes them to favor the much-needed social support that Hamas provides. The Palestinian Authority, known more for its corruption than its social services, created over time a humanitarian vacuum filled—and exploited—by Hamas. But as in any good racketeering syndicate, no favor comes without an expected favor in turn. Whether this comes in tacit or tangible support, Hamas counts on the Palestinian people to support its terrorist activities in exchange for social services. In addition to purchasing goodwill, charities also create a built-in logistical support umbrella underneath which terrorist operations are sheltered and operate. Because the dawa network is used to aid terrorist activities, it is an essential component in any accounting of the cost of Hamas terrorism.

There are two types of foreign charitable foundations that finance Hamas from abroad: those directly tied to Hamas and those that support any number of radical Islamic elements worldwide, including Hamas. As indicated above, an Israeli report estimates that charities tied directly to Hamas raise

$25 million to $30 million a year and include groups like Interpal and the al-Aqsa International Foundation, both of which are banned by the U.S. government as terrorist organizations.[10]

As they are a major component of Hamas' overall fundraising apparatus, the budgets of the dawa are illustrative of the high level of costs required to fund the organization. For example, the Holy Land Foundation for Relief and Development (HLFRD) collected $57 million between 1992 and 2001, according to a federal indictment. It transferred over $6.8 million to Palestinian charities from January 1997 to September 2000, and its transfers to Hamas charities increased each year, from $900,000, in 1997, to a projected $2.4 million in 2000. At least one of these charities, the Sanabil Association for Relief and Development in Lebanon, was later designated by the U.S. government as a Specially Designated Global Terrorist entity. According to its 2000 tax return, the HLFRD's total revenue exceeded $13 million, up from about $1 million in 1993–1994. (At the time, its Jerusalem bureau was using $80,000–$120,000 per year just on routine office expenditures.) In a detailed forty-nine-page memorandum, the FBI claimed that HLFRD funds were used by Hamas to support schools that sometimes indoctrinated children into careers as suicide bombers. The FBI reached a similar conclusion about charitable money dispersed by HLFRD to families of suicide bombers: "by providing these annuities to families of Hamas members, the HLFRD assists Hamas by providing a constant flow of suicide volunteers and buttresses a terrorist infrastructure heavily reliant on moral support of the Palestinian populace."[11]

Documents found in the offices of the Ramallah-al-Bireh branch of the al-Islah Charitable Society offer a window into the financing priorities of Hamas charitable organizations—and insight into the larger question of how much it costs to run Hamas. One document, an expense report recording al-Islah's spending over a forty-one-day period in November and December 2000, is particularly revealing. A breakdown of the charity's main expenses falls into several clear-cut categories:

- Aid to families of Hamas "martyrs," prisoners, and wounded operatives;
- Administrative costs tied to running the Hamas charity's office and similar expenses; and
- Social welfare support to Hamas social service organizations.

Over the course of these forty-one days, the charity dispersed $4,990 in financial aid to the families of martyrs (including suicide bombers), $16,257 directly to prisoners, $17,275 for prisoner's families, and $3,833 for wounded militants. The charity even spent money on gifts to families commemorating their suicide bomber relatives; papers seized from the al-Islah charity show a series of small gifts—$100 each—presented to the families in celebration of the three-day Eid al-Fitr holiday in 2001. Spending on supporting terrorists and their families represented 46 percent of al-Islah's spending over that time period, compared to 43 percent ($39,537) on social welfare. The charity also spent $9,719 on office space, equipment, travel, and salary. Extrapolating this data over a one-year period suggests that al-Islah's annual expenses would amount to $508,265 for the support of terrorists and their families, and $474,450 for Hamas social welfare institutions. Even if these figures are slightly inflated (the projections are based on a forty-one-day period that overlapped with the Islamic month of Ramadan, when Muslim charitable giving and social spending peaks) they are nonetheless instructive as ballpark expenditure figures, and for the insight they provide into the breakdown of the Hamas charity's disbursement priorities.[12]

Hamas contributes a substantial amount of money to martyrs' families, prisoners, prisoners' families, and wounded operatives in relation to the average monthly wages of the typical Palestinian worker. For example, in 2005 the average monthly salary for an average worker in the Gaza Strip was $372 and $516 for an average worker in the West Bank. By comparison, over the forty-one-day period in 2000, the al-Islah Charitable Society provided an average stipend of $328 to the families of martyrs, $170 to detained prisoners, $201 to the families of prisoners, and $508 to wounded operatives.[13]

A document found in the Tulkarm charity committee office marked "Arab Bank" outlined financial requests the Hamas charity made to the Union of Good, a consortium of more than fifty Islamic charities around the world. The document included the cost of food and financial aid for families: a minimum of 5,000 food packages per month and financial aid for 2,000 families. Money was also needed for 17,000 school bags, school uniforms, and school fees. The Tulkarm committee also requested money for several construction projects, including schools, cultural centers, mosques, orphanages, and for hospital equipment and treatment costs. They also requisitioned money to subsidize Palestinian agriculture. While these uses might themselves be considered attempts at harvesting grassroots support, the Tulkarm charity also requested money for public relations, comprising funds for public libraries, dawa publications, audiocassette tapes used for indoctrination, and a local TV station. Notably, it asked for more money to be provided to prisoners and the families of martyrs or suicide bombers.[14]

The Cost of Compensating Terrorists' Families

Speaking in 2001, Hamas founder Sheikh Ahmed Yassin asserted that Hamas distributes $2 million to $3 million in monthly handouts to the relatives of Palestinian suicide bombers, "martyrs" killed in attacks on Israelis, and prisoners in Israeli jails. An Israeli government report found that families of Hamas activists killed or wounded while carrying out terror attacks—and of those imprisoned for their involvement in such attacks—"typically receive an initial, one-time grant of between $500–$5,000, as well as a monthly allowance of approximately $100." Significantly, the Israelis found that "the families of Hamas terrorists usually receive larger payments than those of non-Hamas terrorists."[15]

Documents captured during Operation Defensive Shield revealed that the al-Tadhoman Charitable Society, another charity operating under the Union of Good umbrella, also provided funds for the families of Palestinians "martyred" in suicide bombings or clashes with Israeli forces. One document featured a table listing all the suicide bombers and other "martyrs" from the Nablus district between January and March 2002. Most of these were Hamas operatives, though the list also included operatives from the al-Aqsa Martyrs Brigade, Palestinian Islamic Jihad, the Popular Front for the Liberation of Palestine, and even members of the various Palestinian security organizations. The last column of the table describes the circumstances of the terrorist operation carried out by each qualifying operative, making clear that the employees of both al-Tadhoman and the Union of Good fully understood that funds from their charities were used as rewards for the families of suicide bombers. Another document, entitled "Table of Al-Tadhoman Martyrs in Nablus for whom an allotment of 500 Jordanian dinars was not paid," further illustrates the dynamic of providing economic benefits to terrorists and their families. The ages of the terrorists in this list ranged from 15 to 42, the average age being 25.9 years old. When compared to the average monthly wage in the Palestinian territories—roughly 1,500 Israeli shekels (under $400) per month—payments of up to $5,000 represent more than a year's pay and therefore serve as an important financial incentive for Palestinians to conduct attacks. While the amounts of money transferred to the family of wounded and killed operatives vary, they still serve the same function. The dawa essentially removes one disincentive from the psychology of a suicide bomber by providing sustenance for the families of terrorists.[16]

Seized lists of people supported by the Holy Land Foundation for Relief and Development revealed that "favored individuals" received more generous stipends (of $300 or more). An analysis of these lists notes that these more fortunate recipients included "numerous individuals involved in Hamas activity." They include:

- The mother of Ahmad Shukri, a Hamas terrorist sentenced to a life term for murdering an Israeli and attempting to force a public bus off the road in 1989;
- The father of Mohammad Shawan, a Hamas terrorist who murdered two grocers in 1993 and was killed in a shootout with Israeli forces in 1994;
- The wife of Abd al-Rahman Aruri, a Hamas terrorist killed in a clash with Israeli forces in late 1993;
- The family of Suleiman Idan, a Hamas terrorist who died in a car bomb attack in 1993;
- The mother of Ashraf Ba'aluji, sentenced to a life term for murdering three Israelis in 1992;
- The wife of Jamil al-Baz, a Hamas terrorist sentenced to a life term for running over an Israeli soldier in Gaza in 1991;
- The wife of Majdi Hamad, a Hamas terrorist sentenced to a life term for killing fellow Palestinians—presumably suspected informers—in Gaza;
- The family of Yasser Hajaj, a Hamas terrorist sentenced to a life term for placing a bomb on a Tel Aviv beach that killed a Canadian tourist;
- The brother of Raid Zakarna, a Hamas terrorist who carried out a suicide attack at a crowded bus stop in Afula on April 6, 1994, killing eight people and wounding over forty others, including many children.[17]

The Cost of Other Dawa Projects

Other dawa projects, such as the construction of the nine-story "orphan's village" that Hamas' Orphan Care Society built in Bethlehem, can also be very expensive. The structure, completed in 2004, was intended to house 1,000 orphans, as well as a Hamas school, clinic, kindergarten, libraries, and more. It is impossible to quantify the logistical benefits (recruitment, radicalization, building grassroots support, supporting the families of killed or captured terrorists) Hamas accrues from such an investment, nor is it possible to put a price on the operational benefits provided by such a facility (such as use as a safe house, dead-drop, or weapons cache). No algorithm calculating the cost of carrying out an attack can account for the monetary value to terrorism of long-term dawa investments like the Hamas orphans' village.[18]

Hamas operatives have been vocal about the centrality of dawa activity in Hamas' overall strategic vision, and some figures are available on the cost of running such wide-ranging and large-scale social welfare projects. In 1992, for example, a Hamas activist wrote to Mousa Abu Marzook seeking funds and bemoaning the financial distress the group was enduring at the time. "We have many large projects and projects of the dawa which have been affected by the tardy allowances," one letter states. "We are in dire need of every cent we are supposed to get," it continues, "in order to support our brothers and our dawa." The theme is reiterated in another letter:

> As to the budget, we hope that Allah gives us generous support and releases us from the distress we are in, which constitutes a genuine tragedy we are now living through. Because the money is the dawa's life-line and without it there is no giving or doing. We are therefore asking you to hurry and send us the funds and what we require from you as a budget for the past months and for the current month, a considerable sum which would enable us to solve all our problems and return all our debts, which are accumulating and worrying us day and night, since they are hampering our progress and forcing us to calculate everything.[19]

According to another letter, "the monthly budget for the dawa alone is not less than 150 thousand for all the regions, beside their apparatuses, that receive some of the budgets monthly." (The currency was not specified, but presumably was either U.S. dollars or Israeli shekels since the letter was sent from Bassem Musa in the West Bank to Marzook in the United States.)[20]

Hamas' prolonged terror campaign is not a thrifty operation. Considering the costs of bomb belts, payments to terrorists and their families, and even bribery, Hamas' outlays are far greater than the price of a cheap explosive. This is why the dawa is so critical to Hamas' survival: not only does it provide legitimate cover in which to operate, launder money, and recruit, but it promotes suicide and other operations by removing the deterrent of leaving one's family destitute.

ECONOMIC JIHAD: TITHING FOR TERROR

Dawa organizations are key nodes in what radical Islamist leaders frequently describe as the "economic jihad" (*al-Jihad bil-mal*), a phrase that features prominently in their fundraising techniques. The concept is simple in practice. Radical leaders claim their followers have a religious duty to engage in jihad—either by physically fighting Islam's enemies or by supporting those who do. Proponents of this logic ground their position in a Koranic verse in Surah 9 (*al-Tawbah*) Verse 41: "Fight with your possessions and your souls in the way of Allah." Typically, "possessions" translates into "money," for purposes of expediency.

Zakat: How Alms Become Arms

Charities in general, and *zakat* (charity) committees in particular, are especially susceptible to abuse by terrorists and their supporters for whom charitable or humanitarian organizations are particularly attractive front organizations. Indeed, terrorist groups have long exploited charities for a variety of purposes. Charities offer a veil of legitimacy for terrorist fundraising, attracting unwitting donors who are unaware that monies they donate for humanitarian purposes fund terror. Those social welfare organizations funded by the terrorist groups engender grassroots support for said groups and create fertile spotting and recruitment grounds.

Charities are also ideal money laundering mechanisms. They tend to operate in zones of conflict and traditionally involve the flow of money in only one direction, both of which are characteristics that would arouse suspicion in other organizations. They enable terrorist groups to move personnel, funds, and matériel to and from high-risk areas under cover of charity work, and provide terrorist operatives with day jobs that provide both salary and cover, facilitating their terrorist activities. Moreover, terrorists co-opt charitable giving through a range of diverse tactics. Some charities are founded with the express purpose of financing terror, as authorities believe was the case with the U.S.-based Benevolence International Foundation (al-Qaeda), the Holy Land Foundation for Relief and Development (Hamas), and the Islamic Committee for Palestine (Palestinian Islamic Jihad). Others are infiltrated by terrorist operatives and supporters and co-opted from within. For example, the Islamic Red Crescent has been infiltrated by al-Qaeda and Palestinian terrorists. Recognizing that analysis of this particular preferred means of terror financing demands a discerning and discriminating level of analysis approach, Ambassador Francis X. Taylor, then the State Department's Coordinator for Counterterrorism, noted in 2002 that "any money can be diverted if you don't pay attention to it. And I believe that terrorist organizations, just like criminal enterprises, can bore into any legitimate enterprise to try to divert money for illegitimate purposes."

Not only are donors more willing to give to humanitarian causes, but in the Muslim world they often do so as part of their religiously mandated annual zakat contributions. Such donations have long been known to lend themselves to abuse, and not only by terrorists. In Pakistan, for example, scholars note that zakat recipients have included "orphans" with living parents, "impoverished women" decorated in gold jewelry, and "old people" who had long since died. The mixing of funds across different Hamas wings also shields the group's terrorist activities under a veil of political and humanitarian legitimacy, as discussed in more detail below.[21]

Jihadist Rhetoric: A Call to Alms

The call to wage economic jihad is a staple of statements from Islamist leaders of various stripes. For example, speaking of the need to support Palestinian militants in a "Jerusalem Day" speech in December 2003, Hezbollah leader Sheikh Hassan Nasrallah said, "All the institutions, committees, parties, private and collective initiatives throughout the Moslem world must be spurred on to collect money, everywhere in the world, and to bring that money to Palestine. With it they will buy bread and rebuild their houses. The money will bandage their wounds. With that money they are assured of the ability to buy weapons, for the men and women of Palestine will not be weakened. The [challenge] of our era is found today in Palestine. . . . If we cannot give them arms, we can give them the money to buy them."[22]

Sheikh Nasrallah's position mirrors that of Hezbollah's benefactor, Iran's Ayatollah Khomeini. A Syrian Ministry of Information publication records Khomeini as saying that it is the duty of all Muslims "to get rid of that germ corruption [Israel] in any way possible," and that to achieve that goal "it is not enough to extend practical support to [Palestinians to achieve] the goal but to direct resources to that end from the zakat and other Islamic charity monies."[23]

Sheikh Yusef Qardawi, a prominent Muslim Brotherhood theologian who founded the Union of Good, has also issued numerous calls for economic jihad. Though better known for his religious rulings (*fatwa*) calling on Muslims to murder American and other civilians in Iraq and justifying Hamas suicide bombings against Israeli civilians, Qardawi has also decreed that it is more important that Muslims donate money to "support Palestinians fighting occupation and other struggles of Muslim populations, such as in Bosnia" than that they make the Hajj (the pilgrimage to Mecca required of every able Muslim at least once in his or her life). In an interview with the *Palestine Times,* he said of Islamist resistance in Lebanon and the Occupied Territories, "if we can't carry out acts of *jihad* ourselves, we at least should support and prop up the *mujahideen* financially and morally so that they will be steadfast until God's victory." A more calculating variation on Qardawi's theme was played by Sheikh Omar Bakri Mohammad (whose fundraising for Hamas is also discussed in Chapter 6). Speaking to followers in his hometown of London, the sheikh said, "The market of *jihad* has opened. Now all we need is the people who are the merchandise, the ones who want to buy *jennah* (paradise). If you cannot do it physically, do it verbally, do it financially, but do it."[24]

In addition to proclamations and exhortations by individual religious leaders, the call to wage economic jihad is tacitly endorsed or explicitly expressed by foreign governments, most notably by elements within the government of Saudi Arabia. According to a 2005 report released by the nongovernmental organization Freedom House, titled "Saudi Publications on Hate Ideology Fill American Mosques," clergy at Saudi-sponsored mosques in the United States have encouraged worshippers to send money to foreign jihadists. Freedom House's researchers discovered a fatwa promoting economic jihad at the Islamic Center of Washington, a high-profile Saudi-funded mosque that was visited by President George W. Bush in the week following the September 11 terrorist attacks. Prepared by the Saudi government's so-called Permanent Committee for Scientific Research and the Issuing of Fatwas, the decree was in response to an inquiry as to whether the transfer of charitable donations (zakat) from the United States to Islamic countries is permissible. The Saudi committee wrote, "Transfer of zakat from country to country is allowed when legitimate, such as when those to whom it is transferred are in greater need or in legitimate jihad." In another document, in which a senior Saudi cleric ruled that Muslims should not, as a general rule, use banks that offer interest on their accounts, the scholar ruled that "there is an exception if the banks offer interest without prior agreement or knowledge on the Muslim depositor's part, it is proper to take the money provided it is spent on helping the poor or those engaged in *Jihad* against the infidels."[25]

Even secular Muslim leaders have echoed the call of economic jihad. Former Iraqi dictator Saddam Hussein argued in 2002 that Arab leaders should shun further peace plans and commit "to support the Palestinian people in armed fighting." He added, "If we are incapable of offering aid to the armies, our support should be by [giving] money or buying them arms, or by giving Muslims and Arabs the option of volunteering [to help the Palestinian people]."[26]

Economic Jihad and Palestinian Radicalism

Palestinian groups such as Hamas have perfected the technique of raising funds by calling on supporters to engage in an economic jihad. For example, the Halhoul charity committee—which received over the years at least $100,741 from the Holy Land Foundation for Relief and Development—issued a letter of thanks to the U.S.-based foundation in May 2000. This letter was subsequently included in a booklet marking the foundation's "Ten Years of Achievement." Quoting a saying of the Prophet Mohammad (*hadith*), the letter expressly echoed the theme of economic jihad: "[The Prophet Mohammad,] may Allah bless him and grant him salvation, said: 'Whoever strives for the widow and the poor is like a person engaged in a holy war [*jihad*] in the way of Allah.'" Similarly, a pamphlet produced by a Koranic memorization center sponsored by the Ramallah-al-Bireh charity committee lists thirty ways to enter heaven, including "*Jihad* for the sake of Allah by fighting with one's soul and money."[27]

Fawaz Damrah took a page from the same radical Islamist book in his fundraising pitches to U.S. audiences of radicalized Muslims. Damrah was the imam of Cleveland's largest mosque and a major fundraiser for Palestinian Islamic Jihad before his conviction in 2004 of unlawfully obtaining citizenship via false statements to immigration officials, including failure to note affiliations with terrorist groups. His investigation by federal authorities provides a model of how an Islamist fundraiser used religious rhetoric to drum up financial support for Palestinian terrorism. Transcripts of phone conversations between Damrah and senior Islamic Jihad officials and fundraisers along with videos of Damrah sharing the dais with them at Islamic Jihad conferences were key pieces of evidence at the trial.[28]

For example, at a "Round Table Discussion About Jihad and the Intifada" held in Cleveland, Ohio, on April 7, 1991, Damrah was videotaped saying, "God says, . . . '[w]hoever equipped a raider for the sake of God, has himself raided.' Whoever donates for a *mujahid* so that he may throw stones, as if he too is fighting the Holy War, and will be rewarded like him, even if he stays home."[29]

When he lobbied for donations at fundraisers, Damrah often promised that the funds would go to Islamic Jihad. "O brothers," he said at one event, "I would like to open the door to donations . . . to the Intifada, to Islamic Jihad in Palestine." At another fundraiser he enticed potential donors to give in the name of an Islamic Jihad martyr: "I ask you to donate to Islamic Jihad," Damrah said, "Nidal Zalloum, of Islamic Jihad, who grabbed a dagger and stabbed four Jews in the courtyard of the Holy Sanctuary. Nidal Zalloum, from Islamic Jihad, is saying to you, 'Be compassionate upon my blood. Avenge my blood.' And that *mujahid,* who took the bus and killed more than twenty Jews. He is from Islamic Jihad. This is the Islamic Jihad movement. I say to you donate so that this money will serve you with God. I am offering the chance for this medal so that a brother steps forward and donates for the sake of God." Damrah then presided over an auction of a medal in honor of the martyrs.[30]

While fundraisers frequently frame their fundraising pitch in terms of the terrorist group's humanitarian support activities, sometimes—especially before the extra scrutiny brought on by the attacks of September 11—they have also called on donors to fund overtly violent, militant activities. Such calls to economic jihad include comments made by Damrah and other Islamic Jihad officials at a conference hosted by the Islamic Committee for Palestine (ICP, a since defunct front organization for Islamic Jihad) in Chicago in December 1989. Responding to a question from the audience, Islamic Jihad co-founder Bashir Nafi said, "If the problem, as far as you are concerned, is the problem of weapons . . . how would weapons reach the Occupied Territories, then meet me outside the conference." Damrah himself explained at the same conference that "The first principle is that terrorism, and terrorism alone, is the path to liberation. . . . The second principle is that 'settlement is decided by the sword.'" At another point, Damrah clarified, "If what they mean by *jihad* is terrorism, then we are terrorists!"[31]

In November 2002, Hamas took the concept of economic jihad one step further, issuing a communiqué on one of its websites calling on supporters worldwide to atone for their sins and ensure themselves a place in heaven by helping to finance Hamas. "We call on you," the statement read, "my brother the *Jihad* fighter and my sister the *Jihad* fighter to donate part of your money to the *Jihad* fighters who are protecting the honor of the Islamic nation. . . . Even if you cannot participate yourselves alongside us in the *Jihad,* your [financial] donation to us from the money that Allah gave you is not less important [than participating in the *Jihad*]."[32]

Such techniques are used not only by radical leaders and fundraisers seeking support for Hamas, Hezbollah, and Islamic Jihad but by al-Qaeda boosters as well. Indeed, as highlighted in the case of Sami Omar al-Hussayen, radical individuals and organizations often issue calls for an economic jihad on behalf of both Hamas and al-Qaeda. Though he was ultimately acquitted (primarily on technical legal grounds), the trial evidence left no doubt that the websites al-Hussayen managed directly supported terrorism and violence, specifically in Israel, the West Bank and Gaza Strip, and Chechnya. On the one hand al-Hussayen sent a "Monthly Reminder" to all members of a virtual e-mail group—as he regularly did at the beginning of each month—in which he urged readers to donate money to support those participating in violent jihad, "providing them with weapons and physical strength to carry on with the war against those who kill them." On the other hand, a page devoted to violent jihad in the Palestinian territories found on the Islamway website al-Hussayen managed expressly called on readers to donate funds to Hamas.[33]

Of course, Hamas not only is focused on securing major donations; it also places collection boxes in storefronts and mosques. The Holy Land Foundation distributed charity boxes in the United States, and Palestinian security officials noted that Hamas charities in the West Bank and Gaza Strip did the same. For example, the Orphan Care Society distributed as many as 450 collection boxes—decorated with a small child stretching out a hand for donations—in the Bethlehem area alone.[34]

FROM MOSQUE TO MORGUE: FOLLOWING THE HAMAS MONEY

Hamas operatives and organizations in the West Bank, Gaza, and abroad form a vast financial support network. This network not only performs the yeoman's work of raising funds for Hamas, it also provides the equally crucial service of laundering and transferring those funds—from the United States, Europe, and the Persian Gulf to Hamas leaders in Syria and Lebanon, and ultimately to terrorist operatives in the West Bank and Gaza Strip. As one concerned columnist writing in the Arabic daily *al-Sharq al-Awsat* noted in October 2004, "Money laundering has not stopped and it will continue in the future, by means of [collecting funds] for humanitarian purposes for the poor and the needy, fast-breaking dinners, dialyses and excavation of wells; however, these funds ultimately end up in terrorists' houses. Even though officials [in the Arab world] say they have established rules and set inspectors, it will be almost impossible to monitor hundreds of associations and thousands of donors and collectors."[35]

If money is the lifeblood of a terrorist network, then stanching its flow is naturally a priority of those who oppose terrorism. Numerous investigations into Hamas activity in the United States have led American law enforcement to conclude that chasing down the money flowing through the dawa system can be particularly effective in preventing Hamas attacks. Even tracking small financial transactions suspected of supporting terrorism is important because terror funds are usually transferred around the world in small denominations. Such transfers are intended to evade detection, and often do, and therefore require no large-scale laundering operations. As one U.S. expert put it, "the most serious threat to our well-being was now [post-9/11] clean money intended to kill, not dirty money seeking to be rinsed in a place of hiding."[36]

In September 2003, FBI Assistant Director John Pistole testified before Congress that FBI investigations into the financial activities of terrorist supporters in the United States helped prevent four different terror attacks abroad. According to Pistole, at least a portion of contributions made to Hamas charities directly support the group's military wing, while the remainder of raised funds indirectly support Hamas attacks. By Pistole's reasoning, "any contribution to Hamas, for any purpose, frees up other funds for its planned violence."[37]

This logic is borne out by Hamas leaders themselves, who acknowledge using social services funds for military purposes and vice versa when necessary. Consider the letter Hamas operative Bassem Musa wrote to Mousa Abu Marzook in October 1992. Complaining of a lack of funds, Musa lamented the financial shortfall for both the dawa and the military, or "positive." Musa wrote: "We take not less than 50,000 from the monthly allowance of the 'dawa' for the 'positive.' This is what we did before this apparatus received its own budget. Moreover, the monthly budgets we allocated to the 'positive' from 'al-dawa' are much larger than that the part [sic] we give to 'dawa' from their allowance in most cases." At another point in the letter, Musa reported receiving 370,000 for "the positive," but he added, "we were forced to allocate some of it for the 'dawa' because their budget was late, otherwise the funds for the 'positive' would have reached their destination without complications."[38]

To be sure, even when not facing a shortage of funds, Hamas launders money to terrorist cells through its charity organizations. Jamal Tawil, the Hamas military commander in Ramallah introduced in Chapter 2, readily acknowledged founding the al-Islah charity as a purportedly legitimate front through whose accounts he could launder the monthly fund transfers he received from Hamas. A report produced by the Palestinian Authority General Intelligence in Gaza in late 2000 notes that several Hamas leaders—not just Tawil—made a strategic decision to transfer to the Qassam Brigades charitable funds originally earmarked for social services. Another Palestinian intelligence report dated December 10, 2000, notes that Hamas officials decided that charitable donations "will not be sent to the PA, but deposited in the accounts of Usama Hamdan [the Hamas representative in Lebanon] and Khaled Mishal [Secretary General of Hamas]." Part of these funds, the report made clear, "will be allocated to support the Hamas' military arm 'inside.'"[39]

In another case, Palestinian security officials determined that the Ramallah-al-Bireh zakat committee laundered and transferred funds raised abroad (particularly from Jordan, Saudi Arabia, the United Arab Emirates, and Qatar) through local banks, moneychangers, and businesses with ties to Hamas. Palestinian security officials found that "the committee works with a number of banks in Ramallah, particularly the Arab [Bank] of Jordan and Beit al-Mal." (In the United States, federal investigators opened an investigation into the Arab Bank in 2004, the same year victims of Hamas attacks filed suit against the bank for its reported ties to Hamas. As described in greater detail below, Beit al-Mal was banned by Israel in 1998 and the United States in 2001 because of its ties to Hamas.) Beit al-Mal and its officials have appeared in several investigations. Palestinian investigators identified a company called Sunuqrut and the al-Ajouli moneychangers as "among the most important companies the committee works with" to launder and transfer funds. According to Israeli experts, Ghazi Ajouli is a well-known West Bank moneychanger tied to Hamas, and Sunuqrut is a company owned in part by Mazen Sunuqrut, a Hamas activist who also served as president of the board of directors for Beit al-Mal—and was appointed PA Minister of Economy in February 2005.[40]

Fungibility of Funds: How Hamas Is Designed for Internal Money Laundering

In 2003, Assistant Secretary of State E. Anthony Wayne told a congressional committee, "If you are funding the organization [Hamas], even if there are many charitable activities going on, there is some fungibility between funds. You are strengthening the organization." It is precisely this ease and readiness with which Hamas transfers money from putatively charitable or political funds to military ones that belies any moral separation between the organization's various branches. Hamas' ability to shift funds across its various wings is critical to its mission, because it facilitates the organization's most effective means of raising funds for terrorist purposes: through humanitarian channels. The mixing of funds across different Hamas wings also shields the group's terrorist activities under a veil of political and humanitarian legitimacy. The coordinator of the Justice Department Terrorist Financing Task Force highlighted this phenomenon, noting that people who support groups like Hamas or Palestinian Islamic Jihad in the United States typically choose charities as their front organization of choice because charities "give them the cover of apparent legitimacy and the benefit of tax deductions to their donors."[41] Finally, mingling funds across the organization allows for maximum cash flow and enables Hamas to spend available money on the particular needs of the moment. Because of these advantages, Hamas leaders promote fungibility of funds and do not require local cells or departments to create financial reports or receipts for how monies are spent. In part, this is because mingling funds is legitimate in the eyes of Hamas, which sees the social services it provides as a jihadist extension of its terror attacks. This shared mission was on full display on the "Islam Online" website in July 2002, which featured a special page glorifying suicide attacks. The page stressed the need not only to support Palestinian armed struggle but also youth education, social activity, and economic assistance as a means of participating in the "economic jihad." The site then provided a long list of European, American, South African, and Arab social organizations, whose function, according to the site, is to transfer funds to the charitable associations Hamas recommends.[42]

Terrorist Fundraising via Criminal Enterprises

FBI investigations in the United States reveal that Hamas also draws funding and support from criminals who are either directly associated with Hamas members or who harbor sympathies toward its ideology. According to the FBI, "these investigations have uncovered a myriad of criminal activities used to generate funds, a portion of which is then forwarded to NGOs associated with Hamas. Some examples include, but are not limited to, drug trafficking, credit card fraud, counterfeit products, fraudulent documents, cigarette tax fraud and stolen infant formula." A Drug Enforcement Administration (DEA) investigation into a pseudoephedrine smuggling scam in the American Midwest led investigators as far as Jordan, Yemen, Lebanon, and other Middle Eastern countries, including bank accounts tied to Hezbollah and Hamas. DEA chief Asa Hutchinson confirmed that "a significant portion of some of the sales are sent to the Middle East to benefit terrorist organizations." As noted in a U.S. General Accounting Office (GAO) report published in November 2003, according to officials from the Bureau of Alcohol, Tobacco, Firearms and Explosives, "Hizballah, Hamas, and al-Qaeda have earned assets through trafficking in contraband cigarettes or counterfeit tax stamps."[43]

Hamas and other groups also fund themselves with the proceeds of pirated multimedia. Copying intellectual property brings in millions of dollars a year from "royalties" collected from criminals engaged in the counterfeit multimedia business. Hamas, Fatah, and even senior members of the Palestinian Authority are suspected of participating in such activities in the West Bank and Gaza. In the United States, law enforcement officials opened an investigation into a variety of criminal enterprises suspected of funding Middle East terrorist groups, including the stealing and reselling of baby formula, food stamp fraud, and scams involving grocery coupons, welfare claims, credit cards, and even unlicensed t-shirts. Hamas activists are also suspected of engaging in credit card fraud to fund their activities. In October 2005, a man described as "a suspected Palestinian supporter of Middle Eastern terrorist groups" posted credit card numbers online with instructions on how to steal active credit card numbers off American businesses' databases.[44]

U.S. officials believe "a substantial portion" of the estimated many millions of dollars raised by Middle Eastern terrorist groups come from the $20 million to $30 million annual illicit scam industry in the United States. In South America, widespread criminal activity also finances terror. The GAO report noted above also reports that much of the financial support activity on behalf of Hamas (and Hezbollah) conducted in the so-called Tri-border area, where the borders of Brazil, Argentina, and Paraguay converge, involves criminal activity. Likewise, the DEA identified Hamas as one of several terrorist groups suspected of drug trafficking in the Tri-border region. Ali Nizar Dahroug, together with his uncle and a key Tri-border Hamas activist, Mohammad Dahroug Dahroug (believed to have since returned to the Middle East), is suspected of financing Hamas through the proceeds of counterfeit goods. When Ali Nizar was arrested in the Paraguayan border town of Ciudad del Este in June 2002, authorities found "numerous counterfeit goods, false packing devices, and documents showing wire transfers to his uncle." Authorities there say Ali Nizar transferred between five and ten million dollars to accounts worldwide in 2000 and 2001. (In a disturbing twist, Mohammad Dahroug's name was found in the address book of senior al-Qaeda commander Abu Zubayda.)[45] In January 2004, U.S. law enforcement agencies uncovered another typical case of criminal activity tied to Hamas. According to the Directorate of Border and Transportation Security (BTS) Daily Operations Report for January 10, 2004, four days earlier agents from the Bureau of Immigration and Customs Enforcement (ICE) and the Los Angeles Joint Terrorism Task Force (JTTF) had arrested a group of Jordanians involved in a scheme to sell adulterated oil. According to the report, officials believed one of the Jordanians was also a member of Hamas:

> On 6 January, in Los Angeles, ICE and JTTF agents arrested Jordanian nationals Hussam Ahmad Khalil, Emad Takleh Khalil and Hattim Haleem for violating state trademark regulations related to adulterated oil. Reportedly, Khalil has gained substantial profit from this venture and has sent $30,000–$40,000 per month to the Middle East. Khalil, who is believed to be a member of Hamas (a designated foreign terrorist organization), is also suspected of involvement in wire fraud, trademark violations, alien smuggling, harboring of illegal aliens, narcotics smuggling, and visa fraud. Agents also arrested Omar Okour, Mahmoud Khalil and Ziad Saleh for unlawful presence in the United States. Khalil and Saleh claim to have paid $10,000 to a smuggler in Mexico to transport them into the U.S.[46]

EVIDENCE OF TERRORIST MONEY-LAUNDERING BY HAMAS

Much of what we know about the transfer of money from Islamic charities to Hamas military cells comes from various U.S. investigations into such laundering activities, investigations concluding that donations to charities frequently find their way directly to the Qassam Brigades, where they are used to fund Hamas attacks. The State Department has determined that "there can be no doubt . . . that donations to Hamas for charitable purposes free up funds for use in terrorism." In an example cited by the U.S. Treasury Department, Ali Muqbil, described as "General Manager of the al-Aqsa International Foundation office in Yemen and a Hamas official," transferred funds to Hamas and other Palestinian groups to assist "Palestinian fighters," while recording these disbursements as "contributions for charitable projects." Similarly, according to information cited by the U.S. government, Osama Hamdan, a "senior Hamas official based in Lebanon," and Khaled Mishal, the head of Hamas' political bureau in Damascus, both received "funds transferred from charitable donations to Hamas for distribution to the families of Palestinian 'martyrs'" that were transferred to their personal bank accounts, and then "used to support Hamas military operations in Israel." Hamas leader Mousa Abu Marzook is also "implicated in receiving funds for Hamas terrorist attacks, funds that have been used to mobilize activity inside Israel and the West Bank/Gaza." Then there is the case of Haldon Barghouti, a Syrian citizen of Palestinian descent, who delivered $80,000 from Hamas officials in Damascus to a Qassam Brigades cell in Ramallah. Barghouti personally couriered some of these funds in cash he carried across the Allenby Bridge connecting Jordan to the West Bank, while the rest was sent as a wire transfer to an account in Barghouti's name in Ramallah. The Ramallah cell used the funds Hamas leaders in Damascus sent via Barghouti "to acquire war materiel, vehicles, cellular telephones, etc. and to disburse to its members [sic]." Following are several case studies of individuals who used Hamas-connected charities to launder money to terrorist operatives.[47]

Abdelhaleem al-Ashqar

One especially blatant case of a Hamas charity funding the group's terror cells is that of Abdelhaleem al-Ashqar, head of the defunct al-Aqsa Education Fund (AAEF). According to an internal FBI communication dated February 8, 1993, the Bureau had "reason to believe that instant subject [al-Ashqar] is or may be engaged in international terrorism or activities in preparation therefore, or knowingly aiding or abetting a person in the conduct of these activities, at the direction of a foreign power." Al-Ashqar opened a Suntrust Bank account under the name "Abdelhaleem Hasan Ashqar for Al-Mojamaa al-Eslami—Gaza Strip, account 16811688." As we have seen in the previous chapter, al-Mujama was one of the primary Hamas dawa precursors operated by Sheikh Ahmed Yassin. FBI files include statements of Hamas militants arrested by Israeli authorities who detailed al-Ashqar's activities on behalf of—and his senior role in—Hamas. According to one such statement cited by the FBI, "Ashqar arranged a transfer of Hamas funds totaling 41,200 Jordanian Dinars to [Hamas militant Sufian Abu] Samara through a resident of [the West Bank town of] Sajaiyah." In two other cases he transferred $35,000 and $300,000 respectively (the latter in two installments of $200,000 and $100,000). Al-Ashqar made a point of detailing how the transfers totaling $300,000 should be spent, telling Samara that the transfers were for "Hamas activity."[48]

Mahmud Rumahi

Another self-confessed Qassam Brigades activist in the West Bank, Mahmud Rumahi, was recruited into Hamas by his brother-in-law, who gave him al-Ashqar's U.S. telephone and fax numbers "so he could obtain 'money and pamphlets' from Ashqar," according to an FBI memorandum. Al-Ashqar also sent a representative from the U.S. "to obtain detailed reports on Hamas activities in his [Rumahi's] region." Rumahi visited the U.S. in July 1991 to meet with al-Ashqar, who also facilitated a meeting between the

Hamas operative and Mousa Abu Marzook at a Tennessee airport where Rumahi reported on his cell's terror activities. A year later, in April 1992, Rumahi was dispatched on a forty-five-day international trip for Hamas, including a stop in London where he gave Hamas operatives named Said and Ibrahim "a full report about Hamas activities in the occupied territories," and then made additional stops in Italy and the United States. According to Rumahi, he participated in a meeting in Washington, D.C. "I want to mention," Rumahi stressed to Israeli police interrogators, "that this was a meeting with the Hamas leaders in the USA."[49]

Rumahi's confession offers one of the most clear-cut admissions that funds sent from Hamas fronts abroad directly fund the group's terror attacks. In his statement, included in FBI files on Hamas activities in the United States, Rumahi said that "until April 1992 the money that financed my activities arrived in the name and account of Ala Anwar Aql, 28 years old, from al-Bira, recruited by Hamas. His role was to take the money from his account and give it to the militants in my area. Ala was recruited to Hamas by Mahmud Qazim, my brother-in-law. After a while, the money started to be transferred to my account, $10,000 each month, for a total of $100,000."[50]

Mohammad Salah

According to the FBI, even as Marzook and several colleagues, including Nasser al-Khatib and Ismail Elbarrase, were investing seed money in the Holy Land Foundation for Relief and Development (HLFRD) and other Hamas charities based in the United States, they were also providing funds to the Izz al-Din al-Qassam Brigades via Mohammad Salah. As previously noted, Salah was convicted in Israel of funding Hamas terror squads and designated a Specially Designated Terrorist by the U.S. government in 1995. At the time of his arrest in Israel in January 1993, Salah had $97,000 in cash in his possession and admitted to already distributing approximately $140,000 to Qassam Brigades activists. Salah had already provided funds to a Hamas military cell the previous year. Salah Arouri, the Hamas recruiter and commander to whom Mohammad Salah provided these funds, admitted receiving "approximately $96,000 to procure weapons from Abu Ahmed [Salah] in August 1992" and providing "$45,000 to Musa Muhammed Salah Dudin to be used for weapons to conduct attacks." Dudin purchased several weapons from Sheikh Hussein Awada, including one M-16 rifle, two Kalashnikov rifles, two Uzi submachine guns, two or three 8mm and 9mm pistols, one Carbine rifle, and rounds for each. Dudin and others then used these weapons in attacks on Israelis, including the murder of Yuval Tutange on December 12, 1992. Informed that another one of his associates, Mohammad Bashirat, "would mount a suicide attack" with an M-16 rifle he provided, Arouri prayed that "Allah should help you perpetrate the attack and that you not die and that Allah will protect you" but also assured Bashirat that "we the Hamas, and I being responsible in the Hamas, will help your family, don't worry." Salah had been employed at the Quranic Literacy Institute (QLI), whose founder, Ahmad Zaki Hammad, was an early Bridgeview mosque prayer leader. In December 2004 a Chicago court found QLI liable for financing Hamas in a civil case and ordered the institute and other defendants, including Salah, to pay $156 million to the victim's family. In December 2003, the Family Bank and Trust Co., the Bridgeview mosque's main bank in suburban Chicago, closed all accounts associated with the mosque due to its connections to terrorist financing.[51]

Sufian Abu Samara

Starting in 1989, in the wake of an Israeli crackdown on Hamas, Marzook traveled to Gaza and personally recruited new cadre to replace the scores of Hamas activists recently arrested. One of these recruits, Sufian Abu Samara, was himself arrested by Israeli forces in early 1991 and gave a full confession. Samara headed the Hamas security apparatus responsible for the group's counter-intelligence efforts and for dealing with collaborators. He also told Israelis that he established terror cells, and "aided in transferring money to the families of the movement's detainees." According to his statement, "after the wave of arrests inflicted on Hamas he [Marzook] initiated approaching many people to fill up the vacuum created after the arrest of the organization's activists. . . . Mousa [Abu Marzook] also warned against the collapse of the movement if no new infrastructure is established." Marzook recruited Samara and others, instructing them on how to receive money from operatives abroad, including Abdelhaleem al-Ashqar.

During one such meeting with his new recruits in Gaza, which Marzook held to "reestablish the connections and set up Hamas again," Samara said that Marzook "requested that we at first carry out some operations" and leave the propaganda effort of distributing leaflets to others for the time being. Given responsibility for Hamas operations in "Gaza South," Samara proceeded to recruit two teachers at the Islamic University of Gaza, Mahmoud Muqdad and Zuhadi Abu Nameh, and tasked them each to recruit more operatives. Samara was told the locations of Hamas dead letter boxes for secret communication with other operatives and cells. Almost all of these were located in mosques run by the Hamas dawa, including the Great Mosque in Bureij, the mosque in the al-Amal quarter in Khan Yunis, the al-Huna or al-Auda mosques in Rafah, and the al-Yarmuq mosque on al-Yarmuq Street and the al-Rahman mosque on al-Ansar Street, both in the Nasser neighborhood of Gaza City, among others. Samara detailed how operations funded by activists like Marzook and al-Ashqar were frequently planned by jailed Hamas commanders in Israeli prisons who communicated through letters smuggled out by relatives working for Hamas. For example, Munir Qatifan's instructions arrived from jail via his brother, Hanu; Hassan al-Sibi passed messages through his brother, Bassam.

Sufian Abu Samara also told Israeli authorities that Marzook gave him signed checks drawn from U.S. banks and that Marzook "used to deposit funds into the checking accounts that he left us." According to Samara, Palestinian moneychangers like Salah Harzallah or unnamed Jewish moneychangers then cashed these checks. Samara admitted receiving over two hundred thousand dollars in this manner, which he then transferred on to regional Hamas leaders like Abu Anas al-Faluji, Zuhadi Abu Nameh, and Mohammad Maqdid, "who are the ones in charge in the Gaza district of distributing them [the funds] to the families of Hamas detainees."

Samara also recounted meeting a Hamas operative who, at the direction of Hamas political and dawa leaders like Marzook and al-Ashqar, provided him a bag full of cash totaling 41,200 Jordanian dinars. "Another way to get money," Samara explained, "is getting money from [West Bank or Gaza] residents traveling abroad [who, while] outside the country they get money from the movement." Despite the evidence of his frenetic activity financing Hamas operations, Marzook commented self-deprecatingly in a 1997 interview, conducted while he was imprisoned in New York on immigration charges, that fundraising was beyond his ability. "As to fundraising, this is not my work. . . . I don't know how to do it, I don't have the skills or personality to do it."[52]

Mohammad Qassem Sawalha

Marzook's efforts to revitalize the Hamas military wing through dawa activists included a European angle that made news as recently as early 2005. Mohammad Qassem Sawalha, a Hamas activist and longtime Muslim leader in Britain, was appointed a trustee of the radical Finsbury Park mosque in London in February 2005. The mosque was closed in 2004 because it had come under the influence of Abu Hamza al-Masri, a radical Islamic cleric arrested in Britain and charged with sixteen offenses, including incitement to murder and possession of a document useful to someone plotting terrorism, among other counts. Sawalha was named one of five trustees designated to lead the mosque when it was reopened in early 2005. His appointment, however, was not likely to mark a change in direction from al-Masri's leadership, if Sawalha's own decade-long history of supporting Hamas terrorist operations was any indication. An August 2003 indictment against Hamas activists in the United States named Sawalha as a co-conspirator. He was accused of providing assistance to those indicted on racketeering and conspiracy, among other charges. According to the indictment, before Sawalha moved to London in the early 1990s he was a Hamas leader in the West Bank. The indictment goes on to cite several cases in which Sawalha allegedly conspired with others to support Hamas terrorist operations.

For example, while in London Sawalha met with Mohammad Salah (one of the defendants) and Mohammad Jarad, who were passing through London en route to Israel. According to the indictment, Sawalha provided the two men with instructions on "Hamas-related activities they were to carry out while in Israel, the West Bank, and the Gaza Strip." The indictment further describes how, in August 1992, Sawalha met with Marzook and Salah to discuss the need to "revitalize Hamas terrorist operations in the West Bank." At that meeting Sawalha suggested specific Hamas members in the West Bank on whom Salah and Jarad might rely to help energize Hamas' terrorist activities. Less than six months later, in January 1993, Sawalha and Salah met yet again in London. At this meeting Sawalha specifically directed Salah to "provide money to various Hamas members in the West Bank and Gaza Strip."[53]

Ahmad Mohammad Abdallah al-Sharuf

In another case, Hamas operatives made use of a Palestinian furniture store owner's frequent travels between Bethlehem and the northern Israeli-Arab town of Um el-Fahm to raise funds for Hamas among Israeli-Arabs—and transfer those funds back to the West Bank. According to a 1998 intelligence report produced by the Bethlehem Directorate of the Palestinian Preventive Security Headquarters, based on "information passed on to us from one of [our] sources in the Hamas movement," Hamas activists affiliated with charitable front organizations in the West Bank and Israel used the al-Nubani furniture store to further Hamas fundraising efforts. The storeowner was Ahmad Mohammad Abdallah al-Sharuf, a Hamas activist and assistant director of the Bethlehem Orphan Care Society, identified by Israeli and Palestinian authorities as a Hamas front organization. Al-Sharuf's frequent travels into Israel on behalf of his furniture business provided cover for regular meetings in Um el-Fahm with al-Haj Abd al-Latif, a leader of the Islamic Movement in Israel and head of the Orphan and Prisoner Association. (The northern wing of the Islamic Movement, headquartered in Um el-Fahm, is closely tied to Hamas. In fact, Israeli authorities shut the Orphan and Prisoner Association in 1996 for serving as a Hamas front.) After these meetings, according to the report, al-Sharuf would take money raised by the Islamic Movement and turn it over to Hamas via his furniture salesman, who also happened to be the treasurer of the Bethlehem Orphan Care Society. According to another Palestinian intelligence report dated July 1997, al-Sharuf "is politically oriented toward Hamas" and "all his children belong to Hamas."[54]

Mazen Sunuqrut

As noted above, Palestinian intelligence reports document their belief that the Sunuqrut Global Group was "among the most important companies the [Ramallah/al-Bireh zakat] Committee works with" to launder funds for Hamas. But Mazen Sunuqrut, part owner of the company, did not only use the family business to benefit Hamas, he also used personal bank accounts in London for that purpose. According to a retired Israeli intelligence official, Sunuqrut "was arrested in the early 1990s, during the first Intifada, and in his interrogation confessed that he used his private bank accounts in the UK to transfer money for Hamas. He gave many details about the finance [sic] of Hamas at that time. Due to his cooperation in the interrogation he was not tried and was released." In a similar case, an Israeli report on the raid of the Holy Land Foundation Jerusalem office notes that money raised in the United States "was transferred to the [recipient] *zakat* committee by means of [Hamas activist] Salah Harzallah's account in London."[55]

Jamil and Salah Sarsour

Other Hamas supporters also used London as a transit point for Hamas communications and funding. In 1990, Hamas operative Sheikh Mohammad Abu Tair moved to Great Britain. After a trip to the West Bank to visit his family in 1994, Hamas supporter Jamil Sarsour—a co-owner in a family furniture store in Milwaukee—was asked to take a package back to his home in the United States and mail it from there to Abu Tair in Great Britain. Asked why he was requested to do this, Sarsour replied, "I don't know why, but when people ask for a favor, one should try to help them out." Indeed, Hamas relies heavily on this sentiment in its efforts to draw logistical support from everyday Palestinians and Hamas supporters alike.[56]

Israeli authorities later arrested both Jamil and his brother Salah Sarsour, for supporting Hamas. Salah Sarsour and Adel Awadallah were cellmates in an Israeli prison and became close friends. At the time, Adel and his brother, Imad, headed the Qassam Brigades in the West Bank. According to Jamil Sarsour, "I had already declared that I have given [Hamas] money in 1991. Adel Awadallah asked me to help out with money again, and told me Israel and the Palestinian authorities were after him. I passed money over to Adel Awadallah several times, and my brother sent money to him through me several times too." The Sarsour brothers passed the Awadallah brothers $2,000 to $3,000 at a time drawn on their furniture store's business account because "we didn't want to use personal checks from either of one of us so that the government shouldn't trace the checks back to us personally. We did it this way so we could take checks abroad and send money to Adel Awadallah."[57]

As detailed in Chapter 4, the role of the Hamas dawa in the group's terror attacks was especially evident in the string of suicide bus bombing attacks in February and March 1996. In the wake of this series of attacks, Israeli authorities identified specific Hamas logistical support networks that facilitated the attacks. Prime Minister Shimon Peres told the Israeli Knesset: "Hamas has established charitable organizations in order to camouflage its true nature. These charitable organizations raise funds abroad, supposedly to aid orphans, but in fact they use the contributions to purchase explosives." Indeed, these charities—and the funds they raise—also recruit, employ, and hide Hamas militants and provide essential administrative support to terrorist cells.[58]

4

the logistics of terror:
tactical uses of the dawa

In addition to financing Hamas attacks, dawa activists frequently play essential tactical roles in Hamas terrorism. Among their tactical functions are collecting pre-operational intelligence on potential targets, leading suicide bombers to target sites, and bolstering the cover identity of suicide bombers en route to attacks. Following a Hamas suicide bombing at Jerusalem's Mahane Yehuda outdoor market in July 1997, the Israeli Shin Bet (Israel Security Agency) wrote an intelligence estimate on the types of preventive missions the agency should conduct "for the purpose of preventing and foiling a bombing attack." The report found that time and again investigations into Hamas "military infrastructures" revealed that military cells "were aided and prepared for their missions by the [logistical] infrastructures."[1]

> Starting from the beginning of 1996, Hamas infrastructures in Jerusalem and Judea [the southern West Bank] were exposed which were involved in a number of far reaching plots. The infrastructures were involved over the years with the setting up of a wide logistical network which produced explosive materials, located suicide bombers, prepared safe houses, rented and bought vehicles, helped transfer wanted suspects, and purchased electrical, electronic, and chemical equipment for the purpose of preparing an explosive device. The infrastructure included Hamas operatives from all levels of operations that are known to us inside the Hamas organization, starting with individual operatives from the mosque and dawa levels and up to the core of wanted suspects, each of whom was essential in the military operations that led to the bombing attack.[2]

The report concluded, "there exists an *essential need* to strike/foil the human infrastructure of Hamas in the area in all its echelons and operational levels" (emphasis in original). Though frequently misrepresented as Hamas' "civilian" wing, to distinguish from its explicitly military cells, the Hamas dawa serves as the ideal logistical and support infrastructure for a terrorist network. By its very nature the dawa operates overtly, offering an extensive and entrenched network of charities, social service organizations, mosques—and employees, members, donors, and service recipients—available to facilitate Hamas activities. Many dawa employees and beneficiaries enthusiastically support Hamas terrorist operations; others do so unwittingly or as a quid pro quo for charity or social services. Either way, as noted in a report on suicide bombings in the *Economist,* "because [terrorist groups] are corporate enterprises, disrupting or preventing attacks is not just a question of catching the bomber: there are also recruiters, trainers, reconnaissance agents, bomb-makers and safe houses." In this chapter, we borrow the magazine's corporate metaphor and examine how the dawa fulfills many of the logistical, human resource, and infrastructural needs of the group's primary terrorist mission. We conclude with a case study of the West Bank al-Tadhoman Charitable Association, a model of how a Hamas social services organization serves an integral tactical component of the group's military mission.[3]

HUMAN RESOURCES

The network of charitable organizations affiliated with Hamas fulfills three primary human resource functions critical to its military success: recruiting, employing, and providing a cover of legitimacy for terrorists. To fully appreciate how effective Hamas' network of charitable organizations is at fulfilling these functions we must first understand just how extensive this network is. While the network has grown significantly since then, a noncomprehensive list of Hamas organizations presented by a Hamas official in 1993 marks a useful starting point. Speaking at a meeting of Hamas leaders from North America held in Philadelphia, Hamas operative Muin Shabib, visiting from the West Bank, offered a presentation on "the situation in Palestine" and the status of "Islamic works" tied to Hamas. According to the FBI transcript of his lecture, Shabib described the institutions tied to Hamas as falling under the following classifications: educational (schools, universities), social and charitable (refugees, orphans, relief), cultural, health institutions (clinics, medical centers), public syndicates, technical institutions, sports clubs, media, religious institutions, and women's institutions.[4]

Shabib then proceeded to list specific institutions tied to Hamas, which he described as "our institutions."[5]

In the Gaza Strip:

1. The Islamic University
2. The Islamic Complex
3. The Islamic Association
4. Al-Salah Association
5. The Young Woman Association
6. Al-Wafa Association for the Elderly
7. The Orphans Center
8. Some al-Zakah [zakat] committees
9. Some general service committees that received new licenses, such as the organization of the Truth and the Law

In the West Bank:

1. Al-Zakah Committee (Shabib did not specify which zakat committee, but he did add that "it has investments and other activities. In reality, we, the Islamists, do have much presence in this committee.")
2. Al-Tadhoman Al-Eslami Committee
3. Al-Tadoman Charitable Association
4. Al-Zakah Committee in Jenin (which "established a hospital" and is "controlled by the Islamists")
5. Al-Aqsa Institutions (which "should have a big role and we can benefit from controlling these institutions")
6. The Association of Islamic Studies and Cultures in Jerusalem
7. Al-Zakah Committee in Ramallah (where "we have [additional] active institutions")[6]

Shabib also cited the Ramallah Islamic syndicate and the Islamic Youth Association as Hamas institutions, adding that employees of Hamas-run organizations such as these have been arrested or deported for getting "mixed up" in Hamas "organizational work." In the discussion that followed Shabib's lecture, the al-Islah charity, student unions (described as "completely controlled by us"), and commerce syndicates were also mentioned as Hamas organizations. Taken together, Shabib's rundown of "our" organizations and the list of typical syndicates and unions run by Hamas provide a clear picture of the pervasiveness of Hamas institutions that are available to facilitate the group's recruitment of future members and its provision of employment and cover for existing ones.[7]

Recruitment

The charity committees, mosque classes, student unions, sport clubs, summer camps, and other organizations run by Hamas are places where recruiters (usually themselves dawa activists) recruit Palestinian youth into Hamas—whether into other dawa positions, or for suicide and other terror attacks. As a senior U.S. State Department official noted, funding any part of Hamas enhances the group's credibility and provides it "the opportunity to recruit people through its charitable activities."[8]

In their analysis of interviews with jailed terrorists, including Hamas members and others, academics Jerrold Post, Ehud Sprinzak, and Laurita Denny found that the "pre-recruitment" social environment for members of Islamist groups like Hamas "was dominated by the mosque, religious organizations and religious instruction." According to their report, "For the Islamist groups, almost 50 percent cite the mosque, Moslem Brotherhood or other religious influence as central. Another 20 percent cite their experience at the university or other professional school as of primary importance." Moreover, "the recruitment process is predominantly a casual or informal process among both secular and Islamist groups," to the extent that "over half the members of each group type knew their recruiter prior to recruitment." In the words of one Islamist interviewed for the above study:

My initial political awareness came during the prayers at the mosque. That's where I was also asked to join religious classes. In the context of these studies, the sheik used to inject some historical background in which he would tell us how we were effectively evicted from Palestine. The sheik also used to explain to us the significance of the fact that there was an IDF military outpost in the heart of the camp. He compared it to a cancer in the human body, which was threatening its very existence. At the age of 16 I developed an interest in religion. I was exposed to the Moslem Brotherhood and I began to pray in a mosque and to study Islam. The Koran and my religious studies were the tools that shaped my political consciousness. The mosque and the religious clerics in my village provided the focal point of my social life.[9]

The above confession could have been uttered by any number of Hamas militants. Hamas bomb maker and head of the Jenin charity committee Ahmed Saltana acknowledged recruiting young men into Hamas while they were working for the charity committee. Saltana is a prime example of the dual social activist/militant operative common in Hamas. He was imprisoned between 1993 and 1995 "for his activities in the Izzedine al-Qassam Battalions, Hamas' terrorist-operational wing" and was a contact person for Hamas financiers in Saudi Arabia. Like Saltana, Nasser Khaled Ibrahim Jarrar, a founder of the Jenin charity in charge of its orphans department, also split his time between social activism, terrorist recruitment, and fundraising. According to Israeli intelligence, Jarrar "was active in recruiting terrorist-operatives and in locating and dispatching suicide bombers, and planned a series of deadly attacks against Israeli targets." On top of his other activities, Jarrar also traveled abroad on behalf of the charity committee to raise funds for Hamas.[10]

The soccer team of the Hamas-affiliated Jihad mosque in Hebron was another breeding ground for militants. From its athletic ranks came several Hamas terrorists, responsible for a string of attacks conducted over the first six months of 2003. Five of these were suicide bombings executed by team members. (The team shirt featured a picture of a hand holding an axe with an inscription reading, "Prepare for the enemy and to fight the occupation.") Another sports club is infamous for producing six different suicide bombers. To facilitate such recruitment opportunities Hamas sponsors not only individual teams but soccer tournaments as well. Under the heading of "various activities of Hamas in the area," a 1999 Palestinian security surveillance report noted, "a soccer [tournament] was organized in the Beit Sahour region by the Islamic Revival club."[11]

Palestinian security officials have long observed the Hamas trend of dawa installations serving as recruitment centers. In Gaza, the Dab al-Rakmah school is located in a large building that doubles as a cultural center. But the school is widely known to be tied to Hamas, which uses the building as a place to spot new recruits.[12] Fares Sarfandi, a Hamas operative recruited by Qassam Brigades commander Imad Awadallah, acknowledged participating in dawa activities through the al-Ayn mosque even as he engaged in parallel terrorist operations. Additionally, Sarfandi noted he "was charged with finding suitable Hamas candidates from among the mosque activists."[13]

The PA's General Nizar Ammar explains how Hamas spots potential recruits at local mosques:

> Hamas members are there and notice him looking anxious, worried, and depressed and that he's coming every day. It's a small society here—people tend to know each other. They will ask about him, discover his

situation. Gradually they will begin to recruit him. They talk to him about the afterlife and tell him that paradise awaits him if he dies in the jihad. They explain to him that if he volunteers for a suicide bombing, his family name will be held in the highest respect. He'll be remembered as a *shadhid* (martyr, hero). He'll become a martyr and Hamas will give his family about $5,000, wheat flour, sugar, other staples, and clothing. The most important thing is that the family's status will be raised significantly—they too will be treated as heroes. The condition for all this: he is not allowed to tell anyone.[14]

Hamas spotters also recruit new members on university campuses. In a statement to Israeli police in January 1993, Qassam Brigades member Salah Arouri noted that he, like many others, was first recruited into Hamas at Hebron University. Arouri recounted for Israeli police his [first] meeting with recruiter Muin (Muayn) Shabib in 1991: "Muayn told me that there was authorization for military activity and gave me a code word for an anonymous person that would come to him which was 'Abu Hani sends you his regards and wants to make a license.'" When the unnamed man arrived in July or August 1991, Arouri continued, he made contact at the university. "He came to the University in Hebron and gave me the code word," Arouri recalled, and then assigned Arouri "to recruit a squad in Hebron and to obtain weapons."[15]

Arouri's experience at Hebron University is hardly surprising; the university faculty contains several Hamas activists. Since June 1999 Sheikh Azzam Naman Abd al-Rahman Salhoub has been the head of the Islamic Law department there. In 2002, Salhoub was arrested by Israeli authorities for Hamas activity, including holding regular meetings with other Hamas operatives like Sheikh Yunes al-Assa al-Ubeidi, a senior Hamas leader in Bethlehem.[16]

Employment

Hamas terrorist operatives frequently hold day jobs within the dawa system. In addition to providing a salary, these jobs offer militants both legitimate standing as employees of charitable and humanitarian organizations, as well as cover for activities related to plotting and carrying out terror attacks. An Israeli analysis concluded that one of the ways Hamas dawa institutions serve as the group's terrorist support apparatus is "by creating jobs and employment opportunities for them (and sometimes also for their family members) in many 'charitable societies' and other institutions which comprise its civilian infrastructure." In so doing, the group provides the operatives an apparently legal cover. In one example cited by Israeli intelligence officials, Hamas operatives were listed as employees of a tailor shop that paid them regular salaries although they never showed up to work. Further investigation revealed that Hamas, not the tailor shop, paid the salaries. In another instance, documents seized from the offices of the Islamic Relief Agency (IRA) in raids conducted in July and November 1995 revealed that the salaries of ten West Bank Hamas military activists were being paid through the charity. The placement of such battle-hardened operatives in key dawa positions also streamlined the organization's ability to skim and launder funds from charities and social service organizations to military operations. Operating under the cover of legitimate employment is critical for terrorist operatives engaged in covert activity. For example, in Nablus a homeowner rented an apartment to someone he was told was a schoolteacher. In fact, the schoolteacher proved to be a Hamas fugitive bomb maker who used the apartment as a safe house and bomb production lab. The pretense only became clear after the apartment was wrecked and the tenant killed when the explosives he was handling detonated prematurely.[17]

The importance of such cover was underscored in a 2002 ruling handed down by an American court that found Iran responsible for a 1996 Hamas suicide bus bombing that killed American citizen Ira Weinstein. The court determined that Iranian money "supported Hamas terrorist activities by, for example, bringing Hamas into contact with potential terrorist recruits and by providing legitimate front activities behind which Hamas could hide its terrorist activities."[18]

Indeed, intelligence agencies have identified many current and former members of the Qassam Brigades—active militants who have participated in suicide bombing and other attacks—who hide in plain view by melting into the community through employment in Hamas dawa organizations, including local zakat committees. For example, Nur al-Din Kamal Asad Tahaina, the computer specialist for the Jenin charity committee, was arrested in 1994 for aiding a Hamas suicide bomber who carried out an attack in the northern Israeli town of Afula. Fadel Mohammad Salah Hamadan, a member of the Ramallah charity committee, was "directly connected with the planning of suicide attacks and the spiritual preparation of suicides (including the Mahane Yehuda attack in July 1997)." Under interrogation, detained Hamas activists have identified many other Hamas members employed by charitable organizations tied to Hamas in the West Bank and Gaza. One particularly fruitful interrogation was of Mahmud Rumahi, who listed eleven Hamas activists employed by a single charity. According to Rumahi, Hamas activists were also employed by social service organizations that benefited from these charities. Among these were Ziyad al-Ghani, the supervisor of the Tiba hospital in Jenin; Dr. Idris Abu Samaha, the supervisor of the Tulkarm hospital; and Hafiz al-Sadr, the supervisor of the Red Cross Station in Nablus. Rumahi added that the Hamas chief for the Ramallah region, Ahmad Mustafa, also worked for an unnamed charitable organization there. Eventually, Rumahi conceded: "There is a medical center in Ramallah that belongs to the charitable organization [tied to Hamas]. I am the medical director at that center."[19]

While employed by the Ramallah clinic, Rumahi oversaw the Hamas military spending for the area, including providing three operatives $10,000 a month "for the funding of their activities, as well as to the arrested Hamas militants to pay their lawyers. The families of the arrested men received about 300–400 [Israeli] shekel each month." A significant amount of the funding at his disposal came from Hamas members in the United States who deposited money in a First Wisconsin Bank account Rumahi opened while visiting Chicago in 1992. "Through this account Abu Ahmed [Mohammad Salah] transferred me money," Rumahi said, "and I withdrew it through money exchange offices in Ramallah until the day I have been arrested. I withdrew through them about $100,000, and I gave the money, cash, to the militants."[20]

Sheikh Hassan Yusef, a Hamas spokesman in Ramallah and a prominent figure in the group's public political and social welfare activities, provides another case study of the same phenomenon. Rumahi noted that Yusef played an active role in restructuring the leadership of the Hamas military wing in late 1992, even assuming the position of Rumahi's deputy after the previous deputy, Mazin Haga, was arrested. Khaled Mishal had also identified Yusef as one of the "next generation" of Hamas leaders. According to Hamas activist Akram Harubi, in his day job Yusef served as the representative of the central region of the West Bank to the Hamas public relations and media committee.[21]

Dawa-affiliated offices abroad also employ seasoned Hamas activists in leadership positions:

- The U.S. Treasury Department noted that Mahmoud Amru, the director of the al-Aqsa International Foundation's Germany offices, "is an active figure in Hamas."
- Abdelhaleem al-Ashqar of the defunct U.S.-based Hamas front al-Aqsa

Educational Fund (AAEF) was so senior a Hamas official that he "sent a representative from the United States to Israel" in April 1991 "to obtain detailed reports on Hamas activities in [Mahmud] Rumahi's region."

- Haitham Maghawri, the HLFRD's executive director, admitted to U.S. immigration officials that he had been arrested in Lebanon several times, once for placing a car bomb.
- Muin Kamel Mohammad Shabib, a participant at the 1993 Hamas planning meeting in Philadelphia, was identified by one of the Izz al-Din al-Qassam operatives he recruited as "being involved in the Hamas terrorist apparatus."[22]

Prior to his assignment to the Hamas dawa fundraising effort, Shabib was in charge of the Hamas central sector (Ramallah-Jerusalem), where he recruited leaders for Hamas terrorist cells. According to FBI agents who interviewed Shabib in Falls Church, Virginia, on March 16, 1994, "Shabib advised that he supports Hamas both financially and politically but does not support the violence associated with Hamas." Shabib also conceded knowing Hamas co-founder Sheikh Jamil Hamami, who was then traveling across the United States raising funds for Hamas. According to the FBI report, "Shabib advised that he has had no contact with Hamami since he has been here. (Note: WFO [Washington Field Office] knows this to be untrue.)"[23]

And Shabib is no exception: Hamas social welfare activists running the group's local charity organizations in the West Bank and Gaza are frequently current or former members of Hamas terror cells. Consider the following examples cited by the FBI:[24]

- Fadel Mohammad Salah Hamadan, a member of the Ramallah charity committee, was "directly connected with the planning of suicide attacks and the spiritual preparation of those about to commit suicide attacks, including the Mahane Yehuda attack in July 1997."
- Ahmed Salim Ahmed Saltana, head of the Jenin charity committee, was involved in transferring bomb-making materials for the preparation of explosives in 1992 and participated in a car bombing in 1993.
- Khalil Ali Rashad Dar Rashad, an associated member of the Orphan Care Society in Bethlehem, was known to provide shelter and assistance to Hamas fugitives, including Hamas bomb maker Muhi al-Din al-Sharif and Hassan Salameh, the commander behind the string of suicide bus bombings in February and March 1996.
- Nur al-Din Kamal Asad Tahaina was in charge of the Jenin charity com-

mittee computer. Tahaina was imprisoned from July 1994 to December 1994 for "'aiding' one of the suicide bombers in the 1994 terrorist attack against an Israeli bus in Afula" and again from January 1995 to January 1996 "for conducting Hamas activities."

- Nasser Khaled Ibrahim Jarrar, another member of the Jenin charity committee, was detained for three months in April 1994 "for recruiting young men to the Hamas terrorist wing" and again in January 1998 "for his connection to one of the suicide bombers in the 1994 terrorist attack against an Israeli bus in Afula, as well as his assistance to other Hamas operatives."

- Abd al-Jaber Mohammad Ahmed Jarar, also a member of the Jenin zakat committee, was arrested in May 1993 "for transferring weapons to Hamas recruits who subsequently conducted terrorist attacks."

- Fawaz Hamdan, active in both the Jenin zakat committee and the Hamas-funded al-Ghazi Hospital there, "was imprisoned for his activities in connection with Hamas, which included aiding fugitives and funding weapons purchases."

- Adnan Abd al-Hafez Musbah Maswada, directorate co-chairman of the Islamic Charity Association (a.k.a. The Islamic Charitable Society in Hebron), was detained for several months in 1989 and again in 1994 "for Hamas activity." According to the Government of Israel, "Maswada is a member of Hamas headquarters in Hebron and is connected to Hamas terrorist activities against settlers." Maswada was therefore included among the Hamas and Islamic Jihad leaders Israel deported to Lebanon in 1992.

Beyond the members of the Qassam Brigades embedded within the dawa, Hamas charities also provide the group's terror cells a ready pool of Palestinians unaffiliated with the Qassam Brigades but prepared to serve logistical and operational functions such as leading suicide bombers to their targets. Hamas operatives told one such group of logistical volunteers supporting militant cells in Bethlehem, Hebron, and Ramallah to "welcome the suicide bomber, outfit him and direct him to his target." Jamil Sarsour, the Hamas activist from Milwaukee, not only provided Hamas with tens of thousands of dollars, he also volunteered to help facilitate the escape of Adel Awadallah, a Hamas terrorist commander and fugitive wanted for his role in Hamas suicide bombings. Before flying to Israel, Sarsour reportedly swallowed a note—presumably from Hamas activists in the United States—instructing Awadallah on how to obtain a passport to evade Israeli authorities and flee the country. Sarsour also purchased four wigs for Awadal- lah in Milwaukee, brought them to the West Bank, and, in a typical example of how Hamas uses its dawa members to support the Qassam Brigades, had them delivered to Awadallah by the mother of another Hamas activist.[25]

Hamas' use of the dawa infrastructure to recruit militants has been es- pecially troubling to the secular Palestinian Authority, which—as its name suggests—is the ostensible authority over Palestinian society. When Hamas social services organizations take care of people the PA government cannot, or will not, the Authority has been weakened in the eyes of its constituents. When Hamas has used its charitable network to further its terrorist mission, the reputation of the PA is severely damaged. For this reason, Palestinian in- telligence agencies have quite rigorously investigated the existence of Hamas military agents embedded within so-called charitable organizations.

Consider, for example, Palestinian intelligence reporting on the Or- phan Care Society. In April 2002, Israeli forces seized a Palestinian intelli- gence report on Hamas institutions in the Bethlehem area. The document noted that the Orphan Care Society in Bethlehem tended to the needs of both average orphans and the children of Hamas "martyrs" and prisoners. According to the document, the institution's governing board "is com- posed entirely of Hamas activists in Bethlehem, prominent among whom is Dr. Ghassan Issa Mahmoud Harmas, considered to be the Hamas politi- cal leader in Bethlehem." As of January 2005, the association was still being directed by senior Hamas leaders—namely, Harmas (also known as Abu Tayib) and his deputy (and chairman of the association's board of gover- nors) Hajj Ahmed al-Sharouf. Harmas was included among the 415 Hamas and Islamic Jihad members deported across the border to Marj al-Zhour, Lebanon, in December 1992 and was briefly arrested again in 2002. Hajj al- Sharouf is the father of two known Hamas operatives.[26]

Because of the Orphan Care Society's central role in Hamas activities, Palestinian Intelligence made it a focus of their intelligence collection ef- forts. Palestinian Intelligence services ran sources within the Orphan Care Society who reported that Hamas activists employed there raised funds from various charities and foundations. One Palestinian intelligence re- port, written by the Political Security Department of the Preventive Secu- rity Service in Bethlehem, identified ten Hamas members affiliated with the Society. The report notes that the Society's objective is "to care for or- phans and the children of Hamas members who are imprisoned and *Sha- heeds* (martyrs)." In 2004, the Orphan Care Society completed construction of the Omar bin Khutab building, a nine-story structure described as an "orphan's village" intended to house 1,000 orphans, a Hamas school, clinic, kindergarten, as well as libraries and more.[27]

Palestinian security also highlighted the strong Hamas affiliation of the administrative officers at the Orphan Care Society. A Preventive Security Service report lists the names of the Society's members who both work there and have "administrative authority." Of the eleven officers, ten are listed as Hamas operatives. The Society's objective, according to the Palestinian report, is "to care for the orphans and the children of Hamas members who are imprisoned and martyrs." Stacking the Society's leadership with Hamas operatives enables the purported charity to easily launder funds. Thus, in a classic money-laundering maneuver, the report noted that "the Society does not have a specific bank account number. A thorough investigation revealed that some of the Society's employees have accounts at various banks in the district." The result is that funds donated to the Society—such as $38,435 raised in the United States and donated to the Society by the Holy Land Foundation between January 1997 and September 2000—could end up funding military or any other Hamas activity just as easily as it could fund the care of the children of killed or imprisoned Hamas operatives.[28]

Palestinian intelligence reported similar concerns about the Beit Fajar Charitable Society, also in the Bethlehem area. The head of the charity is Dr. Issa Thawabtah, a senior Hamas activist arrested first by Palestinian and later by Israeli authorities. Dr. Thawabtah previously served as the head of another Hamas front, the al-Islah Charitable Society, but left in February 2001 and was replaced at al-Islah by Sheikh Anwar Zaboun, another Hamas activist from the neighboring town of Beit Sahour. Palestinian security officials assessed that "an office of the Beit Fajar Charitable Society in Bethlehem was opened as a result of intense pressure exerted by Dr. Issa Thawabtah and because Dr. Issa Thawabtah plays a central role in bringing [in] support funds to Hamas institutions in Bethlehem."[29]

Palestinian authorities had no doubt about the Hamas connections of either the Orphan Care Society or the Beit Fajar Charitable Society. Palestinian intelligence officers documented a disagreement between Harmas and Thawabtah over the allocation of Hamas funds in the Bethlehem area, and over who should be the point of contact with foreign charities. According to a Palestinian intelligence report, Harmas argued that decisions about how to spend funds received from foreign charities (most of which are tied to Hamas) "is exclusively the business of the Hamas directorate in Bethlehem," which Harmas heads. Responding to Thawabtah's complaint that his charity received less than its share of funding, Harmas asserted, "I distribute the money as I see fit."[30]

Hamas-run charities were a matter of concern to Palestinian intelligence not only in the Bethlehem area but throughout the West Bank and Gaza Strip. In Ramallah, Palestinian intelligence was especially interested in the Charity and Contribution Committee of Ramallah-al-Bireh and the Surrounding Area (*Lajnat al-Zakat wal-Sadaqaat Ramallah wal-Bireh wal-Liwaa*), more commonly known as the Ramallah-al-Bireh zakat committee. Though nominally headed by Dr. Abd al-Qadir Abu Awad, a respected physician, the Palestinian General Intelligence noted in a report that the charity "supports the families of imprisoned and deported individuals" and that the "higher echelons of this society and others like it belong to Hamas, and some of them are movement [Hamas] activists." Thus, the committee's expense report for November and December 2000 reveals that among the families who benefited from the committee's financial aid were several senior Hamas operatives, including Abd al-Aziz Arouri, Rafat Mohammad Awad, Mundhir Abd al-Jabbar, Murad Sakhafi, and Amad Atshan. The expense report includes entries such as 10,000 Israeli shekels in "aid for a *shaheed* [martyr] family in Jericho"; 2,927 shekels to rent temporary office space for Beit al-Mal, the Hamas-run bank banned by Israel and the United States; "aid to wounded/Ibrahim Muteir"; and "aid to family of *shaheed/ Najwa al-Anati*."[31]

While the Ramallah-al-Bireh committee was ostensibly headed by respectable figures, another Palestinian intelligence report listed its active members (including the charity's administrative director and accountant) and concluded that "all the aforementioned are considered Hamas activists and we have files on them." After listing some of the charity's investments and programs, the report noted, "the committee is run by Hamas in a sophisticated manner. Its main activity is transferring funds from the 'outside' [funds raised abroad] into Hamas's coffers [in the West Bank]." Yet another Palestinian intelligence report features a table listing seven committee activists, including the committee's chairman. Under the column for "affiliation," all seven are listed as Hamas members, and three are marked as having been arrested at one time or another by Palestinian security. In fact, the report notes that after one Hamas-affiliated committee member, Mahmoud al-Rahmi, was arrested by Israel, and after other steps were taken against committee activists, its activities on behalf of Hamas decreased. "Our investigation of the Committee," the Palestinian intelligence report concluded, "made it clear that it was transferring funds from abroad to Hamas." These conclusions were apparently based on documents seized in their own raids, since the reports added, "We paid a surprise visit to the Ramallah office and confiscated a number of documents."[32]

Meanwhile, similar Palestinian investigations were under way in Hebron where Palestinian authorities found that senior Hamas activists ran the Islamic Charitable Society there. Adil Numan Salm al-Junaydi was the head of the society until his arrest for Hamas activity in December 2004. According to the Palestinian news agency *Wafa,* al-Junaydi was arrested along with six others in a sweep of fifteen houses in the Hebron area. Junaydi was among the senior Hamas and Islamic Jihad leaders deported to Lebanon in 1992. He served as the assistant administrative director for another Hamas charity, the al-Islah Charitable Society, before joining the Islamic Charitable Society in Hebron. Another former head of the society, Abd al-Khaliq al-Natsheh, was also arrested for his Hamas activities. Al-Natsheh was also among the 1992 deportees, and was imprisoned twice for terrorist activities, once in 1996 and again in 1998. After his release from an Israeli prison in 1998, al-Natsheh accepted an offer from Hamas political leader Khaled Mishal to assume the position of Hamas spokesman in Hebron. In this capacity, al-Natsheh would later confess, he referred several Hamas members interested in carrying out attacks to leaders of Hamas terror cells within the Qassam Brigades. Al-Natsheh oversaw an extensive terrorist infrastructure in Hebron that was responsible for many terrorist attacks carried out within Israel. These include the April 27, 2002, attack targeting Israelis in the community of Adora, which resulted in four deaths, including the death of a five-year-old girl, as well as the attack at Karmey Tzur on June 8, 2002, in which two were killed and five wounded.[33]

In 2002, Israeli authorities raided al-Natsheh's office at the society and found a letter from Hamas activists abroad that revealed in the clearest of terms how critical the dawa infrastructure is to Hamas terrorist activity. "The Intifada," the letter stated, "needs both wings, the popular one which supports it and the military which promotes the Intifada and the spirit of resistance." To facilitate continued "resistance" operations, the letter opined that the group needed an "organizational network which would cover all fields of necessary activity when needed, such as commerce, schools, mosques, neighborhood affairs, societies and universities, etc."[34]

Disguise

Hamas relies on the seeming legitimacy of its dawa network to deflect investigations of Hamas front organizations as "witch hunts" or efforts to subjugate Palestinian society. The organization actively campaigns for grassroots support on the platform of its overt social welfare programs, while at the same time soliciting backing for its less benevolent activities. In January 2005, Mohammad al-Masri, a Hamas candidate in municipal elections in the northern Gaza town of Beit Hanun, anticipated that Hamas' strong record in the field of dawa activities would lead to electoral success: "Everybody knows Hamas as a resistance group but Hamas is much more than that. We have a reputation as professionals in the social field, providing health and education services as well as welfare support." If the group's success in these municipal elections is any indicator, al-Masri is right. A Palestinian Authority intelligence report notes that Palestinians appeared quite eager to support a known Hamas charity in Bethlehem—despite its widely know ties to Hamas terror—"because of the humanitarian slogans it both utters and applies."[35]

Indeed, it is this professional reputation—and the cover of apparent legitimacy such a reputation provides—that has enabled Hamas institutions to receive funding and support from a variety of unwitting sources. For example, until Israeli authorities brought the issue to their attention in January 2001, Citibank in New York maintained an affiliation with Beit al-Mal, a bank described by the U.S. government as having "extensive ties to Hamas." Israel shut down the bank's operations there in 1998 and arrested several of the bank's officials, including the president of its board of directors, Mazen Sunuqrut, and Sulayman Aghbariyah, an Israeli-Arab who would be indicted a few years later on charges of financing Hamas. According to the U.S. Treasury Department, which designated both Beit al-Mal and the affiliated al-Aqsa Bank as terrorist entities in December 2001, "the majority of [Beit al-Mal's] founders, shareholders, and employees are associated with Hamas. Persons identified with Hamas hold a majority of the company's stock, and it has invested in projects in Gaza and the West Bank that are owned or managed by Hamas activists." Moreover, "Beit al-Mal transfers money to and raises funds for associations that the Palestinian Authority itself has identified as belonging to Hamas, and to known Hamas activists and convicts who are members of Hamas." In a letter to the Treasury Department, Citibank's parent company, Citigroup, stressed that it had been unaware of these banks' terrorist ties. "Let me be clear," wrote a managing director of Citigroup, "Citibank would never knowingly do business with a terrorist organization."[36]

In another case, several Hamas institutions in the Palestinian territories received donations from the United Nations Development Programme (UNDP). In at least one instance, UNDP continued to fund the Jenin and Tulkarm charity committees—both of which are intimately tied to Hamas—for four months after Israeli authorities raised the issue with U.N. officials. The veil of legitimacy the Hamas dawa draws over the rest of the group's activities is so thick that Peter Hansen, the former head of the United Nations Relief Works Agency (UNRWA)—the U.N. agency created to address the needs of Palestinian refugees after 1948—openly conceded that Hamas members were likely employed by UNRWA. "Oh I am sure that there are Hamas members on the UNRWA payroll and I don't see that as a crime," Hansen told the Canadian Broadcasting Corporation in October 2004, adding, "Hamas as a political organization does not mean that every member is a militant and we do not do political vetting and exclude people from one persuasion as against another." But in recent years there have been numerous cases of Palestinian terrorists employed by the UNRWA or using UNRWA facilities, equipment, and vehicles to carry out terror attacks. Between 2000 and 2004 thirteen Palestinians employed by the UNRWA were arrested for alleged involvement in terror activities on behalf of a variety of terrorist groups, including Hamas.[37]

In one example, Nahed Rashid Ahmed Attalah, director of food supplies for Gaza Strip refugees in the UNRWA office there, used United Nations vehicles and his U.N. free travel permit (*laissez-passer*) to aid the terrorist activities of the Popular Resistance Committees (PRC) in Gaza, a motley crew of radicals from a variety of groups, including Hamas. Indicted in September 2002, Attalah admitted to using his U.N. vehicle on multiple occasions that summer to transport arms, explosives, and armed PRC activists to carry out terrorist attacks. Attalah also confessed to using his U.N. laissez-passer to travel to Egypt, Lebanon, and Syria, where he contacted members of the Popular Front for the Liberation of Palestine (PFLP) "in order to obtain money for transferring arms to the Gaza Strip as assistance for the PRC."[38]

PHYSICAL AND ADMINISTRATIVE RESOURCES

In addition to helping Hamas recruit, employ, and disguise militants, the dawa also functions as the physical and administrative backbone of the organization's terrorist operations. Hassan Salameh, the Hamas military commander behind the string of suicide bus bombings in early 1996, openly acknowledged the support he received from Hamas facilitators, "from contacts to recruiting, to locating the places and all these matters." After sneaking into Israel from Gaza, Hamas dawa facilitators ferried Salameh across Israel's midsection into the West Bank, avoiding Israeli checkpoints as they traveled from town to town in the West Bank before arriving in Jerusalem. According to Salameh, Hamas operatives provided him with safe houses, scouts to identify targets, and recruiters to find the individual suicide bombers. These operatives were drawn from dawa activists at West Bank colleges and vocational schools. The safe houses where he was sheltered included private homes and, in at least one case, a Ramallah mosque, where Salameh met a potential suicide bomber for the recruit's final vetting and assignment. Hamas logistical operatives drove Majdi Abu Warda, one of the suicide bombers, to a Jerusalem safe house where others shaved his beard and dressed him to look like an Israeli. The following morning, Abu Warda boarded the number 18 bus on Jerusalem's Jaffa Road and detonated his explosive vest, killing twenty civilians (including three Americans) and wounding ten.[39]

Among Salameh's logistical supporters was Muayyad Mahmud Salah al-Din, a dawa operative active in the Hamas-dominated student council at Bir Zeit University. According to an article in the Hamas publication *Filisteen al-Muslima,* at the time of the 1996 attacks, Salah al-Din had "joined the student [council]'s activity in order to prepare the hearts and minds [of the students] to adhere to the right form of Islam." On November 8, 2001, Salah al-Din carried out a suicide bombing of his own in an attack near the Israeli-Arab villages of Baqa al-Gharbiya and Baqa al-Sharqiya.[40]

In another case, Jamal Abd al-Shamal Abu Hija, a senior terrorist operative in the Jenin area, simultaneously served as a supervisor for a center for Koran memorization and as a member of the Jenin charity committee. According to Israeli authorities, Abu Hija "was in charge of groups responsible for sending terrorists into Israel to perpetrate suicide bombing attacks." Another member of the Jenin charity committee, Ibrahim Hassan Ali Jaber, was also involved in "planning attacks, transporting explosive devices, giving military training and possessing weapons."[41]

An entire logistics cell such as this was wrapped up in one night on November 30, 2003. That night, Israeli forces detained several logistical support activists "involved in assisting the senior wanted terrorists" from the Ramallah sector. During the same security operation, Israeli forces arrested or killed several Hamas terrorism commanders, uncovered explosives labs, and seized suicide bombing belts and other explosives (including bombs concealed in basketballs).[42]

These cases are not aberrations; crossover between the social, political, and military wings is common. In fact, Hamas leaders have openly called for "civilian" (i.e., dawa) support for Hamas terrorists wanted by authorities. In August 2003, Hamas leader Abdel Aziz al-Rantissi urged average Palestinians to help Hamas fugitives, writing that "protecting the fighters and to offer them support is part of our religion, is part of the holy war."[43]

Hamas uses its civilian infrastructure as meeting places; it hides fugitives in the homes of its dawa activists and supporters, and has buried caches of arms and explosives under its own kindergarten playgrounds. In one such case, referenced by the State Department in its annual report on international terrorism for the year 2000, Palestinian security forces arrested members of a Hamas cell from the Israeli-Arab town of Taibeh in the nearby West Bank village of Kalil near Nablus. Under interrogation, the arrested Hamas operatives informed that the explosives they intended to use in a series of bombing attacks were cached in a Hamas kindergarten in Gaza. Palestinian security chief Jibril Rajoub recounted that "one of the men we arrested in Nablus confessed that they have explosives hidden in a kindergarten in Shati [refugee] camp in Gaza. We found in that hideout 32 kilos of explosives in the kindergarten yesterday. It belongs to Hamas."[44]

Hamas actively solicits the assistance of "civilian" Hamas supporters to provide logistical support or even facilitate its terror attacks, especially those who can make use of their places of employment to serve the needs of the Qassam Brigades. For example, a Hamas cell led by Sheikh Ibrahim Hamad smuggled contraband weapons in the garbage truck that one of its cell members, Majdi Na'asan, drove for a living. The cell later plotted to kidnap Israeli soldiers on patrol in the Ramallah area by staging an accident with the garbage truck, hiding up to three soldiers in the garbage truck, and decapitating any additional soldiers that would not fit in the truck. (In an archetypal example of the crossover between dawa and terrorist activity, Hamad is a close associate of Jamal al-Tawil, the Hamas operative and al-Islah head in Ramallah profiled in Chapter 2.) Another Hamas military cell caught in February 2005 was found to be using the West Bank welding shop owned by one of its members, Atzam Shafik al-Kader Samar, as a weapons laboratory where the cell manufactured explosives and homemade Qassam rockets. The cell, led by Yihiya Sayid Mussa Zivad, a senior Hamas military commander in the northern West Bank area, was believed to be directly

funded by Hamas leaders abroad. It planned to fire Qassam rockets at Israeli communities from positions within the West Bank.[45]

Sometimes, the support provided by Hamas dawa operatives is as simple
as printing or photocopying Hamas material. Taher Abd al-Aziz Dandis, a
member of the Islamic Charity Society in Hebron and a Hamas activist, allowed the printing office he owned to be used to print Hamas material. In
1989, Hamas operatives in Gaza found themselves in need of a place to
safely photocopy Hamas pamphlets (containing claims of responsibility
for attacks, political messages, and other propaganda). The Gaza cell commander ended up photocopying the materials himself "in the library on
Omar al-Muranawi Street beside the court house of appeals through a fellow named Nazim who works as a caretaker there as a cover for his Hamas
activity." Hamas so valued its access to the library, and the services Nazim
was able to provide, that it worked to solidify the position of their Hamas
agent. "We helped him buy books for four hundred Dinars" for the library
and "bought a photocopying machine for 4,000 [Israeli] Shekels and saw to
it that it was taken to the library."[46]

Indeed, libraries—along with hospitals and mosques—tied to Hamas
have proven to be particularly useful physical resources supporting the
group's terrorist activities.

Libraries

Islamist libraries in Arab villages routinely sell videocassettes of radical sermons featuring anti-Semitic themes and explicitly calling for terrorist actions against Israel. Recognizing the utility of libraries for logistical support,
propaganda, and radicalization efforts, the Tulkarm charity committee highlighted "support for the construction of public libraries and mosques"
among a list of programs for which it sought financial support from the
Union of Good, an umbrella organization for groups raising funds for
Hamas abroad. In fact, Hamas has funded several library projects in the
West Bank. These include the al-Anwar al-Ibrahimi Library in Hebron (described by the FBI as "controlled by Hamas" and funded by the Holy Land
Foundation, a Hamas front organization shut down in December 2001),
and the Orphan Care Society's library in Bethlehem (supervised by Walid
al-Bastanji, described by Palestinian Preventive Security as "a close associate"
of Ghassan Harmas, the head of the society and a senior Hamas activist).
The Ramallah-al-Bireh charity committee funded another library at the
Grand Mosque in al-Bireh, described by Israel as "a center for Hamas ac-

tivity," while the Islamic Center in the Jenin refugee camp, tied to Palestinian Islamic Jihad, also ran a public library funded in part by Hamas.[47]

Hospitals

Among the most prized physical assets of the Hamas dawa are hospitals. These public institutions are used by Hamas to build grassroots support, procure chemicals used in the production of explosives, and facilitate attacks. In the early 1990s the head of Hamas' Jenin charity committee, Sheikh Ziad Zakarna, approached Israeli authorities for a permit to build a hospital in Jenin specializing in optometry. He said a Palestinian expatriate living in Saudi Arabia was prepared to donate the land for the hospital, and that other foreign donations were available for its construction. Israeli officials were wary of the request, however, on two counts. First, the general hospital already functioning in Jenin at the time was both underutilized and under-equipped. Why invest in a new, specialized hospital when the existing one was in need of funds and had open beds? Second, Hamas had recently built a large social service center in Jenin, which included a mosque, library, and medical clinic complete with an X-ray machine. Several people affiliated with the new center had already been arrested by Israeli police for questioning about their affiliation with Hamas, and Israeli investigations into people affiliated with the proposed eye hospital revealed still more ties to Hamas.[48]

Over the next decade, Israeli suspicions about Hamas' use of hospitals in Jenin and elsewhere would prove well founded. In June 2002, Israeli authorities arrested Mustafa Amjad, a doctor at the al-Razi Hospital in Jenin. Amjad had been recruited by Hamas and told to exploit his freedom of movement as a medical professional to help smuggle Hamas suicide bombers into Israel from the Jenin area. Like the eye hospital proposed a decade earlier, the al-Razi Hospital is affiliated with the Jenin charity committee, a Hamas charity. After his arrest, Amjad confessed to helping Hamas terrorists enter Israel while delivering medicines. According to information cited by the FBI, another hospital, the Dar al-Salam Hospital, "was founded in 1995 with Hamas funds and protection. The building is located on the land of a Hamas-associated family by the name of Al-Bata from Khan Yunis."[49]

According to FBI records, between January 1997 and September 2000 Dar al-Salam Hospital received $317,222 in funding from the Holy Land Foundation. Dr. Mufid Mahlalati, director of the Dar al-Salam Hospital, who also ran a health center in Gaza, was identified by Israeli authorities as a Hamas activist, and was closely tied to the Holy Land Foundation. Simi-larly, Israeli authorities identified Dr. Hafez Abd al-Nabi Salah Nahsha, the director of the al-Ahli Hospital, as a Hamas activist with ties to the Holy Land Foundation's Jerusalem office.[50]

In addition to hospitals, ambulances are also frequently used by Hamas operatives for meetings, and to transport terror-related matériel and people. For example, Nasser Nazal, a senior Hamas operative in Qalqilya, took ad-vantage of the fact that his brother, Nidal, enjoyed "freedom of passage" rights as a Palestinian Red Crescent ambulance driver. Nidal transferred weapons and messages in his ambulance from one Hamas cell to another across the West Bank. In another case, Hamas commanders Khaled Abu Hamed and Said Kutab recruited Rashed Tarek al-Nimr, a chemist employed at hospitals in Nablus and Bethlehem, to procure chemicals for Hamas bomb making. Nimr first met these and other wanted Hamas men while they were hiding out inside hospitals where Nimr worked. Over a period of months, Nimr provided Hamed with six containers of hydrogen peroxide, a precursor ingredient used in the production of the TATP explosive fa-vored by Hamas. In at least one instance, Hamed solicited Nimr's help with the promise that "there would be a large explosion in Israel in the near fu-ture." Nimr agreed to help find a safe place to store the chemicals, and of-fered to covertly transfer them to Hamas in a Palestinian ambulance. In their last request, made just days before his arrest in November 2003, Nimr's handlers tasked him with procuring nitrous acid and hydrogen sulfide, chemicals used to make nitroglycerine explosives.[51]

Mosques

According to Palestinian scholar Ziad Abu-Amr, Hamas' use of mosques was honed during the first Intifada when "Hamas used the mosque as a platform and turned it from a place of worship into a center of learning, and later on a place for political organization." In general, Abu-Amr notes, "the mosque has been one of the most effective means of expanding Is-lamic influence. Unlike other institutions, the mosque remains open all the time. Being a sanctuary, the mosque could be used as a place for political work and organization, away from the eyes of interference of the Israeli au-thorities. Religious functions and activities are not subject to the same re-strictions to which nationalist or political activities are subjected." Pales-tinian intelligence officials have highlighted the fact that mosques (as well as universities, student organizations, and other parts of the Hamas dawa) serve as a prime recruitment environment. According to Israeli officials, Palestinian intelligence efforts targeted such venues in "a consecutive, clinging, and documented intelligence follow-up of the activities of a big portion of these institutions."[52]

Operational meetings are frequently held in mosques run by Hamas members or sympathizers. For example, a Palestinian intelligence surveillance team reported in 1999 that Hamas activists in the Bethlehem area regularly met at the mosque after prayers. Israeli authorities have highlighted the al-Ein mosque in al-Bireh (in the West Bank, near Ramallah) as a location "exploited by Hamas operatives as a place to hold meetings to coordinate military activities." Israel has also identified two of the al-Ein mosques' preachers, Bassem Nihad Ibrahim Jarrar and Fadel Mohammad Salah Hamadan, as "senior Hamas members, well known in the region of Ramallah." In another case, Mohammad Salah—the Hamas leader from Chicago—met Qassam Brigades recruits at several mosques, including the al-Bireh mosque and the al-Nasser mosque. According to Qassam activist Salah Arouri, "I received 96,000 American dollars from Abu Ahmad [Mohammad Salah] which he gave me personally in the Abd al-Nasser mosque in al-Bireh. He told me that the money was meant for our weapons procurement activity." As highlighted in the case of the Park Hotel suicide bombing, mosques run by Hamas also serve as preferred locations for "dead letter boxes" (DLBs), an espionage term referring to physical locations where matériel is transferred without direct contact between two parties. For Hamas, DLBs ensure secure communication between cells. Locating their DLBs in mosques provides Hamas operatives with a drop site that is as easy for them to access as it is difficult for Palestinian or Israeli authorities.[53]

Some Hamas institutions are co-located in mosques affiliated with the group. For example, the headquarters of the Orphan Care Society in Bethlehem is located at the Salah al-Din mosque. Even while under Palestinian intelligence surveillance and outlawed by Israeli authorities for its ties to Hamas, the society utilized the mosque as a center of Hamas activity.[54]

Mosques associated with Hamas also serve as safe houses and meeting places for Hamas fugitives. For example, Arouri recounted hiding Qassam activists Bashir Hamad, Talal Salah, and Imad Aqel in the al-Hares mosque in Hebron in 1991 after three other members of their cell were captured. Mohammad Salah then personally ferried two of these fugitives to Ramallah. From there they were smuggled into Gaza by hiding behind stacks of toilet paper in the back of a delivery truck. In a typical example of how

Hamas terrorists use the dawa, Salah later informed Arouri that the two fugitives left for Egypt using false identification they procured from "a man by the name of Salah from Gaza who studied in a nursing institute in Ramallah and forged the I.D. cards of the fugitives."[55]

Hamas often issues declarations and instructions to followers over mosque loudspeakers; within a week of the publication of the Hamas charter in August 1988 copies were posted in mosques throughout the West Bank and Gaza. In fact, while the Palestinian Authority officially controls and oversees all Palestinian mosques through the Ministry of Religious Endowments (which pays the salaries of most preachers), in reality it has engaged in almost no supervision whatsoever. Imams (preachers) associated with Hamas are relatively free to allow their mosques to be used as meeting places and dead drops by Hamas operatives, to use religious classes as recruiting pools at which new recruits are first spotted, and to deliver radical sermons extolling the virtues of suicide bombers and portraying all Israelis and Jews as mortal enemies.[56]

Khaled Tafesh Duweib, for example, a senior Hamas activist in Bethlehem and close associate of Ghassan Harmas, the head of the Orphan Care Society, served as the imam of the Omar mosque. Duweib regularly preached the virtues of terrorism from his pulpit, including a sermon on November 3, 2000, praising a car bombing in a Jerusalem market that killed two people and wounded eleven the previous day.[57]

CASE STUDY: AL-TADHOMAN CHARITABLE ASSOCIATION

The al-Tadhoman Charitable Society is a model of how Hamas operatives are positioned within the organization's social-welfare institutions. Founded by the Muslim Brotherhood in the 1950s, the al-Tadhoman operates in very close cooperation with two other Hamas charities in the area, the Nablus charity committee and the Jenin charity committee. Sheikh Hamid Bitawi, a senior Hamas official, serves simultaneously as the head of the al-Tadhoman Charitable Society and the vice chairman of the Nablus charity committee, and the two charities' boards of directors share many members. In a sign of his radical Islamist worldview, Bitawi told a crowd of 10,000 Hamas supporters following a suicide bombing at a Tel Aviv café in March 1997, "I have good news. There is a suicide bombing in Tel Aviv." He continued, "This is the only language the occupiers understand, the language of martyrdom." Bitawi is also the chairman of the Palestinian Association of Islamic Scholars, which includes many Hamas members and issued a religious edict (fatwa) praising suicide attacks as "actions [that] are an exalted expression of jihad for the sake of Allah and are not to be considered suicide."[58]

Because of al-Tadhoman's role as a key Hamas front organization, the Palestinian Authority closed its main offices, its sports club, and its medical clinic in December 2001. In September 2002, the chief of Palestinian Preventive Security in Gaza, Rashid Abu Shabak, referred a report to the political security department and the office of Yasser Arafat regarding funds collected for the Palestinian people in Bosnia. A $50,000 donation was apparently supposed to go to the PA but had instead been sent to the Islamic al-Tadhoman Charitable Society. "It should be noted," the report stresses, "that this is contrary to what was agreed upon by the [Palestinian] embassy [in Sarajevo]." The embassy's assumption that the donation would go to the PA was suspect at the outset, however, since the office of the Grand Mufti of Bosnia-Herzegovina coordinated the donation through the office of Sheikh Ikrima Sabri, the Mufti of Palestine and a known Hamas supporter, in conjunction with Sheikh Hamid Bitawi.[59]

The Society's close ties to Hamas are corroborated not only by Muin Shabib's statement to Hamas members in the United States but by other sources as well. For example, an Israeli analysis of al-Tadhoman's board of directors revealed that all the members were Hamas activists. Dr. Abd al-Rahim Radi al-Hanbali, chairman of the Nablus charity committee and a member of the al-Tadhoman board, is described by Israel as "a senior political Hamas activist" whose son, Mohammad al-Hanbali, was "one of the heads of Hamas' terrorist-operational infrastructure in Nablus." Another board member, Haj Adli Rafat Salih Yaish, was deported to Lebanon along with other Hamas officials in 1992; as treasurer of the Nablus charity committee he had been involved in Hamas money transfers. Dr. Muawiyah Rizq al-Masri was a prominent advocate for supporting families of martyrs and "at the end of 2002 he waged a public struggle for the continuation of payments to such families." Members of the al-Tadhoman board are involved with related Hamas institutions too, including the al-Tadhoman medical clinic, the al-Ansar sports club, and the Koran Memorization Committee, among others. Israeli forces killed a former board member—Sheikh Jamal Damouni—in a July 31, 2001, missile strike targeting the Palestinian Center for Studies and Media (a Hamas center run by Jamal Mansour, a senior Hamas leader also killed in the attack).[60]

Sheikh Hamid Bitawi is himself a telling example of the kind of Hamas leadership embedded within the organization's dawa infrastructure. The head of the Association of Religious Clerics in Palestine (also known as the

Council of Sages of Religion of Palestine, the Palestinian Islamic Scholars Association, or the Palestine Association of Religious Scholars), Bitawi enjoys a position of religious prestige and legal authority in the Palestinian territories separate from that earned as the head of the al-Tadhoman Charitable Society. The Association of Religious Clerics was established by prominent Hamas religious figures who saw the need for an organization that would issue religious edicts in support of Hamas' actions, thereby promoting Hamas' ideology of militancy and violence against Israel. Several members of the association are also affiliated with al-Najah University, a Hamas stronghold in Nablus. Several other members are officials of Hamas charities, including Ghassan Harmas, the chairman of the Orphan Care Society in Bethlehem. Bitawi is also a preacher at the famous al-Aqsa mosque in Jerusalem and has held prominent judicial positions such as head of the appellate courts in Nablus and head of the Religious Judicial Council in the West Bank.[61]

Bitawi's institutional authority gives currency to his radical ideas and broadens the Palestinian audience exposed to his message. On more than one occasion, he has voiced his support for jihad and martyrdom—even explaining in one interview why it is religiously permissible for children to take part in jihad and martyrdom missions. In another interview, Bitawi referred to suicide bombers as "angels sent from heaven." He frequently employs religious textual interpretation and edicts to support militancy. In the wake of the death of Hamas bomb maker Muhi al-Din al-Sharif, Bitawi told a crowd of Hamas supporters that "religious rulings dictate that the Palestinian people must conduct acts of Jihad to rock the enemy. We call on the Islamic movement [Hamas] to take its revenge for its martyr." Similarly, at a rally following the Israeli assassination of Sheikh Ahmed Yassin, Bitawi criticized Palestinian officials who urged restraint and "peaceful Intifada," saying, "We want to ask those officials in the Palestinian Authority who speak of a peaceful Intifada: will this Intifada liberate our homeland, oust the occupiers and free our detainees?"[62]

Neither the al-Tadhoman Charitable Society nor Sheikh Bitawi is an exceptional case. An FBI analysis of organizations that received funds from the Holy Land Foundation revealed that a large number of Palestinian charities and service organizations are "controlled by Hamas." Specifically, FBI investigation determined that the following organizations and individuals, employed by or affiliated with these organizations, are tied to Hamas. Each of these organizations received funds from the Holy Land Foundation:[63]

- *Islamic Charity Association* (a.k.a. Islamic Charitable Society in Hebron): Mohammad Ayad Mohammad Missaq; Abdallah Najar; Hashem abd al-Nabi Natshe; Adnan Abd al-Hafez Musbah Maswada; Izzam Naaman Abd al-Rahman Salhab; Hathem Mahmud Hassan Shahada; Taher Abd al-Aziz Dandis.[64]
- *Hebron Library Project* ("presumed to be the al-Anwar al-Ibrahimi Library")
- *Charity Committee in Ramallah* (a.k.a. Ramallah Zakat Committee): Aqel Suliman Mohammad Rabia (a.k.a. Aqal Sulayman Mohammad Rabiyah); Amar Mohammad Ahmed Hamadan; Ibrahim Said Hassan Abu Salem; Fadel Mohammad Salah Hamadan; Mahmud Ahmed Abd al-Rahman Ramhi; Nabil Abd al-Hadi Mustafa Mansur
- *Jenin Zakat Committee:* Ahmed Salim Ahmed Saltana; Ibrahim Hassan Ali Jaber; Nur al-Din Kamal Asad Tahaina; Nasser Khaled Ibrahim Jarrar; Abd al-Jaber Mohammad Ahmed Jarar; Fawaz Hamdan; Professor Khalid Said (a.k.a. Abu Hammam);
- *Al-Razi Hospital* (tied to the Jenin Zakat Committee)
- *Nablus Zakat Committee:* Abd al-Rahim Taha Hanbali; Hamid Sulayman Jaber Bitawi[65]
- *Tulkarm Zakat Committee:* Hammad Mohammed Hamed Qa'adan; Ibrahim Mohammad Salim Salim Nir Al-Shams; Riad Abd al-Latif Abd Al-Karim al-Ras; Husni Hassan Hussein Hawaja; Bilal Hamis Yusef Abu Safira
- *Orphan Care Society,* Bethlehem: Nasri Musa Issa Abada; Ghassan Mohammad Harmas; Khalil Ali Rashad Dar Rashad
- *Qalqiliyah Zakat Committee:* Bilal Abd al-Rahim Mohammad Hanoun; Riad Rashid Hamed Walwil; Ibrahim Zahran; Walid Abd al-Latif Suliman Abu Labadah
- *Halhul Zakat Committee:* Tawfiq Mohammad Ali Atrash; Ahmed Abd al-Rahman Abdallah Jahshan; Ahmed Rashid Ahmed Abu Aroush
- *Hebron Zakat Committee:* Majed Musbah abd al-Fatah Naser al-Din; Mohammad Najab Kamal Sadeq Jabari
- *Dar el-Salam Hospital:* Mufid Mohammad Mahmud Mukhalilati; Naji Mohammad Said Bata; Salah Mohammad Said Bata
- *Islamic Aid Committee (a.k.a. Islamic Relief Agency),* Nazareth, Israel

As part of the Hamas dawa, each of the above organizations was made available to Hamas militants—some of whom are listed above—for day jobs, shelter, funds, or logistical support. Moreover, they each contributed to Hamas' proactive campaign to radicalize Palestinian society, and especially Palestinian youth, to join Hamas or at least support its activities. It is this radicalization function of the Hamas dawa that we explore in the next chapter.

5

teaching terror: how the dawa
radicalizes palestinian society

THE GOAL OF RADICALIZATION

If Hamas has one supreme objective, it is to mutate the essentially ethno-political Palestinian national struggle into a fundamentally religious conflict. Accomplishing this goal entails transforming Palestinian society—a relatively secular culture, compared with other Muslim societies in the Arab world—into a more religiously zealous and politically strident one. Such a project of radicalization is the goal of all violent Islamist groups, from Abu Musab al-Zarqawi's al-Qaeda in Iraq (AQI) to Hezbollah in Lebanon. It is also the fundamental aspiration of other Islamist groups that—unlike Hamas—eschew violence in favor of primarily political means to realize their Muslim utopias. The Islamic Action Front in Jordan, for example, "seeks political power because it believes this will help it to achieve the over-riding long-term goal of 'Islamizing' Jordanian society."[1]

Unfortunately, Palestinians live in an environment that by its very nature creates social preconditions that Hamas is able to use to its advantage in its radicalization campaign. Hamas capitalizes on the suffering and frustrations triggered by Israeli settlement and occupation policies. Israeli settlements—especially those deep in the West Bank (and, until Israel's complete withdrawal in the summer of 2005, in the Gaza Strip)—have long created real and perceived geographic and resource inequities. These, together with roadblocks, curfews, and other measures that are intended to disrupt Palestinian terrorist operations but have the same effect on the everyday lives of average Palestinians, are themselves a significant source of Palestinian anger and radicalization.

Several studies, however, highlight the importance of organized radicalization and recruitment (let alone training and the provision of funds and weapons) in the formation of a terrorist—that is, someone who is not only angry but willing to act on that anger in a violent manner. A Tel Aviv University study of Palestinian suicide bombers reveals the critical role played by the dawa in pushing angry and frustrated Palestinians over the homicide-suicide edge. While they acknowledge that no single psychological profile describes the wide variety of Palestinian suicide bombers, researchers Shaul Kimhe and Shmuel Even developed a series of prototypical categories that combine both clinical and social psychological causes. A telling corollary to their primary findings, however, is that whatever the typology of the potential terrorist—"religious fanatic," "nationalist fanatic," "avenger," or "exploited"—every type requires, according to the researchers, "a social environment that is supportive of such an attack; media that disseminates the information among the supportive population; spiritual leadership that encourages such attacks; and financial and social assistance for families of suicide terrorists after their death." Together, these conditions create a "comprehensive social environment [that] may be referred to as the 'culture of suicide terrorists' that has been created within Palestinian society."[2]

Again, social preconditions by themselves do not make a suicide bomber. While poverty, humiliation, personal suffering, shame, or loss of a loved one can all be powerful radicalizing factors, they almost always require an established terrorist organization to channel that anger and frustration into a desire to kill and maim random civilians (as opposed, for example, to a desire simply to kill oneself). In this book, we have so far focused on Hamas' use of ostensibly humanitarian social and religious organizations to launder its funds and enable its terrorist activity. Now we turn to the advantage the dawa offers to a terrorist group that is actively seeking to radicalize its society. Following our discussion of the manifold goals of Hamas' radicalization efforts, we examine some of the methods by which this radicalization is undertaken. First, though, we look at the aims of radicalization.

BUILDING GRASSROOTS SUPPORT FOR THE ISLAMIST AGENDA

Hamas charitable and humanitarian organizations not only fund the families of Hamas suicide bombers, they finance important health, education, and welfare projects. Projects like these play a critical role in building sympathy and support for the group among the local population. Hamas humanitarian projects are usually couched in Islamist terms and are designed to build grassroots support for its religious agenda. Consider, for example, a letter sent by Hosni Hassan Khawajah, head of the Tulkarm charity committee, to the International Relief Fund for the Afflicted and Needy (IRFAN), a Canadian NGO identified by Canadian, American, and Israeli authorities as a Hamas front. In it Khawajah expresses thanks for IRFAN's funding of eighty packages of food in December 2000 and characterizes the gift in a radical Islamist context. Khawajah wrote: "We would like to take this opportunity to note that your support will increase our motivation and make us all the more determined to continue with our self-sacrifices and daring, to become as mountains planted firmly in the earth [standing] opposed to the abominable occupation, which seeks to uproot us" from the Holy Land.[3]

U.S. officials investigating the Holy Land Foundation noted that Hamas' "benevolent programs are used to enhance its image and earn goodwill in the Palestinian community." To that end, the Holy Land Foundation provided extensive funding to charity committees tied to Hamas. It is the assessment of the FBI that "the civilian [Palestinian] population is aware that the services being provided by the zakat committees, whether it is the distribution of food, medical services or other social services, are being provided by Hamas." According to the Treasury Department, Sanabil, a since-defunct Hamas front organization in Lebanon, increased its influence in Palestinian refugee camps there by first providing basic necessities to needy families and only later requiring these families to fill out application forms noting whether they had ever worked with Hamas. Mousa Abu Marzook himself noted, "If you went [to the West Bank and Gaza Strip] and asked about Hamas' people, you would find that they are widely trusted because of the help they have given to the community. They are the people who built the schools, the universities, the clinics." That exact sentiment was echoed by a Palestinian mother of ten, who told a reporter, "All we know is they [Hamas] are the ones who bring us food."[4]

RADICALIZING HARD-TO-REACH POPULATIONS

For a terrorist organization to have Hamas' spectacular success and influence, it needs to convert to its cause not only disaffected young men, but also children, women, and entire families. These groups are less likely to be attracted by the charms of a street militia, but they are easily reached—and radicalized—by the social services network. Arab citizens of Israel are also a hard-to-reach population that is made more accessible through the dawa.

Children

In the Islamist society idealized by Hamas, the martyr is the most revered citizen; Palestinian children who are caught up in the Hamas dawa are taught to recognize the supreme virtue of death-for-Allah. Once indoctrinated into this belief system, they are more easily exploited as grade-school terrorists. To wit, an Israel Security Agency (ISA) report in 2004 identified a 64 percent increase in the number of minors involved in terrorism compared to 2003. Gaza psychologist Fadl Abu Hein has lamented, "Martyrdom has become an ambition for our children. If they had a proper education in a normal environment, they won't have looked for a value in death." Because they see Palestinian children as legitimate tools in their fight against Israel, Hamas leaders openly discuss how children should be trained and incorporated into the group. On May 26, 2002, Salah Shehadah, a founder of the Hamas military wing, stated in an interview on the Islam Online website that children should be properly trained prior to the execution of terrorist attacks, and that they should be enlisted in a special branch of the military arm of the organization.[5]

Hamas is so enamored of its early education radicalization program that it actively seeks to promote the image that its cadre of adult operatives is composed of members who have been committed to the cause from their early development, inserting this theme into its propaganda even when it is not accurate. For example, before Rim Salih al-Rayashi became the first female Hamas suicide bomber, blowing herself up at the Erez checkpoint in January 2004, the mother of two children filmed a "living will," in which she claimed to have aspired to become a suicide bomber since the second grade:

> God, make me a martyr for your sake. [words indistinct] I have always wished and went too far in wishing that my body would be shrapnel that tear the sons of Zion and to knock the door of heaven with the skulls of the sons of Zion. By God, if you break my bones and cut off my body, you will not be able to change my faith or change my banner. This is my conviction. I have always told myself: Be filled with every possible grudge for the Jews, the enemies of your religion, and make your blood a road leading to paradise. I began to try and do my utmost since the second preparatory grade. I searched on a daily and continuous basis in the hope of finding someone who would guide or help me in anything. By God, my search continued for years, but I did not feel bored even for one second or retreated in my mind.[6]

An Israeli investigation revealed that Rayashi's upbringing contained no evidence of early radicalization, and that she had been coerced into carrying out the attack as a gesture of repentance for committing adultery against her husband, a Hamas member. It is possible that Hamas officials scripted and choreographed Rayashi's videotaped statement in the hopes of using her attack to radicalize other Palestinian children.[7]

Hamas also seeks to equate in the minds of Palestinian parents familial "nurturing" with nursing hatred. In an interview with *National Geographic,* Miriam Farhat, who was elected to Parliament on the Hamas slate in January 2006, admitted that it was she who instilled in her son the desire for martyrdom and "brought them [her sons] up to become martyrs, to be martyrs for the name of Allah." Her "martyred" son Muhammad's old bedroom was adorned with posters of martyred Palestinians and featured a photo of Muhammad on the computer screensaver. Consider also the words of a female adherent of radical London preacher Sheikh Omar Bakri Mohammad, speaking to a group of Muslim women at a conference: "It's important that our children have a passion for jihad. Make sure that you nurture your children. A Muslim woman will say to them (the children): we don't have friendship with the *kufr* [infidel]. We want to put fear into the hearts of the enemy. We want to make sure that our children carry the spirit of jihad in their hearts."[8]

Such rhetoric is standard Hamas fare. In October 2003, Hamas military commander Muhammad Zakarna employed it in recruiting a twelve-year-old Palestinian boy to carry out a terrorist attack. The boy was ordered to courier small arms to Hamas terrorists across the West Bank, to shoot at Israelis traveling West Bank roads, and to carry out a "sacrificial terror attack" (a "death by cop" or "sacrificial attack" scenario in which the perpetrator does not kill himself but expects to be killed in the process) targeting the West Bank settlement of Maale Adumim. In his statement to police, the radicalized child expressed no remorse: "I have no heart, like the Jews have no heart," adding, "I hate Jews, and at any opportunity I have I will kill Jews. I am a *shaheed* (martyr)." At the child's hearing, the judge commented that "from everything taken together, there emerges a picture that in the heart of a young child influenced by the adults around him arouses a hatred that leads him to carry out actions that are among the gravest in the law books."[9]

Desensitizing youth to violence, indeed radicalizing them to glorify and participate in it, is a central objective of the Hamas propaganda campaign targeting Palestinian children. One example is the case of a Hamas member recruited as a street operative in his early teenage years. Arrested years later, the then twenty-seven-year-old Hamas operative was asked to describe how he felt when he was chosen as a suicide bomber. His answer offers a glimpse at the despair that makes Palestinian children susceptible to the consequences of Hamas' religious radicalization program: "A tall, impenetrable wall separates you from heaven or hell, Allah promised one of the two to each of his creations. But this way, by pushing a button, you can immediately open the gate to heaven. It's the quickest way there." His account of Hamas preparation rituals for suicide bombers shows that the group's religious radicalization efforts continue up until the actual attack:

> We were in a constant state of ritual. We told each other that if the Israelis knew how happy we were they would whip us to death. These were the happiest days of my life. The spiritual pulls us upwards, and the material pulls us downward. Someone who is going to become holy is immune to the pull of the material. We floated and swam in a feeling that we were going to enter eternity. We had no doubt. We swore an oath on the Koran, in the presence of Allah, that we would not hesitate. This promise of jihad is called *beit al-riduan*, for the heaven that is reserved for prophets and the sanctified. I know that there are other means of jihad, but this way is sweet—the sweetest of all. Holy acts, if done in the name of Allah, hurt less than a mosquito bite.[10]

Children are desirable operatives, according to the ISA report, because "the innocent appearance of children and young people arouses less suspicion and enables them to more easily blend in crowded places. Moreover, children and teenagers are seen by the terrorist organizations as more easily influenced and constitute an easier recruitment base for suicide attacks." Children who have grown up in the context of the Intifada, whose only point of reference is living under Israeli military occupation and whose lives are disrupted by intermittent closures, are even more susceptible to negative influences than the average child. Because they arouse less suspicion, terrorist organizations often use children's schoolbags and toys to conceal explosives. In April 2002, Israeli soldiers conducted a raid on three explosives laboratories in the West Bank town of Qaliqilya. Among the explosives, suicide belts, hand grenades, and ammunition, the soldiers discovered a child's schoolbag containing explosive charges ready for use. In another case, Hamas operatives ran an explosives factory near a school because they believed authorities would not suspect terrorists would operate a dangerous explosives lab so close to a Palestinian school. According to the

Shin Bet, "Salim Haja, a senior Hamas operative arrested in Operation Defensive Shield, admitted during questioning that he placed a bomb laboratory close to a school, and that the operatives in the laboratory were disguised as pupils carrying schoolbags and books."[11]

Women

The chilling words of Hamas' first female suicide bomber also offer insight into the increasing trend of using women as terrorists. Why would a young Palestinian woman choose to become a suicide bomber? Loss of a spouse or a child, whether in attacks against Israel or Israeli reprisals, can be a powerful motivating factor. But Palestinian psychologist Iyad al-Saraj also explains that, as with Rayashi, death is often a route to redemption, a way to "wash away the shame that has happened to you for your personal or family problems." This theory also helps illuminate why Jala, a young woman from the West Bank featured in the National Geographic documentary "Female Suicide Bombers: Dying to Kill," would attempt a suicide attack. Israeli forces caught Jala before she could execute the assault and imprisoned her for several months. Before she began training to be a suicide bomber, Jala had been abused by her husband—a cousin her family forced her to marry when she was only sixteen years old. She had also been beaten by one of her brothers and sought to escape a painful and miserable life.[12]

Use of female activists in terrorist operations has obvious benefits from Hamas' perspective. The organization can exploit cultural and religious conventions of modesty by using women to smuggle weapons, ammunition, and explosives under their clothing. According to Israeli intelligence, Palestinian terrorist groups deployed fifty-nine female suicide bombers in 2003 and sixty-one more in 2004. A review of these attacks revealed that "in each instance in which women were involved, the terrorists were aware of their need for a disguise that would allow them to blend in on the Israeli street. The terrorists tried to give themselves an overall Western appearance, including by wearing non-traditional clothing such as short clothes, pregnancy outfits and modern hairstyles." In February 2005, Israeli soldiers foiled an attempt by a woman to smuggle a hundred bullets hidden in an apple crate across a checkpoint in southern Gaza. In April 2005, Israeli authorities discovered that the sister of a Hamas gunman hid his gun in her underpants during a search of his home. Lisa Ling, host of the National Geographic documentary, interviewed families of female bombers in the Palestinian, Chechen, and Sri Lankan conflicts. In an interview, Ling explained the advantage of females as suicide bombers: [13]

In the occupied territories [the West Bank and Gaza Strip], for example, the Israelis have really put up some formidable barriers. They check and scrutinize everyone who comes across the border. But women [suicide bombers] are much less detectable. They are like stealth bombers. [The Israelis] often don't check them as thoroughly. One point we're trying to make is that you can't rule anyone out these days. The stereotype of the face of terror is negligible. The people we're least likely to suspect, the givers of life, might be people who are dying to kill.[14]

Ling interviewed a group of Palestinian teenage girls and found each one insisting she was willing to be a martyr, if given the chance. Asked whether she fears death, one girl responded, "No, it's normal for us," and explained that seeing the death of fellow Palestinians is enough to drive them to do "something, anything . . . even if it's your soul." Fatima, a twenty-year-old chemistry student from Rafah, echoed this sentiment to Ling, explaining, "I'm so angry that I'm willing to explode myself" after viewing houses and buildings that were destroyed in her home town by Israeli forces. She highlights the importance of martyrdom in her life, remarking: "All my life I've tried to reach my goal and become a martyr."[15]

While the Hamas charter expressly supports the principle that a woman or a slave "can go out to fight the enemy without her husband's permission," group leaders were publicly reticent about the idea of women serving as suicide bombers, insisting this was the purview of men alone. But as part of the organizational recruitment for which Hamas is famous, leaders like Sheikh Hassan Yusef and Sheikh Ahmed Yassin began issuing statements that women may also be suicide bombers. Sheikh Yassin included a caveat in his opinion, insisting that a female suicide bomber must still be accompanied by a man if the operation were to last more than a day and a night, while Sheikh Yusef insisted "it is Muslim women's right to fight against occupation and no fatwa [religious ruling] forbids them from joining the struggle." Sami Abu-Zuhry, a Hamas official in Gaza, was equally blunt: "Women must decide for themselves what their priorities are, raising children for jihad or participating in acts of martyrdom."[16]

Additional examples of operational support by female Hamas aides are readily available. For example, Ahlam Tamimi, a Jordanian woman working as a journalist in Ramallah, confessed after her capture that she led a Hamas suicide bomber to the Sbarro restaurant in Jerusalem on August 9, 2001. She also admitted to having previously "collected intelligence information concerning the attack site." She noted that she carried a camera and spoke English to the bomber, who carried a guitar case, in an effort to look like tourists. On June 30, 2001, just weeks after being recruited into Hamas, Tamimi played an even more direct role in a Hamas attack by personally placing a bomb hidden in a beer bottle at a Jerusalem supermarket.[17]

Of course, not all female Palestinian suicide bombers belong to Hamas. In a particularly chilling case, eighteen-year-old Ayat al-Akhras, a member of the al-Aqsa Martyrs Brigades, entered a market in April 2002, skirted past a security guard, and detonated a bomb strapped to her body—killing the guard as well as a seventeen-year-old Israeli, Rachel Levy. In an interview with Ayat's parents, who had no idea that their daughter was plotting the suicide attack, her father explained that it was surely the Israeli occupation that drove Ayat to take her own life and the lives of innocent people, and that "the Israelis make everyone go mad out of desperation."[18]

Israeli Arabs

The radicalization efforts of the Hamas dawa are not limited to the West Bank and Gaza; Dawa activists are equally active among the Israeli-Arab population in Israel proper. Khaled Mishal himself dates the group's focus on Israeli-Arabs back to 1967, when Sheikh Yassin traveled to Israeli-Arab communities "and a communication was established between the people in Gaza and the West Bank and the people in the 1948 territories [i.e., Israel]." Criminal investigations by Israeli police revealed that Hamas organizations enjoyed greater success at penetrating Israeli-Arab society than authorities had expected. An Israeli police anti-fraud unit discovered in 1996 that two Israeli-Arab charitable and humanitarian organizations, in Nazareth and East Jerusalem, were financing the families of Hamas suicide bombers with funds received from abroad. The phenomenon was feared to have spread to Israeli-Arab political bodies, including some local Israeli-Arab councils. Indeed, in March of that year Israeli officials detained Dr. Sulayman Ahmad Aghbariyah, the deputy mayor of Um el-Fahm (one of Israel's largest Arab towns) who also served as chairman of the Hamas-affiliated Islamic Salvation Committee.[19]

Palestinian intelligence reports note with concern contacts between Hamas leaders in the West Bank and leaders of the Islamic Movement in Israel, particularly one of its leaders, then Um el-Fahm mayor Sheikh Raed Salah. A captain in the Palestinian Preventive Security service reported to his superior: "[My] sources have informed me that two Hamas members, Ghassan Harmass and Khalded Tafesh Duweib, initiated contacts with Um el-Fahm mayor Sheikh Raed Salah. Their aim was to aid in the collection of contributions from Um el-Fahm, Shefaram, Kfar Kara and Kafar Manda [Israeli-Arab cities] for the Orphan Care Society in the city [of Bethlehem]." The captain added that the meeting had already resulted in a fundraising event at the Great Mosque in Haifa where $24,500 was raised.[20]

UNDERMINING THE PALESTINIAN AUTHORITY

The Palestinian Authority under Fatah has not shared Hamas' Islamist orientation—and therefore must be supplanted for Hamas' vision of Palestinian society to be realized. The dawa is its most successful tool for undermining the PA. According to the State Department, "Hamas has used its charities to strengthen its own standing among Palestinians at the expense of the Palestinian Authority." What the State Department may not have known is how actively Iran was pushing Hamas to make use of this tactic. A Palestinian report submitted to PA Chairman Yasser Arafat in June 2000 described a meeting in Damascus at which Iranian officials and Hamas leaders agreed "to use the dawa in the battle for public opinion." But it was much earlier, during a 1993 Hamas meeting in Philadelphia, where Hamas fundraisers decided that "most or almost all" funds collected from that point on "should be directed to enhance the Islamic Resistance Movement [Hamas] and to weaken the self-rule government [Palestinian Authority]."[21]

That mission statement is as valid today as it was then. A document found in the offices of the Jenin charity committee in October 2003 reveals that in January of that year about $3,700 in donations from the World Assembly of Muslim Youth (WAMY), a Saudi charity tied to Hamas, were transferred to the Jenin charity committee for distribution to members of the Jenin Workers' Union. A couple of weeks later, the Jenin charity committee received another $10,000 for the union. According to an Israeli intelligence analysis of these documents, "The transfer of funds (from charity contributions) to workers' unions is a familiar ploy meant to strengthen Hamas' influence among them, and to extend its power base within Palestinian society. The union in question is one of the strongest in Jenin and is affiliated with Fatah [the traditional backbone of the PA, then headed by Arafat]."[22]

Aware of such grassroots activities, Palestinian analysts readily concur that Hamas has a "project to impose itself as an alternative to the Palestinian Authority although it kept that approach hidden and undeclared." In time, however, Hamas supporters began to speak more openly about their efforts to use their social welfare activities to politically undermine the PA.

Nazir Madi, a high school teacher in southern Gaza and a Hamas supporter, showed journalists the Microsoft Excel database she maintained recording every time Hamas distributed flour, olive oil, or rice to a member
of her extended family. The family subsequently used the list to distribute
Hamas campaign literature in advance of elections in which Hamas fielded
candidates.[23]

Indeed, the PA itself grew concerned about Hamas' successful penetration of the PA Ministry of Education and the group's radicalization of
Palestinian youth in PA schools. Terrorist groups have not only infiltrated
Palestinian ministries, they have co-opted Palestinian intelligence officers
and have obtained critical intelligence simply by bribing Palestinian officials. For the sum of $1,500 to $3,000, Hamas and Islamic Jihad obtained
intelligence from officers affiliated with the Palestinian General and Preventive Intelligence services, including advance warning of pending arrests.
According to an account by a woman who had been employed as a secretary with one of the Palestinian security services, Hamas approached her in
person and on the phone and pressed her to provide the group critical intelligence. After the death of her husband, a Hamas activist, she started receiving phone calls:[24]

> The telephone calls would always begin with a recitation from the Koran
> and the callers always identified themselves as members of Hamas. I re-
> ceived telephone calls several times per week. Each time I received a
> telephone call, the voice was different but the questions were the same.
> A man or woman would ask, "Where are our prisoners?" and would tell
> me, "You should join us." Often, they would say, "This is for our coun-
> try," and, "This is for our religion." They would urge me to take revenge
> for [her husband's] death. Specifically, these telephone callers wanted
> me to provide them with information about who came in and out of the
> [Palestinian security service] office; the whereabouts of Hamas prison-
> ers; and any files or documents that I could steal from the office.[25]

Another time, a man approached this woman at her office asking for
help and for information about detained Hamas members. Following her
continued refusals, Hamas officials harassed the woman and her family, including assaulting her and physically intimidating her family. According to
a PA intelligence report, "the Hamas movement has begun to constitute a
real threat to the PA's political vision, its interests, presence and influence.
The influence of the Hamas movement through its teachers in the [PA]
schools is absolutely clear."[26]

FOMENTING ANTI-CHRISTIAN SENTIMENT
IN THE PALESTINIAN TERRITORIES

Because Hamas' military actions and political rhetoric are focused on the Jewish state and laced with anti-Semitism, its anti-Christian tendencies are sometimes overlooked. But the Palestinian Christian community is as much a target of Hamas' efforts to Islamize society as is the Palestinian Muslim community. In Bethlehem, where about a quarter of the local population (some 40,000 people) is composed of Palestinian Christians, Hamas actively seeks to marginalize and intimidate the Christian population and further radicalize the Muslim population. To this end, the Saudi World Assembly of Muslim Youth (WAMY) funded a Koranic memorization program run by the Bethlehem branch of Hamas' al-Islah Charitable Society. In a letter asking that WAMY's funding for this program continue, the al-Islah charity makes a point of noting that a considerable percentage of Christians live in the area "with their customs and traditions, the exposure to which has a significant influence on our society." The charity asks for continued funding for the program, which is intended to "correct" the behavior of Muslim youth "which is growing lax."[27]

Arab Christians living in Bethlehem feel the ill effect of living among an increasingly radicalized Muslim population. Bethlehem Christians experience a variety of intimidation tactics, including extortion by local officials and unwarranted arrests of businessmen to coerce bribes. For example, several years ago a Christian family alleged that their commercial property was stolen by a Muslim family that had moved to the area from Hebron. The family filed a claim for the return of their property through the Palestinian judicial system and received a favorable ruling. The local police chose not to enforce the ruling, and the Muslim family from Hebron eventually took "legal" possession of the property.[28]

PURCHASING GOODWILL TOWARD HAMAS
BY PROMOTING FINANCIAL DEPENDENCY

Those who benefit from Hamas' largesse support the organization and, frequently, actively facilitate the group's attacks. In the words of an Israeli defense official, "In the territories, there are no free lunches: those who receive help from the Islamic associations pay with support for Hamas." Indeed, Mohammad Anati, the head of the Holy Land Foundation office near Jerusalem, acknowledged to criminal investigators that providing services promotes Hamas interests and earns the support of those who benefit from Hamas aid.[29]

According to Subject [Anati], while working for the HLF, he also promoted Hamas interests secretly. For example, when he helped build an Islamic clinic in a certain area, everyone around knew that it was the Hamas organization behind the clinic; when food was distributed during holidays, the population knew that the Hamas was behind this, too, since both the HLF and Hamas are Islamic organizations.[30]

The al-Tadhoman Charitable Society and the Nablus charity committee highlight Hamas' ability to institutionalize grassroots dependency on the organization's institutions. Not only do these two institutions receive funds from abroad—including the $147,148 the Holy Land Foundation provided the Nablus charity committee between January 1997 and September 2000—they also run profitable businesses. The charities provide jobs through businesses which they own or in which they are partners, including the Yasfa dairy company owned by the Nablus charity committee and the Nablus Mall in which al-Tadhoman is a part owner. They also run several social service branches, including a medical clinic at the al-Rawdah mosque, the al-Tadhoman school, an orphanage, a kindergarten, the al-Ansar sports club, and a club for adults that functions as a community center and a home for the elderly.[31]

The dawa network of charities, services, and employers combines to create a "closed economy" open only to the Hamas activists who are part of this community. An Israeli analysis walks through this Hamas micro-economy:

> For example, a worker who received his salary from the Yasfa dairy company (which belongs to the charity committee) does his shopping at the Nablus Mall (which belongs to the *dawa*). His children go to the kindergarten or school belonging to the Islamic *Riyadh al-Salihin* ["kindergartens of the righteous"] network and when he needs a doctor he is treated free of charge at al-Tadhoman clinic, which was also built by the charity committee.[32]

Other Hamas charities own similar businesses and operate similarly insular Hamas support systems. The Islamic Charitable Society in Hebron, for example, not only runs orphanages, schools, Koran memorization centers, and other typical dawa services, it also owns real estate in Hebron and runs a dairy farm. Hamas also owns a honey bee farm in Tulkarm, a company that operates heavy equipment used in quarries in Jenin, as well as other West Bank businesses, including textile workshops, bakeries, and a discount supermarket.[33]

Recipients of Hamas financial aid or social services are less likely to turn down requests from the organization such as allowing their homes to serve as safe houses for Hamas fugitives, ferrying fugitives, couriering funds or weapons, storing and maintaining explosives, and more. Such beneficiaries are often grateful for the opportunity to do something in return to benefit Hamas. Consider the resident of the Jebaliya refugee camp in Gaza who fed Hamas militants daily: "My son accused me of not paying as much attention to him as I do the fighters," he said. "I told him, 'Yes and there is a reason for that.' These men are protecting us, and protecting him. These men are god's angels on earth." In other cases, recipients simply know better than to ask questions when asked for a favor by Hamas dawa activists. Hamas capitalizes on this passive support, employing "unsuspecting" Palestinians to unknowingly launder and transfer funds on behalf of the group. Sheikh Ahmed Yassin himself proudly noted, "We don't go looking for people, they come to us." Citing one of the many examples of people won over by Hamas financial support, Yassin talked of a family of ten living in one room: "We gave them 1,200 shekels (300 dollars). Sometimes it's a sack of flour, or at the very least the taxi fare home." Considering how many Palestinians enjoy some level of support from Hamas, the group is able to call on a great many Palestinians for support. Consider, for example, that as of June 2002 four thousand people in the Nablus area were reportedly receiving 100 Jordanian dinars a month from Hamas charities.[34]

Hamas social welfare support is largely determined by a cold cost-benefit analysis that links the amount of aid awarded to the support it will buy. According to Hamas founder Sheikh Ahmed Yassin, Hamas distributes $2 million to $3 million in monthly handouts to the relatives of Palestinian suicide bombers, "martyrs" killed in attacks on Israelis, and prisoners in Israeli jails. The al-Islah Charitable Society report for the year 2000 included a picture of two Hamas activists holding a sign thanking the Hamas charity and Interpal, the U.K.-based charity designated as a Hamas front by the United States, for their support for "the unfortunate, the orphans and the imprisoned." According to the FBI, "evidence strongly suggests that the HLFRD [Holy Land Foundation] has provided crucial financial support for families of Hamas suicide bombers, as well as the Palestinians who adhere to the Hamas movement." By providing these annuities to families of Hamas members, the FBI concludes, "Hamas provides a constant flow of suicide volunteers and buttresses a terrorist infrastructure heavily reliant on moral support of the Palestinian populace." Indeed, one captured Islamist terrorist highlighted the significance Hamas aid and prestige carry in recruiting future activists:[35]

> Families of terrorists who were wounded, killed or captured enjoyed a great deal of economic aid and attention. And that strengthened popular support for the attacks. Perpetrators of armed attacks were seen as heroes, their families got a great deal of material assistance, including the construction of new homes to replace those destroyed by the Israeli authorities as punishment for terrorist acts. The entire family did all it could for the Palestinian people, and won great respect for doing so. All my brothers are in jail; one is serving a life sentence for his activities in the Izz al-Din al-Qassam battalions. My brothers all went to school and most are university graduates.[36]

Dr. Ibrahim al-Yazuri, identified as an original participant in the founding of Hamas, offered a particularly candid description of Hamas' philosophy regarding charitable giving:

> Everyone knows that the Islamic Resistance Movement, Hamas, is a Palestinian Jihad movement that strives for the liberation of all Palestine, from the (Mediterranean) sea to the (Jordan) river, from the north to the south, from the tyrannical Israeli occupation, and this is the main part of its concern. Social work is carried out in support of this aim, and it is considered to be part of the Hamas movement's strategy. . . . The Hamas movement is concerned about its individuals and its elements, especially those who engage in the blessed jihad against the hateful Israeli occupation, since they are subjected to detention or martyrdom. The movement takes care of their families and their children and provides them with as much material and moral support as it can. This is one of the fundamental truths of Islamic work and thus represents the duties of the Islamic state. . . . The movement provides this aid through the support and assistance it gives to the zakat (Islamic alms-giving) committees and the Islamic associations and institutions in the Gaza Strip.[37]

Hamas certainly does "take care" of its own. Individuals tied to Hamas receive more dawa assistance than those unaffiliated with the organization; members linked to terrorist activity receive still more. A Palestinian intelligence report from 1999 documents that when Hamas' Orphan Care Society received 200 extra portions of meat to distribute to needy families for a

Muslim feast, "they were distributed to members and those connected to the Hamas movement." The previous year, Palestinian security reported that the same Orphan Care Society distributed meat "to Hamas members" for the Feast of Sacrifice. Meat offerings were also distributed to Sheik Abd al-Majid, a Hamas activist and the head of the Hamas-affiliated Dheishe Charitable Society, and his supporters, not to the poor and needy. According to Palestinian intelligence, "The imams of the mosques were supposed to have given [the meat] to the needy, however that is not what happened."[38]

Corroborating the Palestinian findings, an Israeli government report notes that Hamas charitable organizations "grant preference" to those close to the movement and see to it that those in its favor receive increased financial assistance. According to the report, families of Hamas activists killed or wounded while carrying out terror attacks and those imprisoned for their involvement in such attacks "typically receive an initial, one-time grant of between $500–5,000, as well as a monthly allowance of approximately $100." Significantly, "the families of Hamas terrorists usually receive larger payments than those of non-Hamas terrorists." In late 2001, people in the Tulkarm area who were wounded in clashes with Israel but were affiliated with groups other than Hamas demonstrated against the Tulkarm charity committee. Their claim: that the committee gave preference to supporting members of Hamas.[39]

Materials confiscated in a May 1995 raid of the Holy Land Foundation's office in Beit Hanina outside Jerusalem further confirm the preference Hamas gives to its own members. Israeli authorities seized financial records of fund transfers from the Holy Land Foundation to the Islamic Aid Committee (a.k.a. Islamic Relief Agency, IRA) and lists of the people supported by those funds. FBI analysis of this material revealed that individuals unaffiliated with Hamas received relatively small monthly payments compared to known Hamas members. Families of Hamas terrorists killed or detained in the process of conducting terror attacks received the largest stipends.[40]

Lists of people supported by the Holy Land Foundation seized in the 1995 raid revealed that some "favored individuals" received more generous stipends than others. An Israeli analysis of these lists notes that the more generously compensated included "numerous individuals involved in Hamas activity."[41] As detailed earlier, the extent of the list is revealing:

- The mother of Ahmad Shukri, a Hamas terrorist sentenced to a life term for murdering an Israeli in 1989 and attempting to force a public bus off the road on September 8 of that same year.

- The father of Mohammad Shawan, a Hamas terrorist who murdered two grocers in 1993 and was killed in a shootout with Israeli forces in 1994;
- The wife of Abd al-Rahman Aruri, a Hamas militant killed in a clash with Israeli forces in late 1993;
- The family of Suleiman Idan, a Hamas terrorist who died in a car bomb attack in 1993;
- The mother of Ashraf Ba'aluji, sentenced to a life term for murdering three Israelis in 1992;
- The wife of Jamil al-Baz, a Hamas militant sentenced to a life term for running over an Israeli soldier in Gaza in 1991;
- The wife of Majdi Hamad, a Hamas activist sentenced to a life term for killing fellow Palestinians—presumably suspected informers—in Gaza;
- The family of Yasser Hajaj, who was sentenced to a life term for placing a bomb on a Tel Aviv beach that killed a Canadian tourist;
- The brother of Raid Zakarna, a Hamas terrorist who carried out a suicide attack at a crowded bus stop in Afula on April 6, 1994, killing eight people and wounding over forty others, including many children.[42]

Supporting the families of Hamas suicide bombers denies counterterrorism officials the ability to deter potential bombers by highlighting the hardships their families would incur by their carrying out an act of "martyrdom." Along these lines, Hamas charity committees typically pay the rent for temporary housing for the families of suicide bombers whose homes were destroyed by Israeli forces in an effort to press families to prevent their members from joining terrorist groups. The Jenin charity committee, for example, in cooperation with the Committee for Humanitarian Aid in Israel and the Union of Good in Saudi Arabia (both associated with Hamas) designated a monthly sum of over $18,000 for one such rent project in 2003. The dichotomy—as portrayed by Hamas—is striking: whereas Israel destroys these Palestinian homes to deter future recruits from joining Hamas, Hamas provides temporary shelter and rebuilds new homes, endearing themselves to the population and creating greater incentive to join or support Hamas.[43]

Secretary of State Colin Powell highlighted the twisted nature of such benevolence, saying, "I think it's a real problem when you incentivize in any way suicide bombings." Knowing their families will be provided for after their "martyrdom" by Hamas enables Hamas suicide bombers to focus on their deadly missions. They can carry out their attacks on buses and cafés with the peace of mind that their own families will enjoy the benefits of what amounts to a life insurance policy for Hamas bombers.[44]

METHODS OF RADICALIZATION

The process of becoming an adherent of radical Islam is fundamentally a didactic process, as is the indoctrination to any ideology—whether political, philosophical, or religious. From a very young age, Palestinians who participate in the Hamas dawa, both as agents and subjects, are instructed in the language of radical Islam, schooled in its rationalizations and apologies, and taught its supreme virtue and boundless promise. Such an education program requires the student to be constantly supervised, mentored, cajoled, threatened, and praised. No wonder, then, that Hamas invests so heavily in institutions of secular and religious instruction. Campuses and mosques are controlled environments where impressionable minds are formed, and where people go for salvation, redemption, hope—answers. Our focus in the remainder of this chapter will be on dawa institutions of secular and religious education.[45] At the end of the section, we will also touch upon Hamas' use of traditional and new media to transmit its militant-religious ideology.

Primary Education

In 2001, the Islamic Society (al-Jamiya al-Islamiya) in Gaza held a graduation ceremony for the 1,650 children who attend its forty-one kindergartens. Photographs of the graduation ceremony show preschool-age children wearing uniforms and carrying mock rifles; a five-year-old girl dips her hands in red paint to mimic the bloodied hands Palestinians proudly displayed after the lynching of two Israelis in Ramallah; another child is dressed as Hamas founder Sheikh Ahmed Yassin and surrounded by other children costumed as suicide bombers; yet another child plays the role of Hezbollah leader Sheikh Hassan Nasrallah. The ceremony began with the recitation of Koranic verses and an oath "to pursue jihad, resistance and Intifada." Afterward, individual kindergartens performed for the audience. Preschool students from the al-Imam kindergarten put on a play highlighting the dangers of "the Zionist settlement" and the "obligation to avenge the blood of the *shuahda* [martyrs] and pursue resistance and Intifada." Children from the al-Rahman kindergarten were divided into groups named after Palestinian martyrs killed in the Intifada, and then read excerpts from Sheikh Nasrallah's recent speeches, while waving Hezbollah flags. Hamas makes no secret of the point of such ceremony. After his capture, Hamas activist Ibrahim Abd al-Fatah Shubaka told Israeli authorities that the Islamic Charitable Association in Hebron maintains two orphanages and schools which "instill the pupils with Hamas values, and their graduates include operational Hamas activists."[46]

The radicalization campaign continues through the course of a Palestinian student's academic career, employing materials produced and distributed by the dawa. The Hamas Islamic Student Movement in the Bethlehem area distributed to young students so-called Instruction Cards, bearing the pictures of Hamas suicide bombers and others killed carrying out terrorist attacks and encouraging Palestinian youth to follow in their footsteps. Other "educational material" produced by dawa activists and distributed by Hamas charity committees includes collectable postcards featuring Hamas and Islamic Jihad suicide bombers with rhythmic Arabic inscriptions such as "Oh, Mother, the time for leaving [this world] is quickly approaching," and "Oh, Mother, do not speak of me should I fall and lie dead on the ground." Other cards extol the virtues of the "martyr"-bomber, like the card featuring Issa Khalil Shawkah, a Hamas bomb maker killed when a bomb he was assembling exploded in his hands. An inscription above Shawkah's picture on the Hamas postcard reads, "There is nothing more certain other than that Glory bows down before [the Izz al-Din al-Qassam Brigades, the military wing of Hamas], and only before them." To the right and left of the photo, the captions read, "You were the first to die the holy death of a martyr. You shall always remain the first in the heart of the [Palestinian] people." Hamas propagandists ensure such messages are a part of normal childhood routine. In the al-Fawwar refugee camp, key chains and children's trading cards are handed out featuring suicide bombers. Teenage singing groups like "The Martyrs" sing the praises of their namesakes.[47]

In addition to operating schools, Hamas dawa organizations run summer camps at which Palestinian children are saturated with the group's propaganda and even given semi-military training. On July 22, 2001, Palestinian television broadcast a program on Hamas summer camps that featured a boy reading a poem he learned at camp:

I dedicate this poem to the prisoners, martyrs and the wounded
Oh nation, oh, my people, make your roar and the sounds of thunder
heard
Strike the rock, explode, stop the soldiers' advance
Make your scream of anger heard by everyone everywhere
They planted the enemy amongst us from the days of Solomon and
David

They are our treacherous enemy
Who does not honor treaties and does not recognize the truth
Jerusalem, ask us and we will sacrifice our souls
Today we have been redeemed and bound the wound with shrouds
The decision is in our hands, our only possession
But Sharon, Sharon is intoxicated with power
Perhaps, perhaps he will learn a lesson he will never be able to forget
We have a leader and the entire nation is with him
He commands and all the youth are his redemption
You, mother, make songs of mourning heard
Torches will light the way until we have achieved our purpose.[48]

In July 2003, Hamas hosted a summer camp in Gaza called "The al-Aqsa Intifada Martyrs Summer Camp." The camp was run by Sheikh Ahmad Bahar, head of the Hamas-affiliated Islamic Society in Gaza, which sponsored the camps. Combining childhood recreation with radical indoctrination, the camp environment exposed the children to both active programming in the form of classes on radical Islam and passive indoctrination through the pervasive images of suicide bombers plastered on walls throughout the camp. While all Hamas camps imbue children with radical Islamist ideals, some reportedly also provide young campers with small-arms training. Moreover, many Hamas camps and aftercare programs are run through mosques throughout Gaza, where the curriculum intermingles the religious with secular, recreational with violent: Koran and computers, sports and military training. In the words of Imam Jasser al-Mashoukhi of the al-Farouk mosque in the southern Gaza city of Rafah, "we hire professional captains and teachers to polish up the physical and mental skills of our children, who, God willing, will liberate Palestine."[49]

Donations from dawa charities enable Hamas to provide its campers with luxuries, such as new uniforms, shoes, and books, making the camps especially attractive to parents. Benefits like these draw campers to Hamas summer camps from religious and secular families alike. According to Sheikh Bahar, Hamas summer camps are especially successful at indoctrinating young people. Bahar has explained that teaching children the history of Islam while they are surrounded by pictures of martyrs instills "seeds of hate against Israel."[50]

A reliable indication of the ulterior motives behind Hamas summer camps is the organization's attempt to hide their true nature. In a letter dated May 18, 2003, the Northern West Bank coordinating office of the

Union of Good requested that the Jenin charity committee "formulate a proposal for summer centers" which the coordinating office would then forward on to Interpal, the U.S.-designated Hamas front organization in London. In the letter, the coordinating office suggests:

- The term "summer centers" should be replaced by "guidance training centers."
- The [summer] centers should be limited to educational, cultural and sports activities only.
- Islamic emblems and flags should not be hung [in the centers].[51]

The Union of Good's coordinating committee requested the obfuscation, in both Arabic and English, "in light of the current embarrassing situation of the [charitable] societies in Europe"—an oblique reference to the legal challenges then facing accused Hamas charities in Britain and Germany. The Jenin charity committee's activities were also funded by the Holy Land Foundation, which provided the committee $194,459 between January 1997 and September 2000. Aside from Hamas-run zakat committees, other Hamas institutions operate summer camps at which Palestinian children are inculcated with radical Islamic beliefs. For example, not only do Hamas-affiliated centers for Koran memorization (discussed below) operate summer camps, but the Palestinian security service reported that in 1999 the Women's Hope League, a subsidiary of the Orphan Care Society, "has begun supervising some of the summer centers which the Hamas movement used to supervise under the cover of the League."[52]

Polling data suggest that Hamas' efforts to radicalize children are indeed successful. According to an April 2001 survey conducted by the Islamic University in Gaza, 49 percent of children ages nine to sixteen claimed to have participated in the Intifada—and 73 percent said they hoped to become martyrs.[53]

Higher Education

Radicalization of Palestinian youth is no less prominent at Palestinian institutions of higher learning. Hamas propaganda—pamphlets, posters, and myriad other printed collateral—literally litters Palestinian university campuses. A timetable for university lectures at one campus featured pictures of Hamas suicide bombers. A class schedule distributed at various college campuses included a photo of Qassam Brigades member Karim Nimr Mafarja above the inscription, "The *shahids* [martyrs] are with their Lord and light shines from them." A typical Hamas student kit distributed to students by the Islamic Bloc features pictures of Hamas leaders like Sheikh Yassin and their sayings, such as Yassin's wish that God "allow us to die with [the] honor [reserved for] whoever fights in a holy war [mujahid]." The Islamic Bloc held a fair at al-Najah University in September 2004 to hand out school supplies. Banners at the fair pictured Hamas leaders like Yassin and al-Rantissi alongside Muslim Brotherhood founder Hassan al-Banna. During student elections at Bir Zeit University in 2003, Hamas candidates reenacted suicide bombings by blowing up models of Israeli buses. They also wore mockups of Qassam rockets on their shoulders. In one Bir Zeit campus debate, a Hamas candidate taunted his Fatah challenger by boasting, "Hamas activists in this University killed 135 Zionists. How many did Fatah activists from Bir Zeit kill?"[54]

On special occasions, prominent leaders of Palestinian terrorist groups participate in student rallies. For example, on November 13, 2001, the day after student council elections at al-Najah university, Ramadan Shallah of Islamic Jihad addressed the students via telephone, praising the results of the election: "Yesterday's student council elections were a vote in favor of the Intifada, a vote in favor of the Jihad and the struggle, a vote in favor of the blood of the fallen heroes . . . a vote in favor of the heroic suicide bombers of the [Hamas] Iz Adin al-Qassam battalions and the [Palestinian Islamic Jihad] Jerusalem squads. This is the righteous choice; this is the true referendum . . . a test the students of Al-Najah passed with flying colors." Hamid Bitawi, a top Hamas official, also visited al-Najah to speak at a gathering.[55]

With an estimated 11,000 students enrolled during the 2004–2005 school year, al-Najah University in the West Bank city of Nablus is the largest university in the Palestinian territories. It has produced numerous suicide bombers, including:

- Hasham Najar, who conducted a suicide attack with an explosive belt at a restaurant frequented by Israeli soldiers and Jewish settlers in Mehola on December 22, 2000, wounding three;[56]
- Hamed Abu Hijla, who detonated a car bomb carrying an estimated twenty kilograms (forty-four pounds) of explosives in Netanya on January 1, 2001, injuring nineteen bystanders;[57]
- Jamal Nasser, who detonated a car bomb next to a school bus on April 29, 2001;[58]
- Muayad Salah, who prematurely blew himself up en route to a suicide operation on January 8, 2001;[59]

- Asam Reihan, who attacked a bus near Emanuel with a roadside bomb and automatic weapons, killing ten and wounding thirty;[60]
- Darin Abu Aisha, who blew herself up at the Makabim checkpoint on February 27, 2002, wounding three people;[61]
- Muhammad al-Ghul, who blew himself up on a Jerusalem bus on June 18, 2002, killing nineteen and wounding over seventy people.[62]

The terrorist recruitment, indoctrination, and radicalization of students for which al-Najah is known typically takes place via various student groups. By far the most prominent of these student associations is the Hamas-affiliated *Kutla Islamiya*, or Islamic Bloc. Funded in part through Hamas charities like the Islamic Association of al-Bira, the Bloc has long been a critical component of the Hamas dawa infrastructure. One reason for the success of the Islamic Blocs located on university campuses throughout the West Bank is their history. Even before the Palestinian Muslim Brotherhood adopted the name Hamas, the Islamic Bloc played an important part in the Brotherhood's structure and activities, as Hamas political bureau head Khaled Mishal acknowledged: "Inside, we had several names: the Islamic Movement [Hamas], Muslim Brotherhood, Islamic Front, the (Islamic) Youth Center and the Islamic Bloc. It was one organization with different names." After the founding of Hamas, the Islamic Blocs continued to operate under that name (Kutla Islamiya) but with an overt affiliation with Hamas.[63]

One night in December 1986, Israeli forces raided a room that was being used as a mosque on the campus of al-Najah University in Nablus. By that time Israeli authorities were already conducting searches at al-Najah on a regular basis, despite lacking a clear policy on how to deal with the rise in radical Islamist elements in general and on college campuses on particular. That night, soldiers confiscated radical books, posters, leaflets, and more related to what Israeli authorities now describe as "pre-Hamas Islamist incitement material." Authorities found posters featuring images they had never seen before in the Palestinian context, including one of a globe draped in an Islamic green flag, a ship with the sails of Islam, and pictures of Sheikh Izz al-Din al-Qassam (the namesake of the future military wing of Hamas). Identical material would later be produced under Hamas' name, but this particular raid revealed material that predated the organizational foundation of the group under the name Hamas.[64]

As the student group's emblem suggests—a globe atop a Koran, assault rifle, and jihad flag, with a map of historic Palestine in the background—

the Bloc is deeply involved in militant activity, and many of its members have led Hamas terror cells. Of the thirteen members of al-Najah's 2004 student council, eight—including the chairperson—belong to Hamas' Islamic Bloc. Some of the most notorious Hamas terrorists have held senior positions in the al-Najah faction, including Qais Adwan, a former Islamic Bloc leader and head of the al-Najah student council, who was also the head of the Qassam Brigades in the northern West Bank. Adwan personally prepared suicide bombers for their missions and was involved in the production of homemade explosives and rockets.[65]

Hamas sees the Islamic Bloc student groups as breeding grounds for future terrorists, and has described al-Najah University as a "greenhouse for martyrs." The accuracy of the description was evident in July 2004 when Israeli forces exposed and arrested a Hamas terrorist cell planning kidnappings, shooting attacks, and a suicide bombing in either Netanya or Ariel. The leader of the cell was Alaa Zuharyr Nimr Jayusi, a leader of the Islamic Bloc at al-Najah. Other members of the cell were also Islamic Bloc activists.[66]

Less than a year later additional attacks were thwarted when Said Ikhras, another Islamic Bloc leader at al-Najah, was arrested as he was preparing an explosive device in February 2005. Ikhras had planned a previous suicide bombing attempt targeting Rosh Ha'ayin, near Tel Aviv, which authorities prevented in July 2004.[67]

Membership in the Islamic Bloc is often the first step in a career in the dawa, as typified by the case of Mohammed Anati, head of the Holy Land Foundation office near Jerusalem. Already a low-ranking Hamas activist when he enrolled in the al-Oumah College in the West Bank village of Dahiat al-Barid, Anati was enlisted to help establish the Islamic Bloc at his new campus. Among his fellow members of the Islamic Bloc at al-Oumah College were several other prominent and up-and-coming Hamas activists, including Muhammad Rajub and Abd al-Karim Bader. (Rajub was a Hamas fugitive wanted at the time by Israeli authorities. Bader was a member of the Qassam Brigades who had already been involved in several Hamas operations. He would be killed in 1994 by Israeli forces raiding a Hamas safe house where Bader and other gunmen were holding Nachshon Wachsman, a kidnapped Israeli-American.) Like many other heads of Hamas charities, Anati was recruited to head the Holy Land Foundation office directly after graduating college. Similarly, Muhammad Talaji Jaber, who was in charge of orphans at the Organization for Islamic Studies and Education, had been an Islamic Bloc activist together with Anati in college.[68]

The Islamic Bloc's principal activity on Palestinian campuses is fomenting pro-Hamas sentiment among students, both to encourage them to participate in Hamas attacks and to be supportive of such attacks. Radicalization efforts take many forms. For example, a new student enrolling in the economics department at al-Najah University received a "greeting certificate." Bearing the logo of the "Martyr's Bloc" (*Kutlat al-Shuhadah*), the document welcomed the student, a Fatah commander before enrolling in the university. In February 2005, the Islamic Bloc at Hebron University held a "Palestinian Book Week" featuring Hamas material and pictures of Hamas leaders. After Bloc chairman Hamed Abu Hajlah carried out the Netanya suicide bombing, the group produced an article about him, describing him as a fifth-year engineering student who was devout, popular, and a lover of art. A poster of the members of the al-Najah student council, including Hajlah, employs Jerusalem's Dome of the Rock as a backdrop, complete with rivers of blood flowing from its doors and forming the inscriptions, "There is no God but Allah" and "And Muhammad is his Messenger" on either side of a broken Star of David. The Bloc's official website at al-Najah features a selection of songs, some of which, such as "Ya Shaheed" (O Martyr), glorify martyrdom. One song exalts Hamas leader Sheikh Ahmed Yassin:[69]

> *Ahmed Yassin, the one who stood up despite the disability*
> *You will stay in our souls the highest example*
> *You taught us that the Jihad is our path*
> *You taught us that the issue without effort will not resolve*
> *You taught us despite our sorrow not to despair*

Other songs explicitly glorify violence:

> *Write your life in blood*
> *Be silent*
> *Do not speak*
> *Silence speaks louder than the ring tones*

Such songs and images were present at a 2005 Islamic Bloc rally at Bir Zeit University in Gaza, traditionally a Fatah stronghold. Scheduled to commemorate the anniversary of the death of Yihye Ayash, a notorious Hamas bomb maker known as "the Engineer," the rally also coincided with the Palestinian Central Election Committee's press conference to announce the electoral victory of Mahmoud Abbas as Yasser Arafat's successor. In front of an audience of hundreds, a five-man chorus sang, "Oh suicide bomber, wrap yourself with an explosive belt and fill the scene with blood." Backed by Hamas banners and posters, speakers told the crowd, "Ayyash is alive and don't say he's dead," and described the bomb maker as "the engineer of death for those who deserve to die."[70]

The Islamic Bloc is fond of such theater and performance. At al-Najah, rallies include operatives marching with weapons and student actors demonstrating how to carry out suicide and other attacks. In 2001, the entrance to an Islamic Bloc rally was a recreation of the Sbarro pizzeria in Jerusalem, the scene of an August 2001 Hamas suicide bombing. The attack, at the busy corner of King George Street and Jaffa Road in downtown Jerusalem, was executed by Hamas member Izzadin Masri just before 2 p.m. as the restaurant was full of diners, including many children. Fifteen people were killed, including seven children and an American woman, and approximately 130 others were injured.[71]

The Islamic Bloc not only publicizes the statements of Hamas leaders, it issues violent messages of its own. In late 2002, for example, the Islamic Bloc at al-Najah University issued a statement declaring Hamas would continue to conduct attacks against Israelis and describing Jews in general as "pigs" and "satans."[72]

The Bloc faction at al-Najah maintains its own official website as a vehicle for dissemination of propaganda and the glorification of Hamas martyrs who attended the school. The site links to a variety of terrorist-affiliated websites, including that of the Izz al-Din al-Qassam Brigades, the Muslim Brotherhood website, the Palestine Information Center website, and the web pages of Hamas student groups at other Palestinian universities, such as Beir Zeit University. One page, titled "Kutla Islamiya Martyrs," includes a list of approximately thirty-five martyrs. Each martyr is listed with photos, a brief biography, and sometimes his written will. Many of the photos feature the martyrs in their Qassam Brigades uniform.[73] Consider, for example, just two of these featured martyrs.

On December 12, 2001, Assem Rihan, twenty-three, an engineering student at al-Najah University, was killed when he and two other terrorists attacked an almost full Dan No. 189 bus on the outskirts of Emmanuel. The bus was coming from Bnei Brak, an Orthodox Jewish neighborhood near Tel Aviv. Two bombs exploded alongside the bus, then the terrorists opened fire. Ten died and thirty were wounded in the attack. Three days earlier, Assem Rihan was filmed reading his will, wearing green army fatigues and a helmet and holding a gun. This video is featured on the Islamic Bloc website.[74] An excerpt of the will:

Thank God that made me a Jihadist in his path
Thank God that has made me join the Martyrs ranks
Thank God that made me part of this holy land
Thank God that made me part of Palestine and its Jihadist soldiers
Dear Brothers in the land of Palestine
I cannot but salute you
I congratulate myself and you of the approaching victory
In this holy month, in its last days
I present myself to defend the sand of Palestine
To revenge my brother Mohammad and the hero commander
   Mahmoud Abu Hannoud
I say to Sharon the bastard and all of those that call us terrorist
We are proud that we are engaged in God's path
May all the calls for a cease-fire come to an end
May the sound of bombs grow louder
It's either victory or martyrdom
God is great
Victory to Islam
The living martyr Assem Rihan
Forces of Iz al-Din al-Qassam
Hamas Movement[75]

Also featured on the Islamic Bloc website is a student diary glorifying a Qassam Brigades operative from al-Najah. In January 2002, Karim Nimr Mafarja, a former student of the Islamic Law faculty at al-Najah and a former student council member, was killed in an IDF operation in Nablus. Mafarja, a member of the Qassam Brigades, had been an aide to Yusuf Surkaji, at one time a senior member of Hamas' terrorist network in Nablus, himself involved in the planning and preparation of terrorist attacks. Mafarja's martyrdom was glorified by the Islamic Bloc in various ways, including a student diary featuring Mafarja's photo on the cover, with the caption "Qassam Martyr Karim Mafarja." A printed timetable of lectures features a photo and biographical notes on Mafarja, with a photo of hooded Hamas activists marching in the background.[76] A short poem lauding suicide appears at the bottom of the page:

My life, although one of suffering and strife,
My path crossing places where troubles are rife,
Still I am oblivious to fear and the wicked do not scare me
Since my flesh, like wolves, will tear apart its prey.[77]

Surrounding Palestinians with messages extolling Hamas suicide bombers carries over from campuses to charities. For example, assembly lines of Palestinian men and teenage boys packing food items at the Islamic Charity Society in Hebron do so to the tune of inspirational music praising Hamas. An Associated Press journalist who observed such a scene reported that the lyrics announced "the holy war is calling" and pledged, "We will continue the resistance, the Hamas revolution." The charity, the AP reporter notes, "is believed to be tied to Hamas." And while Islamist activists contend that "politics and charity are two separate matters," the reality is that "the connection is hard to ignore."[78]

RELIGIOUS EDUCATION

Even more than the academic campus, the religious campus is the most influential and important battleground for the hearts and minds of Palestinians, young and old. Complementing the traditional mosque environment are "Koranic memorization centers" that mimic in a religious setting the tight clique-like structure of the terrorist cell.

Mosques

Sheikh Ibrahim Mudeiras' sermons from the Sheikh Ajlin mosque in the Gaza Strip are often broadcast live on Palestinian television. On January 10, 2003, he called for parishioners to "rise up against the Jews and their allies! Let us rise up against the United States of America and its allies. Oh Allah, cleanse [the] al-Aqsa [mosque] from Jewish pollution." Mudeiras insists that "the resurrection will not take place until the Muslims fight the Jews, and the Muslims kill them. The Muslims will kill the Jews, rejoice [in it], rejoice in Allah's victory. The Muslims will kill the Jews, and he [the Jew] will hide." On January 7, 2005, Mudeiras told his television audience that "the Jews are a cancer spreading in the body of the Arab nation and the Islamic nation, a cancer that has spread and reached the Arab institutions, the villages and the refugee camps."[79]

Of course, anti-Israeli and anti-Semitic themes are not surprising from a preacher affiliated with Hamas whose brother, Nabil Mudeiras Awqil, is a Hamas operative schooled in al-Qaeda training camps in Afghanistan. A bit more surprising are the virulent anti-American messages Sheikh Mudeiras includes in his sermons. "The day will come," he preaches, "when, from the pulpits of the mosques, we will proclaim the fall of that evil nation, America, which pretends to rule the world. If America continues its cruelty and oppression, and if it continues to support our enemies against us and against our holy places, with the help of Allah, it will disappear." In May 2005, after several of Mudeiras' anti-Semitic sermons were publicized by non-governmental organizations, the Palestinian Authority finally announced its "concern" with Mudeiras' sermons.[80]

Examples of mosques that function as radical soapboxes are commonplace. In early 2005, Sheikh Yusuf Abd al-Wahab Mahmoud Abu Snina, a Hamas-affiliated preacher at Jerusalem's al-Aqsa mosque, denounced talk of an approaching ceasefire, declaring it "oppressive and cruel to our people and the people of our nation" because it "means our blessed lands will forever be occupied." Such sermons, especially when delivered in such historic locations, may drive parishioners to both support Hamas and carry out attacks on its behalf. Such was the case, at least, with Zaher Yusuf Diav Ali, an Israeli-Arab from the Galilee studying for a master's degree at the Hebrew University in Jerusalem. According to an Israeli Security Agency press release, "While in Jerusalem, he attended various Hamas-affiliated frameworks for Islamic studies on the Temple Mount and at other sites, which preached about perpetrating terrorist attacks against Israel. It was in these frameworks that Ali made contact with Hamas terrorists, including Na'al Jalad." An Israeli investigation into Jalad led them to Ali, who was scouting potential sites for suicide bombings in Jerusalem, including cafés near his university, a popular park, bus routes and bus stops, and a wedding hall that later was targeted by a suicide bomber.[81]

In addition to the radical rhetoric issued from their pulpits, mosques run by Hamas members and sympathizers are often a bulletin board of propaganda, their walls plastered with posters and pamphlets glorifying suicide bombers and jailed Hamas militants. For example, Israeli forces raiding the al-Ein mosque in al-Bireh in September 2003 found posters of suicide bombers on the mosque's front door as well as on walls and notice boards throughout the mosque. One such poster commemorated Hamas suicide bomber Ramez Fahmi Izz al-Dina Salim, who detonated his suicide belt at a Jerusalem café on September 9, 2003, killing seven people and wounding more than fifty others. With Salim depicted in front of the al-Aqsa mosque, the poster's caption reads: "When al-Aqsa mosque cries out: I beg you, come to my aid—all the blood in my veins answers the call." Soldiers also seized a wealth of leaflets and other Hamas propaganda calling for "many spectacular suicide bombing attacks" against U.S. forces in Iraq.[82]

Usra: Religious Study Cells

Religious study groups held at Hamas-affiliated mosques—including the al-Aqsa mosque—have also been identified as sources of recruitment and radicalization. Known as an *usra* (literally, "family"), such a group is typically led by a teacher (*emir*) who is a Hamas member or sympathizer, and is therefore in a unique position to identify members responsive to radical and Islamist messages. Mohammad Anati, the head of the Holy Land Foundation office near Jerusalem, acknowledged being recruited by Hamas operative Musa Acari, the emir of an usra that met in places like the al-Aqsa mosque and the Abu Obeideh mosque in the Shuafat refugee camp outside Jerusalem. Tawfiq Mohammad Ali Atrash, a member of the charity committee in Halhoul, was placed under administrative arrest by the Palestinian Authority for about seven months in 1996 for inciting violence as the emir of an usra.

There are different levels of usras. Intelligence sources believe individuals recruited at a "public" usra may be later selected to participate in a "closed" usra composed of select Hamas members and recruits. For example, over time Anati was gradually invited to participate in more covert usras. The leader of the third usra he was invited to join, an emir named Mahmud Issa, was arrested in 1994 for participating in the kidnapping and murder of Israeli policeman Nissim Toledano. Israeli authorities found Anati's phone number among Issa's belongings and called him in for questioning. Under questioning, Anati attempted to hide either man's participation in a "closed" usra, insisting that he knew Issa only by virtue of working in the same geographic area. An official report of Anati's interview states, "He did not say that he had been in the usra together with Mahmud Issa."[83]

Mosques and Children

When Hamas members spotted a thirteen-year-old boy who demonstrated a proclivity for fiery sermons, they arranged for him to speak at more than forty mosques. Referred to as "the young sheikh" and "the wonder boy of Hamas," the child was endorsed by both Hamas and Islamic Jihad. But moderate Palestinian parents are often unaware of the degree of Hamas rhetoric to which their children are exposed. One mother recounted how her son's behavior changed when he started going to the mosque regularly.[84]

> At first I thought it was normal when my son Mohammed, who is 18, started going to the mosque frequently, but when I found out he was watching films about suicide attacks I was worried. . . . My son was

going to the mosque late at night and early in the morning, adding to our fears. . . . His behavior changed, He became introverted, which made his father and me search his room and spy on his comings and goings. . . . We even locked the door to stop him going out. . . . We later found out that those in charge of the mosque are members of Hamas, which teaches children about jihad and shows them documentaries about suicide bombings.[85]

The father of fifteen-year-old Hamas recruit Musa Ziyada told a similar tale. Originally pleased with his son's growing faith, Hisham Ziyada did not realize Hamas had begun radicalizing his son when the boy was just ten years old and sweeping the mosque floors. Musa would later tell reporters that Hamas "taught me about the heroes of Islam who were killed as saints and how they are now in heaven beside God. . . . I also learned that the Jews have no right to exist on this land, which belongs to Muslims." It is not uncommon for Palestinian parents to lament Hamas' efforts to radicalize and recruit their children. After a thirteen-year-old boy failed to come home at his usual time one day, his mother asked neighborhood children if they had seen him. Several replied they saw him get into someone's car after school. When he returned that evening, he acknowledged that someone had picked him up after school and taken him to the Jamal Abd al-Nasser mosque and that "the future did not matter because it was his future to become a martyr and to go to heaven." The mother said:

This was the first time I heard [my son] say any of these things, and I became afraid that he was being somehow brainwashed. [He] told me the people who took him to the mosque gave him an audio tape, and told him that it would give him courage to fight the Jews. The audio tape is entitled "The Pearl of Al-Aqsa Martyrs" and it contains six songs with lyrics like: "No to the Jews, the descendents of monkeys"; "Peace is meaningless"; "War is Medicine and Death is Eternity"; "Hamas, the Light of the Eye, the Pearl of Jihad"; and "After the stone, a knife, and after that martyrdom." Between what [my son] had told me and the songs on the audio tape, I realized that Hamas had targeted my son for recruitment.[86]

Palestinian parents often seek professional psychiatric help to deprogram their radicalized children. Some have gone so far as to report their children to Palestinian or Israeli authorities for fear they have been recruited as suicide bombers and are about to take their own—and others'—

lives. Dr. Mahmud Sehwail, the general director of the Treatment and Rehabilitation Center for Victims of Torture in Ramallah, commented in May 2002 that "this has been happening more and more often in the last few months as the Palestinian resistance has deepened." Sehwail noted that "the parents say they have detected a significant change in the behavior of their children and they desperately want to know if their children are candidates to become human bombs."[87]

The account of Palestinian police officer Hisham Ziyada, whose son Musa was recruited by Hamas spotters in a local mosque, is particularly telling. According to Ziyada, Musa was selected for a mission, along with at least five other Palestinian boys, and wrote a letter to his family explaining that "he would execute the attack in order to ensure himself a comfortable life in heaven." In retrospect, Ziyada recalled that a few weeks earlier Musa's behavior had changed and he started talking about a desire for "a week long vacation from school in order to spend time with his uncle in the al-Berij refugee camp. This was a red warning light for me," Ziyada noted, since "we [Palestinian police] had been monitoring one of the mosques in al-Berij for quite a while. Hamas instructors lead discussions there with youth candidates for suicide attacks in Israel."[88]

Indeed, the increasing trend in which children are used to carry out acts of terrorism has not been lost on scholars studying trends in political violence. Groups like Hamas have recruited children as young as thirteen to be suicide bombers; eleven-year-olds have been used to smuggle explosives and weapons. According to one scholar's calculation, Palestinian youths carried out more than thirty suicide bombings between the onset of the al-Aqsa Intifada in September 2000 and January 2005.[89]

Koranic Memorization Centers

Koranic memorization centers (*Dar al-Quran*) in the Palestinian territories are institutions that teach Muslim children about their religious heritage. They are also a key component in Hamas' general indoctrination project, one that targets children in particular. Such centers are often the beneficiaries of funding by Hamas front organizations abroad and are usually run out of mosques tied to Hamas. For example, the Ramallah-al-Bireh charity committee ran a Koranic memorization center out of the Grand (Abd al-Nasser) Mosque in el-Bireh, a mosque known as a hotbed of Hamas activity.[90]

In the late 1980s and early 1990s Israeli intelligence received information that Hamas was establishing Koranic centers in villages throughout the West Bank. In most cases these were located in or next to mosques run by Hamas and were growing in importance as centers of incitement, radicalization, and recruitment. Such centers proved difficult to close, however, because they frequently posed publicly as sports clubs. Authorities would find Hamas posters and many copies of the Koran, but also basketballs and judo equipment. Such was the case, for example, when police raided the Dar al-Quran operated by the Salt al-Khuriya charity committee north of Jenin. But by 1993–1994, raids of Koranic centers began to produce more tangible evidence of Hamas activity. A search of the al-Aya mosque and Koranic center in al-Bireh, for instance, revealed Hamas posters, extensive literature, and brochures used for recruitment. More importantly, police inspected the mosque itself and discovered notes hidden in the lip of the carpeting in places where the carpet extended an inch or two up the wall from the flooring. The notes contained secret communications between Hamas operatives. Further investigation revealed that mosque carpeting served as a prominent dead-drop in several West Bank mosques and Koran centers where operatives knew to leave messages for one another.[91]

Hamas used Koranic institutions as cover for the organization's activities in other contexts as well. The Quranic Literacy Institute (QLI), a non-profit organization involved in translations of Koranic texts, was tied to Hamas in the United States. Purportedly established to promote Koranic memorization and translate sacred texts into English, the Chicago-based group also served as a money-laundering clearing house for funds from leaders of the Hamas political committee, especially Mousa Abu Marzook, to military commanders tasked with resurrecting the Hamas military wing in the wake of mass deportations of Hamas and other terrorists from the West Bank and Gaza to southern Lebanon in December 1992. One of these commanders, Chicago resident Mohammed Salah, received funds from Marzook and traveled to the West Bank and Gaza to recruit and train a new generation of Hamas terrorists. In Chicago, Salah was employed by QLI, which arranged for him to receive compensation from Yassin al-Qadi, a wealthy Saudi designated as a terror financer by the U.S. government.[92]

MEDIA JIHAD

In October 2004, several dozen Hamas activists responsible for promoting the group in the media met in what they believed was a closed forum. In fact, the meeting was recorded on videotape. On the tape, Hamas communication chief Fathi Hamad complained bitterly to the group about Islamic Jihad's propaganda dominance, its success at infiltrating the media, and its control of "the agenda." Hamad opened his lecture by describing the media as "the decisive weapon." This is an echo of the Hamas charter, which highlights the importance of having "educators and teachers, information and media people" involved in awakening the masses and resistance. The charter goes on to state that "the book, the article, the bulletin, the sermon, the thesis, the popular poem, the poetic ode, the song, the play and others" are all important vehicles for ideological mobilization. Accordingly, Hamas prints newspapers and leaflets, runs Internet sites, operates a television and a radio station, controls mosques, and even supports singing groups—all of which praise Hamas and espouse its ideology. Three of the Hamas operatives who carried out the 2002 Passover suicide bombing at the Park Hotel in Netanya were members of a Hamas singing troupe.[93]

Losing the battle of the "media jihad" to the smaller Islamic Jihad was therefore viewed as a serious failure in the eyes of the Hamas communication committee. "We outnumber them," Hamad lamented to the propaganda group. "We have many more mosques, and much more commitment, but they are ahead of us in the satellite TV stations, and their websites are much bigger than the group itself." He continued, "They are stealing attacks from Hamas, exaggerate the number of the killed, and inflate the numbers of their street demonstrations as if they are a domestic group, even though they are supported by Hizballah. The media has turned them into the equals of the Muslim Brotherhood [i.e., Hamas]."[94]

For Hamas, the media is an important component of its goal of Islamizing the Israeli-Palestinian conflict and radicalizing Palestinian society. In an interview with a Hamas periodical, Dr. Mamun Jarar, head of the Islamic Literature office in Amman, Jordan, explained that "the dissemination of the jihad literature is one of the most serious reasons for the continuation of the active resistance." What is needed, Jarar continued, is for Muslim writers to "enslave their pens . . . to the service of the Islamic problem in Palestine by inspiring the spirit of jihad and of active resistance to surrender." In January 2006, just days before the election that brought Hamas to power, the group launched al-Aqsa Television. Like Hamas' Voice of al-Aqsa radio station, the television broadcasts aim to spread the group's message to Palestinians and eventually, via satellite, a global audience. The station broadcasts Koranic readings, discussions of Islamist issues, and shows for young viewers like Uncle Hazim, a children's program featuring men in animal suits articulating Hamas' message for Palestinian preschoolers.[95]

Along with posters and other media extolling the virtues of suicide bombers, another typical radicalization tool employed by Hamas social service organizations is the distribution of the last will and testament, or "living will," recorded by suicide bombers—and often broadcast on Arab satellite television networks after the attack. In a typical example, Israeli forces who raided the offices of the Islamic Charity Society in Hebron found a booklet called "In Memoriam" (*al-Tadhkirah*) featuring the living will of Majdi Abu Warda, the Hamas suicide bomber who blew up a Jerusalem bus at rush hour on February 25, 1996, killing twenty-four people and wounding forty-four more. In his statement, Abu Warda praised "the way of jihad," discussed his intent to blow himself up in "a Zionist bus full of passengers," and explained that "the real reward is the reward of paradise."[96]

NEW MEDIA JIHAD

Hamas publishes a weekly online children's magazine—just one of approximately twenty Internet sites the group produces—called *al-Fateh* (The Conqueror). Launched in September 2002, the site links to other Hamas websites and runs benign children's stories alongside articles preaching the value of carrying out acts of terror—casting suicide bombers as ideal role models for young children, and encouraging hatred of Israel and Jews. Issue 38, for example, featured a photograph of the decapitated head of Zaynab Abu Salem, a female suicide bomber from the al-Aqsa Martyrs Brigades (not Hamas) who detonated her suicide bomb belt on September 22, 2004, at the French Hill intersection in Jerusalem, killing two and wounding seventeen. The caption below the gruesome picture reads: "The perpetrator of the suicide bombing attack, Zaynab Abu Salem. Her head was severed from her pure body and her headscarf remained to decorate [her face]. Your place is in heaven in the upper skies, oh, Zaynab . . . sister of men." Interestingly, the fact that Salem was not a Hamas member did not preclude members of the media committee from using her severed head to desensitize Palestinian youth to acts of violence. *Al-Fateh* frequently runs the wills of Hamas suicide bombers recorded before their attacks, in which they glorify the act of suicide-murder they are about to commit. For example, it published the will of Sa'id Hasan al-Houtari, the Hamas suicide bomber who killed twenty-six civilians and wounded eighty-three more—almost all of them teenagers—at the Dolphinarium discotheque in Tel Aviv.[97]

Al-Fateh is only one of many Hamas websites, which typically feature statements and interviews with the group's leaders, martyr photo galleries, as well as articles, posters, and photographs demonizing Israel and glorifying suicide bombers. In some cases, the sites feature video clips of Hamas operatives reciting their living wills. In one such segment, Tarek Hamid reads the text of his living will while sitting on his knees in front of a Hamas flag, holding a rifle in one hand and a Koran in the other. "Today I will drive my detonated car in the name of God almighty," Hamid pledges. "I shall avenge the death of my master, the martyr Sheikh Ahmed Yassin." The clip then cuts to the actual operation, showing a jeep crashing into an armored military vehicle and blowing up.[98]

In addition to incitement, Hamas websites perform the important function of claiming credit for attacks, for attribution purposes by the news media. Hamas even glorifies attacks carried out by other groups as a means of radicalizing its readership. For example, following a suicide bombing in Tel Aviv carried out by Islamic Jihad member Abdallah Badran, a Hamas website featured pictures of the suicide bombing and of Badran posing with a young child. The caption described Badran as "the heroic shaheed [martyr]."[99]

Hamas also uses the Internet to recruit new supporters and members. While some Hamas recruitment efforts are active and tangible, such as spotting potential recruits at mosques and religious classes, the Internet enables groups like Hamas to conduct a virtual recruitment drive that, while passive and intangible, has the capacity to reach out to a far larger audience—one that can be reached at any time of day, in any weather, under any conditions (i.e., even when neighborhoods are under curfew or closure), and anywhere—not just the West Bank and Gaza Strip, but the world entire. To this end, Hamas operates websites in Arabic, English, Russian, French, Farsi (Persian), Urdu, and Malay, which are run off servers in the United States, Russia, Ukraine, and Indonesia.[100]

Through an impressive combination of all these means—including secular and religious institutions, grassroots activism, and globalized media—Hamas successfully radicalizes Palestinians not only to support but to participate in the group's terrorist attacks. And the fact that Hamas, an organization that prides itself on being a local "resistance" organization, targets foreign audiences from America to Malaysia with its web-based messages should not surprise: the vast majority of Hamas' operating budget is raised abroad.

6

foreign funding of hamas

Most of the money—tens of millions of dollars—raised every year on be-half of Hamas comes from outside the Palestinian territories. A table of donors seized in 2004 in the offices of the Ramallah-al-Bireh charity committee offers a typical example of the disproportional representation of foreign fronts that fund the Hamas social welfare and terrorism network. Of the fourteen donors listed, two are Israeli-Arab charities, one is an "internal" sponsor from the West Bank, and the rest are foreign-based foundations, from Jordan, Qatar, Kuwait, Saudi Arabia, Britain, Germany, United States, United Arab Emirates, Italy, and France. In this chapter, we turn our focus to the precise sources of Hamas' foreign funding. As we might expect from an organization that bills itself as a primarily charitable enterprise, most Hamas money is raised by foreign charities that focus on their donors' sincere sympathy for the plight of Palestinian refugees; in some cases they focus more specifically on sympathy for the ideological claims of radical Islam and jihad. But Hamas also raises money around the world directly from wealthy individuals, corporations and criminal enterprises, eventually tapping into the larger financial networks that support other international terrorist groups, including al-Qaeda. Each of these financial founts is treated in turn. We conclude with a discussion of the moral culpability of foreign donors, whose "charitable" contributions are so central to Hamas' terrorist project.[1]

FOREIGN CHARITIES

An Israeli analysis breaks down into categories the foreign charitable funds and foundations that finance Hamas. The first category includes those fronts that are directly tied to Hamas. These typically employ Hamas activists, are established with the assistance of the Hamas political leadership, and see the vast majority of their raised funds dispensed to Hamas charities in the West Bank and Gaza. Such charities bring in an estimated $15 million to $20 million a year and include groups like Interpal and the al-Aqsa International Foundation. The second category includes fronts that support radical Islamist elements generally, but are not Hamas-specific. Most of the fronts in this second category are based in Persian Gulf states, especially Saudi Arabia, and most of the funds they send to the West Bank and Gaza are also channeled through Hamas organizations there.[2]

Of the various means terrorist groups use to raise funds, holding fundraising events and soliciting charitable donations are among the most successful. Some donors know they are funding terrorism, while others believe they are supporting legitimate organizations that merely tend to the humanitarian needs of the needy. Whatever the motivation, abuse of the collection of *zakat* (an obligatory 2.5 percent charitable tithe of a Muslim's earning) is an effective way to raise and launder money for use by Islamist militant organizations. According to a report authored by a research associate at an Islamist think tank in Virginia identified by the U.S. government as tied to Hamas, "pro-Hamas Islamists, in coordination with the [Muslim] Brethren, collect zakat via local committees." Charity work, according to the report, "is conducted in cooperation with other Islamic centers sympathetic to Hamas." As a U.S. government analysis of Hamas concluded, "charitable donations to non-governmental organizations are commingled, moved between charities in ways that hide the money trail, and then often diverted or siphoned to support terrorism." There's no better proof of the efficacy of charities at raising terrorist dollars than the sheer size of the global Hamas charity-fundraising network itself. And the evidence of such a network's existence is overwhelming.[3]

A CIA report on charitable organizations that finance terror refers to Hamas operatives and front organizations operating throughout Europe, including the United Kingdom, Denmark, Austria, and Croatia. Made public in 2003, the report was written in 1996, revealing that already in the 1990s American authorities were aware that Hamas fronts like Human Appeal International (HAI, *Hayat al-Amaal al-Khayriyah*) were operating offices in Europe, the Middle East, Asia, and Africa. Also in 1996, Western intelligence services determined that the International Islamic Relief Organization (IIRO) and the World Assembly of Muslim Youth (WAMY), both Saudi charities associated with al-Qaeda, were funding Hamas through Interpal, a U.S.-designated Hamas front organization in London discussed in detail below. Other examples of purportedly charitable organizations cited by the CIA for financing Hamas (and, more often than not, other terrorist groups as well) include the Kuwaiti Joint Relief Committee, the Saudi High Commission (in Bosnia), and the Qatar Charitable Society (*Jamiyyat al-Khainyyah*).[4]

Documents seized by Israeli forces in West Bank raids confirm the CIA conclusion that Hamas is largely financed by global charities. Some charities, like the United Arab Emirate Friendship Association, explicitly funded the families of martyrs and demanded that a copy of the death certificate accompany each application form. Other prominent Middle Eastern charities whose ties to Hamas are clear from these seized documents include the Kuwaiti al-Mounasara Fund (and many of its Middle East branches such as the Aid Committee, or *Lajnat al-Mounasara*, in Jordan); the Palestine Charity Committee (PCC) of the Kuwait-based International Islamic Charitable Organization (IICO); and the Fund for the Care of Families (*Wakfiat Ria'at El Usra*) in Lebanon.[5]

HAMAS CHARITIES IN THE UNITED STATES

Despite his assertions that "Hamas itself has never collected or received money in the United States or any other country," former Hamas chief Mousa Abu Marzook was personally involved in establishing the Hamas fundraising infrastructure in the United States. On December 4, 2001, the United States shut the Holy Land Foundation for Relief and Development (HLFRD), designating the foundation a terrorist entity for being the major front organization for Hamas then operating in America. Five days before the September 11 attacks, the FBI raided the offices and froze the assets of Infocom, an Internet company located across the street from the HLFRD that shared personnel, office space, and board members with HLFRD. The two organizations were formed in California around the same time, and both received seed money from Marzook. At the same time that he was providing startup funds for Hamas fundraising organizations in the United States, Marzook was already funneling significant sums of American money to Hamas himself. According to Israeli information cited by the FBI, "In early 1989, Abu Marzook sent some tens of thousands of dollars . . . from the U.S. with his brother-in-law Bashir Elashi who is also a Hamas activist." Bashir Elashi's brothers, Bayan, Ghassan, Basman, Hazim, and Ihsan, would all be indicted in 2002 on terrorism charges related to the Infocom investigation.[6]

After their arrests, the Richardson mosque—also known as the Dallas central mosque—hosted fundraising events with the goal of collecting $500,000 for the Elashi brothers' defense fund (established as the Muslim Legal Fund of America two weeks after the government shut down HLFRD). The fund distributed a leaflet, produced by a company run out of the home of Shukri Abu Baker, HLFRD's former CEO, calling for a "Cash & Gold for Justice" drive and urging members of the local Muslim community to raise $500,000 in five months. The mosque had been a client of Infocom's, and had personal ties with at least two of the Elashi brothers: Basman Elashi was a former board member of the mosque, and Ghassan Elashi was active in an affiliated Islamic school. This same house of worship would later be implicated in the distribution of Islamist material produced and distributed by extremist Saudi sheikhs. In December 2003, a document was found at the mosque titled "Patriotism and Its Requirements In Light of Islamic Teachings," which told faithful Muslims: "[W]e consider ourselves to be in a continuous war against the Zionist enemy in every way until we achieve the hopes of the Arab nations driving the occupier out."[7]

The Holy Land Foundation for Relief and Development and the al-Aqsa Education Fund

According to its 2000 tax return, HLFRD's total revenue exceeded $13 million that year. In a detailed forty-nine-page FBI memorandum, the U.S. government determined that these funds were used by Hamas to support families of suicide bombers and to finance Palestinian schools that teach reverence and sympathy for suicide bombers. "By providing these annuities to families of Hamas members," the report asserts, "the HLFRD assists Hamas by providing a constant flow of suicide volunteers and buttresses a terrorist infrastructure heavily reliant on moral support of the Palestinian populace." Citing information from the Treasury Department, a General Accounting Office report agreed with the FBI, concluding that "evidence shows that Hamas used some of the money that the Holy Land Foundation raised to support suicide bombers and their families."[8]

The Holy Land Foundation operated in conjunction with the rest of Hamas' international fundraising machine. The FBI tied HLFRD to Interpal (the U.S.-designated Hamas front in London discussed in the following section), discovering, for example, that "a review of the HLFRD's financial records shows that on April 11, 2000, the HLFRD wired Interpal $66,000.00." Beyond the links to Interpal and other European charities that authorities have tied to Hamas, investigations tie the HLFRD to a long list of other terrorist operatives and fronts. For example, financial transactions link the HLFRD to an al-Qaeda-associated front in Chicago called the Global Relief Foundation, and to the chief Hamas fundraiser in the Tri-border area of South America, Ayman Ghotme.[9]

Although it was the largest and most successful, the Holy Land Foundation is by no means the only U.S.-based organization to have raised, laundered, and transferred significant amounts of money to Hamas. According to Israeli police interviews cited by the FBI, Abdelhaleem Hasan al-Ashqar "transferred hundreds of thousands of dollars on behalf of Hamas" in the late 1980s and early 1990s at the direction of Sufian Abu Samara, an admitted West Bank member of the Izz al-Din al-Qassam Brigades. At the time, al-Ashqar was head of the al-Aqsa Educational Fund (AAEF) in the United States, an organization that played a central role in the Hamas dawa. In October 2003, al-Ashqar was indicted on criminal contempt charges in Chicago for refusing to testify before a grand jury on Hamas activities in the United States. More recently, he ran as a candidate in the January 2005 Palestinian presidential elections even as he faced criminal charges of supporting Hamas in an updated federal indictment. FBI electronic surveillance of al-Ashqar and others revealed that in 1994 Mousa Abu Marzook ordered curtailing the AAEF as the primary Hamas fundraising entity in the United States and replacing it with the HLFRD. The decision to shutter the AAEF and streamline Hamas fundraising in the United States under the HLFRD was highly successful: Holy Land Foundation blossomed into the largest Islamic charity in the United States until the U.S. Treasury Department froze its assets in 2001.[10]

The Philadelphia Meeting

One of the earliest known incidents of Hamas fundraising activity in the United States is a 1993 conference in Philadelphia at the Marriott Courtyard Hotel on Bartram Avenue minutes from Philadelphia's international airport. According to an FBI report describing the conclave, the seventeen attendees "discussed the 'Holy Land Fund' and the 'El-Aqsa Fund'" and also held a brief discussion about "collecting money in an effort to support uprisings in the West Bank and Gaza." The participants decided on five central goals: (1) "Support the holy struggle, Jihad"; (2) publicly distance their movement from Hamas "to avoid media criticism and negative public perception"; (3) effect "Mass mobilization"; (4) "Actively solicit contributions and fundraising" for Hamas; and (5) "Influence the public opinion and the news media in the United States."[11]

The participants at the Philadelphia meeting were individuals described by the FBI as "senior leaders of Hamas," including heads of organizations believed to be fronts for Hamas like the HLFRD and the Islamic Association for Palestine (IAP). They included Abdelhaleem Hasan al-Ashqar, Akram Kharroubi, Mohammad al-Hanooti, Ismail Elbarasse, Muin Kamel Mohammad Shabib, HLFRD CEO Shukri Abu Baker, executive director Haitham Maghawri, chairman of the board (and later vice president of international marketing) Ghassan Elashi, and others. During the meeting, these participants took great pains to disguise their association to Hamas by making a concentrated effort not to refer to the organization by its full name or its more recognized acronym. Instead they referred to it simply as "the Movement" or as "Samah" (Hamas spelled backwards).[12]

According to a summary and analysis written by an FBI translator who listened in on the meetings, the participants "believe that the Palestinian cause is only a small part of the Islamic cause. They believe that somehow, their cause are (sic) connected with the Islamists causes in Egypt, Algeria and Tunisia. They believe that the trust of the new world order which was promoted by the [first] Bush administration is to destroy Islam." Accordingly, the participants agreed that future funds should be allocated only to Islamic causes, and not to "certain funds [or] activities that will enhance economic position [sic] of the self rule administration [i.e., the Palestinian Authority] such as the needy, the poor, the refugees, the camps and the like." In their words, "the objective is to weaken the self rule administration, not to strengthen it. Therefore the funds should be directed towards the Islamic projects that follow, enhance, promote (sic) the Islamic cause such as Islamic universities and Islamic schools."[13]

The Philadelphia group determined to be more discreet than had been Sheikh Omar Abdel Rahman, the so-called Blind Sheikh convicted in plots to bomb New York landmarks, including the United Nations headquarters. The Philadelphia participants had no issue with Rahman's goals, but with his "method," which was "wrong, unsophisticated. It resulted in labeling him a terrorist." One participant commented that Rahman "didn't commit crimes"; his problem was that "he was not able to defend himself against the media." Another point made during the discussion was concern that American and Israeli investment in Palestinian areas was "absorbing the Palestinian anger, desperation, revolution by raising the standards of living of the Palestinians." It was the hope of the men assembled in Philadelphia that "the failure of the self rule administration to solve the problems of the Palestinian population and providing the needed services to them will be detrimental to the peace accord." To hasten the fall of the Palestinian Authority and the peace process they concluded "to defeat the [Oslo] accord we [Hamas] should make services available to the population." Such charity would be doled out primarily to Islamist organizations within the Palestinian public: "Our relation has to be good with everyone," noted one participant, "but we can give the Islamists 100,000 and 5,000 to the others." An FBI summary of another speaker's remarks reveals an even more explicit commitment to raising U.S. money with the explicit aim of financing Hamas terror attacks. The FBI translator's summary noted:[14]

> He said we should concentrate our efforts on supporting Jihad (holy war) in the occupied lands. This can be done, he said, through concentrating our financial resources on those directly connected with Jihad, such as to injured, the martyrs, their families and the prisoners. Other needed services can be provided by other organizations, those who receive assistance from the United States and UN agencies. But we should focus on those people who are directly connected with Jihad.[15]

The Islamic Association for Palestine

In its effort to Islamize the Palestinian national struggle, Hamas invests significant resources in Palestinian popular culture and society. Indeed, experts have noted that giving the Palestinian cause an Islamic flavor is part of Hamas' effort "to link the particular Palestinian struggle with the wider Islamic wave in the Muslim world." In the United States, authorities believe the Islamic Association for Palestine (IAP) is the primary organization responsible for fulfilling this function, though it also raises funds for Hamas in cooperation with HLFRD.[16]

The IAP has operated under the name of several related entities, including the American Muslim Society (AMS) and the American Middle Eastern League for Palestine (AMEL). The IAP is intimately tied to the most senior Hamas leadership; in fact it was originally formed in 1981 by Dr. Aly Mishal at the personal direction of Khaled Mishal (who was then a senior Muslim Brotherhood activist and would later become secretary general of Hamas). The founding of the IAP six years prior to the official formation of Hamas is still further indication of Hamas' roots in the Muslim Brotherhood. When the group's leaders in Gaza made the decision to officially found Hamas in 1987, the IAP became the group's mouthpiece in North America. For example, the FBI noted that IAP officers were among the "senior leaders of Hamas" who participated in the 1993 Hamas planning meeting in Philadelphia. At one time Hamas leader Mousa Abu Marzook was himself a member of the IAP's Board of Directors. In January 1990, Marzook—who was then living in northern Virginia—opened a bank account in the name of IAP. At the same time that Marzook was providing seed money to the HLFRD and operational funds for Mohammad Salah to deliver to Hamas operatives in the West Bank, he was also providing startup funds for the IAP. Bank records show that over the course of 1990 and 1991 seven checks totaling $125,000 were deposited into this account.[17]

Since the creation of Hamas in 1987, the IAP has published Hamas communiqués calling its followers to jihad. It published and distributed the Hamas charter, which included the address of the Occupied Land Fund, HLFRD's former name. It also held conventions and conferences at which pro-Hamas speakers and singers rallied support for Hamas. For example, the 1988 IAP conference in Oklahoma City featured Abdallah Azzam, Osama bin Laden's spiritual mentor. The 1989 IAP convention in Kansas City, Missouri, held in honor of Azzam, who had recently been killed by a rival Islamist faction, featured a hooded Hamas activist who called for financial assistance for terror attacks and Yusef Qardawi, the Islamic cleric who issued a *fatwa* (religious edict) permitting Muslim women to engage in suicide attacks. A banner at the front of the room proclaimed: "Islamic Palestine from the river to the sea" in Arabic, while another banner bore Hamas' name in Arabic. A video tape of the 1989 IAP convention ends with a solicitation to send donations to the Occupied Land Fund (HLFRD). Sheikh Mohammad Siyam, an admitted Hamas leader whose fundraising trip to the United States was paid for by the HLFRD, also spoke at the 1989 IAP conference. The IAP also organized support rallies for jailed Hamas members, including Hamas leader Mousa Abu Marzook and Chicago operative Mohammad Salah.[18]

In the United States, the Hamas magazine *Filisteen al-Muslima* (Muslim Palestine)—which pays glowing tributes to Hamas suicide bombers, justifies their attacks, and suggests they be models for future suicide bombers—was distributed by the IAP. The IAP distributed many fliers and communiqués, some on behalf of Hamas and others supporting and raising funds for Hamas. A December 1989 communiqué, for example, states that "the only way to liberate Palestine, all of Palestine, is the path of Jihad," and declares that "Hamas is the conscience of the Palestinian Mujahid people." It goes on to invite its readers "to perform jihad for the sake of God with your money and donate as much as you can to support the Intifada in Palestine" and directed donors to send funds to the Occupied Land Fund

(HLFRD). Another communiqué, issued in February 1989, was distributed on IAP letterhead but signed "The Islamic Resistance Movement (HAMAS), Palestine." Part of this statement, printed in the United States, demanded that "our brothers in the PLO stop the dialogue with the American enemy."[19]

While the IAP's primary function was to serve as the public voice of Hamas in the United States, it also assisted HLFRD in its fundraising efforts. For example, the IAP included solicitations for HLFRD in many of its letters and publications, and negotiated fundraising contracts by which the HLFRD paid the IAP $40,000 a year for the IAP's fundraising services. In February 1996, an FBI source reported being told by a Hamas activist who had been affiliated with the IAP for about a decade that the IAP "donates to the Palestinian arena approximately $3 million per year. These donations were reportedly sent to the Holy Land Foundation in Palestine, and the money goes to Hamas."[20]

KinderUSA

Even after the closure of the Holy Land Foundation in 2001, other U.S.-based charities continue to fund Hamas. One organization that has appeared to rise out of the ashes of the HLFRD is KinderUSA. According to one of its press releases, KinderUSA was formed in early 2002, "in response to dual challenges posed by the state of Muslim charities in America and the rapidly deteriorating humanitarian picture in Palestine." In January 2005, the group suspended its activities for fear it was under FBI surveillance. "In recent weeks," a press release read, "we have discovered that the federal government has targeted KinderUSA for investigation. This has taken the form of unwarranted and obtrusive surveillance by the FBI, wiretapping, attempts to bribe and subvert our employees (which has caused them to resign in fear), spreading of malicious disinformation about the organization, and the possible invasion of our office space."[21]

Ties between KinderUSA and HLFRD are evident in their shared leadership. For example, Dalell Mohmed, executive director of KinderUSA, was HLFRD's project coordinator. Likewise, Dr. Riad Abdelkarim, KinderUSA's president, was a member of HLFRD's governing board. Both were arrested in Israel in May 2002 (and subsequently released and deported) after Mohmed filed to register KinderUSA as a charitable organization there on May 3, 2002, and opened a bank account in its name in Jerusalem. Israeli authorities denied the request and deported Abdelkarim and Mohmed, believing the group was tied to Hamas. The formation of KinderUSA highlights an increasingly common trend: banned charities continuing to operate by incorporating under new names, either in response to designation as terrorist entities or in an effort to evade attention. This trend is also seen with groups raising money for al-Qaeda.[22]

Council on American-Islamic Relations

KinderUSA's Abdelkarim also worked as the western region communications director for the Council on American-Islamic Relations (CAIR). Several CAIR officials have been identified as Hamas supporters, including CAIR executive director Nihad Awad and Holy Land Foundation's vice president of international marketing, Ghassan Elashi, who also founded CAIR's Dallas office.[23]

CAIR, which describes itself as "established to promote a positive image of Islam and Muslims in America," was co-founded by Omar Ahmed. Ahmed also co-founded the Islamic Association for Palestine (IAP)—the same organization that first published the Hamas charter in English— together with Hamas leader Mousa Abu Marzook. CAIR takes pro-Hamas and pro-Hezbollah positions, regularly rising to the defense of terrorism suspects and openly supporting designated terrorist groups. For example, Nihad Awad, CAIR's executive director and a former IAP employee, is a self-identified "supporter of the Hamas Movement." But the group's ties to terrorism are not limited to mere lip service. CAIR employee Randall "Ismail" Royer was indicted in 2003 for his role in a northern Virginia jihad network that visited terrorist training camps in Pakistan and conspired to fight Indian forces in Kashmir. Royer and Elashi are not the only CAIR officials to be arrested or indicted since September 11, 2001. In another case, Bassem K. Khafagi, then CAIR's community affairs director, was arrested in New York in January 2003 for his alleged role in a terror financing plot involving the Islamic Assembly of North America.[24]

Other Hamas Fundraisers in the United States

Federal investigators have uncovered a surprisingly large number of front organizations supporting Hamas in the United States. On September 30, 2003, U.S. authorities detained and indicted Abdurahman Mohammad Alamoudi, head of the American Muslim Foundation (AMF) and also associated with several other charities, on charges of engaging in financial transactions with Libya, a state sponsor of terrorism subject to U.S. sanctions. Alamoudi was already a known quantity among terror supporters in the United States, especially after his comments at a rally outside the White House in 2000, where he announced: "We are all supporters of Hamas.

Allahu Akhbar! [God is great] ... I am also a supporter of Hezbollah." Alamoudi is also known to have attended a conference of major Islamic terrorist groups in Beirut in January 2001. The case that led to his eventual incarceration, however, is particularly revealing. According to court documents, $340,000 in cash was seized from Alamoudi on August 16, 2003, as he attempted to board a plane in London bound for Damascus. An unidentified Libyan had delivered the cash to Alamoudi in his hotel room the previous night. According to the U.S. Bureau of Immigration and Customs Enforcement (ICE), the money may have been "intended for delivery in Damascus to one or more of the terrorists or terrorist organizations in Syria." Alamoudi has publicly lauded Hezbollah and Hamas, expressed his preference for attacks that "hit a Zionist target in America or Europe or elsewhere but not like what happened at the Embassy in Kenya," and was an officer of charities in northern Virginia tied to Hamas and al-Qaeda. In an allusion to Hamas, one of Alamoudi's prosecutors said, "in addition to dealing with Libya, [Alamoudi] has a more direct connection with terrorist organizations designated by the United States government." In requesting that Alamoudi be held without bail, the U.S. government further charged that Alamoudi had laundered and transferred hundreds of thousands of dollars through charities to terrorist groups, including al-Qaeda and Hamas. In 2000, for example, a group that received $160,000 from a charity run by Alamoudi was subsequently implicated in the millennial terrorist plot foiled in December 1999. Later, in 2002, two of Alamoudi's other organizations (the Success Foundation and the Happy Hearts Trust) sent $95,000 to Hamas front organizations in Jordan and Israel. Court documents assert that tens of thousands more dollars were funneled through other Alamoudi-led organizations to Hamas.[25]

In June 2004, Alamoudi pled guilty to charges of violating sanctions against Libya. Alamoudi's agreement revealed that he was also involved in a Libyan plot to assassinate Saudi Crown Prince (now King) Abdullah in 2003. The plot involved Alamoudi, Libyan intelligence officials, and Saad al-Faqih, a Saudi dissident tied to al-Qaeda who was based in London. Alamoudi was sentenced to twenty-three years in jail, fined $750,000, and had to forfeit $910,000 in monies gained due to these illicit activities. Later, in July 2005, the U.S. Treasury Department revealed that in 2003 Alamoudi contributed approximately $1 million to the Movement for Islamic Reform in Arabia (MIRA). MIRA, a Saudi oppositionist organization based in Britain, was run by Saad al-Faqih, the al-Qaeda associate who was also involved in the plot to assassinate the Saudi crown prince. Faqih was himself designated as a terrorist supporter by the United States in December 2004. On July 14, 2005, the U.S. Department of Treasury added MIRA to its list of terrorist organizations and froze its U.S. assets. According to the Treasury Department, Alamoudi's 2003 arrest in the United States was a serious blow not only to Hamas but to al-Qaeda because of his ties and financial support for both groups.[26]

In court documents stemming from another terrorism case, this one in Boise, Idaho, the U.S. government charged that the Islamic Association of North America (IANA) "provided a number of Internet websites and other internet-related outlets for disseminating information regarding Islam, as well as for soliciting and receiving donations of monies both from within the United States and without." The websites "included materials intended to recruit and to raise funds for violent jihads," including the one pursued by Hamas against Israel. According to the indictment, the website, titled www.islamway.com and registered to the IANA, "included a specific solicitation of donations to the Islamic Resistance Movement, also known as Hamas, and provided a link for that purpose to a website it characterized as the official mouthpiece of Hamas." There is reason to believe IANA knew such donations would fund Hamas' terrorist activities; the website's director and administrator, Sami Omar al-Hussayen, was discovered in receipt of an e-mail purporting to be from the Hamas Qassam Brigades, "stressing the need for money in order to arm fighters against the 'Zionist occupiers.'" While al-Hussayen was ultimately acquitted on technical legal grounds of charges that he provided material support to terrorist groups, this evidence was never disproved.[27]

HAMAS FRONTS IN EUROPE

At the 1993 Hamas meeting in Philadelphia, one participant stressed that while the United States "is a secure place for the movement . . . Europe also can play the same role." Hamas support networks are indeed active across Europe, where their ostensive social welfare mission is more sympathetically received by governments that oversee rapidly increasing (and increasingly disaffected) Muslim immigrant communities.[28]

Al-Aqsa International Foundation

One useful gauge of terrorist-fundraising trends is law enforcement activity. By that measure, the al-Aqsa International Foundation in Europe was a critically important financial conduit for Hamas. Over the course of 2003, authorities in the United States, United Kingdom, Germany, Denmark, the

Netherlands, Luxembourg, and Switzerland all took action against the foundation (also referred to as the al-Aqsa Fund or the al-Aqsa Charitable Foundation). With operations in Europe, South Africa, Pakistan, and Yemen, al-Aqsa was during its heyday a major Hamas fundraising front and raised millions of dollars per year. The organization was first outlawed in Israel in 1997 and declared a terrorist organization there the following year. According to a statement issued by Britain's Treasury Ministry in May 2003, "strong evidence from international law enforcement agencies links al-Aqsa Foundation with terrorist activity." A Canadian intelligence report also lists al-Aqsa as a charity providing "fundraising and propaganda activities for Hamas."[29]

In January 2003, the head of al-Aqsa's Yemen office, Sheikh Mohammad Ali Hassan al-Moayad, was arrested in Germany. According to court documents filed in support of his arrest warrant, Moayad offered an FBI informant a receipt showing that he had transferred $70,000 to Interpal, the U.S.-designated Hamas front in London, as proof of his ability "to get money to the Jihad." Moayad also told FBI informants he had provided $3.5 million to Hamas and $20 million to al-Qaeda. A Palestinian intelligence document dated July 2000 and seized by Israeli authorities two years later included the al-Aqsa Charitable Foundation in a list of foreign institutions that support Hamas. Indeed, documents seized from the offices of Hamas charities in the West Bank revealed significant funding was received from the al-Aqsa Foundation. While some of these documents refer to otherwise innocuous donations such as "food packages" and "holiday packages," many specifically note "the project of assistance to the families of the martyrs, the wounded and those who sustained damage." In one case, evidence uncovered at the al-Islah Charitable Society in Bethlehem documented donations for thousands of dollars earmarked for the families of martyrs. The money was described as coming from the al-Aqsa offices in Germany, Holland, and South Africa, as well as from Interpal (which also coordinated the donations).[30]

Al-Aqsa has had a rather dramatic history in Germany. In August 2002 the German Ministry of Interior issued a decree banning al-Aqsa's activities because of its ties to Hamas. A German court repealed the ban in July 2003, in response to an appeal by the foundation. Then, in December 2004, the higher Administrative Court overturned the lower appeal court's ruling and upheld the government's original ban, effectively shutting down the al-Aqsa Charitable Foundation in Germany. The Administrative Court found that the al-Aqsa Foundation "supported the activity of an organization [Hamas] outside the Federal Republic that instigates and supports killing of people and damage to property." The ruling continued:[31]

> By its continuing and extensive financial support to welfare organizations that belong to Hamas, the Palestinian resistance movement [Hamas], the Petitioner [al-Aqsa Foundation] disrupted the understanding and peace between the Israeli and Palestinian peoples. In that, it concurrently supported Hamas' violent activities against the Israeli people. While it is impossible to prove that the funds transferred to the welfare organizations were used (in part) indirectly by Hamas' military activity, Hamas must be viewed as a single structure, with no distinction between its social work and the military sphere.[32]

After being banned in Germany, al-Aqsa shifted the bulk of its European fundraising operations to Holland, "where it raised approximately 600,000 Euros in 2002 and $650,000 in 2001," according to an Israeli government report. It continued to operate in the Netherlands throughout 2003, but changed its name to ISRA to avoid scrutiny by local law enforcement. By December 2004, ISRA's funds in Denmark and Holland had been added to the European Union's list of terrorist organizations and were prohibited from transferring money to the Palestinian territories. The most significant impact on the fund's Dutch branch may have less to do with government action and more do to with the public pressure that ensued after the Dutch television station Nova TV ran a segment investigating the group in 2001.[33]

Evidence of al-Aqsa financing of Hamas is extensive. In the second half of 2003, Israeli authorities detained two al-Aqsa employees who arrived in Israel to meet with and/or fund Hamas charities. On May 1, 2003, Israeli authorities arrested Lis Ben Khaled, a French citizen of Algerian descent, who "arrived in Israel with 11,000 Euros and contact details for someone in Jenin." Under questioning, Khaled provided detailed information regarding the activities of the various al-Aqsa Foundation offices, including their money transfers and other connections to Hamas charities in the West Bank and Gaza.[34]

The evidence tying al-Aqsa and its most senior officers to Hamas is also extensive. Particularly damning information was provided to Israeli authorities by Abd al-Hakim Mohammad abd al-Fatah Abd al-Rahman, a Hamas activist from the Palestinian village of Bir Naballah near Jerusalem, in 1993. Under interrogation, Abd al-Rahman revealed that before he left for Germany to pursue his studies, he approached Sheikh Jamil Hamami—

a senior Hamas leader in the West Bank—about joining Hamas. Hamami instructed Abd al-Rahman to contact Mahmoud Amru, the head of the al-Aqsa Foundation in Germany, who Hamami described as a senior Hamas activist in Aachen, Germany. Abd al-Rahman contacted Amru though the local Islamic center, and continued to be in touch with him throughout the course of his studies in Germany. Amru served as his contact with other Hamas activists in Germany, provided him with ideological materials, and helped him contact Hamas activists in Jordan.[35]

Al-Aqsa also served as a clearinghouse for smaller organizations supporting Hamas. U.S. officials noted in May 2003 that the Islamic League in Norway sent funds, gold, and jewelry it collected to the al-Aqsa International Foundation offices in Sweden "to be provided to Hamas." In another instance, in late 2001, the Islamic League sent funds to the al-Aqsa Foundation office in Sweden via human courier. Unlike many other Hamas fronts whose leaders are publicly circumspect about the final destination of the funds they solicit for Hamas, the Islamic League openly acknowledged such funds were intended to support terrorism. At its May 2002 annual conference, the League's secretary general called on "all Muslims to provide support and to participate in continuing the suicide operations against Israel."[36]

Interpal

Like many European charities tied to Hamas, the al-Aqsa International Foundation operated in close cooperation with Interpal, identified by U.S. and other international services as an influential Hamas front in London. Founded in 1981 as the Palestine and Lebanon Relief Fund in Manchester, the group assumed the name Palestine Relief and Development Fund, or Interpal, in November 1994 and is now headquartered in London. Beyond the funds Interpal raises on its own—its 2001 income was in excess of £4 million—authorities believe the organization serves as a global "clearinghouse" for charitable money earmarked for Hamas that is raised in Western Europe, Saudi Arabia, and other Gulf states.[37]

On August 22, 2003, the U.S. Treasury Department added Interpal and several other Hamas charities in Austria, France, Switzerland, and Lebanon to its terrorism list. The other charities were the Comité de Bienfaisance et de Secours aux Palestiniens (CBSP) in France, the Association de Secours Palestinien (ASP) in Switzerland, the Palestinian Association in Austria (PVOE), and the since-defunct Sanabil Association for Relief and Development in Lebanon. On November 21, 2003, Australia followed suit and listed these same Hamas fronts, along with six Hamas leaders, as terrorist entities and seized their funds. Canada has also cited Interpal and CBSP as Hamas fronts. The ties between Interpal and Hamas front organizations in the West Bank, Gaza, and Israel have been established not only through receipts found in Hamas charities, but also via telephone intercepts introduced in the case of Sheikh Raed Salah, an Israeli-Arab leader charged with funneling money to Hamas. Transcripts reveal that Salah communicated extensively with Interpal officials while laundering and funneling money received from Interpal through charities to Hamas institutions in the West Bank and Gaza.[38]

Virtually all the money raised or filtered by Interpal ends up—usually via bank transfer through the Arab Bank—at West Bank and Gaza charities affiliated with Hamas. According to an Israeli analysis of a 2002 Interpal trustees report, every one of Interpal's twelve "local partner" charities listed in the report is "affiliated with Hamas or works on its behalf, not only with regard to humanitarian issues but as part of its terrorism-supporting apparatus." Overall, Interpal appears focused on the Intifada against Israel, not on the humanitarian crisis faced by Palestinian refugees generally; though it officially claims to operate in refugee camps in Lebanon and Jordan, Interpal's website lists forty "local partners" in Palestine and only five in Jordan or Lebanon.[39]

Despite extensive public evidence of its ties to Hamas, Britain's Charity Commission for England and Wales gave Interpal a clean bill of health in 2003—just weeks after Interpal was designated a terrorist entity by the United States. Coming on the heels of the European Union's September 6, 2003, decision to include Hamas on its list of banned terrorist groups, the U.K. Charity Commission's decision to unfreeze Interpal's accounts was considered by many a setback to the international effort to sideline Hamas and resurrect the Middle East peace process. The British Charity Commission claimed U.S. authorities failed to provide evidence to substantiate charges that Interpal had financial ties to Hamas. "In the absence of any clear evidence showing Interpal had links to Hamas' political or violent military activities," the Commission concluded, Interpal's accounts deserved to be unfrozen. But the Commission arrived at this conclusion despite having found that Interpal received funds from the al-Aqsa Foundation in the Netherlands, already banned as a Hamas front by several countries—including Britain. The Commission excused the transaction because "the funds received were in respect of humanitarian work already carried out by Interpal and then invoiced to The al-Aqsa Foundation."[40]

Apparently what inhibited Commission action against Interpal was the conventional wisdom that the charitable, political, and military wings of a terrorist group are morally distinguishable. But even if Interpal were not tied to Hamas' political and violent activities, Interpal's support for the terrorist group's social service infrastructure ought to have been reason enough to ban Interpal; as observed in previous chapters, the Hamas dawa is the bedrock of Hamas' terrorist activities. At the very least, the sheer quantity of funds funneled from Britain to Hamas might have given the Commission pause. According to a Palestinian General Intelligence report from the late 1990s titled "Who Finances Hamas?" about $12 million of Hamas' estimated $60 million to $70 million annual income came from Britain.[41]

Evidence of the central role Interpal plays in Hamas financing confirms the Palestinian estimate. For example, Interpal transferred $33,800 through the City Bank of New York to the Hamas-controlled al-Islah Charitable Society in Ramallah. Among the documents seized from the charity's office was a receipt dated January 15, 2001, for this donation—the receipt was printed on Interpal stationery and signed by Jamal Mohammad Tawil, a senior Hamas operative and founder of the al-Islah charity. As noted above in Chapters 2 and 3, Tawil received funding for Hamas terrorist operations directly from Hamas leaders in Damascus through the al-Islah charity; he used the charity to launder funds for Qassam Brigades operations in which he was personally involved. More than perhaps anything else, Tawil's own history puts the lie to contrived distinctions between Hamas charity and Hamas terrorism; he was involved in planning several suicide bombings, including the car bomb attack in Jerusalem's Ben-Yehuda pedestrian mall in December 2001, which killed 12 people and wounded 180 more.[42]

Other interesting papers seized from the al-Islah charity document a series of small gifts—$100 each—presented by Interpal and the World Assembly of Muslim Youth (WAMY) to the families of suicide bombers in celebration of the three day Eid al-Fitr, marking the end of the holy month of Ramadan in 2001. Over two dozen families received the holiday gift, including families of Hamas and Islamic Jihad operatives—among them several suicide bombers. Interpal's ties to Hamas charities not only are widely documented by Israeli and American intelligence reports but have warranted special attention from Palestinian authorities. A Palestinian intelligence report dated July 1, 1999, details the Orphan Care Society in Bethlehem and its "connections with Hamas." The report, which highlights the

activities of Hamas activists Ghassan Harmas (a representative of the Orphan Care Society) and his ties to other Hamas charities like the Islamic
Charitable Society in Hebron, concludes by adding, "It should be noted
that the Islamic Charitable Society in Hebron receives support from Interpal in London, where Essam Yussuf, who lives in London, is its head."[43]

As noted above, United States and German investigators have also tied
Interpal to Sheikh Mohammad Ali Hassan al-Moayad, the head of the
Yemen office of the al-Aqsa International Foundation. Al-Moayad was arrested in Germany, in large part for providing money, arms, communication gear, and recruits to al-Qaeda. As proof of his ability "to get money to
the Jihad," al-Moayad offered an FBI informant a receipt from early 2001
showing that he had transferred $70,000 to Interpal. In contrast to Arafat's
Fatah party, which al-Moayad stressed he did not consider "to be Muslim
followers," al-Moayad highlighted Interpal as an example of an organization through whom money goes to Hamas. When the informant confused
the Hamas front Interpal with the European law enforcement agency In-
terpol, al-Moayad corrected him, saying, "No, no, no, it's Interpal, it's a respectable company, which I visited in London and I sat with them, they're
doing well." When the hotel room service knocked on the door just seconds
later al-Moayad immediately gathered up the receipts and told the others
in the room, "remove everything, remove them," instructing them to look
like all they had been doing was translating the Koran together.[44]

Other European Charities in the "Union of Good"

Other, less well known European charities and humanitarian organizations
are also suspected of serving as Hamas front organizations, such as the
Associazione Benefica di Solidarieta con il Palestinese (ABSPP), the Italian
branch of the U.S.-designated Hamas front CBSP operating in France.
French officials have long resisted banning CBSP, creating little incentive
for officials in places with CBSP-affiliated offices, like Italy, to take action
themselves. As with Britain's attitude toward Interpal, French officials cite
Hamas' social welfare work as the reason for their refusal to act against local
Hamas fronts, even after the EU has banned them. A French government
position paper sites "reticence" to ban Hamas among "a certain number of
EU member countries," including France, and highlights "the movement's
social activities, which partially but significantly make up for some of the
Palestinian Authority's difficulties in guaranteeing essential services to Pales-
tinian society." Despite the EU ban, the paper explains, "France continues

to oppose the inclusion on the list of the Committee for Palestinian Charity and Aid (CBSP), which raises funds for social actions in the Palestinian territories. Several administrative and judicial investigations have produced no evidence that this group uses such funds for terrorist purposes." In contrast, U.S. officials maintain they have provided "indisputable" evidence of the links between Hamas and European fronts like the CBSP. Israeli authorities point to documents seized in raids in Jenin and Ramallah showing bank transfers between the CBSP and Hamas-run welfare groups. The transfers reportedly include the transfer of €45,000 in the first half of 2004 alone. Moreover, other intelligence services, including the Canadian Secret Intelligence Service, have also highlighted CBSP's ties to Hamas.[45]

Both the French and Italian branches of CBSP, as well as Interpal in London, the al-Aqsa International Foundation branches throughout Europe, and many others, belong to an umbrella organization called the Union of Good (*I'tilaf al-Khayr*, also known as the Charity Coalition). It was founded in October 2000 by Sheikh Yusef Qardawi, the radical Islamist sheikh highlighted in Chapter 3 for his religious rulings (fatwas) legitimizing suicide bombings against Israeli civilians, and for calling for attacks on Americans—military and civilian alike—in Iraq. The date of the organization's inception is significant, coming as it does right on the heels of the outbreak of the al-Aqsa Intifada, the second Palestinian uprising that followed the breakdown of the Camp David peace talks in September 2000. The timing provides insight into the organization's underlying purpose, which is "to serve as an umbrella organization for a global Islamic fundraising drive for Palestinians in the PA-administered territories." Noting its ties to Hamas, Israel outlawed the Union of Good in February 2002.[46]

Sheikh Qardawi's vision was to place the Palestinian cause squarely into the context of global Islamic radicalism, thus opening Hamas, Palestinian Islamic Jihad, and other groups to the financial largesse of radical Islamists worldwide. In transcripts of covertly recorded conversations, Mohammad Ali Hassan al-Moayad, the head of the al-Aqsa Foundation office in Yemen, described Qardawi and his assistant, Issam Kashashani, as people who "support the entire Jihad movement." In a different exchange with an undercover American source, or cooperating informant (marked CI-1), Moayad and his assistant, Sheikh Mohammad Zayed, discussed Qardawi and his support for a variety of jihadist organizations:

Moayad: Yusef . . .

Zayed: He's a religious scholar.

CI-1:   And he is a good, religious man and he is supporting, uh . . .
           He also supports Hamas?
Moayad: He supports all of Islam. He works toward the unanimity of
           all Muslims.
CI-1:   He is supporting Hamas and the other Islamic Jihad—
Moayad: Jihad.
CI-1:   —movements.[47]

The Union of Good began life as a limited 101-day fundraising drive
chaired by Qardawi. It was so successful, however, that it became an institution unto itself and now works with over fifty Islamic foundations
worldwide. According to Palestinian intelligence, "The Union [of Good] is
considered—with regard to material support—one of the biggest Hamas
supporters." Qardawi recruited Essam Yusef, until then the head of Interpal
in London, to serve as the Union's operative director (Yusef retains his affiliation with Interpal, serving as its vice chairman of the board of trustees
as well as its managing trustee). In a 2001 television interview Yusef reportedly described Sheikh Qardawi as "Sheikh al-Mujahideen" (sheikh of
the holy warriors). And in a telling indication of the cooperation between
Hamas fronts abroad, one of Sheikh Moayad's deputies at the al-Aqsa
Foundation, Ali Muqbil al-Jawabirah, is described in a Palestinian intelligence document as the "director-general" of the Union of Good in Yemen.[48]

Also affiliated with both the Union of Good and Interpal is a smaller
Islamic charity called Muslim Aid. Founded by former pop music icon and
Muslim convert Islam Yusef Islam (formerly Cat Stevens), Muslim Aid and
Interpal have collectively raised funds for the Hamas-run Ramallah-al-
Bireh charity committee. Citing suspected financial ties to Hamas and Sheikh
Omar Abdel Rahman (the "Blind Sheikh" serving a life sentence for plot-
ting to bomb New York landmarks), the United States denied Yusef Islam
entry into the United States in September 2004. He had been denied entry
to Israel in 2000 on similar grounds.[49]

Funds raised under the auspices of the Union of Good and its con-
stituent organizations like Interpal and Muslim Aid make their way to
Hamas through local charity committees, the vast majority of which are affiliated with Hamas. According to an Israeli assessment, by December 2004
the Union of Good had transferred tens of millions of dollars to the Palestinian territories, via local Hamas charities. These purportedly charitable
donations were then "exploited by Hamas to finance its apparatus (i.e., financial and material support given to the families of martyrs and prison-

ers), as well as the welfare and health projects which reinforce its status among the Palestinian population." To facilitate such large-scale funding, the Union of Good split its operations in the Palestinian territories into four administrative districts with one in Gaza, and three in the West Bank. While the organization has its own representative office in Gaza to distribute aid there, its operations in the three West Bank districts are run through the offices of local Hamas charity committees. The al-Tadhoman organization in Nablus coordinates distribution in the northern West Bank, while activities in the central West Bank are run through the al-Islah committee in Ramallah and in the southern West Bank through the Hebron Islamic Charity Society. As discussed in previous chapters, each of these organizations is intimately tied to Hamas. Al-Tadhoman, for example, is headed by senior Hamas official Sheikh Hamid Bitawi, who also serves as one of three Union of Good trustees in the West Bank. Also on the organization's board of trustees are Sheikh Ikrima Sabri, the Mufti of Palestine and frequent preacher at Jerusalem's al-Aqsa mosque, and Sheikh Raed Salah, the head of the Israeli-Arab Islamic movement in northern Israel who was convicted of transferring funds to Hamas via charities he ran.[50]

Even projects funded by the Union of Good with no direct tie to Hamas, such as the group's financing of large infrastructure projects, function to bolster the terrorist group's reputation in Palestinian eyes. "The projects are carried out through [Hamas-affiliated] institutions and improve [Hamas'] standing among the population," according to an Israeli report, "helping Hamas to present itself as a potential radical Islamic alternative to the more secular-oriented Palestinian Authority." But some of the funds dispersed by the Union of Good are explicitly funneled to Hamas operatives. Under interrogation by Israeli authorities, Hamas activist Ashraf Muhi al-Din Mohammad Sawafteh described receiving money from the Union of Good. A Hamas political leader in the Jenin area, Sawafteh had already planned to join the group's Qassam Brigades when he was arrested. Sawafteh further laundered the funds he received through a branch of the Palestinian Association of Workers, General Services and Manufacturing Institutions, which he headed. The Union of Good boasts ties to a litany of known and suspected terrorists, including Hamas activists, radical Arab leaders (including a former Sudanese president, a Jordanian minister, and the speaker of the Yemeni parliament), and other radical Islamist individuals and organizations tied to global jihadist groups. Included in this last category, for example, is Sheikh Abdel Majid al-Zindani, a Specially Designated Global Terrorist accused by the U.S. government of "actively recruiting for al-Qaeda training camps" and playing "a key role in the purchase of weapons on behalf of al-Qaeda and other terrorists."[51]

WEALTHY INDIVIDUALS AND CORPORATE DONORS

While most Hamas money raised abroad comes by way of charities that rely on relatively small donations from hundreds or thousands of Palestinian sympathizers, significant funds also come from the personal resources of individual terror financiers—and the coffers of the corporations they run. According to Hamas spokesman Ibrahim Ghosheh, "the fact of the matter is that Hamas receives modest support from many Muslims in the Gulf states, Saudi Arabia, Iran, Jordan, Yemen, Turkey, and many others." For example, Yassin al-Qadi, a prominent Jedda businessman and head of the now-defunct Muwafaq Foundation, is accused of supporting a variety of terrorist groups, from al-Qaeda to Hamas. According to U.S. court documents, in 1992 al-Qadi provided $27,000 to U.S.-based Hamas leader Mohammad Salah and lent $820,000 to the Quranic Literacy Institute (QLI). Based on these connections to Hamas, the U.S. government froze the assets of both Salah and QLI. Many of the individuals who finance Hamas do so from the proceeds of their otherwise legitimate businesses. Businessmen like Yassin al-Qadi are able to draw on extensive business holdings and investments, but less prominent funders also make serious contributions to Hamas. For example, in January 2003 Jamil Sarsour, a grocer from Milwaukee who owns several properties there, was charged in the U.S. with money-laundering offenses related to his funding of Hamas military activists in the West Bank. Sarsour pleaded guilty and served four years' time in an Israeli jail for providing $40,000 to Adel Awadallah, a Qassam Brigades fugitive wanted for planning suicide bombings. These funds are suspected to have come, at least in part, from the Sarsour family's business holdings. When Israeli authorities first arrested Sarsour in October 1998, they found almost $10,000 in cash and over $60,000 in personal checks, cashier's checks, and money orders, as well as two American passports in his name. Sarsour's brother, who runs a furniture business in one of the family properties, was also arrested in Israel for funding Hamas with family money.[52]

Hamas has proved itself well aware of the advantages of capitalist enterprise, going so far as to establish its own banks and financial houses. For example, investigators revealed that Beit al-Mal Holdings, a public investment company in the West Bank and Gaza, is controlled by Hamas and funds the group's activities. The U.S. government has concluded that "although its stated business activities are making loans and investing in economic and social development projects, Beit el-Mal has extensive ties to Hamas." A majority of the bank's founders, shareholders, and employees are Hamas associates, while the bank has funded projects in the Palestinian territories "that are owned or managed by Hamas activists," according to the United States. The al-Aqsa Bank, described by U.S. authorities as "a financial arm of Hamas," is partly owned by Beit el-Mal, with which it also shares senior officers and directors. Like Beit al-Mal, a majority of the al-Aqsa Bank's shareholders and senior officials have ties to Hamas. According to U.S. officials, "Individuals associated with the Bank have been previously arrested and charged with financing Hamas activities in the Middle East. Soon after the bank opened in 1998, its connection to Hamas extremists became evident and a number of banks refused to clear its transactions."[53]

In the United States, Beit al-Mal operated under the name Beit al-Mal, Inc., or BMI. Founded by Soliman Biheiri in 1985, the New Jersey–based holding company operated several subsidiaries, including BMI Leasing, Inc., BMI Real Estate Development, Inc., and BMI Trade and Investment, Inc. One of Biheiri's real estate companies invested in housing developments on behalf of Hamas and its leader, Mousa Abu Marzook, including a housing complex in the Maryland suburbs of Washington, D.C. (U.S. law enforcement officials reportedly refer to the Oxen Hill development as "Hamas Heights.") Marzook, also identified as the president of Mostan, another company tied to Biheiri, confirmed the investment to a U.S. government informant.[54]

Other businesses, like Infocom—the telecommunications company jointly established by Mousa Abu Marzook and the founders of the Holy Land Foundation—not only funded Hamas but also provided services to Hamas members, front organizations, and supporters. Infocom engaged in regular financial dealings with Marzook (and his wife, Nadia Elashi), laundered money through the company, provided computer services to several organizations linked to terrorist groups, and exported technology to Libya and Syria in violation of U.S. export control regulations.[55]

Individuals, charities, and banks tied to the ruling class in Saudi Arabia are among the most prolific supporters of Islamist extremism, both Palestinian and global. Members of the al-Raji family have been tied to Hamas funding, as have other members of the Saudi elite, such as Khari al-Agha and Abd al-Rahim Nasrallah, who is believed to have laundered and transferred funds through charitable organizations fronting for Hamas in Europe. Nasrallah was reportedly in direct contact with Ziad Mahmoud

Abd al-Rahim Salameh Zakarna, the head of the Jenin charity committee—
a central node in the Hamas dawa in the northern West Bank. Together, Zakarna and Nasrallah may have arranged for the transfer of hundreds of
thousands of dollars to Hamas. Individual contributions from Saudi Arabia were instrumental in Hamas' development of the Qassam rockets it
routinely shoots into Israel from Gaza. In December 2001, Israeli authorities arrested Hamas operative Osama Zohadi Hamed Karika as he attempted
to leave for Egypt via the Rafah border crossing at Gaza. On his person were
documents detailing the development of the Qassam rockets. Under questioning, he admitted that he was on his way to Saudi Arabia to brief unidenti-
fied persons on the development of the rockets and to obtain their continued funding for the project. Karika also told his Israeli interrogators that
Saudi Arabia was where he had personally secured initial funding for the
rocket program.[56]

In October 2002, Treasury Department undersecretary for enforcement Jimmy Gurule traveled to Europe armed with a list of "about a dozen
of al-Qaeda's principal financial backers, most of them wealthy Saudis."
Gurule went to present his European counterparts with "specific information on selective, high-impact targets" in an effort to have them "designated
terrorist financiers and have their assets blocked." Many of these individuals also fund Hamas, prompting Gurule to press his European counterparts
"to reconsider the common European and official E.U. distinction made
between political or social wings and military or terrorist wings of organizations such as Hamas."[57]

Aware that authorities in Europe, the Middle East, and elsewhere frequently turn a blind eye to such activity, prominent Islamist leaders openly
call for financing Hamas. For example, the day after the July 31, 2002, Hamas
bombing at Jerusalem's Hebrew University (which killed seven civilians,
including five Americans, and wounded eighty-six others), the Jordanian
Islamic Action Front (IAF) sponsored a mass rally in Amman. IAF leaders
proudly and publicly lauded the university bombing as a "bold, heroic operation" and highlighted the IAF's commitment to supporting Hamas.
Speakers asserted that the Hebrew University attack cost $50,000, adding
that "this necessitates giving large financial aid to the Palestinian people to
carry out more operations of this kind." Jordanians and the larger Arab nation were urged "to contribute generously to the Palestinian people so that
they could buy the weapons and necessary equipment for confronting the
Israeli arrogance."[58]

Fundraising for Hamas by wealthy individuals also occurs outside the

Middle East. A Canadian intelligence report declares that "Hamas supporters and fundraising activity also appear to be present in the tri-border area of Brazil, Paraguay, and Argentina. . . . Reporting indicates funds are regularly sent to groups in the Middle East, including Hamas, from supporters in the tri-border area." U.S. officials agree, noting that a prominent Sunni cleric in the Tri-border area, Sheikh Khaled Taqi al-Din, "is primarily affiliated with Hamas."[59]

FUNDING FROM OTHER TERRORIST NETWORKS

Hamas funding also comes from sources more closely tied to other groups, especially al-Qaeda, substantiating the comments of terrorism scholar Rohan Gunaratna that al-Qaeda's "modus operandi is fully compatible with that of other terrorist groups such as the Tamil Tigers and Hamas." Indeed, despite their not sharing any formal affiliation, there is enough significant overlap in Hamas and al-Qaeda's financing networks that informal person-to-person cooperation in this area is probably inevitable. Take for example Muhammad Zouaydi, a senior al-Qaeda financier in Madrid whose home and offices were searched in April 2002. Spanish investigators found a five-page fax dated October 24, 2001, revealing that Zouaydi was not only financing the Hamburg cell responsible for the 9/11 attacks, but also Hamas. In the fax, which Zouaydi kept for his records, the Hebron Muslim Youth Association solicited funds from the Islamic Association of Spain. (According to Spanish prosecutors, "the Hebron Muslim Youth Association is an organization known to belong to the Palestinian terrorist organization Hamas which is financed by activists of said organization living abroad.") Spanish police also say Zouaydi gave a total of almost $6,600 marked "Gifts for Palestine" to Sheikh Helal Jamal, a Palestinian religious figure in Madrid reportedly tied to Hamas.[60]

A particularly interesting link between al-Qaeda and Hamas was revealed when U.S. immigration officials briefly detained Muhammad Jamal Khalifa, Osama bin Laden's brother-in-law and a senior International Islamic Relief Organization (IIRO) official and al-Qaeda financier, in San Francisco in December 1994. Among the material found in his belongings "were extensive discussions of assassination, the use of explosives, military training and jihad as well as details of Islamist movements such as Hamas and Palestinian Islamic Jihad." Even after he left the Saudi charity to open a branch of the Muwafaq Foundation in the Philippines, Khalifa apparently maintained relations with Hamas members working for the IIRO there.[61]

The al-Taqwa banking system has also financed the activities of multiple terrorist organizations, including Hamas and al-Qaeda. Al-Taqwa was added to U.S. terrorism lists in November 2001 for "provid[ing] cash transfer mechanisms for Al-Qaida," and European intelligence services confirm "al-Taqwa used Hamas funds in the late 1990s." Subsequent investigation has determined al-Taqwa was established in 1988 with financing from the Egyptian Muslim Brotherhood. According to the U.S. Treasury Department, "$60 million collected annually for Hamas was moved to accounts with Bank al-Taqwa." Al-Taqwa shareholders include both known Hamas members and individuals linked to al-Qaeda. Ghalib Himmat, noted for his ties to the Kuwaiti-based International Islamic Charity Organization (IICO), is also an executive of the al-Taqwa banking network. Moreover, a 1996 report by Italian intelligence further linked al-Taqwa to Hamas and other Palestinian groups, as well as to the Algerian Armed Islamic Group (GIA) and the Egyptian al-Gama'a al-Islamiyya (Islamic Group).[62]

Further evidence of crossover between Hamas and al-Qaeda financing was exposed in the case of Soliman Biheiri, discussed above in connection with his defunct New Jersey investment company, BMI. Described by U.S. officials as "the U.S. banker for the Muslim Brotherhood," Biheiri's original investors include Hamas and al-Qaeda figures, among them Yassin al-Qadi and Hamas leader Mousa Abu Marzook (both listed as Specially Designated Global Terrorists by the U.S. government), as well as Abdullah Awad bin Laden (Osama bin Laden's nephew and the former head of WAMY in the United States).[63]

THE MORAL CULPABILITY OF FOREIGN DONORS

Having established the massive quantities of American, European, and Middle Eastern "charity" money flowing into Hamas coffers, the logical follow-up question is: do the foreign elements who empty their pocketbooks for Hamas and other radical Islamist networks know they are funding terrorism? An analysis of the index of documents seized by Israeli forces from charity committees across the West Bank reveals that the group's foreign benefactors are often full partners in the use of charitable donations for terrorist purposes. While individual donors are often duped into funding extremism and violence under humanitarian pretexts; the actual fundraisers—and many of their larger donors—frequently fund terrorism knowingly. The index reveals that donors from Italy to South Africa to Qatar contributed millions of dollars through charities that often specified recipients as "the families of martyrs." Hamas front organizations in Europe are prominently featured in these documents, which include accounting spreadsheets, personal letters, and more. The donations themselves came from front organizations in Europe, North America, South Africa, Qatar, and elsewhere, and were usually transferred through local branches of Middle Eastern banks. Interpal, the al-Aqsa International Foundation, the Holy Land Foundation, and many more charities all featured prominently in the material Israeli forces seized in the West Bank.[64]

For example, when Israeli forces raided the Tulkarm charity committee, they found material lauding Hamas suicide attacks and records showing the Saudi International Islamic Relief Organization (IIRO) had donated at least $280,000 to the Tulkarm charity committee and other Palestinian organizations linked to Hamas. Israeli authorities found that many of the checks made out to Hamas organizations were drawn from the corporate account of al-Rajhi Banking and Investment at Chase Bank. Several charitable and banking institutions tied to the al-Rajhi banking family (including the SAAR Foundation in northern Virginia) are under investigation as terrorist fronts.[65]

In another case, Israeli authorities found Saudi texts praising suicide attacks in the West Bank offices of the Koran and Sunna Society—Palestine, which, along with the Dar al-Arqam Model School in Gaza, received funds from the Saudi-based World Assembly of Muslim Youth (WAMY). According to Israeli officials, both Palestinian organizations are tied to Hamas. While authorities determined WAMY was funneling money to Hamas through Interpal as early as 1996, a Palestinian report from 1999 asserts WAMY also funneled money directly to Hamas organizations in the West Bank. "There is a charity located in Saudi Arabia/Riyadh, the World Assembly of Muslim Youth, which supports Hamas members through the school in Hebron which belongs to the Islamic Charitable Society." WAMY, the report continued, "aids and supports the poor, orphans, widows and the families of martyrs and the imprisoned who belong to the Hamas movement." In 2002, the same year Israel outlawed WAMY, Hamas leader Khaled Mishal was an honored guest at WAMY's annual conference in Saudi Arabia.[66]

In the offices of the Islamic Charity Society in Hebron, a Hamas-run charity, Israeli forces uncovered letters demonstrating that Islamic charity money transferred from abroad knowingly and intentionally finances attacks targeting Israel. In one letter, Hamas fundraisers abroad highlight their efforts to "invest efforts in transferring large sums of money for you [Hamas activists in the territories] by charity activity and emergency budgets which we are still attempting to develop. . . . We promise to make efforts to transfer money to the casualties (*shuhada*) and the prisoners by transfer to charity institutions." In another letter confiscated from the Islamic Charity Society, Hamas social welfare activists explain to their benefactors that foreign largesse has enabled Hamas to set up a "special apparatus for the popular resistance." The Hamas activists stress that "this would be coordinated with the military activity, based on the notion that the Intifada needs both arms, the popular supportive arm and its activities, as well as the military arm, which promotes the Intifada and its spirit of resistance, and at the same time spurs the public's motivation in case of calm." One goal, the writers explain, is "to prepare the ground for creating new waves of the Intifada in case it dies down."[67]

7

state support for hamas

Beyond the tens of millions of dollars raised by Hamas each year from foreign charities, individuals, businesses, and criminal enterprises, the terrorist organization is also a massive beneficiary of support from foreign governments. State supporters of Hamas have included Saudi Arabia, Iran, Syria, Lebanon, Libya, Sudan, Yemen, and Qatar. Each country's support of Hamas is different in nature; some nations, like Iran, provide direct state funding, while others help out by providing military training or a safe haven for wanted activists—or by merely turning a willful blind eye to Hamas activity within their borders. Of the countries listed above, Iran, Syria, Libya, Sudan, and Iraq under Saddam Hussein have been designated by the United States as state sponsors of terrorism. Saudi Arabia, Yemen, Lebanon, and Qatar are not so designated by the State Department and are perhaps most accurately described as "facilitators" of Hamas terrorism.[1]

Saudi Arabia and Iran account for the majority of the group's overall financial support, including support for the Hamas dawa, though Iranian support comes directly through state institutions as a function of the government and Saudi support comes primarily through private organizations and individuals—some close to or members of the royal family—whose actions have been tolerated to varying degrees by the regime. Beyond the money raised in the Gulf states, much of the money raised by Hamas institutions elsewhere is funneled to the group's institutions in the West Bank and Gaza via charities based in the Gulf. This accounts for the tremendous number of financial transfers to Hamas from Gulf charities, as highlighted above in Chapter 4.

STATE SPONSORS OF TERRORISM

Iran

The Islamic Republic of Iran is described by the CIA as "the foremost state sponsor of terrorism" and is Hamas' most important and explicit state sponsor. Israeli, British, Canadian, and Palestinian intelligence all concur with the U.S. conclusion that Iran directly aids Hamas with money, training camps, and logistical support.[2]

Estimates of Iran's financial assistance to Hamas vary, but there is unanimity on one score: the sum is significant. According to Israeli estimates, as of 2005 Iran contributes around $3 million a year in direct aid to Hamas. Canadian intelligence cites assessments that Iran transfers somewhere between $3 million and $18 million a year to Hamas. According to the Canadian Secret Intelligence Service, "in February 1999, it was reported that Palestinian police had discovered documents that attest to the transfer of $35 million to Hamas from the Iranian Intelligence Service (MOIS), money reportedly meant to finance terrorist activities against Israeli targets." Palestinian sources estimate Iranian assistance to Hamas "at tens of millions of dollars." According to experts testifying in the case of *Diana Campuzano et al. v. The Islamic Republic of Iran,* Iranian financial support to Hamas in 1995 totaled $30 million and ranged from $20 million to $50 million annually between 1990 and 2000. Expert testimony in another case involving a Hamas attack, *Susan Weinstein et al. v. The Islamic Republic of Iran et al.,* concluded that "the Islamic Republic of Iran gave the organization at least $25–50 million in 1995 and 1996, and also provided other groups with tens of millions of dollars to engage in terrorist activities. In total, Iran gave terrorist organizations, including Hamas and others, between $100 and $200 million per year during this period."[3]

Whatever the specific sum, it fluctuates given circumstances on the ground; Iran is known to employ a performance-based approach to determining the level of funding it is willing to provide terrorist groups. As a U.S. court noted in *Weinstein v. Iran,* the period of 1995–1996 "was a peak period for Iranian economic support of Hamas because Iran typically paid for results, and Hamas was providing results by committing numerous bus bombings such as the one on February 25, 1996." Iran's pay-for-performance funding policy is also evident from its interactions with Palestinian Islamic Jihad. Until Palestinian officials released imprisoned Islamic Jihad bomb makers and terrorist recruiters in 2000 and 2001 (following the collapse of Israeli-Palestinian peace talks), it had been years since Islamic Jihad carried out a successful attack. Islamic Jihad conducted several suicide bombings in 1995 and then not again until September 2000 with the exception of the November 6, 1998, double bombing in the Mahane Yehuda market that injured twenty. Plot after plot failed, either because of terrorist incompetence or successful counterterrorism operations. But once their key operatives were released from jail, Islamic Jihad terrorist activity quickly picked up. In early June 2002, Iran's Ayatollah Ali Khamene'i met with Islamic Jihad leader Ramadan Shallah on the sidelines of a Tehran conference convened in support of the Palestinian Intifada. Khamene'i pledged to separate Iran's funding for Islamic Jihad from that of Hezbollah and to increase Islamic Jihad funding by 70 percent "to cover the expense of recruiting young Palestinians for suicide operations." U.S. officials note that in the period following the onset of violence in September 2000, Tehran instituted an incentive system in which millions of dollars in cash bonuses to Islamic Jihad were conferred to the organization for successful attacks. Tehran often demands of its terrorist beneficiaries videotapes or other evidence of successful attacks.[4]

Iranian funding of Hamas is also affected by the affairs of other states. In the wake of a 2004 internal Saudi crackdown on al-Qaeda terror financing, funding for Hamas from the Kingdom all but dried up for a time. (As it turned out, many of the financiers of al-Qaeda were supporters of Hamas, as well.) Reeling from the loss of Saudi funds, Hamas is believed to have accepted an emergency budgetary supplement from Iran to tide the organization over until alternative means could be found to transfer funds from within the Kingdom to Hamas. This financial support was likely forthcoming thanks to Hamas' successful militarization of the Intifada that followed the failure of Israeli-Palestinian peace talks in 2000. Similarly, Iranian funding to Hamas increased following the U.S.-led coalition's overthrow of Iraq's Saddam Hussein—thereby drying up the generous Iraqi grants to families of Palestinians killed, wounded, or jailed in the course of attacking Israelis. As Israeli journalist Zeev Schiff wrote in the *Ha'aretz* newspaper in May 2004, "Intelligence information also suggests that Iran is passing over millions of dollars to Palestinians via Hizballah contacts. Iran, in effect, is a replacement for former Iraqi leader Saddam Hussein, who subsidized families of Palestinian suicide bombers or those injured in the fighting. In the [Palestinian] territories, the funding is being managed by various Islamic welfare organizations."[5]

Hamas jealously guards its operational independence, and was initially reluctant to accept too much money from Iran and risk becoming—like

Hezbollah and Palestinian Islamic Jihad—a tool of Tehran's Ayatollahs. But the increase in Iranian funding for Hamas in May 2004 not only coincided with the removal of the Baathist regime in Iraq, it also came just weeks after the Israeli assassination of Hamas leader Abdel Aziz al-Rantissi. Coming on the heels of the assassination of Hamas founder Sheikh Ahmed Yassin, al-Rantissi's death left Hamas with no clear internal leadership. In Damascus, Khaled Mishal reportedly sought increased funding from Iran and a direct channel to the Iranian Revolutionary Guards Corp (IRGC) in an effort to contain the impact of the loss of Yassin and al-Rantissi and reinvigorate Hamas' operational cells.[6]

Unlike much of the financing examined so far in this book, Iranian funding of Hamas is generally not laundered through the dawa but directed straight to operational units. According to a December 2000 Palestinian intelligence report confiscated by Israeli authorities, Iran had transferred $400,000 directly to Hamas' Qassam Brigades to specifically support "the Hamas military arm in Israel and encouraging suicide operations," and another $700,000 to other Islamic organizations opposed to the PA. According to a former Jordanian prime minister, "grassroots fundraising is really not enough for big Hamas operations. Most of the support [for such operations] is from Iran. Iran's money is more influential." A senior Fatah official and member of the Palestinian Legislative Council offered a similar assessment, saying that while "some of Tehran's money over the past three years [2001–2004] may go to supporting health and humanitarian services in Gaza," the bottom line is that the "money from Tehran that goes to Hamas is for the political leaders of Hamas and for the bombings, not for the Palestinians." Iran, the official stressed, "is not really interested in the Palestinian cause." Indeed, "the Palestinian agenda and the creation of a Palestinian state is not in Iran's interests."[7]

Palestinian leaders have good reason to resent Iranian influence and pressure on radical Palestinian groups. Consider the contents of a Palestinian report on a May 2000 meeting in Damascus between the Iranian ambassador to Syria and representatives of Hamas, Islamic Jihad, and Hezbollah. According to the report, the Iranian ambassador demanded that the terrorist groups "carry out military operations in Palestine without taking responsibility for these operations." According to another Palestinian intelligence document dated October 31, 2001, officials from Hamas, Islamic Jihad, and Hezbollah had been meeting in Damascus "in an attempt to increase the joint activity inside [i.e., in Israel, the West Bank, and Gaza] with financial aid from Iran." The meeting was held "after an Iranian message had been transferred to the Hamas and Islamic Jihad leaderships, according to which they must not allow a calming down [of the situation] at this period." The Iranian funds, the document added, were to be transferred by Hezbollah. Not surprisingly, U.S. courts have concluded that "Iran provides ongoing terrorist training and economic assistance to Hamas" and found that Iran has "provided material support and resources to Hamas and its operatives, for the specific purpose of carrying out acts of extrajudicial killing."[8]

Jordan's King Abdullah II highlighted one such Iranian-funded operation when he visited President Bush on February 1, 2002. The king reportedly presented the president with evidence that Iran had sponsored no fewer than seventeen attempts to launch rockets and mortars at Israeli targets from Jordanian soil. This was, according to the king, an Iranian plot aimed at undermining the Jordanian regime and opening a new front against Israel. Detained Hezbollah, Hamas, and Islamic Jihad terrorists reportedly admitted to having been trained, armed, and funded by Iranian instructors at Hezbollah camps in Lebanon's Beka'a Valley. This story was raised in passing at a hearing of the House International Relations Committee on February 6, 2002, when Rep. Benjamin Gilman asked Secretary of State Colin Powell to respond to the above reports. Powell replied that the United States was taking the issue seriously: "We are going to make sure that the Iranians understand that this is inappropriate and that there are consequences to bear. . . . We're using the channels that are available to us to bring pressure on the Iranians." In light of the exposure of Iranian-funded Hamas operations on Jordanian soil, it is understandable that a senior Jordanian diplomat conceded being "nervous about Hamas in Jordan" and concerned about the "dirty game" being played by Iran. "Iran plays an indirect role in Jordan," the official said, "mainly through Lebanon. And of course Iran influences Hamas." This is a particular problem, the diplomat noted, because of the large percentage of ethnic Palestinians in Jordan: "If someone sneezes in Gaza, we get the flu here [in Jordan]."[9]

Iranian involvement in the weapons smuggling incident of the Karine-A—a ship loaded with Iranian weapons that was intercepted by the Israeli navy en route to Gaza in 2002—is also well documented. The White House described evidence of Iran's role in the Karine-A incident as "compelling," a conclusion echoed in the statements of CIA head George Tenet, senior State Department officials, and even European officials. Speaking before the European Parliament in Strasbourg in February 2002, European Union head of foreign affairs Javier Solana described the Karine-A as a "link between Iran and the PA," adding that "such a connection had not existed for many years." Hezbollah's role in the affair is also well known; not only did Iran arrange for Hezbollah external operations commander Imad Mughniyeh to purchase the Karine-A, but Mughniyeh's deputy, Haj Bassem, personally commanded the ship that met the Karine-A at the island of Kish (south of Iran) and oversaw the ship-to-ship transfer of the Iranian weapons. But the link extends to Hamas as well.[10]

According to U.S. officials, Iran offered the Palestinian Authority a substantial discount on the arms in return for being allowed to run a hospital in Gaza and other social welfare organizations in the Palestinian territories. By these means, Iran hoped to gain a foothold of its own in the Palestinian territories, through which it could build grassroots support, propagate its anti-Israel message, collect intelligence on the activities of U.S. officials, and provide direct support to Hamas and Islamic Jihad. Outreach to the Palestinians in this fashion would follow efforts by Iran elsewhere to use humanitarian and diplomatic footholds as a cover for the Islamic Revolutionary Guard Corps or MOIS operatives collecting intelligence and supporting local terrorist groups. In 1997, a Defense Intelligence Agency report detailed a similar Iranian initiative in Tajikistan; the MOIS had been collecting information on the U.S. presence there and possibly engaging in "terrorist targeting." In 1998, another such plan came to light in Kazakhstan, where three Iranians were arrested for espionage, possibly in support of a terrorist attack against U.S. interests.[11]

The Karine-A episode stood out not only because of the magnitude and audacity of the scheme (more than fifty tons of weapons valued at over $2 million were destined for Palestinian militants in this one plot), but because of the quality of the weapons. The weapons seized aboard the Karine-A have been described as "force multiplier weapons systems" that would have drastically shifted the balance of power between Israeli forces and Palestinian militant groups. They included 107 mm and 122 mm rockets and launchers with ranges of up to twenty kilometers, antitank launchers, and 120 mm mortars and mortar bombs, antipersonnel mines, small arms and ammunition, and more. Some of these arms still bore serial number markings revealing they were produced in Iran in 2001, including PG-7 Tandem and PG-7 Nader antitank rockets, and YM3 antitank and YM1 antipersonnel mines. While executed by Hezbollah, the entire operation was financed by Iran.[12]

The Karine-A is by no means the only Palestinian weapons-smuggling plot financed by Iran. Hezbollah and the Popular Front for the Liberation of Palestine-General Command (PFLP-GC) were both involved in other maritime smuggling efforts involving the Santorini and the Calipso-2 ships, which between them made three successful smuggling runs to Gaza and the Egyptian Sinai before a fourth attempt was thwarted by the Israeli navy in May 2001. Money from Tehran is believed to have financed these and other plots to arm Palestinian militants. For example, in May 2003, the Israeli navy intercepted the Abu Hassan, a fishing vessel on which Hezbollah was attempting to smuggle to Palestinian militants thirty-six CD-ROMs featuring bomb-making instructions, detonators, and a radio activation system compatible with rockets, suicide bombs, and remote-controlled explosives. The commandos also captured Hamad Abu Amar, a Hezbollah explosives expert, on board the boat.[13]

As part of its agenda to undermine prospects for Israeli-Palestinian peace, Iran actively trains Palestinian terrorist recruits, both directly and via Hezbollah, its primary terrorist proxy. Perhaps the best-known case is that of Hassan Salameh, the Hamas commander who was the mastermind of a string of suicide bus bombings in Israel in February and March 1996. In his statements both to Israeli police and to CBS's *60 Minutes,* Salameh described that after undergoing ideological indoctrination training in Sudan he was sent to Syria and from there transported via an Iranian aircraft to a base near Tehran. Osama Hamdan, Hamas' representative to Iran at the time, met Salameh in Tehran, after which Salameh underwent three months of military training by Iranian experts. With the help of a translator (Salameh did not speak Farsi and his trainers did not speak Arabic well), Salameh learned to handle explosives, automatic weapons, hand grenades, and shoulder-fired missiles. He was trained in ambush techniques, deactivating land mines and extracting their explosive material, and building trigger mechanisms for bombs. By his own admission, Salameh received all his military training in Iran.[14]

Iran also runs terrorist training camps of its own in Lebanon, aside from the Iranian-funded camps Hezbollah operates there. In August 2002, Tehran was reported to have financed camps under General Ali Reza Tamzar, commander of the IRGC activity in Lebanon's Beka'a Valley. These camps were designed to train Hezbollah, Hamas, Palestinian Islamic Jihad, and PFLP-GC terrorists in the use of the short-range Fajr-5 missile and the SA-7 antiaircraft rocket. The IRGC training program, which reportedly costs Iran $50 million annually, was said to include training for Lebanese and Palestinian terrorists to carry out "underwater suicide operations." While training terrorists in the Beka'a Valley, the IRGC and MOIS simultaneously run several terrorist camps in Iran. As of August 2002, more than seventy foreign recruits—mostly Arabs—were reportedly undergoing vigorous training under the command of the IRGC's Qods Force in two camps. At least fifty were being trained at the Imam Ali Garrison in Tehran while another twenty-two were being trained at the Bahonar Garrison, a Qods Force base located north of Tehran. Trainees were instructed to hide their connection to Iran and were warned by a Qods commander that "subsequent to September 11, our activities have become more sensitive."[15]

In an indication of the Iranian leadership's promotion of anti-Americanism and legitimization of acts of terrorism, Iranian hardliners constructed a monument in Tehran at the Behesht-e Zahra cemetery commemorating the Hezbollah suicide truck bombing that killed 241 U.S. servicemen in Lebanon in 1983. The Committee of the Commemoration of Martyrs of the Global Islamic Campaign sponsored the monument and is dedicated to registering "martyrdom seeking" volunteers (i.e., suicide bombers). Within one year the group registered 35,000 volunteers. During one recruiting drive, Maryam Partovi, thirty-one, a mother of two, said, "As a Muslim, it is my duty to sacrifice my life for oppressed Palestinian children." Over 400 "volunteers" signed up at that event, and President Khatami's adviser on women's affairs and a representative of Khamene'i were present, giving official backing to the event. According to the Committee's officials, the group said they would carry out attacks only if Ayatollah Khamene'i authorized them, highlighting the Iranian leadership's direct connection to Iranian-sponsored terror attacks.[16]

Iraq

The former regime of Saddam Hussein disbursed and pledged money to the families of Palestinian terrorists; these funds amounted to an annuity or life insurance policy for Hamas terrorists and served as a financial incentive for Palestinians to engage in acts of terror. Iraq paid $25,000 to the families of suicide bombers, as well as smaller rewards of $5,000 to $10,000 to the families of operatives killed or injured in the course of other terror operations targeting Israel. The funds were disbursed through two pro-Iraqi Palestinian groups, the Palestine Liberation Front (PLF) and the Arab Liberation Front (ALF), both of which maintained headquarters in Baghdad and long enjoyed Iraqi state sponsorship. While these funds were neither distributed by nor earmarked for Hamas—suicide bombers affiliated with any group or, theoretically, a lone suicide bomber operating on his own, would qualify—families of Hamas terrorists directly benefited from

Saddam's largesse. Indeed, Hamas likely benefited more from Iraqi state aid than other groups, given that it has always been the most active and deadly of the various Palestinian terrorist outfits. Evidence sized from ALF offices in the West Bank documents payments made to the families of the following Hamas terrorists:

- Imad Kamal Said Zabidi (who carried out a suicide bombing in Kfar Saba on April 22, 2001, killing one and wounding 38);
- Ashraf Mohammad Sabhi al-Seid (who carried out a suicide car bombing in the Jordan Valley on August 8, 2001, wounding one person);
- Izz al-Din Shuhayil Ahmad Ismail (who carried out a suicide bombing at a Jerusalem pizzeria on August 9, 2001, killing 15 and wounding 85);
- Ra'id Nabil al-Barghuti (who carried out a suicide bombing in Jerusalem on September 4, 2001, wounding 11);
- Mu'ayad Mahmud Eyadah Salah al-Din (whose suicide bomb exploded prematurely on November 8, 2001, when Israeli police officers approached him as he was on his way to conduct an attack);
- Osama Mohammad Id Bahr and Nabil Mahmud Jamil Halbiyyah (who carried out a double suicide bombing in Jerusalem on December 1, 2001, killing 11 and wounding 152);
- Fuad Ismail Ahmad al-Hurani (who carried out a suicide attack at a Jerusalem café on March 9, 2002, killing 11 and wounding 16);
- Shadi Zakariyyah Rida Tubassi (who carried out a suicide bombing in Haifa on March 31, 2002, killing 15 people and wounding 33);
- Nizam Mohammad Sabir Rashid Abu Hamdiyyah (who was wounded in gunfight with Israeli forces on June 3, 2002, and died of his wounds three days later).[17]

The ALF organized public disbursement ceremonies at which families of suicide bombers and other terrorists would pick up their checks and publicly thank Iraq. One such ceremony was held on July 18, 2002, in the Jabaliya refugee camp in the Gaza Strip and broadcast on international news networks. Families of dead terrorists from Hamas, Islamic Jihad, and other groups picked up their checks—$10,000 for the families of ordinary terrorists and $25,000 for the families of suicide bombers. Notable at this event was the participation of the Palestinian Communications Minister, Imad al-Faluji, a former Hamas member, as well as representatives of other militant Palestinian factions. The al-Tadhoman Charitable Society, a Hamas charity in Nablus, also served as an important intermediary for disbursing Iraqi payments. A letter addressed to the ALF found in the charity's files explained that two "martyrs" had not yet received their $10,000 payments and requested that ALF "please take care of this matter."[18]

Hamas leaders openly supported the Saddam regime and publicly expressed gratitude for Iraq's financial support. In June 2002, the ALF wrote a letter to a Ba'ath party official recording "the distribution of grants of the Fighting Saddam Hussein in Gaza." The letter reports on a distribution ceremony held on June 11, 2002, which was attended by several militant groups, including Hamas. According to the ALF account, "the Hamas delegate opened by greeting the families and praising the strong stand of the Palestinians against the Zionist war supported by the Big Satan, the U.S. He also praised the firm stand of the Iraqi people and its leader Saddam Hussein in view of the siege they are under by the imperialist Americans and the Zionists that are attempting to ruin the achievements of the Iraqi people and its scientific development." At a January 2003 rally in Gaza's Jabalya refugee camp, Hamas leader Abdel Aziz al-Rantissi called on Iraqis to emulate the Palestinian suicide bombers Saddam's regime had funded. "I call on Iraq to prepare an army of would-be martyrs and prepare tens of thousands of explosive belts," al-Rantissi said. "Blow yourselves up against the American army. Bomb them in Baghdad. I call on Arab nations to burn the ground underneath the feet of the Americans in all capitals." Saddam Hussein was equally vocal about his determination to support Palestinian terrorism. "The Intifada demands steadfastness. We have asked the [Arab] politicians not to pretend to know better than the Palestinian people what they want and what the fighters want, but to cooperate with them. . . . It is their duty to be [the Palestinians'] partners in blood, money and weapons, as a common fate." Saddam insisted that "the Palestinian people does not need more [peace] plans. We are not interested in [more] plans. Our basic plan is to support the Palestinian people in armed fighting."[19]

At least some of the Iraqi money used to support Hamas and other Palestinian groups came from the proceeds of illegal kickbacks paid to Saddam's regime in violation of the terms of the United Nations' Oil-for-Food program. According to hearings held by the House International Relations Committee in November 2004, "Saddam paid $25,000 rewards to the families of Palestinian suicide bombers through the Iraqi ambassador to Jordan out of accounts in the Rafidain Bank in Amman which held kickback money Saddam demanded from suppliers to his regime." A chart displayed at the hearings demonstrates how funds from several sources, including a 10 percent kickback payment from companies granted Iraqi contracts under the U.N.'s Oil-for-Food program, were deposited into an account at the Rafidain

Bank in Amman under the name of the Central Bank of Iraq and another account at the Rafidain Bank under the name of Iraq's ambassador to Jordan, Sabah Yaseen. Funds for the families of Palestinian suicide bombers were sent directly from Ambassador Yaseen's personal account, sometimes after being transferred to his account from the account held by the Central Bank of Iraq.[20]

Syria

According to the State Department, at least five of the forty terrorist groups recognized by the United States receive some level of sponsorship and support from Syria. Moreover, a number of Specially Designated Terrorists, such as senior Hamas official Mousa Abu Marzook and Palestinian Islamic Jihad leader Ramadan Abdullah Shallah, both work and reside in Damascus. From their Syrian headquarters, the groups and leaders incite, recruit, train, coordinate, and direct Palestinian terrorism. Indeed, since September 11, no fewer than five Damascus-based organizations—Hamas, Islamic Jihad, the Popular Front for the Liberation of Palestine (PFLP), the Democratic Front for the Liberation of Palestine (DFLP), and Hezbollah—have undertaken operations, from suicide bombings to assassinations, resulting in the deaths of dozens of civilians and an Israeli cabinet minister. Despite official protestations that terrorist groups are allowed to maintain only "political offices" in Damascus, Syrian officials actively support the full spectrum of these groups' activities. Consider, for example, the May 21, 2001, meeting between Syrian Defense Minister General Mustafa Tlas and Nayef Hawatmeh, head of the Democratic Front for the Liberation of Palestine (DFLP). According to a DFLP official, the discussions centered not on political or media issues, but "covered ways of supporting the Palestinian uprising and resistance in occupied Palestine against the Zionist aggressions."[21]

While it is far from certain 2002 ceasefire talks would have succeeded, it is certain that the Damascus-based leaders of Palestinian rejectionist groups—especially Hamas and Islamic Jihad—torpedoed efforts to broker a ceasefire between the Palestinian Authority and various Palestinian factions. The Damascus leaders pressured their groups' representatives in the Palestinian territories to not accede to any deal that proscribed suicide and other terrorist attacks. In fact, Syrian officials urged Hamas and Islamic Jihad to step up attacks. In May 2002, Damascus reportedly offered Hamas direct Syrian financial aid if it renewed suicide bombings. Syria's hosting of these group's leaders—providing them with some semblance of political cover, and facilitating their financing and operational planning—regularly frustrated U.S. efforts to de-escalate Israeli-Palestinian violence, establish calm, and initiate reform within the Palestinian Authority. Syria also played a key role in the Santorini and Calipso-2 weapons-smuggling plots, which were prepared and launched from Syria and Syrian-controlled Lebanon.[22]

If early trends are an indication of things to come, Syrian efforts to promote Hamas terrorism are expanding under the rule of Bashar al-Assad. Since Bashar took office, Israeli authorities have uncovered more than twenty Hamas activists who were recruited in various Arab countries and sent to Syria for terrorist training. The recruits received weapons training, as well as lessons in the preparation of explosives, intelligence activities, hostage taking, and suicide operations. The cases of three Hamas recruits who were sent to Syria for military training are particularly revealing. What follows is a summary of their confessions after their capture by Israeli security forces.[23]

In May 2001 Mohammad Abd al-Malk Abd al-Qadr al-Hur mentioned to a friend that he was interested in joining Hamas' Qassam Brigades and executing a suicide attack. By August, the friend had arranged for al-Hur to go to Syria for military training, explaining that al-Hur would then return to the West Bank ready to carry out attacks. Once in Syria, al-Hur and three other recruits were taken to a training camp near Damascus operated by the PFLP-GC. There the trainees underwent basic training in the use of small arms, producing and using explosives, electrical circuitry, and camouflage. In an effort to conceal that his terrorist training took place in Syria, al-Hur was then sent to Saudi Arabia with a cover story—and returned to the West Bank via Jordan. During his stopover in Amman, al-Hur met with Khaled Mahmud (also known as Fares), a Hamas operative assigned to serve as al-Hur's supervisor before crossing back into the West Bank.[24]

In another case, Hamas operative Majdi Abd al-Azim Sadeq Tabesh confessed to completing two sets of terrorist training courses in Syria. While information on his first training experience is unavailable, it was likely a "Terrorism 101" introduction similar to that undergone by al-Hur. Tabesh's second training, in July 2001, was a higher-level course focused specifically on sabotage and operational security. Conceptual learning was done in an apartment near Damascus in the Yarmouk refugee camp, where Hamas, Hezbollah, Islamic Jihad, and several other terrorist groups maintain offices. Practical training was provided at the Durayj army camp, a Syrian army garrison near Damascus. Tabesh learned how to construct improvised explosive devices (IEDs) and how to arm them with either thirty-minute-delay mechanisms or cellular phone activation. He also trained to surreptitiously track and trail suspects and practiced these newly acquired techniques in exercises carried out on the streets of Damascus. Following this second course, Tabesh was officially recruited into Hamas' Qassam Brigades by his Hamas instructor in Syria, Yihye al-Fayad. Tabesh then returned to the West Bank via Jordan with instructions to carry out terrorist operations.[25]

Hussein Zaghal, from a village near Jenin, was also recruited to Hamas and sent to Damascus for military training. In August 1998, Zaghal registered as a Ph.D. student in Islamic Studies at a school in Damascus. For a month and a half, he underwent a thorough curriculum of Hamas theoretical and practical training, averaging three days a week. Zaghal's training mirrored that of al-Hur and Tabesh. He studied the art of conducting and eluding surveillance, surreptitiously detecting and emptying caches (dead-drops), map reading, and secure communications. This regimen was followed by small-arms training at a Syrian army base forty minutes by car from Damascus. Later the following year, Zaghal went to another two-week training course at which previously covered material was reviewed and instruction was provided in the use of light antitank weapons.[26]

Hamas training in Syria is not merely a matter of historical record. In March 2005, Hamas recruit Osama Mattar told journalists how Hamas spotters recruited him at a Gaza mosque in 2003 and in December 2004 sent him to Syria. His mission: to be trained as a trainer for other recruits in Gaza. A former student at Damascus University, Mattar re-enrolled as a cover and waited twenty-five days to be contacted by Hamas operatives who instructed him in basic security procedures. He was then taken to a camp outside Damascus where he was trained "by nine instructors in everything from electronics to weapons." According to Mattar himself, Syrian officials "know very well about the presence of Hamas [in Syria]. What they may not have known about was the presence of a guy from Gaza coming to train at the training camp in Syria."[27]

While Syrian support for Palestinian terror comes primarily in the form of providing groups like Hamas a safe haven and a base for operational planning and training, the state also provides some amount of direct financial support. According to reports in the Arab press in January 2005, regional government authorities in the northern province of Aleppo were said to have instituted an automatic deduction of fifty Syrian pounds (about one dollar) from the paychecks of government employees to support "Palestinian insurgency groups based in Damascus." Syria has steadfastly resisted most international calls to desist its support for terrorism. In the wake of an Islamic Jihad suicide bombing in February 2005, White House spokesman Scott McClellan announced that "Syria continues to support terrorism; Syria continues to allow its territory to be used by terrorists. We have firm evidence now that the Palestinian Islamic Jihad out of Damascus was involved in planning the attack in Tel Aviv. It is unacceptable that terrorists are allowed to operate out of Syrian territory." Even in the wake of this attack, Syria declined to shutter the offices of Hamas, Islamic Jihad, and other terrorist groups in Damascus. As recently as April 2005, Syria was reported to have pressed these groups to lower their public profile there and to refrain from any activity that could "embarrass" the Syrian regime but was not demanding the groups close their Damascus offices.[28]

Sudan

A U.S.-designated state sponsor of terror since 1993, Sudan has long supported a laundry list of international terrorist groups, including Hamas. In the past, Khartoum provided safe haven for secular and radical Islamist terrorist groups, supported these groups with travel documentation and safe passage, and condoned Iranian fundraising and assistance to these groups in Sudan. In June 2003, Foreign Minister Mustafa Osman Ismail claimed Sudan would limit Hamas to conducting political activities. However, Sudanese President Umar al-Bashir, in a 2003 interview with al-Arabiyah television, said that Sudan retained a political relationship with Hamas and, therefore, could not banish Hamas from the country. In October 2003, an article on Hamas' website quoted Ibrahim Ahmed Omar, the secretary general of the ruling National Congress Party in Sudan, through SUNA, Sudan's official news agency, as saying, "Sudan's position toward Hamas and Jihad is clear: these are two Islamic forces struggling for the sake of (liberation of) their homeland. . . . They are not involved in any terrorist activities."[29]

Despite paying lip service to the idea, there is no indication that the Sudanese government has meaningfully limited Hamas' activities within Sudan's borders. Hassan Salameh, the convicted Hamas bomber and terror instructor who led a wave of terrorist attacks on Israel in 1996, received training in Sudanese camps before traveling to Iran for still more training arranged by Hamas leaders there. There he learned to handle weapons, construct and plant bombs, and harvest intelligence. He was also able to obtain a forged passport. Salameh acknowledged both to police and the media that before receiving three months of intense military training in

Iran he traveled to Sudan, where he first received ideological indoctrination to prepare him for his terrorism training and missions.[30]

In 1998, Hamas spiritual leader Sheikh Ahmed Yassin visited Sudan and was promised Hamas would receive access to an office, land, and a farm in Khartoum State to support the "Palestinian struggle." The state's governor, Majzub al-Khalifa, went on to say, "The assistance is in appreciation of Sheikh Yassin's contribution to reviving the Jihad." Since October 2003, Hamas has also had a small public relations office in Khartoum, called "al-Aqsa for Media." The office is run by a Hamas "information officer," Ghalib Hussein, and is overseen by the Hamas "representative" to Sudan, Jumaa Abdel-Fattah. The office sponsors conferences, lectures, and written materials, and functions mainly as a conduit in Sudan for promoting the Hamas position on Palestinian issues and the "Zionist-Palestinian conflict."[31]

Sudan also hosts charities with extensive ties to terror. One of these is the Islamic African Relief Agency (IARA), which funds not only Hamas but also al-Qaeda. In October 2004, the Treasury Department designated the IARA a terrorist organization, as well as five IARA employees—including Mohammad Ibrahim Sulaiman, the secretary general at the group's headquarters in Khartoum. At one point the IARA had an office in Columbia, Missouri, and received donations from former NBA all-star Hakeem Olajuwon's own Islamic charity, Islamic Da'Wah Center, which donated $81,250 to the IARA in hopes of helping needy Africans. In another prominent example, a deposed Sudanese president, 'Abd al-Rahman Siwaral-Dhanab, is second-in-command of the Union of Good charity umbrella, which, as discussed in Chapter 6, funnels money and goods to Hamas-affiliated entities in the Palestinian territories. Dhanab has publicly stressed the importance of "financial jihad," or financial support in furthering violence in the Palestinian-Israeli conflict.[32] Another Hamas-affiliated charity, HRI, also maintained an office in Sudan, underscoring that African country's convenience as a terrorist meeting place. According to Khaled Mishal, the last time he met Sheikh Ahmed Yassin in person was during a 1998 meeting in Sudan, part of a regional fundraising tour the movement organized for Yassin.

Sudan has also been a primary recruiting ground for Hamas. Many volunteers and university students studying in Sudan have been recruited and given basic military training and religious instruction in forty-five-day-long "jihad" camps in Sudan. As an Israeli military intelligence report notes, "Most of the [Hamas] activists [sent for training in Arab states] are students recruited to the Hamas during their studies in Syria, Yemen, Sudan and other Arab universities." In the wake of the global war on terror, fewer operational spaces are openly available for training in Sudan. Terrorist training for Palestinian students recruited into Hamas continues there, but reportedly on a smaller scale. Despite the war on terror, however, Hamas continues to use Sudanese passports to facilitate its operatives' travel across international borders. Moreover, Israeli intelligence officials believe at least some of the weapons Hamas smuggles into Gaza from Egypt originate in Sudan. In 2002, Israeli authorities arrested Muntasar Talab Salamah Frej, a twenty-year-old Gazan who joined Hamas as a dawa activist at age fifteen and transferred to the group's Izz al-Din al-Qassam Brigades when the Intifada began in 2000. According to his indictment, Hamas arranged and financed Frej's academic studies abroad as cover for his tour of terror training camps in Jordan (despite a Hamas statement that "there are no Hamas military people at all in Jordan") and Sudan. In conversations recorded by the FBI, Hamas officials from the United States, the West Bank, and Sudan discussed the logistics and costs of funding Palestinian students "who come from the inside," meaning the West Bank and Gaza. Concerned that Hamas officials in Sudan had no way to verify that applicants from the West Bank and Gaza were in fact Hamas members, the three Hamas officials noted that a decision had been made to screen students in advance, to weed out non-Hamas members. The Hamas representative to Sudan at the time, Mohammad Siyam, warned that Hamas activists in Sudan "will not accept anyone coming from the inside without a recommendation for those in charge abroad." According to Siyam, Hamas officials in Sudan and Yemen were "working to avail opportunities" for Hamas activists in the West Bank and Gaza so that when Hamas students studying in Sudan return to the Palestinian territories "they will act as our eyes and ears."[33]

Other groups have recruited students in Sudan as well, as highlighted by the December 21, 2004, suicide bombing of a U.S. army base in Mosul, Iraq, that killed twenty-two people. The attack, claimed by the al-Qaeda affiliated Ansar al-Sunna, was executed by a Saudi who was a second-year medical student at Sudan's Khartoum University. Radicalized at the university, the student told his family of his intentions to drop out of school and fight in Iraq and did so despite their protestations.[34]

Libya

Libya is perhaps best known for orchestrating the terrorist operations against Pan Am flight 103 (1988) and UTA flight 772 (1989), which killed 270 and

170 people respectively. Throughout the 1990s, Libya also made several public statements in support of violence against Israel. In 2001, the State Department noted in its annual *Patterns of Global Terrorism* report that Libya had "contact with groups that use violence to oppose the Middle East Peace Process." The State Department still lists Libya as a state sponsor of terrorism, even though the most recent report cites improvement. The 5,000 Libyans who assembled in Tripoli to protest the assassination of Hamas leader Sheik Ahmed Yassin suggest that strong sympathies for Hamas still exist in Libya today.[35]

The most clear and recent case of Libyan sponsorship of terrorism is dictator Moammar Gadhafi's involvement in ordering the plotted assassination of Saudi Crown Prince Abdullah. Abdurahman M. Alamoudi admitted in his plea agreement with a U.S. court that he was ordered by Gadhafi to help orchestrate the assassination and was provided by the Libyan leader with $340,000 toward that end. Alamoudi also served as a conduit for Libyan funds intended for Hamas. When Alamoudi was caught, he admitted that he had previously received funds from the World Islamic Call Society (WICS), usually in the range of $10,000 to $20,000. WICS was originally established by Gadhafi to function as a way to export Libya's particular brand of radical Islamic-socialist ideology abroad. A portion of WICS's endowment stems from the Jihad Fund, which was a Libyan payroll tax first levied in 1970 to provide assistance to the Palestinian struggle against Israel. Alamoudi himself was a member of the World Islamic Call Council, which is charged with the duty of implementing the programs drafted by the WICS conference.[36]

Alamoudi deposited funds he received from WICS in banks located in Saudi Arabia. This money would be laundered back to accounts in the United States in smaller sums to be used at the discretion of Alamoudi and the various organizations with which he was associated. A draft letter from Alamoudi (writing as president of the American Muslim Foundation) to Mohammad Ahmed al-Sharif, secretary general of the International Islamic Dawa Association (another name for WICS), states that the AMF used such funds to purchase an office building in May 2002. The building was to serve as the permanent headquarters of the AMF, the American Muslim Council (AMC), and the Hajj Foundation, all organizations under Alamoudi's influence and all suspected of ties to Hamas. The building was bought with interest-free loans from the Saudi Islamic Development Bank and the Saudi Economic Development Company (SEDCO). Money was also transferred from the Success Foundation and Happy Hearts Trust—

two organizations that were also housed in AMC's building and on whose boards Alamoudi sat—to the Humanitarian Relief Association, an organization shut down on suspicion of funneling money to Hamas. Bank records for the Happy Hearts Trust also revealed that funds were transferred to accounts in the names of Human Appeal International-Jordan (HAI) and Association de Secours Palestinien (ASP). HAI has a close relationship to Hamas and the Holy Land Foundation for Relief and Development (HLFRD), which gave large amounts of money to HAI. ASP is the leading Hamas fundraising organization in Switzerland.[37]

Libya has ties to other Hamas activists in the United States as well. The five Elashi brothers involved in the Infocom case (*U.S. v. Bayan Elashi*), who were charged with laundering funds to Hamas, illegally shipped computers to Libya. One of their cousins, Nadia, is the wife of Hamas leader Mousa Abu Marzook; the Marzooks initially invested $250,000 in the company. Interestingly, Marzook and Alamoudi both worked at the Virginia-based United Association for Studies and Research (UASR) in Springfield at the same time. UASR describes itself as a Muslim American think tank, but federal prosecutors and congressional investigators have demonstrated its links to Hamas. Finally, despite recent Libyan efforts to rejoin the international community and escape the shadow of its history of supporting terrorism, Israeli intelligence officials believe that some of the weapons Hamas continues to smuggle into Gaza from Egypt may originate in Libya.[38]

STATE FACILITATORS OF TERRORISM

Saudi Arabia

In 2003, a senior U.S. official assessed that as much as half of Hamas' income may come from the Persian Gulf, much of it from the Kingdom of Saudi Arabia. Indeed, Israeli intelligence analysts calculated in 2002 that at the time as much as 40 percent to 50 percent of the Hamas budget came from the Gulf. According to Israeli information dating from 2003, Saudi Arabian aid to the Hamas dawa alone—aside from any other covert aid directly to Izz al-Din al-Qassam military elements—totaled $12 million a year. Such support came from a variety of sources, including official Saudi government coffers, the accounts of the royal family, and from the largess of wealthy and influential members of the Saudi elite. Whatever the specific source, financing Hamas and other terrorist groups has been possible only because such activity is tolerated by the Saudi regime.[39] As a report authored by the Center for Strategic and International Studies concluded:

Little or no effort was made to monitor the extent to which foreign "charities" raised money for political movements in Europe, the Middle East, and Asia that were far more extreme (and sometimes violent) than would have been tolerated in Saudi Arabia. The government turned a blind eye to the flow of funds to movements like Hamas that mixed charitable with terrorist activities in Israel. Extremists and terrorists learned to exploit this situation, using formal charities or personal requests for charitable aid to obtain money they would never have gotten if they announced their real purpose in seeking funds. At the same time, some real charities had a strong political orientation and often supported extremist movements and some donors knowingly gave money to "charities" that were extremist fronts. This was particularly true in the case of money going to Palestinian causes, after the beginning of the Second Intifada in the fall of 2000. Saudis saw Israel as an occupying nation constantly using excessive force against Palestinian freedom fighters—virtually the opposite image from Americans who saw them as terrorists. The exploitation of individualized charity resulted in massive amounts of money flowing out to extremists, and sometimes terrorist movements, through sheer negligence, fraud, or under the guise of charity.[40]

As early as 1994, Palestinian sources noted that "the widespread belief is that Hamas has received money [from] the governments of Saudi Arabia and some Gulf states," adding that such support was believed to have continued after the Persian Gulf War "as a way of punishing the PLO for its support of Iraq during the Gulf crisis." In 1997, Italian press reports cited unnamed Palestinian officials who complained, "Riyadh's help to Hamas has grown with the opening of new [financial] channels," and revealed that "over 140 billion lire has been collected in Saudi Arabia and the other oil monarchies." In September 2003, U.S. officials noted in congressional testimony that despite some success in curbing terror financing, "by no means have we crossed the bridge of the issue of terrorist financing emanating from Saudi Arabia." In testimony on efforts to target Hamas financing, a senior Treasury official noted that not only is it "not a crime to give to Hamas in Saudi Arabia," but also that "Hamas during the Hajj alone raises enormous amounts of money and sends their political director there." The official went on to confirm that the Saudi royal family "established by royal edict" special accounts for humanitarian assistance to Palestinians called "Accounts 98." These accounts, according to U.S. officials testifying in September 2003, "are alive and well" and are still feared to be sources of Hamas "blood money."[41]

Beyond raising funds at the Hajj, Hamas also recruits Palestinians making the religious pilgrimage to the Saudi Arabian city of Mecca. For example, in July 2003, Israeli officials arrested four members of a Hamas cell in the Galilee, two of whom were Israeli Arabs recruited in Mecca. Other Palestinian terrorist groups have also used the Hajj as a recruitment venue. For example, in October 2001, the Israeli Shin Bet arrested Hezbollah member Suleiman Ahmad Suleiman Rizek of Jerusalem for allegedly spying on Israel and recruiting other terrorists. It came out after his arrest that Rizek was recruited by Hezbollah while attending the Hajj in February 2001. A year after Rizek's arrest, the Shin Bet arrested a Hamas member in the Gaza Strip named Ahmed Awiti, who was also recruited by Hezbollah during the Hajj and subsequently underwent military training in Lebanon. Palestinian Islamic Jihad recruited an Israeli-Arab making a pilgrimage to Mecca in 2002, and upon his return to Israel, the man in turn recruited his cousins to assist him in scouting locations for suicide attacks. The cousins were arrested in March 2003.[42]

Canadian intelligence identifies Saudi Arabia as a crucial source of Hamas' foreign funding. A 2002 Canadian Secret Intelligence Service (CSIS) intelligence report, *Terrorist Group Profiler: Hamas,* notes that "financial support is also received from the government of Saudi Arabia, as well as charities in France, Britain, Germany and North America." According to Israeli intelligence analysts, some charities in Saudi Arabia and elsewhere in the Gulf fund Hamas out of affinity with the group's Muslim Brotherhood ideology. In other cases, "Hamas members [are] believed to have infiltrated humanitarian organizations in the Gulf."[43]

Palestinian sources have long complained about Saudi funding of Hamas, which both bypassed and undermined the Palestinian Authority. In January 1999, Palestinian security officers reported to their superiors that Hamas's Orphan Care Society in Bethlehem "received the sum of $35,000 from Saudi Arabia without informing the [Palestinian] Ministry of Endowments." In response, the officers were instructed a few days later to "thoroughly investigate the information and supply us with your results as soon as possible, since the matter is extremely important." In 2000, long before his brief tenure as Palestinian prime minister or his subsequent election as Palestinian president, Mahmoud Abbas complained to Saudi authorities about the Kingdom's direct funding of Hamas. Israeli forces uncovered a letter from Abbas to Prince Salman, the governor of Riyadh, complaining about Saudi funding for Hamas. In the letter, dated December 2000 and marked "personal," Abbas noted that "the Saudi committee responsible for transferring the contributions to beneficiaries is sending large sums to radical committees and associations including the Islamic Association [al-Jamiya al-Islamiya] which belongs to Hamas, the al-Islah Society, and brothers belonging to the Jihad in all areas."[44]

While much financial aid for Hamas from within the Kingdom is not directly tied to the government or the royal family, some of it is. Among the documents seized by Israel were thank-you letters from heads of Hamas-affiliated West Bank charity committees addressed to Saudi officials, including King Fahd, thanking the regime for its support for the orphans of martyrs and for fighters wounded in the Intifada. Israeli forces also found an internal Palestinian Preventive Security Apparatus memorandum dated February 2001 noting that "about a month ago, financial aid was transferred to detainees in prisons [in Israel]. The source of this aid is in Saudi Arabia. Saudi Arabia refused to give this money to the Palestinian Authority out of fear that the money may not reach the detainees." The Saudi Committee for the Support of the al-Aqsa Intifada, a governmental committee established in September 2000 and headed by Saudi Interior Minister Prince Nayef bin Abdel Aziz, reportedly raised more than $100 million in its first two years of operations, much of which went directly to Hamas. According to a sworn declaration by the chief banking officer of the Arab Bank made on November 11, 2004, "beginning in December of 2000, the Saudi Committee made approximately 200,000 payments into Palestine through Arab Bank branches totaling over US$90,000,000." The Committee's website declared that it provided $5,333 to the family of every Palestinian killed in the Intifada—regardless of whether those killed were victims or died in the process of trying to kill others—totaling disbursements of $133 million as of May 2002. The Committee raised most of its funds through fundraising drives in Saudi Arabia but was also a member of the Union of Good, the umbrella organization funding Hamas.[45]

Between the time of its founding and August 2000, the Saudi Committee for the Support of the al-Aqsa Intifada transferred funds to Palestinian families either directly into the bank accounts of the families of martyrs, prisoners, and wounded, or through Hamas charitable fronts in the PA-administered territories, which served as intermediaries. The al-Tadhoman Charitable Society, a Hamas organization in Nablus, was one of the intermediaries used by the Saudi Committee to disburse funds to families in the Nablus area. Al-Tadhoman's collaboration with the Saudi Committee is evident from documents contained in an al-Tadhoman folder detailing the transfer of funds from the Saudi Committee to Palestinian families. Tables found in this folder include lists of martyrs' names, personal information about the martyrs, the beneficiaries' names, the bank in which the money was deposited, and how much money the beneficiary was awarded. For example, among the beneficiaries of the Saudi committee were Ashraf Mohammad Subhi Mahmoud Sayyid and Hamed Falah Mustafa Abu Hajlah. Sayyid killed an Israeli civilian in a Hamas suicide bombing in the Jordan Valley on August 8, 2001. Abu Hajlah wounded sixteen Israeli civilians in a suicide car bombing in Netanya on January 1, 2001.[46]

In early 2002, Crown Prince Abdullah was reported to have officially withdrawn the Kingdom's support for Hamas. But the "Accounts 98," created by the government to funnel money to Palestinian organizations, continued to fund groups like Hamas. In fact, ten months after the crown prince supposedly withdrew his support for Hamas, the group's leader, Khaled Mishal, was an honored guest in Saudi Arabia at the annual conference of the World Assembly of Muslim Youth. The following year the crown prince personally attended the Sharm al-Sheikh peace summit convened by President Bush. There the president stressed the need for Arab states to crack down on funding and other support for terrorist groups like Hamas. Bush specifically thanked the Saudi crown prince for attending the summit and noted that all the leaders at the summit "declared their firm rejection of terror, regardless of its justifications or motives." The president added, "they've also committed to practical actions to use all means to cut off assistance, including arms and financing to any terror group, and to aid the Palestinian Authority in their own fight against terror." But later that same month, Saudi spokesman Adel al-Jubeir conceded that "a lot of the [Palestinian] institutions" that continued to be funded by Saudi Arabia "may be run or managed by the political wing of Hamas."[47]

Ironically, the Saudi decision to tolerate (and at times participate in) Hamas fundraising in the Kingdom turned out to be a double-edged sword. By turning a blind eye to the jihadist militarism they were supporting, Saudi authorities indirectly contributed to the radicalization of Saudi society and the proliferation of violent jihadists within their own borders. In the wake of the September 11th attacks, and especially after the al-Qaeda attacks in Saudi Arabia in May and November 2003, the ramification of this policy came full circle. As a report by the Center for Strategic and International Studies notes, "The Saudi security services failed to fully appreciate the threat posed by the flow of Saudi money to Palestinian groups like Hamas, and Palestinian Islamic Jihad, and other hard-line or violent Islamic elements in countries like Egypt, and failed to detect a significant flow of arms, explosives, and terrorist supplies into Saudi Arabia from neighboring countries like Yemen."[48]

A 2004 Council on Foreign Relations report on terror financing notes Saudi progress in the war on terror financing, but adds that "in Saudi Arabia, whose people and organizations may contribute as much as 60 percent of Hamas's annual budget, the government still does not recognize Hamas as a terrorist organization, notwithstanding important recent steps, such as the announced cessation of official efforts to raise money for the families of Palestinian suicide bombers." Writing in October 2004, well after the onset of a severe Saudi counterterrorism campaign targeting militants and curbing terror financing, the Arab columnist Abd al-Rahman al-Rashed wrote, "Now, many cases have been uncovered where the people's money was found in the terrorists' pockets—[Saudi] Riyals and Dollars—some of it still inside charity boxes labeled 'Palestine' and 'Chechnya.'" Predicting a long and difficult road ahead in the war on terror financing, the journalist concluded: "In the Persian Gulf countries, as long as the preachers associated with those [terrorist] movements are able to find sufficient money and enthusiastic youngsters, they will have the means to perpetrate acts of terrorism against those who previously assisted them." A former senior U.S. official in charge of combating terror financing described Saudi cooperation on terror financing in the period leading up to the May 2003 al-Qaeda attack in the Saudi capital this way: "selectively cooperative leaning on the disingenuous."

Following that and subsequent terrorist attacks within the Kingdom, Saudi authorities took action against al-Qaeda financiers and, consequentially, severely curtailed the funding these financiers provided to Hamas as well. By restricting Islamist charities that fund both al-Qaeda and Hamas, like the World Assembly of Muslim Youth (WAMY) and the International Islamic Relief Organization (IIRO), funding for Hamas from the Kingdom all but dried up for a while. According to an Israeli report, in the second half of 2004 "Saudi authorities began severely limiting charitable money transfers from their country to Hamas institutions in the PA-administered territories." But while Saudi authorities did take several proactive steps against terror financing—including restricting charities to maintaining a single account from which funds can be withdrawn, and eliminating cash disbursements from charitable accounts—many of their most significant anti-terror promises were not implemented. Saudi authorities had committed to setting up a Financial Intelligence Unit (FIU) but failed to do so; an oversight commission for charities was also promised but was not established. In any event, the commission would have been of limited use even if established because some of the most significant charities in need of oversight, including WAMY and the Muslim World League, were expressly excluded from the commission's purview.[49]

Funding for terrorist groups, including Hamas, continues to flow from within the Kingdom—albeit at a slower pace. Thus in April 2005, while the president hosted the crown prince at his Texas ranch, a bipartisan coalition of twenty-two legislators sponsored a bill in the United States Congress sanctioning Saudi Arabia for failing to put an end to the financing of terrorist groups from within the Kingdom. "Saudi Arabia has pledged for years to put an end to its support of terror," the coalition's statement read. "But Saudi Arabia provides more than 50 percent of funding to the Palestinian terrorist organization Hamas, as well as financial support to the families of Palestinian suicide bombers."[50]

If anything, Hamas activity within the Kingdom appears to be on the rise. In September 2005, Israeli authorities announced the arrest of an Israeli-Arab Hamas activist who played central militant, political, and financing roles for the group in coordination with a "Hamas command in Saudi Arabia." Until he was arrested in August 2005, Yakub Mohammad Yakub Abu Etzev was in contact with senior Hamas officials in Saudi Arabia via e-mail. According to Israeli authorities, "Abu Etzev confessed that he received hundreds of thousands of dollars from the Hamas HQ in Saudi Arabia as well as instructions that he passed on to Hamas field operatives." These funds entered the West Bank through human couriers and money changers, often under the cover of charity work. The Hamas office in Saudi Arabia reportedly instructed Abu Etzev to open a "communications office" to report on developments on the ground to Hamas operatives abroad. The group's leaders in Saudi Arabia provided the funding for this venture, as well as funding for the families of suicide terrorists and imprisoned terrorists and a variety of Hamas institutions.[51]

Yemen

Hamas maintains an official representation office in Yemen, which functions openly as a legal entity there. The office enjoys close ties to senior Yemeni officials and its head is treated like an ambassador. The office was headed for several years by Sheikh Mohammad Siyam and then by Muneer Sayid. Siyam was described by the head of Hamas' al-Aqsa International Foundation office in Yemen as "the spokesman of Hamas" and was known to travel the world raising funds for the group. Yemen's cozy relationship with Hamas is hardly surprising, given the ideological positions of President Ali Abdullah Salih. In an interview with the al-Jazeera satellite television station just days before the attacks of September 11, Salih acknowledged that his government supports all Palestinian factions, including Hamas and Islamic Jihad, because their "struggle is legitimate." The Yemeni president rejected the premise that Hamas is a terrorist organization and, asked if Yemen supplies Palestinian terrorist groups with weapons, responded, "We supply the Palestinians with money." Answering a caller's question about the Palestinian Intifada, Salih said Arabs should support the Palestinians financially so they may purchase weapons. In 2002, Salih hosted a visiting delegation of Hamas leaders, including Khaled Mishal, Mousa Abu Marzook, Khaled Nazzal, and Muneer Sayid. The delegation met with many other senior Yemeni officials as well, including the vice president, premier, foreign minister, and parliament speaker. Khaled Mishal described Hamas as enjoying "close ties and continuous contacts" with President Salih and "strong ties" with senior Yemeni Sheikh Abdallah al-Ahmar.[52]

The Islah party, the main Islamist party in Yemen, regularly collects donations for the Palestinian cause in the context of helping Palestinian "*mujahideen.*" Support for Palestinian militancy is a regular theme at the party's rallies, such as the 10,000-person-strong rally just a month after September 11th at which demonstrators asked "Arab and Islamic leaders to open the doors for Jihad, stressing it is the only way to restore al-Quds (Jerusalem)." When Sheik Yassin was killed, thousands of Yemenis demonstrated in solidarity, including at a huge protest rally held at the University in Sanaa where thousands of students called for jihad in chanting, "Vengeance, vengeance, oh Ezzedine Al-Qassam Brigades!" In April 2002, the Islah party held a public demonstration demanding the "opening of the army's centers and camps for training the mujahedin and sending them to Palestine."[53]

As with Sudan, Yemeni universities are popular with both Palestinian students and Hamas activists looking for motivated recruits. According to Israeli military intelligence, "Most of the [Hamas] activists [sent for training in Arab states] are students recruited to the Hamas during their studies in Syria, Yemen, Sudan and other Arab universities." Indeed, President Salih's half-brother, General Ali Mohsen al-Ammar, is suspected of overseeing the training of terrorist recruits. A former associate of Osama bin Laden, alongside whom he fought the Soviet occupation of Afghanistan, General al-Ammar is known for relocating from Afghanistan to Yemen those so-called "Afghan-Arab" mujahideen no longer welcome in their home countries. According to press reports citing Yemeni and Western intelligence sources, the general "was in charge of $20 million supplied by Mr. Bin Laden to help settle Arab Afghan fighters in Yemen." General al-Ammar's ties to radical Islamists were solidified by his marriage to a sister of Tariq Nasr al-Fadhli, a prominent Afghan-Arab militant suspected of leading the cell behind one of the first documented al-Qaeda attacks: the failed attempt in December 1992 to bomb two hotels housing U.S. forces en route to Somalia. According to a primer on General al-Ammar, he "trained partly in Iraq and close to the Yemenite Muslim Brotherhood, he commands the artillery units of the Northern army and is responsible for the defense of the Sanaa district."[54]

In surreptitiously videotaped meetings in a Frankfurt hotel room in early 2003, Sheikh Mohammad al-Moayad and his assistant Sheikh Mohammad Zayed discussed the possibility of obtaining compact disks of military training techniques through General al-Ammar for the purposes of training terrorist recruits. Sheikh Moayad commented that they could seek out a Yemeni officer who took military training courses abroad, and "we'll ask him if he has disks . . . What he has in the area of training." Moayad further considered having General al-Ammar purchase such training material under the name of his military squadron and copying the material for the purpose of terrorist training. "Maybe we can buy them [training material on compact disks] from Europe, here, or there. We are not going to buy. We'll contact Commander Ali Muhsin [al-Ammar]. . . . He is a very nice man and he can purchase in the name of the first squadron. . . . He'll buy in the name of the [Yemeni] Ministry of Foreign Affairs and it'll be shipped to them. And they'll copy them for us."[55]

Training terrorist recruits in Yemen is not uncommon. In January 2005, gunmen fired shots and detonated a bomb at a building housing the ruling party in Yemen, the General People's Congress. The attack was apparent retribution for an article that ran on the party's website the previous month which reported that a "military wing" at the Islamist al-Iman University had called for anti-government demonstrations. The university's founder, Sheikh Abdel Majid al-Zindani, designated a global terrorist by the United States in February 2004, denied that the university has a military wing, but his claim is undermined by the fact that many known jihadists spent time at al-Iman University, including "the American Taliban" John Walker Lindh and Yahya Goba, a convicted member of a terrorist cell in Lackawanna,

New York. Al-Zindani himself actively recruited for al-Qaeda training camps and purchased weapons for al-Qaeda and other terrorists. According to the Treasury Department fact sheet released when al-Zindani was designated a terrorist, "al-Iman students are suspected of being responsible, and were arrested, for recent terrorist attacks, including the assassination of three American missionaries and the assassination of the number two leader for the Yemeni Socialist party, Jarallah Omar." As previously noted, Sheikh Moayad headed the Yemen office of the al-Aqsa International Foundation, a Hamas front organization. Like the Hamas political office in Yemen, this ostensibly charitable office also wears its Hamas affiliation proudly and publicly. Speaking of his knowledge of Hamas needs, and his ability to funnel money to Hamas to fulfill those needs, Moayad commented in the Frankfurt meetings, "In Yemen we have good information regarding what they need in Palestine, it is done through Hamas. Hamas studies which I have to get it and study it and prepare it, and so, etc."[56]

Yemen tolerates a wide array of overt Hamas activity. Yahya Goba, the leader of the Lackawana cell, told the FBI about Hamas events in which he participated while in Yemen. Called as a witness in the case against Sheikhs Moayad and Zayed, Goba recounted attending a three-day rally in 1995 that was co-sponsored by the al-Aqsa Foundation and the Charitable Society for Social Welfare. According to Goba, the event included "a march for the cause, also showed videos, attributes of suicide bombers [sic]. The third day was a speech by the Sheikh Siyam over there . . . the representative for Hamas in Yemen." Money raised at the rally went to the al-Aqsa Foundation. Another major Yemeni event chaired by Sheikh Moayad and addressed by Hamas representative Mohammad Siyam was a "group wedding" for young mujahideen. The wedding was reportedly organized for the benefit of young jihadists who could not afford their own ceremony. Held on September 19, 2002, the wedding coincided with a Hamas suicide bombing in Tel Aviv that killed six people and wounded fifty-two more. In a speech later that afternoon, Hamas representative to Yemen Mohammed Siyam drew a parallel between the group wedding in Yemen and the "wedding" (i.e., terrorist operation) in Tel Aviv:[57]

Either those who organized the [group wedding] celebration found out about the timing of Hamas' operation in Tel Aviv, that it will be today, and this is leaking of the news, so they held the wedding here coinciding with the wedding there. An organized operation, God willing you will hear about it, you will read about it tomorrow in the newspapers and hear about it in the media. It brought down many of the invading occupiers, and thanks be to God, Lord of the Universe.[58]

In their videotaped meetings in Frankfurt, Sheikhs Moayad and Zayed were gleeful at the symmetry of these two near simultaneous "weddings."

CI-1:   He [the other confidential informant, CI-2] was very happy to [unintelligible]. He is expressing his own enthusiasm during the wedding and at the beginning, and especially the speech of the [Hamas] representative [Mohammed Siyam] at the opening and as you know, what had happened the same day, it coincided with the

Zayed: —the operation.

CI-1:   The operation.

Zayed: The suicidal one.

CI-1:   —the suicidal one [translator note: said simultaneously] in a—

Moayad: Yes, ha, ha, ha, [clapping].

CI-1:   In Palestine. All that coincided with the wedding.

Moayad: Two weddings in one time.

CI-1:   Two weddings in one time.[59]

Later, the cooperating informant (CI-1) adds that "the future wedding [operation] is going to be a great happy event for all the Muslims, but the most important thing is nothing should happen in America while I am inside it." Moayad and Zayed laugh, and Moayad adds, "God Willing! Or you could die as a martyr."[60]

Qatar

Qatar allows Hamas to maintain official offices in the country, permits Hamas to fundraise there through charities and telethons, and regularly hosts Hamas officials. When Jordan expelled four Hamas leaders in 1999, Qatar offered to host them: political bureau chief Khaled Mishal, spokesman Ibrahim Ghosheh, and political bureau members Ezzat Rushuq and Sami Khater. Though these Hamas officials were formally banned from any political activity, they were given complete freedom of movement, including the right to enter and exit the country at will. Mishal and other Hamas leaders are now believed to split their time between Qatar and Syria, and freely travel between Doha and Damascus. Mishal discussed Qatar in a 2003 interview with the pan-Arab daily newspaper al-Hayat:[61]

The movement established a relation with Qatar ever since Prince Hamad bin Khalifa was the heir to the crown. A good relation developed with the people of Qatar. After he held the reins of power, the relation remained good. I had a personal relation with the Prince and his Minister of Foreign Affairs, Sheikh Hamad bin Jasem bin Jabr. Our relation with Qatar is not new. When Jordan closed the bureaus of the movement at the end of August, when I was on a visit to Iran, I called a number of Arab countries and told them closing the bureaus is an unjustified step and that we do not want to enter in confrontation with any Arab country. I called Sheikh Hamad and told him what happened. I asked him to deploy an effort to settle this situation. Three weeks later, we went back to Jordan and I was jailed in Jouweida prison with Ibrahim Ghosheh.[62]

The target of at least one Israeli assassination attempt while headquartered in Jordan, Mishal feels more secure in Qatar: "There are regions more secure than others. I have limited my choices between Doha and Damascus. I am settled in Doha and Damascus." As for financial support, Mishal maintains that Qatari money for Hamas does not come from the government but "the aids [sic] come from popular committees and charitable foundations. The Qatari TV might organize a day to support the Intifada and collect donations."[63]

Lebanon

One of the reasons Lebanon is a perennial candidate for the State Department's list of state terrorism sponsors is its long history of serving as a platform for terror attacks against Israel. Occupied by Syria for thirty years until the April 2005 withdrawal of Syrian military and intelligence forces, Lebanon remains under the influence of Damascus through Lebanese proxies aligned with Syria. In fact, Damascus' manipulation by Syria is likely the primary reason Lebanon has not been added to the state sponsors list. This political conundrum notwithstanding, the fact remains that Beirut recognizes as legitimate several groups targeting the Jewish state, despite their being designated as terrorist groups by the United States and other Western nations. The 2004 edition of the State Department's annual *Patterns of Global Terrorism* report notes that Beirut continues to demonstrate an unwillingness to rein in terror groups. It allows Hamas and other Palestinian groups to maintain offices in Lebanon, engage in terrorist training, and obtain arms from Iran via the Lebanese Shi'a terrorist organization Hezbollah. The report is corroborated by Canadian intelligence, which also believes Lebanon houses Hamas training camps. And citing "a Western intelligence agency," the *Beirut Daily Star*, Lebanon's English language daily, reported in 2002 that "a detachment of Iranian Revolutionary Guards (IRG) are in Lebanon training elite units of Hizbullah and Palestinian fighters to fire rockets and carry out underwater suicide operations."[64]

Beirut also refuses to take action against Hamas fundraising there. Indeed, the government provides "legal resistance groups" with exemptions from existing money laundering and terrorism-financing laws. In October 2003, the Lebanese National Assembly authorized two bills that were supposed to bolster existing money laundering and terrorist financing laws. A special investigations commission reviewed 245 cases, including 22 linked to terrorist finances. The commission found no accounts used for financing terrorism—as defined by the Lebanese government. In 2003, when the Central Bank requested all Lebanese financial institutions to name accounts held by six Hamas leaders so designated by the United States—Sheikh Ahmed Yassin, Imad al-Alami, Osama Hamdan, Khaled Mishal, Mousa Abu Marzook, and Abdel Aziz al-Rantissi—a public backlash prompted the Lebanese government to shut down the investigation.[65]

Lebanon turns a willful blind eye to the extensive Hamas financial activity in Lebanon. Consider the case of Jamal Tawil, the Hamas military commander from Ramallah profiled in Chapter 2. Arrested in April 2002, Tawil received funds from Hamas political leaders in Syria and Lebanon on a monthly basis. In his interrogation, Tawil informed that starting in March 1998, Abu Ahmed (believed to be Ismael Srour, head of the Hamas propaganda bureau in Lebanon) would send him monthly bank transfers of $12,000 for Hamas activities—first into his personal account and then later onto the account of the al-Islah Charitable Society—the Hamas charity Tawil ran. Hamas also runs charitable front organizations in Lebanon, through which it targets the local Palestinian refugee population to support, if not join, Hamas. For example, the U.S. Treasury Department has highlighted the since-defunct Sanabil charity, which increased its influence in Palestinian refugee camps in Lebanon by first providing basic necessities to needy families and only later requiring these families to fill out application forms noting whether they had ever worked with Hamas. Much like Hamas efforts to buy the support of Palestinians on the ground in the West Bank and Gaza, Hamas largesse in Lebanon is geared toward building grassroots support for the group at the expense of rival Islamist organizations in places like the Ein al-Hilweh Palestinian refugee camp. While Hamas supporters in the camp are known to celebrate Hamas attacks—cars equipped with bullhorns broadcast the news of successful attacks and candy is distributed to passersby—the camp is also the center of intra-Palestinian and intra-Islamist tensions. Hamas and Fatah supporters clash in the camp, as do Hamas supporters and members of the al-Qaeda-affiliated Palestinian group based in Ein al-Hilweh, Osbat al-Ansar.[66]

Osama Hamdan, Hamas' representative in Lebanon, has made comments indicating he has direct command over Hamas terror operations. When asked in October 2004 whether Hamas would strike Israeli interests outside of Israel and the Palestinian territories, he responded, "This issue is being studied now. We hope that the occupation will not succeed in repeating the assassination operation. However, if this happens, it will be one of the factors that influence decision-making. I cannot speak prematurely about what the movement is going to do, but any decision that will be made will be linked to the interests of the Palestinian people and the continuation of the resistance and will provide more protection for the Palestinian people and the resistance." Hamdan has also used the threat of terrorist operations as a negotiating tactic. On March 27, 2002, hours after Saudi Arabia presented a new peace plan at an Arab summit in Beirut, a suicide bomber killed nineteen Israelis at the Park Hotel in Netanya during the Jewish holiday of Passover. Immediately after the bombing, Hamdan appeared on CNN and said, "If they [Israel] continue refusing this proposal, they will not have peace, they will not have security, and the Palestinians will continue their struggle." According to information available to the U.S. government, Hamdan "has worked with other Hamas and Hizballah leaders on initiatives to develop and activate the military network inside the Palestinian territories in support of the current Intifada, including the movement of weapons, explosives and personnel to the West Bank and Gaza for Hamas fighters."[67]

Jordan

Jordan is not properly described as a "facilitator" of terrorism. Hamas activists are active in Jordan, though their activities there are both constrained and closely monitored. Unlike other countries where Hamas is active but enjoys official sanction, Jordan maintains a policy of zero tolerance for Hamas operational or overt logistical or financial support activity there. Despite restrictions, Hamas does conduct clandestine activity in Jordan, including transiting operatives en route to training elsewhere in the Middle

East (especially in Syria, Lebanon, and Iran), financial and logistical support operations, weapons smuggling, ad hoc training in Jordan, and recruitment of Palestinian students studying at Jordanian universities—as was the case with Abbas al-Sayyid, the Hamas commander behind the Park Hotel suicide bombing.

8

will hamas target the west?

On March 22, 2004, Israeli security forces assassinated Hamas founder Sheikh Ahmed Yassin. His deputy and successor, Abdel Aziz al-Rantissi, issued a statement implying that Hamas would avenge Yassin's death with attacks on Israel—and on the United States. "The war against Islam is the same war which is launched in Iraq," al-Rantissi proclaimed. "In Palestine also, there is a war against Islam. So, the Islamic nation should wake up and shake the land under the feet of those Zionists and the Americans who back them." Though al-Rantissi withdrew the threat the next day, the State Department immediately issued a travel advisory warning Americans of possible terrorist threats. The advisory warned: "In the aftermath of the killing of Hamas leader Sheikh Ahmed Yassin, a Hamas spokesman has threatened revenge against Israel and U.S. interests . . . all U.S. citizens [are urged] to depart Gaza as early as it is safe to do so." Four weeks later, on April 17, al-Rantissi himself was killed by an Israeli rocket in a targeted assassination. At the funeral procession, a masked Hamas member in camouflage told the *Washington Post*, "Bush stands next to Sharon and after that they assassinate Rantisi." The militant said he believed it was meaningful that American and Israeli leaders had met just prior to the attack. "We should carry our fight against the Americans as much as we are against Israel," concluded the militant. "Israel and America share the same face." Hamas political leader Khaled Mishal also blamed America for the assassination, suggesting that Bush had endorsed the missile attack during a White House meeting with Sharon. "What Bush told Sharon in the White House three days ago is the clearest green light and cover for Sharon's crimes and for what has happened to Dr. Abdel Aziz al-Rantissi. Thus, it [the United States] is the one responsible for this crime."[1]

U.S. authorities take the Hamas threat seriously, particularly because Hamas has threatened U.S. interests in the past. For example, on December 18, 2001, Hamas issued a statement warning that "Americans [are] now considered legitimate targets as well as Israelis." In June 2002, an official Hamas website featured a chat room discussion in which participants discussed various ways to kill a hypothetical group of American citizens in Israel proper or the Gaza Strip. Among the proposed ways to dispose of the Americans was running over the "American dogs," throwing a Molotov cocktail at their cars, burning them in their cabin on the beach, poisoning them, or shooting them "as an example for others like them." Such murders, said one participant, would make "Americans understand they are not safe in Muslim countries."[2]

Despite such expression of violent anti-Americanism, Hamas has not joined al-Qaeda's global jihad. It has not yet bought into the strategy (shared by many other outgrowths of the Muslim Brotherhood) that militants can best undermine local governments by targeting the Western powers that support them. Despite shared ideological roots with al-Qaeda-affiliated groups like the Egyptian Islamic Group, Hamas sees itself as a local "resistance" organization and has traditionally limited its operations to targeting Israelis in Israel, the West Bank, and the Gaza Strip. While many foreigners have died in Hamas attacks, these have been incidental casualties of the group's indiscriminate terrorist attacks, not intentionally targeted victims. But there is reason to question whether Hamas' local focus will continue, or if—and under what conditions—Hamas may expand its focus to include targeting Western interests. Nor is the prospect of such an expansion of targets determined solely by Hamas' top leadership. Indeed, it is far more likely that intentional attacks on Western interests would be the work of Hamas cells or individual members acting independently—either completely on their own or with tacit approval from Hamas leaders. Not only could a change in Hamas modus operandi occur at multiple decision-making levels, it could target Western interests in one of several ways. Hamas activists may target Israeli or Jewish interests abroad, target U.S. or other Western interests in Israel and the Palestinian territories, or target Western interests abroad.

ANTI-WESTERN RHETORIC

When asked, Hamas leaders typically say the group's terrorist operations are strictly limited to Israel, the West Bank, and Gaza Strip. In a March 2004 interview following the Israeli assassination of Hamas founder Sheikh

Ahmed Yassin, Khaled Mishal insisted, "Our strategy hasn't changed. We will not shift the battle outside of Palestine." That same day, Hamas leaders Abdel Aziz al-Rantissi and Mahmoud al-Zahar also emphasized this position to reporters. Al-Rantissi said, "We are inside Palestinian land and acting only inside Palestinian land. We are resisting the occupation, nothing else. Our resistance will continue just inside our border, here inside our country." Al-Zahar told an American journalist, "You (Americans) are people innocent of the Zionist conspiracy that is fooling you and is stealing your money. You are not our target."[3]

But the string of denials was itself prompted by earlier statements suggesting that Hamas was considering American targets. Immediately following Yassin's assassination al-Rantissi stated, "We knew that Bush is the enemy of God, the enemy of Islam and Muslims, Bush and Sharon. The war of God continues against them and I can see the victory coming up from the land of Palestine by the hands of Hamas." Rantissi quickly withdrew his implicit threat, however, as the implications of making veiled threats to American interests settled in. Within days he issued a new statement, saying, "If they (Americans) are worried, then they are stupid because we have said it many times that we will target only our enemy, the (Israeli) occupiers." Still, al-Rantissi's own promotion of an ideology founded on deep hatred for America and the West belies his supposed indifference to the United States as a target. For example, after the 2003 Columbia space shuttle disaster, al-Rantissi said, "the explosion of the shuttle Columbia is, it is reasonable to assume, part of the divine punishment of America and, together with it, Zionism—because of their massacres of Muslims, the destruction of their lives, the humiliation of their honor, and their desire to globalize corruption." Later, in April 2004, al-Rantissi said, "We say to the Muslim people of Iraq, we are with you in your struggle against American terror and destruction, we are with you in your war in defense of Islam. We say to the fighter and commander Mokutada a-Sadr: Hamas stands by your side and blesses your Jihad and wishes you with the help of God, that you will win and be victorious." In July 2005, a Hamas-run radio station in Gaza, *Sawt al-Aqsa*, broadcast this same anti-American message: "We [Hamas] are with Iraq and with the people of Iraq; we are against America and against Britain. Thus, jihad continues and the Intifada continues, and the next breakthrough will take place in Jaffa." Indeed, there does appear to be an internationalization of the Israeli-Palestinian conflict taking place in the Palestinian territories. In the years following the September 2000 outbreak of the Intifada, pamphlets, posters, and compact disks featuring Hamas leaders alongside leaders of the Iraqi insurgency and Chechen terrorists have appeared throughout the West Bank. Rallies and protests in the West Bank and Gaza Strip increasingly feature protestors chanting anti-American slogans like "Death to America from Jerusalem to Baghdad" in front of burning Israeli, British, and American flags.[4]

Hamas leaders often lay blame for Israeli military operations at the feet of the United States, pointing out that Israel buys most of its advanced weaponry from America. When al-Rantissi was assassinated, Khaled Mishal dubbed Bush's purported support for the assassination a "war declaration (against the Islamic nation) by this evil administration in the United States which is . . . allied with the evil entity led by Sharon." Hamas increased its threatening rhetoric in the months following the Yassin and al-Rantissi assassinations, as Israel expanded the scope of its operations and began targeting the group's operatives not only in the West Bank and Gaza Strip but also in neighboring Lebanon and Syria. In September 2004, an explosion in Damascus presumably coordinated by Israeli agents killed Hamas operative Izzaddin Sheikh Khalil. In December of that year, a bomb nearly killed Musbah Abou-Houwaileh, another Hamas operative in Syria. After the first Syrian bombing, Mousa Abu Marzook said, "now that Israel has expanded its war against Hamas to include neighboring countries, there are many voices calling for attacking Israeli targets abroad." Hamas' Qassam Brigades issued a statement warning that their previous policy of letting "hundreds of thousands of Zionists travel and move in capitals of the world" may have to change now that "the Zionist enemy has opened a new door for the struggle by transferring the battle outside Palestine."[5]

Hamas officials acknowledge they had considered attacks abroad even before the Israeli operation in Syria. In September 2002, Hamas official Mohammad Nazzal declared, "Until today, the issue of carrying the fight outside Palestine is under study and no decision has been taken in that sense." Indeed, the U.S.-led war on terror appears to have instigated an internal Hamas debate regarding the targeting of Americans. On December 17, 2001, Hamas and Palestinian Islamic Jihad operatives released a joint manifesto declaring, "Americans are the enemies of the Palestinian people." The manifesto went on to proclaim that Americans "are a target for future attacks." Also in December, "sources in the Hamas military wing" informed a *Time* magazine correspondent that "somewhere in a Hamas safe house, militants inflamed by the American war in Afghanistan are debating whether it is time to add U.S. targets in Israel and the territories to their hit list." The July 31, 2002, suicide bombing at Jerusalem's Hebrew University was indication to some Hamas-watchers that the hardliners may have gained the upper hand in this debate. Five Americans were killed and four wounded in the Hamas attack, which targeted a location known for its large population of American and other foreign students. According to U.S. officials privy to the investigation into the attack, there was reason to believe Hamas had calculated the likelihood that Americans would be killed or injured.[6]

American authorities take Hamas threats against Western interests seriously, even though such threats have historically proven to have more bark than bite. In April 2004, the FBI noted that Hamas does maintain the capacity to carry out terrorist attacks in the United States. The Bureau concluded that Hamas has operatives stationed in the United States, though the terrorist group did not then appear intent on acting on its military capability. The FBI reasoned that Hamas relies on America primarily as a fundraising base, and is loath to risk its financing infrastructure in the United States; conducting attacks on U.S. soil would place Hamas in the crosshairs of the U.S.-led global war on terror. And indeed, Hamas leaders have a long record of issuing empty threats against Western interests, typically in response to actions that have targeted Hamas leaders. One of the earliest threats Hamas issued against American interests, for example, came after the 1995 arrest of Hamas leader Mousa Abu Marzook in New York City on immigration charges. Marzook was detained for twenty-two months as authorities considered deporting him to Israel to face charges there. A Hamas statement issued at the time warned that the group had taken "the decision to strike and to hit back if the United States makes this move." But in 1997, Marzook was deported to Jordan instead, and nothing came of the Hamas threat.[7]

CAUGHT IN THE ACT

Given their history of empty-seeming threats, the conventional wisdom is that anti-Western rhetoric by Hamas leaders is more designed to radicalize new recruits than promote actual attacks. That assumption came under considerable pressure in 2003, when Israeli officials arrested a man named Jamal Akal and discovered that Hamas had, in fact, planned attacks in North America. In 1999, Jamal Akal left the Nuseirat refugee camp in the Gaza Strip where he was born and emigrated to Ontario, Canada. There he enrolled at the University of Windsor, began studying for a degree in social work, and became a Canadian citizen. Akal appeared to be a model immigrant, and returned to Gaza in October 2003, ostensibly to find a Palestinian bride. It would later come out that his month in Gaza was not devoted to romantic pursuits.[8]

On November 1, 2003, Israeli authorities arrested Akal as he was leaving Gaza en route back to Canada. Israeli authorities charged that Akal's ostensible social visit was a ruse; his real object was not a bride but training for Hamas operations in Canada and the United States. A lawyer hired by Akal's family conceded that Akal had been approached by Hamas operatives in Gaza about conducting operations in Canada. The attorney acknowledged that Akal was trained in the use of small arms during his visit but insisted Akal did not agree to carry out the plans. Whether or not Akal agreed to execute the mission, the admission that Hamas attempted to recruit a Palestinian with citizenship in a Western country to carry out attacks in that country would appear to mark a significant departure in Hamas modus operandi.[9]

According to Israeli authorities, Akal admitted that during his month in Gaza he was trained in explosives production and taught to use an M-16 assault rifle by a Hamas operative named Ahmed Wahabe. Wahabe allegedly tasked Akal to return home and "gather information (via the media) on a senior Israeli official who was arriving in the United States. Wahabe instructed Akal to then monitor the senior Israeli official's movements and attempt to assassinate her in a sniper attack. Wahabe also asked Akal to attack members of the U.S. and Canadian Jewish communities, either by shooting or by bombing their homes and/or cars. According to information released by Israeli authorities, "Wahabe told Akal (inter alia): 'New York is an easy place to find Jews.'" In a statement issued by the Israeli Embassy in Ottawa, an Israeli official confirmed that Akal was to use his Canadian passport to "carry out terrorist attacks in North America against Israeli and Jewish targets. . . . Some of the scenarios for those terrorist attacks were assassinating a high-level Israeli official during his visit to North America, booby-trapping cars that belong to Israeli officials—diplomats—and killing a Jew who would come across Mr. Akal's way."[10]

Akal was specifically instructed to draw on the support of Hamas sympathizers in Canada to fund his attacks. According to an Israeli report, he was to contact worshipers in Canadian mosques and "raise funds, ostensibly for the families of suicide bombers, which he would actually use for purchasing a weapon and financing his expenses in monitoring his prospective targets and in perpetrating attacks." At the time of Akal's arrest, he and Wahabe were allegedly awaiting approval from Hamas political leaders in Damascus to conduct the attacks under al-Qaeda's name, not Hamas', in an effort to evade the potential blowback of conducting such attacks in the West. The arrest of Akal confirmed officials' suspicions that Hamas operatives—acting on their own or in concert with Hamas leadership—are willing and able to execute attacks abroad. But the revelation of Hamas' international intentions was the product of increased Israeli monitoring of suspicious foreigners in the wake of an earlier Hamas attack in Tel Aviv perpetrated by two British Muslims of Pakistani origin.[11]

In the early hours of April 30, 2003, two Britons carried out a suicide attack targeting Mike's Place, a bar frequented by Westerners located next to the U.S. Embassy in Tel Aviv. They sat at a table for several hours, waiting for the bar to fill to capacity. Then Asif Hanif, from West London, detonated his suicide vest just outside the bar, killing three people and injuring sixty-five others. Omar Sharif, from Derby, fled the scene when his explosive device malfunctioned. Sharif attempted to escape by swimming out to sea, but he was found two weeks later drowned off the Israeli coast. The attack marked the first time Hamas ever deployed foreign, non-Palestinian operatives. British officials believe the pair was first spotted and recruited in Britain and subsequently spent time in Syria, where they met Hamas officials and received training. According to British officials, "The training, reconnaissance and equipping are all factors that indicate that these things did not take place during a single trip to the Middle East." Hamas delayed claiming responsibility for the attack for eleven months, possibly to avoid tilting the then ongoing debate in Britain over whether or not to add Hamas to the British list of terrorist organizations. But in March 2004 Hamas released a ninety-minute video of the bombers' joint living will, asserting that the attacks were timed to the one-year anniversary of the assassination of Ibrahim al-Makdeh, the founder of the Hamas Qassam Brigades. Wearing green Hamas bandanas and standing in front of a portrait of al-Makdeh, the two men smiled, embraced, and announced—in English—that it was "an honor to kill one of those [Jews]." Sharif asserted that they "wanted to offer our souls for the sake of Allah and to get revenge against Jews and Crusaders." Hanif offered a prayer: "Who is Tony Blair and George Bush?" he asked. "I wish for the Almighty God either to guide them, or for his wrath to come down upon them."[12]

According to British authorities, Hamas' decision to recruit, train, and deploy foreign Hamas operatives was a direct result of Israeli counterterrorism measures. In March 2002, attacks on Israeli civilians led to a series of Israeli counterterrorism operations culminating in the reoccupation of several West Bank cities. By the second half of 2002, Israeli military engineers began constructing a security fence separating the West Bank from Israel. As a result of these measures, Hamas and other terrorist groups suddenly found it much harder to execute suicide bombings in Israel. But with their foreign passports, Hanif and Sharif were able to enter Israel from Jordan and cross in and out of the Gaza Strip with ease. Indeed, in the statement it released together with the videotaped living will, Hamas' Qassam Brigades confirmed that the use of foreigners was meant to evade Israeli counterterrorism measures. According to the statement, the use of foreigners as suicide bombers was a message "to the Zionists that Qassam Brigades have many options to fight you as long as you occupy our land and commit massacres."[13]

HAMAS' GLOBAL REACH

The recruitment of British bombers abroad is just the latest evidence that Hamas maintains an international presence capable of facilitating attacks at home or carrying them out abroad. Hamas' international activities explain the group's designation by the U.S. Treasury Department as a terrorist group of "global reach." In 2003, the National Security Council terrorism czar Richard Clarke testified, "al-Qaeda is a small part of the overall challenge we face from radical terrorist groups associated with Islam. Autonomous cells, regional affiliate groups, radical Palestinian organizations, and groups sponsored by Iran's Revolutionary Guards are engaged in mutual support arrangements, including funding." Indeed, the FBI has long warned of the presence of Hamas and other terrorist groups in the United States. In 1999, the FBI's Counterterrorism Threat Assessment and Warning Unit published a report titled "Terrorism in the United States: 30 Years of Terrorism, A Special Retrospective Edition." The report analyzed the U.S. presence and threat from state sponsors, formal terrorist organizations, and loosely affiliated extremists. "Extremist groups such as the Irish Republican Army, Palestinian Hamas, the Egyptian al-Gama al-Islamiyya (IG), and the Lebanese Hizballah have supporters in the United States," the report noted. "The activities of these U.S.-based cells," it continued, "revolve primarily around fund-raising and low-level intelligence gathering." By describing the activities of groups like Hamas as "primarily" involving fundraising and intelligence activities, the report implicitly acknowledged that already in 1999 the FBI was aware such groups were also engaging in other, secondary activities of a potentially operational character. The reference to groups like Hamas engaging in "low-level intelligence gathering" suggests at least some of these groups had an interest in securing pre-operational surveillance for off-the-shelf contingency planning. In other words, while they expressed no immediate interest in conducting operations, they wanted short-notice operational capability should conditions change. The real question, then, is under what conditions might groups like Hamas, that have not traditionally targeted U.S. or Western interests, decide to conduct operations against Western interests?[14]

Testifying before Congress in February 2002, the director of central intelligence, George Tenet, expressed his concern that conditions for such attacks could be in the making. Tenet warned that if groups like Hamas, the Popular Front for the Liberation of Palestine (PFLP), or Palestinian Islamic Jihad "feel that U.S. actions are threatening their existence, they may begin targeting Americans directly, as Hizballah's terrorist wing already does." An internal FBI review concluded in early 2002—right around the time of Tenet's testimony—that 50 to 100 Hamas and Hezbollah operatives had infiltrated into the United States. While primarily engaged in fundraising and logistics, these operatives were reportedly graduates of terrorist and military training camps in Lebanon and other Middle Eastern countries.[15]

To be sure, the phenomenon of mixing terror activity and dawa activism, especially charity work, is not unique to the West Bank and Gaza. Hamas activists working for foreign charities tied to the dawa have also engaged in planning terror operations. According to a 1996 CIA document released in 2003, Mohammad Sa'd Darwishy al-Shazy, a suspected Hamas operative and Human Relief International (HRI) employee in Croatia, plotted terror attacks there in 1993 and used a local charity office and mosque to "promote ideas for terrorist acts." The CIA report cited intelligence indicating that "al-Shazy's group was considering committing anti-Jewish bombings there, and included the heads of the Zagreb offices of the Saudi High Commission and the Kuwaiti Joint Relief Committee, the head of the HRI's Vienna office, and members of the Saudi-based International Islamic Relief Organization and the privately-run Qatar Charitable Society." Also in Croatia, according to the CIA report, the director of the Zagreb office of the Kuwaiti Joint Relief Committee, Professor Sheikh Abu Adil Uthman al-Haydaer, "was described by an associate as a 'powerful Hamas and Muslim Brotherhood member.'" The group also reportedly planned to assassinate a former Algerian prime minister, PLO Chairman Arafat, and to conduct bombings to support the "brother Algerians" in Croatia. Another member of this group, also identified in the intelligence report as a "Hamas official," was listed as a staff member at the HRI (as well as the Qatar Charitable Society) at the time of the above 1993 terror planning meetings.

Though none of the plots discussed by members of this group appear to have been carried out, their intentions, terrorist affiliations, and planning meeting are illuminating.[16]

The CIA report tracked Hamas activity not only in the Balkans but in the Philippines as well. The report warned that the International Islamic Relief Organization (IIRO) office in Manila employed "the majority of Hamas members in the Philippines" and that a "high ranking" IIRO official led Hamas meetings there. Subsequent investigation in several countries, including the United States and Saudi Arabia, has uncovered that the IIRO has ties to al-Qaeda, Hamas, and other groups. Following the December 2005 tsunami that devastated Southeast Asia, the IIRO was reported to have expanded operations in hard-hit parts of Indonesia where it spread an extremist strain of radical Islam. Such activity, U.S. officials warned, has the potential to "justify and support terrorist activities." The CIA's documentation of Hamas activity in Asia correlates with Israeli intelligence assessments that "Hamas officials in Syria are in contact with Islamic organizations in Asia." As noted earlier, American authorities have long been interested in the IIRO; the man who ran some of the charity's offices in Southeast Asia was arrested by U.S. immigration officials and briefly detained in San Francisco in December 1994. Muhammad Jamal Khalifa, bin Laden's brother-in-law and a senior IIRO and al-Qaeda financier, was in the middle of a U.S. fundraising tour when he was detained. Among the material found in his belongings "were extensive discussions of assassination, the use of explosives, military training and jihad as well as details of Islamist movements such as Hamas and Palestinian Islamic Jihad." Khalifa maintained relations with Hamas-affiliated IIRO employees in the Philippines even after he left his position with IIRO to open a local branch of the Muwafaq Foundation.[17]

To be sure, Hamas maintains financial, logistical, and even operational links to a wide array of international terrorist groups. A Hamas delegation participated in the 1995 Islamic People's Congress in Sudan, where they met Osama bin Laden and representatives of Algerian, Pakistani, Tunisian, and other terrorist groups. In Pakistan, the leader of a jihadist organization there openly admitted to having "person-to-person contacts" with other groups, adding, "sometimes fighters from Hamas and Hezbollah help us." Asked where contacts with groups like Hamas and Hezbollah are held, the Pakistani answered, "a good place to meet is in Iran." Offering insight into the importance of interpersonal relationships between members of disparate terrorist groups, he added, "We don't involve other organizations. Just individuals."[18]

In another sign of the group's global reach, Romanian intelligence in 2002 reportedly investigated seventy-three Hamas supporters there, mostly on university campuses. Hamas operatives in Romania were said to operate there "under the screen of the Islamic and Cultural League in Romania." According to their investigation, Romanian intelligence concluded that "Hamas benefits from the logistics of the Islamic and Cultural League" and that Hamas posed a "potential threat" in Romania, "fueled by the possibility of [Hamas] carrying out attacks on Israeli and U.S. interests or objectives worldwide." According to a Romanian security official, Hamas has maintained a presence in that country since 1992. Several leaders of Hamas cells there were expelled over the next decade, and by 2004 leading Romanian officials felt comfortable saying, "the Hamas following within the local Palestinian community is now paralyzed. They are incapable of presenting any danger to Romanian national security."[19]

Hamas supporters abroad have also played distinctly operational roles in Hamas terrorist attacks. Consider the case of Mohammad Qassem Sawalha, the Hamas activist and longtime Muslim leader in Britain highlighted in Chapter 3. According to a U.S. indictment, Sawalha and his co-conspirators actively assisted Hamas activists planning terrorist attacks. Similarly, Marwan Ismail Dahman, a Palestinian-born Spanish engineer, was jailed in May 2005 on suspicion of having helped design a new Qassam rocket for Hamas and Palestinian Islamic Jihad. Police found copies of rocket designs Dahman reportedly faxed to terrorist operatives, as well as corresponding receipts for these faxes in his home in eastern Spain. Dahman admitted to the presiding judge that he approached Hamas and offered technical assistance in redesigning an enhanced rocket after Israel's 2004 assassination of Adnan al-Ghoul, the original architect of the Qassam rocket.[20]

DISINCENTIVES AGAINST ATTACKING THE WEST

Despite its international presence, Hamas has never actually carried out a terrorist attack beyond its traditional area of operations in Israel, the West Bank, and Gaza Strip. Hamas believes itself to be engaged in "resistance," not terrorism. Many supporters of Hamas and other Palestinian terrorist groups condemned the September 11 attacks in the United States (2001), the March 11 attacks in Spain (2004), and the July 7 attacks in Britain (2005). Clearly, maintaining this distinction is paramount for Hamas and its supporters. In assessing the potential threat from Palestinian groups that rely on American dollars, FBI officials concluded that their "extensive fund raising activity itself acts as a disincentive for operational terrorist activity in the United States." Hamas leaders have verbalized this sentiment. According to an FBI summary transcript of the 1993 Hamas meeting in Philadelphia, the participants mentioned "all the [support] activities they are talking about pertain to the activities within the United States. They also mentioned it is not to this best interest [sic] to cause troubles in the American theater."[21]

But U.S. actions taken against Hamas operatives and organizations in the United States in the wake of the September 11 attacks may be slowly removing this disincentive from the Hamas calculus. Chief among these actions are the closure of the Holy Land Foundation for Relief and Development (HLFRD) in December 2001 and issuance of indictments in Dallas and Chicago against prominent Hamas operatives. The Chicago indictment in particular lays bare the myth that Hamas limited its activity in the United States to financing terrorism through charity. The indictment of Abdelhaleem al-Ashqar, Mohammad Salah, and Mousa Abu Marzook (the latter two already listed as Specially Designated Terrorists) outlines in detail a fifteen-year period during which Hamas supporters in Louisiana, Illinois, and Virginia not only raised funds but also played proactive roles in all facets of the Hamas decision-making process—including preparation for actual terrorist attacks. Indictments like these force authorities to consider the possibility that in the future Hamas and other groups may not only plan attacks abroad from the comfort of their American homes, the groups—or elements within them—may resort to plotting attacks in the United States. Consider just a few examples of the well-publicized, overt American actions targeting Hamas operatives and organizations in the United States since September 2001:[22]

- Five days before the September 11 attacks, FBI and U.S. Customs Service agents raided the offices and froze the assets of Infocom, an Internet company linked to Hamas leader Mousa Abu Marzook, who has been listed as a Specially Designated Terrorist by the U.S. government.
- On November 26, 2001, the Immigration and Naturalization Service deported Ghassan Dahduli. Dahduli was a longtime leader of the Hamas-associated Islamic Association for Palestine and an associate of convicted al-Qaeda operative Wadi al-Hage.[23]
- On December 4, 2001, the Bush administration froze the assets of the

Holy Land Foundation for Relief and Development, labeling it a Hamas front organization. Included in the freeze were two financial institutions linked to Hamas and based in the Palestinian territories: the al-Aqsa International Bank and the Beit al-Mal Holdings Company.[24]

- On June 5, 2002, Joyce and Stanley Boim were awarded $156 million after a jury in Chicago found the HLFRD and the Quranic Literacy Institute liable for the death of their teenage son, David Boim. He had been shot by Hamas militants while waiting for a bus in Jerusalem in 1996. The two charities were forced to pay after prosecutors successfully proved they were guilty of illegally funding a terrorist organization.[25]

- On August 22, 2003, the U.S. Treasury Department designated Sheikh Ahmed Yassin, the spiritual leader of Hamas, and five other senior Hamas officials as Specially Designated Global Terrorists. Their assets were frozen and all financial transactions with them by American nationals were prohibited.[26]

- On July 27, 2004, five former leaders of the HLFRD were arrested on charges of providing financial support for Hamas. The men were charged with raising $12.4 million and then funneling it to Hamas.[27]

- In August 2004, a federal indictment unsealed in Chicago charged Hamas leader Mousa Abu Marzook, Mohammad Salah, and Abdelhaleem al-Ashqar with racketeering conspiracy and using bank accounts in a variety of U.S. states to launder millions of dollars to support murders, kidnappings, and assaults perpetrated by Hamas. Salah was also charged with providing material support for terrorism and obstruction of justice, and accused of recruiting and training new members of Hamas in the United States. Al-Ashqar was already was under house arrest on related charges of contempt and obstruction of justice. Salah and al-Ashqar were arrested in Illinois and Virginia respectively; Marzook resides in Damascus and is considered a fugitive by the U.S. government.[28]

- On February 8, 2005, a federal judge ordered Abdel Jabber Hamdan deported from the United States. The court determined Hamdan understood—or should have understood—that the money he was raising for the HLFRD was being used to support Hamas. Hamdan had been held on immigration violations since July 2004, the same day an indictment was unsealed against HLF.[29]

Shuttering front organizations, seizing their assets, and prosecuting and deporting their members are all key measures necessary to curb the activities of terrorists and their supporters within the United States. Ironically, taking these steps may also contribute to removing at least some of the disincentives that militated against Hamas carrying out an attack against U.S. interests.

ANALYSIS: THE LIKELIHOOD OF A HAMAS ATTACK ABROAD

Facing the removal of such disincentives to attack, might Hamas now decide to target U.S. or other Western interests? Analyzing that likelihood demands a "levels of analysis" approach that acknowledges the various levels of decision making inherent in large terrorist groups. Some decisions are made at the group's headquarters level by a governing council, political bureau, or secretary general. Others may be decided at the level of a regional commander in charge of a network of cells, by a single rogue cell acting on its own, or even by groups of individuals or single members operating on their own as "lone wolves." Each of these scenarios presents counterterrorism officials with especially thorny problems, both in terms of the tactical operational options available to counterterrorism forces, as well as the political options available to decision makers.

The Jamal Akal story is a case in point. Interviews with several senior Israeli intelligence officials produced a variety of opinions regarding what level leadership was aware of the plot to dispatch Akal to North America as a Hamas sleeper agent. According to the public statements of an Israeli official, Hamas leaders in Damascus not only were aware of the plot but were asked to approve the idea of executing an attack and issue a claim in the name of al-Qaeda, not Hamas. An Israeli official described Akal as a "sleeper" agent who was trained and "told to wait for instructions." Akal's family and friends, the official added, included known Hamas military operatives. Another senior Israeli intelligence official echoed this assessment but added, "Akal was an extraordinary departure." This official added that the issue of conducting attacks abroad "had come up before, and Hamas leadership has said 'No attacks versus [the] U.S.'"[30]

But other Israeli intelligence officials came to a slightly different conclusion. They noted that within Hamas "there are no rogue operations, but cells do push the boundaries" in terms of how they carry out their approved operations. The Akal operation, these officials assessed, was more of a "local initiative" than a plot approved by the Hamas leadership. According to one Israeli intelligence official, the Akal plot was developed under the operational oversight of Qassam Brigades commander Mohammad Deif, a senior official with close ties to Hamas leaders abroad. Still other Israeli government analysts concluded that the Akal episode was an example of how operational activists "can and do act beyond the guidance of head-quarters." The cell that trained and attempted to dispatch Akal, these analysts added, was a local element, insufficiently subordinate to Hamas' overall leadership, carrying out a rogue action. It is not uncommon, said the analysts promoting this interpretation, for local cells to engage in this kind of unilateral contingency planning for potential operations at a later date.[31]

Likelihood of Attack Against U.S. Ordered by Hamas Leadership

On November 26, 2004, the State Department issued a travel warning for Israel, the West Bank, and Gaza. Not only did the alert warn against indiscriminate terrorist attacks—the warning expressly prohibited American officials from using public transportation—it specifically warned of the possibility of Hamas attacks targeting U.S. interests. "The U.S. Government has information," the report stated, "indicating that American interests could be the focus of terrorist attacks, including within Israel." The report noted that "since October 2003, militants on several occasions have temporarily abducted Western personnel, and spokesmen for the Hamas terrorist organization have made statements threatening attacks against U.S. interests." Five months earlier a senior Palestinian security official had warned Americans to avoid the Gaza Strip. "I encourage the Americans not to come here," he said. "I cannot ensure their safety."[32]

In fact, Hamas leaders have been threatening U.S. interests since long before 2003. In 1994, when Sheikh Mohammad Siyam was the Hamas representative to Sudan, he told the Sudanese weekly *Drapur al-Jdida* that any U.S. action against Hamas would lead the group to retaliate "against American interests in the world." While noting that Hamas had not yet targeted U.S. interests, Siyam kept that door open. "We are connected to international justice, which gives every nation the right to oppose and fight occupation, and we are not afraid of the American threats, or those from other countries." Siyam continued, "We advise the U.S. to keep its distance from us. General Farah Aydid, with his muddy boots, shortened the noses of Clinton and George Bush in Somalia. We have many militants of this type in the Hamas." Hamas clearly supports the efforts of other groups who would attack U.S. interests. Its leader al-Rantissi published an article on a Hamas website in April 2003 titled "Why Shouldn't We Attack the United States?" arguing that such an action was not only "a moral and national duty—but, above all, a religious one." Al-Rantissi reiterated this sentiment in the context of the U.S.-led war in Iraq. He said: "I call on Iraq to prepare an army of would-be martyrs and prepare tens of thousands of explosive belts. Blow yourselves up against the American army. Bomb them in Baghdad. I call on all Arab nations to burn ground underneath the feet of the Americans in all capitals."[33]

In 1997, Hamas did consider attacking Western interests in Israel. Late that year, Hamas operatives planned to storm an unspecified Western diplomatic mission in Jerusalem and take hostages in an effort to gain the release of Hamas members in Israeli jails. According to Israeli prosecutors, Hamas operative Abdallah Bakri planned the operation to be similar to the seizure of the Japanese embassy in Lima the previous year. Bakri worked closely with senior West Bank Hamas leaders Muhi al-Din al-Sharif and Imad Awadallah, both of whom he admitted hiding in his home for several weeks. Years later, Hamas nearly succeeded in executing a terrorist attack targeting Israeli tourists vacationing in Egypt's Sinai peninsula over the Jewish High Holiday period in September 2004. Shin Bet director Avi Dichter reported to the Israeli cabinet at the time that his service shared actionable intelligence with Egyptian authorities who took preemptive action to thwart the attack. Dichter added that an Israeli air raid on a Gaza soccer field where Hamas operatives were training for the mission a week earlier also helped foil the plot. More recently, Ahmed Azzuz, Antwerp head of the European Arab League, warned of a possible Hamas plan to attack foreign targets in response to the Israeli assassination of Sheikh Yassin, adding, "Antwerp is an obvious target." Azzuz explained that "the diamond sector openly supports the Zionist regime and don't forget that every year, 200 Belgian-Israeli reservists leave for Israel to kill innocent civilians."[34]

Despite rhetoric and even contingency plans to do so, Hamas has not attacked Western or Jewish interests abroad. Still, experts fear there are several red lines that, if crossed, could push Hamas over this dangerous Rubicon. For example, there is good reason to fear that Hamas would target American soldiers if they participated in an international intervention force (IIF) stationed in the West Bank and Gaza Strip. From Lebanon to Somalia to Iraq, terrorism looms large in the recent history of U.S. military intervention in the Middle East. During the early 1980s, for example, the deployment of U.S. and other foreign forces to intervene between warring parties in Lebanon proved a costly experience. Even military operations of a purely humanitarian nature have been treacherous for U.S. forces. In Somalia, for example, the U.S. military suffered significant losses, many in attacks orchestrated by al-Qaeda elements. These experiences show that militants will not hesitate to target international forces on humanitarian or peacekeeping missions if doing so can further the militants' own agenda. In the case of the West Bank and Gaza, where an IIF would be tasked with targeting local terrorist organizations and rooting out their support networks, militants would carry out such attacks out of simple self-preservation; indeed, they would see such attacks as "resistance" to an "occupying" force. Palestinian terrorists have already responded to the presence of international diplomats and observers with violence. For example, on March 26, 2002, Palestinian Islamic Jihad terrorists attacked members of the Temporary International Presence in Hebron (TIPH), murdering two observers (Jinjis Twintuk of Turkey and Catherine Broyikes of Switzerland) and injuring a third (Hussein Asraslan of Turkey).[35]

Historically, there have been moments when Hamas attacks abroad have appeared likely. The March 2004 assassination of Sheikh Yassin caused Israeli analysts particular concern because Yassin was one of the most vocal opponents to targeting Western interests among senior Hamas leaders. There was therefore significant debate within the Israeli intelligence community over whether to assassinate Yassin. Without Yassin to restrain more globally oriented jihadists within Hamas, Israeli intelligence officials feared the Hamas response to Yassin's assassination might have included an attack on Jews or Israelis abroad (Israeli security officials describe attacks on Jewish targets abroad as Israel's "soft underbelly"). According to one senior Israeli official, the fact that Hamas did not carry out such an attack following the attack on Yassin "strengthens the assessment that it would really take a great deal to make Hamas—as an organization—cross the threshold and conduct operations abroad."[36]

This issue came up again a few months later when Israeli agents carried out a series of bombings targeting Hamas leaders in Syria and Lebanon in late 2004. Some of these attacks failed, but one senior Hamas operative, Izzaddin Sheikh Khalil, was killed in Damascus in September 2004. One mourner at Khalil's funeral was among those calling for Hamas to conduct attacks abroad, insisting, "We want to fight them [the Israelis] outside Palestine through their embassies, airline agencies and even their places of worship." Hamas threats to conduct attacks abroad, explained one analyst, "were a direct effort against Israeli attacks abroad." According to this school of thought, failure to respond to Israeli strikes against Hamas leaders abroad would "undermine Hamas' deterrent message." But, once again, Hamas did not conduct attacks abroad following these Israeli strikes either.[37]

On several occasions Hamas leaders have debated the issue of conducting operations abroad, according to a senior Israeli security official recounting intelligence reports on these debates. To date, four central arguments against such action have prevailed in these discussions. On ideological grounds, most Hamas leaders are adamant that the group focus on its specific mission of liberating Palestine. On practical grounds, operational leaders stress that the group has limited resources and argue against dispersing the group's capabilities abroad. Hamas leaders are also very wary of carrying out any action that may undermine their claim that Hamas "resistance to occupation" is inherently different from al-Qaeda-style terrorism. And from a public relations and financial and logistical support perspective, Hamas leaders are careful not to draw the ire of the international community or alienate Palestinians, most of whom would oppose operations abroad.[38]

According to some Israeli analysts, if Hamas leaders were to sanction an attack abroad it would therefore not target Western interests. A Hamas attack abroad, these experts concluded, would not be executed al-Qaeda-style to kill as many random people as possible; it would be a focused attack on an Israeli or Jewish target. It is also likely that a Hamas attack abroad would not be claimed by Hamas, as appears to have been the intention in the case of the foiled Jamal Akal plot in North America. There is no unanimity of opinion among Israeli analysts regarding the likelihood that Hamas would conduct attacks abroad. But, according to these analysts, there are "fragments of information and intelligence assessments" suggesting Hamas could conduct attacks abroad. While some Hamas leaders, including operational commanders and senior leaders outside the West Bank and Gaza Strip, were considering the idea of conducting attacks abroad "very seriously" in 2005, these experts stress that they have traditionally focused on developing contingency plans that have yet to be acted on. A greater threat, these and other analysts suggest, comes from semi-independent or rogue cells.[39]

Likelihood of Hamas Attack from Semi-Independent Cells

"The biggest concern," one Israeli official has said, "is about rogue cells and Hamas individuals close to al-Qaeda" carrying out attacks on their own. And elements of Palestinian terrorist groups have in the past carried out attacks without the knowledge of the entire group. Sometimes such operations are carried out by cells without informing senior leadership; in other cases one part of a group's leadership will task a cell with a mission without the knowledge or approval of other parts of the group's decision-making apparatus.[40]

In August 2003, an Israeli-Palestinian ceasefire was abruptly undermined by a Hamas suicide bombing in Jerusalem that killed 18 people (including several children) and wounded over 100 more. Even as Hamas political leaders in the Gaza Strip denied the group was behind the attack, other Hamas members issued a claim of responsibility for the bombing. Hamas leader Abdel Aziz al-Rantissi initially asserted that Hamas was not involved, saying, "We are committed to the truce. I don't know who carried out this action." But Israeli police quickly identified the suicide bomber as a Hamas operative after finding his identity card at the scene. Hamas' Qassam Brigades later released a videotape of the bomber, Raed Abdel Hamid Misek, in which he declared his intention to carry out the suicide operation in revenge for the pre-ceasefire killing of a Hamas leader in Hebron. Misek's suicide bombing is indicative of the splits that exist within Hamas and suggests that elements of the group may carry out attacks without the knowledge of other cells or leaders.[41]

Indeed, it is not at all rare for Hamas cells to operate on their own, or independently of sister cells and some leaders. Consider the Hamas military cell caught in February 2005 that planned to fire Qassam rockets at Israeli communities from positions within the West Bank. That cell, led by Yihiya Sayid Mussa Zivad, a senior Hamas military commander in the northern West Bank area, was believed to be directly funded by Hamas leaders abroad and operated independently of other military cells in the West Bank. According to a statement issued by Israeli security services, "The investigation of the terrorist network reveals that this was an operation carried out with an unusually high level of secrecy, in that it involved only a selective number of terrorists from the network, with centralized management by Yihie Zivad." Such cases highlight the ability of particular segments or factions within a group to carry out operations on their own without the approval of the full spectrum of the group's leadership. It is therefore insufficient to note that Palestinian groups traditionally have not targeted Americans or Westerners, or to quote the statements of certain group leaders insisting they never would, since decisions are sometimes made by segments of these groups that act on their own without consulting the group at large.[42]

Likelihood of Hamas Attacks from Rogue Cells

Rogue cells, operating at their own initiative and without the knowledge or approval of more senior operational or political decision makers, represent another level at which terrorist groups are capable of conducting attacks abroad. Commenting on an Islamic Jihad suicide bombing that threatened to unravel the Israeli-Palestinian ceasefire in February 2005, Nasser Juma, a leader of the al-Aqsa Martyrs Brigades, noted that even if the "main groups" agreed to a ceasefire, a "lone bomber" or "militant cell" could still carry out an attack. That same month Hamas leader Khaled Mishal said that Hamas fugitives would not sign pledges to cease attacks either, rejecting an Israeli proposal to stop hunting fugitives if they signed a pledge to halt attacks and turn in their weapons.[43]

Rogue terrorist elements tied to Hamas have already targeted Western interests. On October 15, 2003, Palestinian militants attacked a clearly marked American diplomatic convoy with a roadside bomb in Gaza. Ironically, the convoy was composed not of security officers, but of State Department officials on a mission to identify potential Palestinian recipients of Fulbright Scholarships. This was the first lethal roadside bombing of an American convoy, but it was not the first attempt. In June 2003, another marked U.S. convoy narrowly escaped injury in a similar attack when unknown assailants detonated two roadside bombs. Within twenty-four hours of the October bombing, described by the State Department as "the most lethal attack ever to directly target U.S. interests in Israel, the West Bank, or Gaza," Palestinian security forces arrested several suspects, including members of the Popular Resistance Committees (PRC). The PRC, a motley crew of loosely associated radical Palestinians from Hamas, Islamic Jihad, Fatah, and the various Palestinian security services, claimed responsibility for the attack. According to an Israeli report, during the period of calm (*tahdiya*) to which Hamas agreed to abide in the spring and summer of 2005, the PRC served "as Hamas' forward operational arm." Although it later rescinded its claim of responsibility, the PRC is known for the kind of powerful remote-controlled roadside bomb used to attack the U.S. convoy; its operatives perfected the technique over the two previous years, destroying three Israeli tanks in Gaza with the same type of explosive. According to the State Department, the PRC remains the primary suspect in the attacks. Similarly, the Ahmed Abu Rish Brigades—a Gaza Strip–based collection of disaffected Fatah operatives with close ties to Hamas—has abducted foreigners in Gaza and announced that its jihadist ambitions go far beyond Israel. According to group spokesman Abu Haron, "our banner is jihad everywhere, even Chechnya. Our aim is to liberate every piece of land in Palestine, including what is now called Israel."[44]

The threat is no less real within the United States. According to FBI officials, some 50–100 Hamas and Hezbollah members with military training are present in the United States. In 2004, former FBI counterterrorism agent Kenneth Piernick warned that such operatives could quickly become operational. According to Piernick, "Where there are cells of supporters, with not too much additional energy applied by motivated recruiters or leaders, they can shift them into a more operational posture. In the United States up until recently we have not seen that shift from either Hamas or Hezbollah. But that doesn't mean they are not able to do that. They are very able to do this. And second, they are not going to do it in a way that we are likely to see it. It will be subtle and secretive."[45]

Likelihood of Hamas Attacks from "Lone Wolves"

Lone wolves, terrorists with no ties to a group—or those acting completely independently of the group to which they belong—represent a particularly difficult threat to preempt. Lone wolves tend not to appear on the radar of counterterrorism officials until they are well into the planning stages of an attack, or later. As explained by FBI official M. E. Bowman, the greatest threat is from someone "who, while otherwise leading a normal life somewhere in the world, decides to become a terrorist." Bowman describes such a terrorist as "the proverbial needle in the haystack" and laments this "occasional, or the part-time, or the one-time terrorist on whom we have limited ability to focus intelligence efforts."[46]

Consider, for example, the case of Ali Hassan Abu Kamal, the gunman who opened fire on tourists at the Empire State Building in New York in February 1997. Apparently distraught and in debt, Kamal killed a Danish national and wounded six other people before killing himself. In a two-page "Charter of Honour" he left behind, Kamal asserted that the Americans, British, and French are the "first enemy" for "turning the Palestinians homeless" and said that his "restless aspiration is to murder as many of them [Zionists] as possible, and I have decided to strike at their own den in New York, and at the very Empire State Building in particular." In July of that same year, two Palestinian men were arrested in their apartment in New York City, accused of plotting an attack on New York City subways. New York police raided the Brooklyn apartment of Gazi Ibrahim Abu Mezer and Lafi Khalil, both from the West Bank, and found several pipe bombs, including some wrapped together and equipped with toggle-switch detonators—the type of explosives often used for suicide bombings. When the officers entered the apartment, one of the suspects attempted but failed to detonate one of the explosives. Abu Mezer later confessed that the plan was to detonate the explosives on a busy New York City subway. While a law enforcement official reported that Abu Mezer and Khalil were tied to Hamas, the head of the FBI's New York office quickly issued a correction saying that investigators had not yet linked the suspects to Hamas. Police found a note in the apartment denouncing U.S. support of Israel and demanding that several Arabs held in U.S. and Israeli prisons on charges of terrorism be released.[47]

More recently, in April 2004 a Lebanese-Canadian firebombed a Jewish school in Montreal in retaliation for the assassination of Sheikh Yassin. The nineteen-year-old attacker, Sleiman Elmerhebi, was not affiliated with any group but left a note outside the burned school warning that "our [sic] goal was only to sound the alarm without causing deaths . . . but this is just the beginning. If your crimes continue in the Middle East, our attacks will continue." And in August 2004, U.S. law enforcement officials arrested a man plotting to bomb a federal office building in downtown Chicago. In the process of planning his attack, the man, Gale Nettles, asked an FBI informant posing as an accomplice to put him in contact with a member of either al-Qaeda or Hamas.[48]

While none of these were Hamas operatives, per se, each acted in perceived concert with the objectives of Hamas, in retaliation for attacks on Hamas, or in attempted cooperation with Hamas. In February 2005, FBI director Robert Mueller testified before Congress that "currently, the most likely threat of terrorist attacks from Palestinian groups to the U.S. homeland is from a 'lone wolf' scenario." Such an attack would be carried out by individuals, Mueller said, "who may embrace the ideology of a Palestinian terrorist group, but act without assistance or approval of any established group."[49]

Likelihood of Attacks from Non-Hamas Jihadists

Early in his career, Sheikh Abdallah Azzam, a Palestinian militant and co-founder of al-Qaeda, coordinated attacks on Israeli targets from Jordan. Only later did he move to Afghanistan and become a leading light in the jihad against the Soviet Union and in the formation of the Afghan jihad's international support network that would later morph into al-Qaeda. Hamas activists see their jihadist ideology as a direct outgrowth of the militant ideology Azzam promoted. Today, many radicalized Palestinians make the same leap Azzam did from engaging in a "near jihad" against Israel and secular Palestinians to a "far jihad" against the "head of the snake"—America and other countries seen as supporting Israel. There are many Palestinians in positions of authority within al-Qaeda, and individual relationships between al-Qaeda operatives and Hamas members are common. According to a January 2001 National Security Council memorandum, al-Qaeda had "recently increased its contacts with the Palestinian rejectionist groups, including Hizbollah, Hamas and the Palestinian Islamic Jihad." These relationships are to be expected, since many of the Muslim Brotherhood–affiliated terrorist front organizations financing al-Qaeda also provided funding to Hamas. In December 2002, for example, Israel deported a visiting Palestinian-American who had been in contact with Hamas activists and institutions. But the man was not a Hamas activist; he worked at the Global Relief Foundation, an al-Qaeda-affiliated front organization based in Chicago, until the foundation was shut down following the September 11 attacks.[50]

To be sure, the plight of Palestinians is an issue that resonates with Muslims worldwide. It is also an issue eagerly manipulated by extremists seeking to radicalize potential recruits. According to 9/11 mastermind Khaled Sheikh Mohammad, his original plan for the September 11 attacks involved hijacking ten commercial airplanes. Nine would be crashed into predetermined targets, and the tenth—commandeered by Mohammad himself—would land at an unspecified U.S. airport. After killing all the adult male passengers and notifying the media, Mohammad would deliver a speech condemning the United States for its support of Israel, the Philippines, and dictatorial Arab regimes.[51]

It should therefore not surprise that the Palestinian cause is a motivating factor for Islamist militants, even among militants primarily involved in more global jihadist activities. Yahya Goba, a convicted member of the Lackawanna jihad cell in upstate New York, testified that he first met cell leader Kamal Derwish at "a rally for Palestine" in 1998 in Brooklyn, New York. Derwish had already fought as a mujahid in Bosnia in 1996 and eventually convinced Goba to take a more active role in jihad. Specifically, he urged Goba "to train, prepare for jihad" by obtaining "military training." In early 2000 Derwish arranged for six members of the group to attend an al-Qaeda training camp in Afghanistan, complete with cover stories, visas, and funding. Similarly, Mohammad Bouyeri, who was collecting unemployment benefits from the Dutch government at the time he assassinated Theo van Gogh, experienced an Islamist awakening during seven months in a Dutch prison for a prior crime. He also developed a distinct anger over the plight of Palestinians and was "sympathetic to Hamas." Surrounded by posters glorifying Palestinian and Chechen suicide bombings alike, and hearing sermons about a purported American war on Islam in Hamas-controlled mosques, Palestinians are increasingly drawn to global jihadist activity. In

May 2005, for example, Iraqi security forces investigating a market bombing in Baghdad arrested five suspects, four of whom were Palestinians.[52]

Still more disturbing, U.S. intelligence agencies report that after four years of successive losses in the ongoing global war on terror, al-Qaeda operatives are actively seeking to lure Hamas activists to replenish al-Qaeda ranks. According to FBI director Robert Mueller, the Bureau is concerned "about the possibility that individuals who are members of groups previously considered to be peripheral to the current threat, could be convinced by more radical, external influences to take on facilitation or even worse— an operational role—with little or no warning." That already appears to be happening.[53]

The same day that charges were unsealed against Hamas activists in Chicago in August 2004, Ismael Salim Elbarasse, a "high-ranking" Hamas operative named as a co-conspirator in the indictment, was arrested in Maryland on a material-witness warrant related to the Chicago case. His arrest occurred after police witnessed his wife videotaping the Chesapeake Bay Bridge from his vehicle. The tape featured close-up footage of the bridge's cables, upper supports, and joints, all unusual preoccupations for a tourist. A former director of the Islamic Association for Palestine—a suspected Hamas front with offices in Chicago and Dallas—Elbarasse worked as an assistant to Marzook and shared a bank account with him that was "used to transfer substantial sums of money to Hamas members," according to the Chicago indictment. In its affidavit for a warrant to search Elbarasse's car, the FBI noted that, while Hamas does not typically target U.S. interests, conspirators from Hamas and several other jihadist groups were behind a 1993 plot to bomb New York landmarks. It also noted, "al-Qaeda commanders and officials stationed in Western countries, including the United States, have recruited operatives and volunteers to carry out reconnaissance or serve as couriers." According to the affidavit, the post–September 11 crackdown on al-Qaeda has spurred the organization to place "renewed emphasis" on finding "confirmed jihadist supporters in the United States by trying to enlist proven members of other groups such as Hamas to make up for the vacuum on the field level."[54]

Then there is the case of Nabil Awqil, who was trained in al-Qaeda camps in Afghanistan and returned to the Gaza Strip to conduct operations against Israeli interests in Israel (see Chapter 2). In September 2005, Israeli prosecutors charged another Palestinian, Mahmoud Waridat, with receiving training in small arms and bomb making at al-Qaeda's al-Farouq camp in

Afghanistan in 2001. Waridat reportedly declined to join al-Qaeda following the training, preferring to put his skills to use in his native West Bank.[55]

CONCLUSION

Israeli analysts believe that while it is currently still not in Hamas' interest to conduct attacks against Western interests, those interests are likely to change. "It is a matter of time," a group of senior analysts concluded in November 2004. Among Palestinian terrorist groups, the analysts noted, Hamas is the most active abroad. And while there is no specific evidence of operational ties between Hamas activists and global jihadist elements, there is a "critical mass of sporadic indications" of such links. It is less likely that a Hamas attack would be called for by senior Hamas leaders and approved by the group's Shura Council, and more likely it would involve individual activists or cells acting on their own—or through their own personal connections to more globally oriented jihadists. Their conclusion on the question of Hamas carrying out an attack abroad is disconcerting: "The clock is ticking—it will happen."[56]

Several factors loomed large in the Israeli analysis, but none more than the Hamas radicalization campaign overseen by the Hamas dawa. When angry, frustrated, or humiliated Palestinians regularly listen to sermons in mosques in which Jews, Israelis, and even Americans are depicted as enemies of Islam and Palestine, Hamas' official policy may not restrain individual enthusiasm. Also, recent events may convince elements within Hamas to break with the group's traditional modus operandi and attack Western interests. Some of the more radical leaders may feel that Israeli attacks on Hamas leaders abroad leave them little choice but to respond with similar attacks on Israelis or Jews abroad. Certainly, any tangible counterterrorism action taken against Hamas by American or other Western forces—such as a Western-led international intervention force—would lead hardened Hamas operatives to respond with attacks against those forces. Likewise, progress toward peace could marginalize Hamas and cause hardliners within it to break with moderates. Those hardliners may well choose to increase the number and lethality of attacks, and could also shift the group's targeting to include Western interests.

In the wake of the Israeli withdrawal from the Gaza Strip, and as Israel completes the construction of a security barrier around the West Bank, Hamas may find it increasingly difficult to infiltrate suicide bombers into Israel. According to the Israeli army, Palestinian groups executed fifty-nine "successful" suicide attacks in 2002. By 2004, that number had dropped by 75 percent. While attacks on the remaining Israeli settlements and military installations in the West Bank are expected, such operations lack the effect of terrorizing Israeli society in the same way that bombings of Israeli cafés and buses do. Should Hamas find itself incapable of mounting attacks on Israeli territory from the West Bank and Gaza Strip, its default option may be Israeli or Jewish targets abroad.[57]

Finally, Hamas has made inroads in Palestinian refugee camps outside the West Bank and Gaza Strip, particularly in Lebanon. Sanabil, a Hamas charity in Lebanon that was designated a terrorist entity by the U.S. Treasury Department, was especially active in militant Palestinian camps like Ayn al-Hilweh until it closed. In the likely event that a negotiated two-state agreement between Israel and the Palestinian Authority does not meet the full expectations of Palestinians living in refugee camps abroad, some of these neglected Palestinians—many of whom have ties both to Hamas and global jihadist groups in Lebanon like Osbat al-Ansar—may decide to conduct attacks on Israeli, Jewish, or Western targets abroad. Should any of these scenarios materialize, Hamas could easily draw on its grassroots dawa organizations around the world to help facilitate its operations.

While Israeli analysts remain skeptical that Hamas will target Western interests in the near term, some analysts close to Hamas believe such an attack will happen sooner rather than later. Writing in the *Palestine Chronicle* in July 2004, an author tied to the United Association for Studies and Research (UASR; founded by Hamas leader Mousa Abu Marzook) concluded: "Sixteen years after Hamas' establishment, the world will probably see an attack [by Hamas] on foreign soil for the first time. Leaders of Hamas' military wing will now seek the expansion of their war against Israel. The Zionist state's interests—embassies, consulates, cultural centers, diplomats—across the globe are potential targets."[58]

9

displacing the hamas dawa

What flows from the analysis thus far is the centrality of Hamas social welfare activity to the success of the group's political and military activities alike. The dawa provides Hamas with both popular support and ample opportunities to carry out attacks. Critically, academic studies have identified the decline of both popular and logistical support as key prerequisites for the demise of terrorist groups. Denying Hamas the logistical, financial, and recruitment networks provided by its dawa infrastructure would therefore go far toward disrupting its ability to carry out the suicide bombings and other attacks that are its hallmark.[1]

Despite the fact that Hamas cynically uses social services and charity to promote radicalism and support murder, shutting the group's social service organizations must be accompanied by a parallel effort to assume responsibility for the provision of these services. The need for humanitarian support activities is indeed acute in the West Bank and Gaza Strip, but Hamas' efficient exploitation of this need should not amount to a free pass for the terrorism the group carries out and the political violence it espouses.

Moreover, while counterterrorism campaigns against active terrorist groups demand ongoing tactical operations of a preemptive nature (including military, intelligence, and law enforcement activities), these are incapable of undermining the underlying support for such groups without simultaneously targeting the group's base of social and political support. Crackdowns alone, while preventing attacks, do nothing to encourage a split between the group's committed radicals and its more moderate members and supporters who lend their support for reasons other than the Hamas violence (such as anticorruption or humanitarian need). Without such a split, attempting to accommodate or reform radical groups like Hamas while they are still committed to violence and hate based on an extremist religious ideology is both unprincipled and doomed to fail. Disrupting the Hamas dawa is the most effective way of weakening Hamas as an organization, undermining its base of public support and denying its operatives critical logistical and financial support. As such, empowering responsible, nonviolent Palestinian entities—both public and private—to assume the responsibility for (and enjoy the resulting public support from) public works and social and humanitarian services should be a central goal of counterterrorism officials, peace negotiators, economists, and development experts alike.[2]

NO FORGIVING TERROR FOR GOOD WORKS

Sadly, academics, journalists, and policy makers all too often downplay the role that the Hamas social welfare network plays in radicalizing society and financing, supporting, and facilitating Hamas terror attacks. Despite the plethora of evidence to the contrary, they subscribe to the myth that Hamas charity is disconnected from Hamas terror.

For example, the highly respected International Crisis Group issued an April 2003 report which, while condemning Hamas terror attacks, implicitly concluded that the social welfare services provided by humanitarian organizations associated with Hamas somehow legitimize the organization overall. Along these lines, the *Washington Post* ombudsman wrote a column explaining that, since Hamas is a "nationalist movement" engaged in "some social work," the perpetrators of Palestinian suicide and other attacks should be described in the press as "militants" or "gunmen" while those who execute attacks in the name of al-Qaeda should be identified as "terrorists." The *Boston Globe* ombudsman wrote much the same, arguing that to "tag Hamas, for example, as a terrorist organization is to ignore its far more complex role in the Middle East drama."[3]

In contrast, David Aufhauser, then general counsel to the Treasury Department and chair of the National Security Council's policy coordinating committee on terrorist financing, described the logic of making distinctions between terrorist groups' charitable and military wings as "sophistry," adding, "the idea that there's a firewall between the two defies common sense." Hamas leader Dr. Mahmoud al-Zahar makes the same argument: "Hamas responds to all questions related to the life of the citizens not only in case of confrontation but also in the political, economic, social, health, and internal relations fields. This movement has proved that it is one organic unit. Mistaken is the one who thinks that the military wing acts outside the framework of Hamas or behaves recklessly."[4]

To be sure, Palestinians face dire social welfare needs unaddressed by the infamously corrupt Palestinian Authority, creating an opportunity Hamas eagerly exploits. In January 2006 Hamas rode a wave of frustration over these and other inequities to victory at the polls. Tolerating this exploitation is neither in the interest of Israeli-Palestinian peace nor Palestinian humanitarian assistance. Social welfare organizations that contaminate their benevolent activities with support for terrorism muddy the waters of charitable giving and good works, making the job that much harder for those simply trying to better conditions in the West Bank and Gaza Strip. In the words of the State Department, "as long as Hamas continues to rely on terrorism to achieve its political ends, we should not draw a distinction between its military and humanitarian arms, since funds provided to one can be used to support the other." The Treasury Department was clearer still, saying, "No matter how terrible the plight of the Palestinian people, there can be no justification for the killing of innocents. In our view, toleration of such terror by anyone is nothing short of complicity."[5]

It is critical that the international community insist that humanitarian support for Palestinians be organized, comprehensive, and divorced from support for terrorist activity. This is necessary both to obstruct Hamas efforts to torpedo progress toward peace and to clear the names of humanitarian groups untainted by terror. Aufhauser hit the nail on the head when he said, "No one is at war with the idea of building hospitals or orphanages or taking care of people who are displaced. But the same people that govern how to apply the money to hospitals govern how to apply the money to killing people, and you cannot abdicate responsibility for one and celebrate what you're doing on the other: it remains blood money." For any future peace initiative to take hold, the international community must endorse this basic principle. Recognizing this, President Bush issued a call on June 25, 2003, for "swift, decisive action against terror groups such as Hamas, to cut off their funding and support." Such cooperation, however, remains elusive largely due to the veil of legitimacy Hamas charitable work provides for its terror attacks. It is this flawed attitude, a Treasury official concluded, which leads countries to "stand on the sidelines refusing to act because the purpose of acts of terror are believed to be politically laudable, not withstanding the moral obscenity of the means of reaching any such goal."[6]

INTERNATIONALLY REGULATED HUMANITARIAN SUPPORT

Detaching humanitarian support for needy Palestinians from terrorist activity can only be accomplished if there are transparent mechanisms for providing aid. The United States, European Union, Gulf states, and other donors should vet potential recipient organizations and strictly regulate which Palestinian charities receive international aid. Freezing out front organizations for Hamas and other violent groups from the pool of foreign funds available for support to Palestinians would go a long way toward deflating Hamas' successful support infrastructure. But as suspect fronts collapse for lack of funds or are shut down by authorities, there must be a parallel effort on the part of the moderate Palestinians, Israel, the Quartet peace sponsors, and the international donor community to fill the gap and provide organized humanitarian aid for needy Palestinians in a way that does not support terrorists.

To date, none of these parties can boast of a positive record in this regard. For example, in August 2003 Palestinian authorities shut down several Hamas-run charities suspected of financing terrorism. But the PA neglected to assume responsibility for the humanitarian services provided by these charities and the international community failed to offer its assistance to facilitate the PA's ability to do so. This had a radicalizing effect on a great many Palestinians, including those stripped of badly needed support and others angry on their behalf. The closures were followed by a series of "widows and orphans rallies" organized by Hamas and attended by a cross-section of Palestinian society calling on the PA to reopen the charities under slogans such as "Feed Our Children" and "Cancel the Freeze." Despite its inability to pay its employees, the al-Salah Islamic Society, one of the Hamas charities whose accounts were frozen, continued providing assistance to needy Palestinians. In stark contrast to the PA, which failed to assume responsibility for the social services previously provided by the banned Hamas charities, al-Salah borrowed money from local banks to continue providing free and discounted services. Though suspicious of the rampantly corrupt PA, the banks willingly provided lines of credit to the famously honest al-Salah Society. "Al Salah's aid and activism," one reporter noted, "are deeply appreciated by people who have rarely felt so abandoned." Stripped of the assistance these Hamas charities provided, and without supplemented funding from the PA to compensate them for the loss of funds, frustrated beneficiaries of al-Salah and other Hamas charities joined Hamas activists and attacked the car of PA Minister of Public Works

Abdel Rahman Hamad. Hamas knew the PA would fail to pick up the short-fall in social services and appears to have been prepared to use these closures in an organized public relations campaign to further discredit the PA. The reason Hamas knew this in advance is that it happened before. The PA briefly shut several Hamas-run charities in September 1997. At the time, Hamas leader Ismail Abu Shanab insisted that "closing them does not affect Hamas—it harms the people. So Arafat ended up creating more of a crisis for the poor, and his own popularity suffered as a result." Then too, the PA failed to see to the continued provision of social services and, succumbing to public pressure, quickly unfroze the charities' accounts.[7]

Shutting the Hamas dawa, therefore, must be accompanied by a cooperative effort on the part of the international donor community to create a trustworthy, transparent humanitarian relief system that does not promote support of "martyrs' families" but fills the welfare void exploited to date by Hamas. Cognizant of the need for transparency and public trust, the European Commission drafted a set of recommendations in July 2005 "to promote transparency and accountability best practices" for non-profit organizations. Noting the evidence that "non-profit organizations have been exploited for the financing of terrorism and for other kinds of criminal abuse," the draft report called for non-profits to apply high standards of transparency and accountability. But the report was based on the assumption that non-profit organizations would adhere to its proposed code of conduct out of their own self-interest. While true for legitimate organizations seeking to protect themselves from abuse or infiltration by radical or criminal elements, the same can not be said for those knowingly fronting for Hamas or other violent groups. Indeed, according to European officials, EU efforts in early 2005 to find legitimate charities and humanitarian organizations on the ground in the Gaza Strip that were not tied to Hamas or other terrorist groups failed. In some cases, EU officials found that international organizations that bothered to have their books audited hired accountants tied to Hamas because of the group's trustworthy reputation. Therefore, any such effort would have to start from scratch with new government offices unaffiliated with Hamas partnered—or "twinned," to borrow a technical EU term—with Western experts capable of providing technical expertise as well as new private institutions overseen by outside regulators.[8]

CRACKDOWN AND AID

On balance, there can be no doubt that crackdowns on the Hamas social welfare network, unaccompanied by a parallel effort to assume responsibility for the humanitarian support this network provides, only inflames passions, hurts the poor, and, in the final analysis, strengthens Hamas. As long as Hamas remains in the terrorism business, any organization that finances, facilitates, or supports the organization must be shut; the social services it provides, however, must continue. Were an international aid effort organized to proactively build and fund new, local institutions that could fill this gap, moderate Palestinian leaders would be empowered to crack down on Hamas without fear of driving its constituency further into the group's arms. There is no doubt that Hamas' terrorist infrastructure can be dismantled only with the full cooperation of an empowered Palestinian Authority—an impossible task while Hamas is in power. Israel cannot battle Hamas alone—militarily or otherwise—and the concept of a third-party international intervention force for the Palestinian territories is as misguided as it is alluring.[9]

On the flip side, increased aid alone will not end Palestinian suffering without a crackdown on terrorism. According to a report the World Bank issued in 2003, even doubling donor disbursements to $2 billion in 2003 and 2004 "would only reduce the [Palestinian] poverty rate by seven percentage points by the end of 2004." The key to a revival of the Palestinian economy, the 2003 World Bank report concluded, was the removal of internal closures and the facilitation of Palestinian exports. But however undesirable they may be, the roadblocks, closures, and curfews that curtail such free movement are unintended consequences of security measures implemented to prevent suicide bombers from gaining access to Israeli population centers.[10]

At the June 2005 G-8 summit in Gleneagles, Scotland, former World Bank leader James Wolfensohn (by then serving as U.S. Special Envoy for Disengagement) secured an agreement from the world's economic powers to invest $3 billion in the development of a sustainable infrastructure for unoccupied Gaza. But as Wolfensohn made clear, the Gaza disengagement would prove successful only if a realistic hope for increased prosperity were created for Palestinians following Israel's departure. He emphasized the relationship between quality of life issues and issues of peace and security, and highlighted the absolute necessity to facilitate the free movement of people and goods throughout Palestinian areas. One economist, echoing Wolfensohn's theme of free movement, wrote that, in the case of aid to Palestinians "it's not the total amount of aid that's a problem; it's the way that aid is distributed." The key to accomplishing efficient distribution of aid, this analyst concluded, is "in a word: security."[11]

Had the international community empowered the PA through a transparent, regulated aid program that provided Palestinians the services they need and deserve, the PA would have been far better positioned to enforce law and order (targeting criminals and terrorists alike), eliminating the need for closures and roadblocks. According to World Bank estimates from mid-2003, facilitating the free passage of goods by removing such barriers could have led to a surge of about 20 percent in Palestinian GNP in 2003 and a reduction of the poverty rate by 19 percent by the end of 2004.[12]

Empowering and funding reformed Palestinian institutions and new, transparent NGOs to provide basic public and social services would complement this priority because the free movement of people and goods is a function of the security situation on the ground. The more alert Israelis have to be to the potential infiltration of Hamas suicide bombers the less flexible they can be about removing checkpoints and barriers. Had the Palestinian Authority assumed responsibility for providing its citizens a social safety net it would have enjoyed the gratitude and public support that instead went to Hamas at the expense of moderate Palestinian leaders.

INTERNATIONAL COORDINATION

Were a new, moderate Palestinian government to come to power instead of Hamas a renewed international aid effort would surely follow. To succeed, however, an internationally organized and regulated aid effort would have to be a cooperative one coordinated among donor nations. Indeed, unilateral efforts to enforce transparency and regulate the terms of foreign aid to Palestinian organizations have fared poorly. For example, the vast majority of Palestinian NGOs refused to sign a 2004 U.S. Agency for International Development (USAID) pledge not to "provide material support or resources to any individual or entity that advocates, plans, sponsors, engages in or has engaged in terrorist activity." Palestinian groups like the Non-Governmental Organization Network, an umbrella group of eighty-nine Palestinian welfare organizations, urged fellow Palestinian organizations not to sign the pledge, called the Anti-Terrorism Certificate (ATC), which is a prerequisite for USAID funding worldwide. Protesting that "the USAID document describes the Palestinian resistance and Palestinian factions as terrorist groups which we reject completely," the NGO Network encouraged Palestinian groups to seek alternative funding from Europe, Japan, Gulf states, and elsewhere. Even Hassan Asfour, head of the Palestinian Authority for NGO Affairs, called on the few Palestinian NGOs that signed the USAID document not to give in to "U.S. extortion" and to rescind their pledge. A coordinated international effort would deny those non-profits disinclined to commit to a basic code of conduct the ability to seek support from donors requiring no such commitment.[13]

Another problem has been the PA's inability to effectively absorb a significant influx of funds. Historically, such aid has gone to waste, fed corruption, or made its way into the pockets of radicals like Hamas or Fatah's al-Aqsa Martyrs Brigades. Internationally organized transparency and oversight would therefore be a prerequisite both for finding willing donor partners and for successful distribution and implementation on the ground.[14]

International aid must also be coordinated multilaterally in nature to succeed. In July 2003, for example, Washington decided to bolster then Prime Minister Mahmoud Abbas and undermine Hamas by providing direct humanitarian aid to the Palestinian Authority Finance Ministry under Salam Fayad. The initial sum, a relatively meager $20 million, was not accompanied by similar pledges from other donor countries and was therefore mostly symbolic in nature. Moreover, when outside auditors were sent to check on how the funds were spent they were prevented from entering the building where they believed the records were being kept. Were such aid coordinated as part of an international effort combining a serious crackdown on the Hamas dawa with a massive donor program overseen, regulated, and managed by the international community, it could have had a much more tangible, verifiable, and lasting effect.[15]

QUALITY AND QUANTITY OF AID

But money is not the issue. The $3 billion increase in aid to the West Bank and Gaza Strip that Wolfensohn secured at the June 2005 G-8 summit is vastly more than what Hamas spends on its dawa, even considering that much of this money is intended to rebuild Gaza's devastated infrastructure. The problem has been the PA's inability to use aid efficiently and transparently. Given Hamas' relatively small budget compared to existing and pledged funds, a serious international aid effort funding reformed Palestinian service providers could dwarf the Hamas dawa with qualitatively and quantitatively superior services. A serious international aid effort should not just replace the tens of millions of dollars Hamas invests in its dawa activities, but rather invest hundreds of millions of dollars and replace the comparatively meager services provided by Hamas with far more comprehensive services. For example, instead of merely replacing Hamas clinics with similar clinics providing similar services, the international community could pull the carpet out from under Hamas by building technologically advanced clinics capable of providing far more than just free medical exams. Coupling active steps to shut down Hamas dawa agencies with effective international aid and reformed Palestinian social service organizations would serve to crowd out Hamas' competing services and would create much-needed jobs in the process.[16]

This is not as massive an undertaking as some suspect, as the amount of money Hamas actually spends on social welfare is relatively small compared to U.N. and other international aid. According to Israeli intelligence estimates, Hamas' annual budget is, at most, between $70 million and $90 million, 80–85 percent of which is spent on the group's political and social welfare activities and the remaining 15–20 percent on terror operations. By this calculus, Hamas spends between $56 million and $76.5 million annually on its political and social welfare activities. Applying this formula to U.S. estimates of Hamas' annual budget, which are closer to $50 million, translates into $42.5 million to $62.5 million in annual social welfare expenditures. This pales in comparison to the amount of funding Palestinians receive from the U.N., EU, and other sources. According to a June 2005 World Food Programme report, "international development assistance [for Palestinians] totals $1.3 billion per year through the Palestinian Authority, the United Nations and NGOs." The UN Relief and Works Agency for Palestine Refugees in the Near East's (UNRWA) cash budget for 2005 was $339.3 million, almost 4.5 times the high-end estimate of Hamas dawa expenditures. On top of this aid, the U.N. Development Programme (UNDP) budgeted $41 million in international development assistance to the Palestinians in 2005; in 2004, the U.N. Children's Fund (UNICEF) ran 100 camps for over 17,000 Palestinian children.[17]

Many countries provide bilateral assistance to Palestinians through UNRWA, like the $50 million grant Japan provided in September 2005, while others donate through other international organizations like the EU. The European Commission allocated €192 million (or $240 million) in aid to the Palestinians in 2003 and provided approximately €250 million (or $312 million) in aid in 2004. In 2005, the EU gave $606 million in aid to the Palestinians. Monetary aid allocated through the European Commission does not include substantial bilateral contributions of individual EU member states, and accounts for about a quarter of the total international donor assistance to the West Bank and Gaza Strip.[18]

According to the World Bank, one reason the Palestinian economy continued to function in 2003, despite teetering on the brink of collapse, was that it was still able to deliver basic services. Indeed, subsidies to the Palestinian budget took up 60 percent of the $1.026 million in foreign aid disbursed in 2002, enabling the PA to employ 26 percent of the people working in the West Bank and Gaza and to pay 40 percent of all domestic wages. (This often amounts to unsupervised handouts though, since U.S. officials note that only 20,000 of the 58,000 Palestinian security personnel on the payroll show up for work.) But while foreign funding kept the PA afloat and provided basic wages to large segments of the population, by 2004 approximately 47 percent of Palestinians in the West Bank and Gaza Strip were still living below the poverty level. In light of such economic conditions, Palestinians are frequently unable to pay even minimal fees for health, education, and social services, and the PA is incapable of filling the gap. Hamas, meanwhile, charges nothing or almost nothing for the same services.[19]

Meanwhile, UNRWA reported a deficit of $20 million against its $313 million 2002 budget, broadening the gap in services available for Hamas to exploit. So, while its overall spending may pale in comparison, Hamas eagerly and competently fills the wide gap that remains despite massive UNRWA and other international aid. While a social welfare budget ranging from about $40 million to $75 million is not a terribly significant amount of aid, it helps many Palestinians make ends meet and certainly was enough to jolt officials within the Palestinian Authority. Peter Gubser, president of American Near East Refugee Aid (ANERA), recounts that in 1999 Yasser Arafat complained to him that the Saudis had just sent Hamas $50 million, without distinguishing between the group's terrorist and charitable activities. Arafat added, "How can I compete with that sort of money?" In fact, he could not—but not because of the amount of money. While the PA and United Nations spend more money and provide more social services than Hamas overall, that assistance is often not enough for needy Palestinians to get by without the additional support provided by Hamas. Moreover, while the notoriously honest Hamas is perceived as doing all it can for Palestinians, the PA under Fatah did more overall but was infamously corrupt, wasteful, and seen by its constituency as failing to address even the most basic needs.[20]

Traditionally, Hamas has not been expected to provide Palestinians with a social safety net, and therefore it was celebrated for whatever assistance it did provide without being held accountable for any remaining shortfall. Making up the difference between international aid and life above the poverty line, Hamas successfully builds grassroots support, radicalizes society, and provides a logistical support network for its operations along the way. Hamas earmarks the majority of its financial resources for "those directly connected with Jihad, such as the injured, the martyrs, their families and the prisoners" in an effort to maximize the support such aid buys the group. Services for other sectors of Palestinian society, a group of Hamas activists concluded, "can be provided by other organizations, those who receive assistance from the United States and UN agencies. But we should focus on those people who are directly connected with Jihad."[21]

STUNTING HAMAS' POLITICAL GROWTH

Denying Hamas the ability to play both humanitarian and terrorist roles simultaneously would also force the group's more moderate members to choose between terrorism and political violence on the one hand and Islamic proselytizing, social communal activity, and political activism on the other. As Hamas activists enter Palestinian politics, fostering such splits within Hamas is especially critical. Having members elected to official office should not on its own legitimize Hamas as long as the group continues to engage in terrorism, political violence, and hateful incitement. As EU foreign policy chief Javier Solana asserted, "Hamas must transform itself into a political party and begin by disarming. A political party cannot bear arms; this exists in no democracy." French President Jacques Chirac was equally unambiguous on the issue of Hamas engaging in parallel political and violent activities. On a state visit to Israel in July 2005, just ahead of the evacuation of Jewish settlers from the Gaza Strip, Chirac said, "Hamas is a terrorist organization that cannot be an interlocutor of the international community as long as it does not renounce violence and does not recognize Israel's right to exist. This is the unambiguous position of the EU and it will not change."[22]

In fact, Hamas' decision to participate in Palestinian elections came only after the group canvassed its field operatives. According to Hamas operative Yakub Abu Etzev, arrested in August 2005, this input was then forwarded to Hamas operatives in Saudi Arabia for a final decision. Once Hamas militants made the conscious decision to participate in elections, operatives like Yakub Abu Etzev were then personally involved in the logistical preparations leading up to elections. For example, Abu Etzev funded the creation of local Hamas committees in towns and villages with funds from Hamas' Saudi office. Having made the decision to run, many Hamas activists realized that openly running as a Hamas candidate could do more damage than good. Ali Mahmoud Akel, a Hamas dawa activist who headed an Islamist school in the West Bank, ran for the Halhul town council in December 2004. Akel noted that Hamas members are known for shunning corruption, "and that's what the public is interested in." Nonetheless, he added, "I'm not saying 'I'm a Hamas activist' in my campaign because it could hurt me." Several Hamas activists running for public office were arrested by Israeli authorities in December 2004, though Israeli authorities insisted these were activists involved in terrorist activity. In fact, the vast majority of Hamas candidates ran for office unmolested by police or intelligence agencies even though most Hamas candidates ran under the translucent cover of political slates with names like "The Reform Bloc" or "The Islamic Bloc for Change." In case there was any doubt regarding their stance on continued bloodletting, their main campaign slogan was "Partnership in blood and partnership in decision-making."[23]

Using these slates as fronts for what were widely known as Hamas entities, Hamas candidates won about 35 percent of the 306 individual races and took control of nine municipal councils in December 2004 municipal elections. A year later, in January 2006, Hamas won a landslide victory over the incumbent Fatah, taking control of 74 seats (out of 132, or 56 percent) in parliamentary elections that included both national and district lists. Local politics, clan and family affiliation, and a significant protest vote against the ruling Fatah party all played large roles in these victories. Still, the group's grassroots dawa activities translated into an especially strong political following at the local level.[24]

Hamas' participation in politics, whether of a local, national, or regional nature, is premised on the group's central objectives of undermining secular authorities and furthering the group's violent Islamist agenda. In the words of Hamas leader Mahmoud Zahar, "Hamas' participation in the parliamentary election will completely destroy the Oslo Accords." Hamas recognizes the utility of promoting this agenda through multiple channels, including political, social, and military activities. Perhaps the most insightful view into Hamas' political calculus comes from an internal Hamas report circulated by the group's dawa leadership to local dawa activists in November 2002 regarding Hamas' participation in political discussions with the PA in Cairo. The internal memorandum was seized by Palestinian Preventive Security in the Gaza Strip and immediately forwarded to Rashid Abu Shabak, head of Preventive Security. The purpose of these political discussions, according to the Hamas memo, was to improve the movement's position in the eyes of Egypt—a key regional player and host of the talks—and to influence a weak PA leadership. Specifically, Hamas proposed a three-pronged political plan:[25]

1. The integration of the PA and its [security] apparatuses in defending the Palestinian people.
2. Giving political patronage to the resistance and stopping the [PA's] condemnation of the terrorist attacks.
3. Stopping the security coordination [with Israel].[26]

Despite this myopic focus on furthering violent conflict with the Jewish state—which is all the more disturbing and revealing coming from dawa, not military, activists—Hamas is by no means a monolithic movement. To be sure, there are multiple fault lines within Hamas, including tensions between the group's internal and external leadership, between leaders affiliated with Khaled Mishal's Kuwaiti group and leaders with roots in the Gaza Strip, and between ideological moderates and true zealots. These fissures have been exacerbated since the assassinations of Yassin and al-Rantissi, which left a gaping hole in the Hamas leadership structure on the ground in the Gaza Strip. While Mahmoud Zahar and Ismail Haniyeh assumed leadership of the movement's overt political wing, several protégés of al-Rantissi's more militant school aligned themselves with Mohammad Deif, the head of the Qassam Brigades in Gaza. This more radical group reportedly only follows instructions from outside leaders like Mishal and Imad al-Alami. For example, former longtime Hamas dawa activist Sheikh Nizar Riyan openly challenged the public statements of Haniyeh and others claiming Hamas would cease firing mortars at Israel from Gaza. The pledge came in response to complaints from local Palestinian businessmen frustrated by the damage Israeli reprisal attacks against Qassam manufacturing and launching sites did to their businesses and the local economy. In response, Riyan publicly paraded through the streets of the Jabalya refugee camp carrying weapons. A prominent al-Rantissi protégé, Riyan then held a press conference at his mosque where four masked Qassam Brigades militants dismissed Haniyeh's remarks, displayed a variety of weapons, handed out pamphlets documenting Hamas attacks, and announced that Qassam rockets capable of reaching the Israeli city of Ashkelon were under development.[27]

The most significant fault line within Hamas is between those Palestinian Islamists for whom the Palestinian cause comes first and those for whom the Islamist cause takes precedence. And while many supposed "moderates" still support terror attacks under certain conditions, there is a current within the Hamas movement calling for a cessation of military activity and a focus on Islamist political and social activity along the lines of the Jordanian Muslim Brotherhood. Traditionally, Muslim Brotherhood movements have, over time, sacrificed their covert military cells for public political activity, as has been the case in Jordan and Egypt. And while there were radical elements who refused to renounce violence in each of these cases, many experts believe it is only a matter of time before Hamas develops into a nonviolent Islamist movement. According to one Israeli expert, an internal memorandum proposing Hamas give up its "secret underground apparatus" was circulated around the Gaza Strip in October 2004 by a senior Hamas leader there. While many Hamas leaders in the West Bank reportedly supported the idea, it was shouted down by Hamas leaders in Gaza and by the senior political leadership outside the Palestinian territories. According to Ehud Ya'ari, one of Israel's preeminent journalists, this explains why "strong trends within Hamas" were willing to agree to a ceasefire in early 2005.[28]

> The movement has been dramatically weakened in the West Bank and its leaders there realize they cannot put it back together under the present circumstances, and will consider switching to political activity as the Palestinian branch of the Muslim Brotherhood. Its people in the West Bank are beginning to say, maybe we have overplayed our hand, and Hamas has to revert back to becoming the Muslim Brotherhood, under whatever name.[29]

Fostering such splits within Hamas is critical, especially following its rise to political power, and can be best accomplished by undermining the Hamas dawa. Palestinian moderates argue that it is Hamas' social welfare activities, not its suicide bombings, which translate into grassroots and electoral support for the organization at the expense of moderate Palestinian groups. In the words of Palestinian President Mahmoud Abbas, "We understand that the success of Islamic organizations is the activity of their social welfare institutions. We pray silently for support for our public institutions in all areas through which we can reach the masses." Indeed, many of Hamas' more successful newly minted "politicians" are longtime dawa activists parlaying their reputation for delivering social services into political gain. For example, until he was elected mayor of Deir al-Balah in the Gaza Strip in February 2002, Ahmad Kurd spent twenty-eight years running the al-Salah Association—one of the Hamas fronts shut down by the PA in August 2003. "The affection and confidence of voters is not bought in an hour," Kurd explained. "It is something that takes years to develop."[30]

For moderate Palestinians to compete politically with radical Islamist groups, services and public projects that impact people's lives will have to be delivered by the Palestinian government as such, not by Hamas as an independent entity. "A strengthened Hamas poses real challenges for Palestinians and Israelis alike," an Israeli expert noted, adding that the way to halt the organization's increasing momentum is "by giving the entire Palestinian population access to a new, modern welfare infrastructure, one that could gradually replace the services provided by Hamas." American experts agree, noting that Palestinian moderates need to "neutralize Hamas and other militant groups with a new political and economic strategy." One of the reasons Hamas swept municipal elections in Gaza just two weeks after Mahmoud Abbas won a clear majority in presidential elections there is "thanks to its track record of providing essential social services, for health care to education, not being delivered by the government."[31]

ORGANIZING AID AND TRANSPARENCY

Organizing international aid and transparency to displace the Hamas dawa would not be as difficult as many presume were Hamas not in control of the PA. An international fund to fill the niche in Palestinian social welfare assistance provided by Hamas could be overseen by an organization like the World Bank, perhaps with an oversight board composed of donor nation representatives. Indeed, in December 2003 the bank offered to oversee just such a trust fund for aid to the Palestinian Authority. "If it is the wish of this group that there be a transparent and single trust fund," the bank's president James Wolfensohn offered at a Palestinian donor meeting in Rome, "we in the bank are prepared, alone or with partners, to lead such a trust fund and add whatever confidence that comes from having the World Bank present in the operations." Such oversight is necessary not only as a means of enforcing transparency but also to coordinate the assistance of an increasing number of donor countries. For example, since the onset of the current Intifada in September 2000, individual Arab countries pledged hundreds of millions of dollars to the PA through the Arab League. Efforts to coordinate these pledges to ensure they are complementary, not redundant, were facilitated through World Bank and United Nations working groups and consultative committees such as the Ad Hoc Liaison Committee. These were coupled with informal NGO working groups and channeled giving routes such as the World Bank's Holst Peace Fund. None of these, however, served the critical function of enforcing transparency at both the giving and receiving ends of the donor spectrum to ensure intended humanitarian assistance was not diverted or otherwise manipulated by corrupt officials or terrorist elements.[32]

Indeed, expert reports reveal the need for regulation, and transparency is imperative not only to thwart the diversion of monies to fund terrorism but also to prevent corrupt officials from enriching themselves at the expense of the Palestinian public. A 2003 International Monetary Fund (IMF) report revealed that $900 million was diverted from PA accounts from 1995 to 2000. And in a January 2004 Palestinian Legislative Council (PLC) session, Azmi Shuabi, chairman of the Palestinian Legislative Council's Economic Committee, exposed an embezzlement scheme within the PA Ministry of Transportation that may have cost the Palestinian treasury $17 million to $18 million.[33]

Similarly, in February 2003 the European Union's Anti-Fraud Office (OLAF) opened an investigation into "allegations of misuse of funds donated by the European Union in the context of EU budgetary support to the Palestinian Authority." The European Parliament has therefore pressed for EU contributions to go only to "identified purposes" instead of general budgetary support, and Britain's international development minister expressed "reservations about providing direct budget support [to the PA] in the form that we do with other countries, because we have to go through a process of satisfying ourselves that the systems and structures are in place to account for how that money is spent."[34]

An oversight body of representatives from donor nations could provide transparency for the fund and political cover for its members. Saudi participation in particular would serve as a welcome and tangible demonstration of the Saudi government's oft-stated commitment to curb the financing of terror from within the Kingdom's borders without having to shut aid efforts specially geared toward assisting Palestinians. Instead, monies from government-sponsored telethons, "Account 98" bank accounts earmarked for aid to Palestinians (including Hamas), and pseudo-governmental charities could all be channeled to an international fund for humanitarian assistance to needy Palestinians. By playing a defining role in this international effort to assist Palestinians, Riyadh could save face at home and deflect criticism from radical religious elites by portraying itself as a driving force uniting the international community together in support of Palestinian humanitarian assistance. To be sure, Saudi participation would set a powerful precedent for other Arab and Muslim states to follow suit.

FINDING ALTERNATIVES TO HUMANITARIANISM TAINTED BY TERROR

Significant investment in medical clinics, early childhood centers, nursing homes, and a liberal education system—facilities and services that not only match but surpass those provided by Hamas—would go a long way toward meeting the challenge posed by Hamas and its social welfare network. But finding alternative mechanisms untainted by terror or corruption that are capable of absorbing the vast amount of international funding available is easier said than done. Short of finding such a mechanism, even significant funding for donor programs will be ineffective. James Prince, a consultant to the Palestine Investment Fund, claims that "many of the donor programs have not only been ineffective, they have harmed the [Palestinian] economy."[35]

In response to this problem, Palestinian officials initiated a trial program in early 2005 to establish a mechanism to deliver humanitarian aid safely and effectively in the West Bank and Gaza as an alternative to the assistance provided by groups like Hamas. The program aimed not only to undermine the infrastructure and financial support for Hamas but also to provide donors interested in contributing funds to needy Palestinians a reliable mechanism to do so. As Hamas began to challenge the Palestinian Authority at the ballot box, drying up support for Hamas became a priority for Palestinian Authority officials. Social welfare officials envisioned doing this by increasing official government welfare rolls from 20,000 to 60,000 people and by monitoring charities tied to Hamas. The new effort, called The Social Fund, was conceived as a means of providing monthly welfare income to the poorest Palestinians who otherwise get by only with the assistance provided by Hamas. But the pilot program never grew into a more robust strategic plan. Filling this void would have denied Hamas a critical base of grassroots political support and undercut its operational support network.[36]

To be sure, resolution of the Israeli-Palestinian conflict will primarily be a function of progress toward a political settlement, not simply a function of security or humanitarian efforts. But reaching a political settlement is contingent on undermining groups like Hamas that are bent on obstructing peace. Hamas, it should be clear, does not carry out suicide bombings for lack of progress toward peace but rather to thwart such progress. And Hamas activists themselves describe the periodic ceasefires (hudna) or periods of calm (tahdiya) to which they subscribe as tactical responses to outside pressure and as "a time-out for the fighters" during which they can rearm and regroup. "This calm," said a Qassam Brigades leader in March 2005, "is not a gift to the occupation. We will work on and prepare ourselves. Disbanding the armed wing of Hamas is absolutely out of the question." In the days leading up to Israel's final departure from Gaza, Hamas distributed 250,000 copies of a bulletin—also posted on its websites—promising continued attacks against Israel after the "expulsion" of Israel from Gaza. Entitled "Dawn of Victory," the cover of the bulletin was a picture of Hamas militants hoisting the green Hamas flag while standing on bloodstained bodies of Israeli soldiers and the rubble of Israeli settlements. Just days earlier Hamas military commander Mohammad Deif appeared on a video released to the media threatening, "You [Israelis] are leaving Gaza today in shame." He continued, "Today you are leaving hell. But we promise you that tomorrow all Palestine will be hell for you, God willing." Hamas promised to do so using traditional and new tactics, including tried and true suicide bombings, a brigade of female Hamas trainees called "Qassamits," and a new missile named the *Sajil* with a reported range of fifteen kilometers. The fact that Hamas suicide bombings continue despite intermittent truces, that Hamas prepares explosives during periods of calm, and that progress toward peace and even territorial withdrawals do not placate Hamas calls for bloodletting, demonstrate that Hamas cannot be co-opted into moderation simply by virtue of its entry into Palestinian electoral politics.

PALESTINE'S "PARTY OF GOD"

Analysts expected Hamas to fare well in the January 2006 elections, but no one—including Hamas—anticipated it would emerge as the dominant political party and form a ruling cabinet. Overnight, Hamas went from planning how to operate as a parliamentary opposition to President Mahmoud Abbas' Fatah party to being asked by Abbas to form a cabinet and appoint a prime minister. But Hamas has a course to follow as it attempts to navigate the political waters between its rigidly conservative ideology, its stated intention to continue carrying out attacks, its need to actually govern, and Western calls for divorcing politics and violence. As it calculates how to balance these apparently competing interests, Hamas will look north to Lebanon's Hezbollah (Party of God) for a working model of a militant Islamist group that balances its political, charitable, and violent activities.

Although its presence in the Lebanese government is small, Hezbollah has held seats in the Lebanese parliament since 1992 and, in the wake of elections that followed Lebanon's 2005 "Cedar Revolution," the party joined the ruling coalition and assumed a cabinet seat. Despite its participation in mainstream Lebanese politics, Hezbollah maintains a large, independent militia deployed throughout southern Lebanon, as well as one of most formidable international terrorist capabilities under the direction of Imad Mughniyeh, one of the FBI's most-wanted terrorists. Like Hamas, Hezbollah seeks to Islamize Lebanese society (though in its case to the Shi'a branch of Islam) and destroy Israel. And like Hezbollah, Hamas is loath to forgo its jihadist agenda for the sake of political participation.[37]

Indeed, for Hamas and Hezbollah alike political participation is just another means—alongside good works and militancy—to achieve their goals. Even were Hamas to agree to a long-term hudna with Israel, this would not indicate an end to its struggle against Israel but a shift in the prioritization of its means of doing so. Abbas al-Sayyid, the convicted Qassam Brigades commander behind the Park Hotel Passover massacre (who simultaneously served as the political leader of Hamas in Tulkarm), explained that a long-term hudna is merely a temporary truce, adding, "I will struggle to get back what is rightfully mine, and if I can not then maybe my son or grandson will." A hudna, al-Sayyid explained, "is the truest solution for those of faith. Hamas is ready for a period of time of truce—but [it] can not agree to Israel taking Islamic lands, for religious reasons." In the final analysis, "No Palestinian can accept a two state solution forever," he said, adding, "this is very sensitive."[38]

Hamas has long cooperated with Hezbollah operationally, and in the lead-up to Palestinian elections it already began implementing a Hezbollah-style model in Gaza. Fathi Hamad, director of Hamas' al-Aqsa television station, noted that the success of Hezbollah's al-Manar satellite television was a key factor leading Hamas to open a television station of its own. Hamas has often issued claims of responsibility on al-Manar for its attacks and, taking another page from Hezbollah's trade book, filmed living wills of suicide-bombers-to-be that were then aired on al-Manar.[39]

Despite its militia and terrorist activities, Hezbollah is perceived in much of Europe and elsewhere as a political organization. While the European Union has designated Hamas as a terrorist organization, it has not so designated Hezbollah. In an attempt to reinvent itself as a political organization in Hezbollah's image, in January 2006 Hamas went so far as to hire a media consultant to improve its image at home and in Western capitals. For a reported $180,000 spent in the weeks leading up to the January elections, Hamas bought such advice as "Say you are not against Israelis as Jews," "Don't talk about destroying Israel," "Do talk about Palestinian suffering," "Don't celebrate killing people," and "Change beard color" (from the henna coloring preferred by Islamists).[40]

But beyond mimicking Hezbollah's propaganda techniques, Hamas also began to structure its militant components along the lines of Hezbollah's parallel standing militia and terrorist elements. Like Hezbollah's guerilla militia in South Lebanon and its Islamic Jihad Organization terrorist network, Hamas established a standing militia in Gaza in 2003 to complement its terrorist Qassam Brigades. Creating an army has long been a dream of Hamas leaders, who often justify suicide bombings as a poor man's F16. The day before the group's electoral victory, Hamas leader Khaled Mishal indicated Hamas' intention to unify all Palestinian factions under a "national liberation army that would continue the liberation march."[41]

Hamas' emulation of Hezbollah underlies the most significant parallel between the two militant Islamist groups: tactical flexibility should not be mistaken for strategic change. Both organizations see politics, charity, political violence, and terrorism as viable, legitimate tools to pursue their goals. At times they stress certain tools over others, but at no time do they see these as mutually exclusive. Thus, after casting his own vote in the parliamentary elections that brought his party to power, Hamas leader Mahmoud Zahar pledged, "Hamas will not turn into a political party. Hamas plays in all fields. It plays in the field of resistance." As the Hamas charter stresses, there is a need for resistance through multiple, concurrent channels, including military, political, social, cultural, propaganda, and other fields. Zahar was very precise in his campaign speeches, telling one crowd, "We are entering the legislative council to make it a project of resistance." Underlying that theme, Zahar promised that Hamas "will not change a single word in its covenant," which calls for the destruction of Israel.[42]

Meanwhile, Hamas remains an extremely capable opponent to both Israel and moderate Palestinians. Between the money it receives from radical Islamist NGOs, "charitable" donations, and the stipends of state sponsors like Iran, Hamas is as well funded and capable as ever before. Cutting off the flow of funds to Hamas, and replacing its largesse with an organized and regulated international aid effort to address the real and immediate needs of the Palestinian people, is therefore more urgent than ever.

Cracking down on terrorism is critical to meeting the social welfare needs of Palestinians in the West Bank and Gaza, providing Israeli civilians a measure of security, and, should political conditions improve, returning to negotiations over a viable political settlement. To pursue these goals, donor countries must not be distracted from debunking the myth that Hamas conducts legitimate political and charity work parallel but unrelated to its suicide terrorism. It is worth recounting that Hamas activists meeting in Philadelphia in 1994 feared that American and Israeli investment in Palestinian territories would undercut "the Palestinian anger, desperation, revolution by raising the standards of living of the Palestinians" and hoped "the failure of the self rule administration to solve the problems of the Palestinian population and providing the needed services to them will be detrimental to the peace accord." Therefore, they concluded, "to defeat the [Oslo] accord we [Hamas] should make services available to the population." Indeed, for Hamas political activism and social welfare support are both tactical (as a financial and logistical support network) and strategic (as a means of undermining the PA and thwarting progress toward peace). For that reason, senior U.S. officials have stressed the need to "come up with a way to get [social welfare support] to the [Palestinian] people in some mechanism other than Hamas. We need to come up with an alternative to ensure that money still gets to the people who need it." Similarly, it is critical that the international community keep to the pledges of leaders like British Prime Minister Tony Blair and American Secretary of State Condoleezza Rice that Hamas must, in Blair's words, "choose whether they want a path of violence or a path of politics." Having "one foot in terrorism and the other foot in politics," Rice warned, "simply does not work." Failure to live up to such standards would leave Hamas unfettered to continue undermining moderate Palestinians, radicalizing Palestinian society, and killing Israelis. The sad reality is that nothing undermines the legitimate goal of establishing a secure and independent Palestinian state that lives in peace side-by-side with its neighbors more than Palestinian terrorism.[43]

ACKNOWLEDGMENTS

This book is the product of three years of research, including several trips to the Middle East and Europe. It draws on newly declassified intelligence, seized Hamas documents, and dozens of interviews on three continents with experts and officials and imprisoned Hamas operatives. Compiling and organizing this data, and then writing, editing, and rewriting the manuscript, was an all-encompassing task made possible only through the kind and generous assistance of a great many people. The few people I can thank by name are mentioned below. But a great many people asked to remain anonymous because of the nature of their professional positions. To all of you, and you know who you are, I extend my sincerest gratitude and friendship. I am grateful to all the experts, government officials, and intelligence analysts who gave so generously of their time, experience, and insights. I am equally grateful to the great many people who helped me gain access to declassified intelligence reports on Hamas. So many people helped me discover, understand, debate, shape, and articulate the material presented in this book and I thank you all.

This project was only possible because The Washington Institute for Near East Policy graciously afforded me the time, space, support, and funding to research and write this book, including funding several research trips abroad. I am especially grateful for the support of the Institute's Executive Committee and Board of Trustees, its Executive Director, Dr. Robert Satloff; its Counselor and Ziegler Distinguished Fellow, Ambassador Dennis Ross; its Deputy Director for Research, Dr. Patrick Clawson; and the entire Institute staff. The Institute's senior research staff was a constant source of support and I am a wiser, better person for having had the opportunity to be a part of this truly remarkable intellectual community. Special thanks go to David Makovsky, Martin Kramer, and Mike Herzog for their constant input and insight, and to Ambassador Ross for his input and the foreword he wrote for this book.

I owe a special thanks and acknowledgment to the various research assistants and interns at The Washington Institute who at some point over the past few years put their hearts and souls into this study, including Sarah Dabby, Andrew Eastman, Anna Hartman, Yonatan Levy, and Joshua Prober.

But among the Institute's cadre of fantastic researchers, two people stand out for their contributions to this book. I could never have produced this book without the tireless efforts of research assistants Julie Sawyer and Jamie Chosak. From arranging travel to transcribing interview notes, from organizing data to editing an endless number of drafts and finally formatting the final manuscript, Julie and Jamie both became full partners in this research project, and I am truly grateful for their contributions.

I am also grateful to the experts at the Intelligence and Terrorism Information Center at the Center for Special Studies in Israel for granting me access to primary source documents seized in Israeli military raids of Hamas and Palestinian Authority offices. My thanks to the center for granting permission to use pictures of materials seized in these raids; the pictures can be seen online at www.yalebooks.com/hamas.

My book agent, Robbie Hare, worked long and hard to find the perfect publisher for this study, and I am very grateful to her for making the match with Yale University Press. I am grateful to Lara Heimert and Molly Egland, my first editor and assistant editor at Yale, and to Chris Rogers and Ellie Goldberg, who picked up as my new editor and assistant editor and saw the book through editing and publication. I am still amazed at the incredible editing job performed by Gadi Dechter, who carved a readable book out of a policy monograph. Thank you, Gadi.

Finally, I am eternally grateful to my family—including my parents, in-laws, children, and, most of all, my wonderful wife, Dina—for their unending support and patience. I am truly blessed.

NOTES

INTRODUCTION

1 For Zahar and Farhat quotes, see Anne Barnard, "Hamas Hardens Campaign Rhetoric: Leaders Praise Jihad and Renew Calls to Fight Israel," *Boston Globe*, January 24, 2006.

2 Salah Montasser, "Shadowy Samsons," *Al-Ahram* no. 729, February 10–16, 2005, http://weekly.ahram.org.eg/2005/729/op8.htm.

3 U.S. House Committee on Financial Services, Subcommittee on Oversight and Investigations, *Testimony of David Aufhauser*, 108th Cong., 1st sess., September 24, 2003, http://www.treas.gov/press/releases/js758.htm.

4 Unless otherwise noted, the information in this section on the Park Hotel bombing comes from the author's prison interviews with Abbas al-Sayyid and Fathi Khatib, November 18, 2004; from the Israeli military indictment against Fathi Kahtib, Samaria Military Court, September 7, 2002; and from C.S.S. Special Information Bulletin, *Passover Eve Massacre at Park Hotel in Netanya: Analysis of a Mass-Murder Terror Attack as a Case Study of the Terrorist Nature of the Hamas Movement and the Involvement of Its Political Leadership in Operational Terrorist Activity*, May 2004, http://www.intelligence.org.il/eng/sib/6_04/park_h.htm.

5 Human Rights Watch, *Erased in a Moment: Suicide Bombing Attacks Against Israeli Civilians* (New York: Human Rights Watch, 2002), 31.

6 Dan Ephron, "Passover Bomber Kills at Least 19 Israelis," *Washington Times,* March 28, 2002. Having taken ill, suicide bomber Nidal Qalq dropped out of the operation believing that a sick "martyr" is impure and therefore ineligible for a "death of the righteous" and entry to heaven. Al-Sayyid planned to dispatch Qalq in a subsequent suicide bombing which was thwarted by their capture. See Khatib indictment.

7 Author interview with Israeli intelligence officials, November 18, 2004, Tel Aviv.

8 Information regarding al-Sayyid and Mansour and the al-Ansar singing troupe is from an author interview with Israel intelligence officials, Tel Aviv, November 18, 2004. Regarding the Tulkarm cell, see "Background Information: Head of Hamas Terrorist Organization in Tulkarm Arrested in Joint IDF and GSS Operation," *Independent Media Review Analysis (IMRA)*, December 3, 2004. For Odeh posters, see Khaled Abu Toameh, "PA Tournament Named for Bomber," *Jerusalem Post*, January 22, 2003.

9 Hamas is an acronym for *Harakat al-Muqawam al-Islamiyah,* or Islamic Resistance Movement.

10 World Bank, "Palestinian Authority: World Bank Launches Multi-Donor Trust Fund to Support Reform Program," April 27, 2004; and United Nations Development Programme, *Arab Human Development Report 2003* (New York: United Nations Publications, 2003), 25; and Steve Franklin, "Health Plight Rises for Palestinian Kids," *Chicago Tribune,* June 28, 2001.

CHAPTER 1 **ORIGINS OF THE HAMAS DAWA**

1 Canadian Secret Intelligence Service (CSIS), "Terrorist Group Profiler," June 2002, author's personal files. The report is referenced in Stewart Bell, "Hamas May Have Chemical Weapons: CSIS Report Says Terror Group May Be Experimenting," *National Post* (Canada), December 10, 2003. For the Hamas Charter, see the Avalon Project at Yale Law School, "The Covenant of the Islamic Resistance Movement," *Hamas Covenant 1988,* http://www.yale.edu/lawweb/avalon/mideast/hamas.htm.

2 Jihad quote culled from John Esposito, "Understanding Islam," al-Jazeerah, July 18, 2003, http://www.aljazeerah.info/Opinion%20editorials/2003%20Opinion%20Editorials/July/18%20o/Understanding%20Islam,%20By%20John%20Esposito.htm. Koranic excepts from Abdul Hadi Palazzi, "The Islamists Have It Wrong," *Middle East Quarterly* 9, no. 3 (2001).

3 Zvi Barel, "Hamas Is Even Prepared to Go 'Legal,'" *Ha'aretz,* March 16, 2005.

4 Yusef quote in Danny Rubenstein, "You Can't Get Rid of Us," *Ha'aretz,* April 14, 2005. Information on Hamas military wing from International Policy Institute for Counter-Terrorism (ICT), "Harakat al-Muqawamah al-Islamiyya (HAMAS)," *Terrorist Group Profiles,* http://www.ict.org.il/organizations/org_frame.cfm?orgid=13.

5 Author interview with Israeli intelligence analysts, Tel Aviv, November 16, 2004. Members of the Kuwaiti group include Khaled Mishal, Osama Hamdan, Mohammad Nazzal, and Ibrahim Ghawsah. The most senior members of the Gaza faction are Mousa Abu Marzook and Imad al-Alami.

6 ICT, "Harakat al-Muqawamah al-Islamiyya (HAMAS)."

7 CSIS, "Terrorist Group Profiler"; Bell, "Hamas May Have Chemical Weapons."

8 Palestinian Academic Society for the Study of International Affairs (PASSIA), "Sheikh Izz al-Din al-Qassam," *Palestine Facts: Personalities,* http://www.passia.org/palestine_facts/personalities/alpha_q.htm; and Ziad Abu-Amr, *Islamic Fundamentalism in the West Bank and Gaza: Muslim Brotherhood and Islamic Jihad* (Bloomington: Indiana University Press, 1994), 98–99. Hamas quickly followed the Shorshan murder with additional attacks, including the murder of an Israeli border guard in Jerusalem and an attempted car bombing in the Ramat Efal community near Tel Aviv. See ICT, "Harakat al-Muqawamah al-Islamiyya (HAMAS)."

9 Regarding Mehola attack, see Jon Immanuel, Michael Rotem, and David Rudge, "Only Luck Prevents Disaster in Suicide Car-Bomb Attack in Territories," *Jerusalem Post,* April 18, 1993. Regarding Afula attacks, see Karin Laub, "Car Bomb Explodes in Northern Israel, Eight Killed, 44 Wounded," Associated Press, April 6, 1994.

10 Database of attacks compiled by author.

11 Israel Ministry of Foreign Affairs (MFA), "Hamas Terrorist Attacks," *Terror Background,* March 22, 2004, http://www.mfa.gov.il/MFA/Terrorism-+Obstacle+to+Peace/Terror+Groups/Hamas+terror+attacks+22-Mar-2004.htm.

12 MFA, "Summary of Terrorist Activity 2004," *MFA Library 2005,* http://www.mfa.gov.il/MFA/MFAArchive/2000_2009/2005/Summary%20of%20Terrorist%20Activity%202004.

13 Agence France Presse, "Chinese Worker, Palestinian Killed in Gaza Settlement Attack," June 7, 2005; "The Family of Nations Under Fire: Victims of Palestinian Violence from 18 Countries," *Beyond Images,* March 2, 2004, http://www.beyondimages.info/b79

.html; "Palestinian Suicide Bombings 1994–2004: Don't Let the World Forget . . . ," *Beyond Images*, September 2, 2004, http://www.beyondimages.info/b78.html.

14 Yassin quote on popular defense from Amit Cohen, "Hamas Setting Up Army in the Gaza Strip," *Ma'ariv*, March 7, 2004.

15 Translated text available in "Israeli Paper Says Hamas Setting Up Army to Fill Vacuum after Gaza Pullout," *BBC Monitoring Middle East—Political, BBC Worldwide Monitoring*, March 7, 2004. Ya'ari quote from Ehud Ya'ari, "Keep the Gloves Off," *Jerusalem Report*, April 19, 2004. Israeli intelligence comment on recruits of popular army are drawn from author interview, Tel Aviv, May 13, 2004. Jabr and Deif roles in popular army are drawn from author interview, Tel Aviv, May 13, 2004.

16 Matthew Levitt, "Designating the al-Aqsa Martyrs Brigades," *Washington Institute for Near East Policy Policywatch* 371, March 25, 2002.

17 Israel Defense Forces (IDF), "Jenin, the Palestinian Suicide Capital," April 18, 2002.

18 IDF, "Iran and Syria as Strategic Supports for Palestinian Terrorism (Based on the Interrogations of Arrested Palestinian Terrorists and Captured Palestinian Authority Documents)," September 2002.

19 For Shami, see Keith Richburg, "Arafat Turns to Militants in Uprising—Freed Extremists Become Part of Palestine 'Resistance,'" *Washington Post*, October 25, 2000; and "Arafat making tactical alliance with Islamic Jihad and Hamas," *International Herald Tribune*, October 25, 2000. For Ghosheh, see "Ghoushe: We Are Committed to Launching Martyrdom Operations—Coordination with Fatah Helped in Expanding Confrontations," *al-Mostakbal*, March 3, 2001. For al-Zanun, see Reuters, "Islamic Jihad Urges Muslims to Fight Israel," April 25, 2001.

20 Regarding "combined force" and "joint operations room," see IDF, "Jenin, the Palestinian Suicide Capital." For officials and weapons supply, see IDF, "The Fatah and the PA Security Apparatuses in the Jenin Area Closely Cooperate with PIJ and Hamas," April 9, 2002. These security officers included Jamal Switat, deputy head of PA Preventive Security in Jenin, and a man named al-Rah. Regarding al-Quds Brigade's attack, see Israel Defense Forces Spokesperson's Unit, "Following in the Steps of Hamas and Fatah, Islamic Jihad Has Also Added the Manufacture of Weapons, Intended for Terror Attacks against Israel, to Its Products," May 27, 2002.

21 For October 2003 interview, see Ramit Plushnick Masti, "Palestinian Militant Groups Join Forces, Get Help from Hezbollah," Associated Press, October 28, 2003. Regarding military wings deal see Ehud Ya'ari, "The Hamas Jihad Axis," *Jerusalem Report*, November 17, 2003.

22 For dawa definition, see R. Hrair Dekmejian, *Islam in Revolution: Fundamentalism in the Arab World* (Syracuse, N.Y.: Syracuse University Press, 1985), 44. Quote regarding waqf from Michael Dumper, *Islam and Israel: Muslim Religious Endowments and the Jewish State* (Washington, D.C.: Institute for Palestine Studies, 1994), 1–2.

23 See Robert Worth, "The Deep Intellectual Roots of Islamic Terror," *New York Times*, October 13, 2001; *Wikipedia Online Encyclopedia*, s.v. "Salafi," http://en.wikipedia.org/wiki/Salafi.

24 John Esposito, *Islam: The Straight Path* (Oxford: Oxford University Press, 1988), 200; Christopher M. Blanchard, *Al-Qaeda: Statements and Evolving Ideology*, Congressional Research Service, CRS Report RL32759, February 4, 2005, http://www.fas.org/irp/crs/

RL32759.pdf. For an insightful discussion of Salafi means of spreading Islam, from dawa to violent activity, see Quintan Wiktorowicz and John Kaltner, "Killing in the Name of Islam: Al-Qaeda's Justification for September 11," *Middle East Policy* 10, no. 2 (2003), http://www.mepc.org/public_asp/journal_vol10/0306_wiktorowiczkaltner.asp.

25 Carrie Rosefsky Wickham, "Islamic Mobilization and Political Change: The Islamist Trend in Egypt's Professional Associations," in Joel Beinin and Joe Stork, eds., *Political Islam: Essays from Middle East Report* (Berkeley: University of California Press, 1997), 124.

26 For comment regarding finding staples on sidewalk, see Isabel Kershner, "Hamas in Manger Square," *Jerusalem Report,* June 13, 2005; Palestinian Center for Policy and Survey Research (PSR), "Exit Polls—Results of PSR Local Elections' Exit Polls (May 2005)," PSR Survey Research Unit, http://www.pcpsr.org/survey/polls/2005/exitlocal2 .html.

27 For Qutb quote, see Dekmejian, *Islam in Revolution,* 91; Olivier Roy, *The Failure of Political Islam,* trans. Carol Volk (Cambridge, Mass.: Harvard University Press, 1994), 57 and 70.

28 General Intelligence and Security Service, "From Dawa to Jihad: The Various Threats from Radical Islam to the Democratic Legal Order," *Netherlands Ministry of the Interior and Kingdom Relations* (December 2004): 7 and 27, http://www.minbzk.nl/contents/pages/42345/fromdawatojihad.pdf.

29 MWL objectives listed at "About the Muslim World League," http://www.arab.net/ mwl/about.htm (accessed March 2003). For treasury designation of Wal Jlaidan, see U.S. Department of the Treasury, Office of Foreign Assets Control, *Terrorism: What You Need To Know About U.S. Sanctions,* Washington, D.C., August 1, 2005, http://www .treasury.gov/offices/enforcement/ofac/sanctions/terrorism.html. For IIRO and MWL raids, see Judith Miller, "Raids Seek Evidence of Money-Laundering," *New York Times,* March 21, 2002. For information on the Muslim World League's ties to terrorism, see U.S. Senate Committee on Banking, Housing, and Urban Affairs, Subcommittee on International Trade and Finance, *Testimony of Matthew Levitt,* "Charitable and Humanitarian Organizations in the Network of International Terrorist Financing," August 1, 2002, http://www.washingtoninstitute.org/templateC07.php?CID=138. See also Sworn statement of David Kane, senior special agent with the Bureau of Immigration and Customs Enforcement (ICE), *United States of America v. Solimam S. Biheiri,* Case No. 03-365-A, Redacted Sentencing Declaration (U.S. District Court for the Eastern District of Virginia, Alexandria Division), December 10, 2003.

30 For more on legitimate dawa activity as NGOs, see U.S. Senate Committee on Banking, Housing, and Urban Affairs, Subcommittee on International Trade and Finance, *Testimony of Quintan Wiktorwicz,* "Prepared Statement to a Hearing on the Role of Charities and NGO's in the Financing of Terrorist Activities," August 1, 2002, http://banking .senate.gov/02_08hrg/080102/wiktorow.htm. For MB ties to suspect NGOs, see, for example, Edward Alden, Mark Huband, and Mark Turner, "Al-Qaeda 'Financiers' Active in Europe: A UN Report Reveals a Lack of Action over Youssef Nada and Ahmed Idris Nasreddin," *Financial Times,* November 14, 2003. See also U.S. Senate Committee on Banking, Housing, and Urban Affairs, *Testimony of Matthew Levitt,* "Untangling the Terror Web: The Need for a Strategic Understanding of the Crossover Between International Terrorist Groups to Successfully Prosecute the War on Terror," October 22, 2003, http://www.washingtoninstitute.org/templateC07.php?CID=15.

31 See Hamas document "al-Haqiqa wal-Wujud" [Truth and existence] (a semi-official history of Hamas), 1990, part I, as cited in Shaul Mishal and Avraham Sela, *The Palestinian Hamas: Vision, Violence, and Coexistence* (New York: Columbia University Press, 2000), 18. Officially, the group was founded the day after a key planning meeting held in the home of Hamas founder Sheikh Ahmed Yassin to decide how best to take advantage of the day-old rioting that developed into the first Intifada; see Abu-Amr, *Islamic Fundamentalism in the West Bank and Gaza*, 63, 80; The Avalon Project at Yale Law School, "The Covenant of the Islamic Resistance Movement."

32 *Columbia Encyclopedia*, s.v. "Muslim Brotherhood," accessed via the Academic Search Premier Database. For Abdel Rahman al-Banna's visit with the Mufti of Jerusalem and MB volunteers fighting Israel, see Abu-Amr, *Islamic Fundamentalism in the West Bank and Gaza*, 1–3.

33 The Avalon Project at Yale Law School, "The Covenant of the Islamic Resistance Movement."

34 Meir Hatina, *Islam and Salvation in Palestine*, Dayan Center Paper 127 (Tel Aviv: The Moshe Dayan Center for Middle Eastern and African Studies, Tel Aviv University, 2001), 18. See also Abu-Amr, *Islamic Fundamentalism in the West Bank and Gaza*, 28.

35 Ghassan Charbel, "The Khaled Mishaal Interview (2 of 7)," *Dar al Hayat*, December 15, 2003, http://english.daralhayat.com/Spec/12-2003/Article-20031215-7a215ab8-c0a8-01ed-0015-c5ece4bc1b17/story.html.

36 Hatina, *Islam and Salvation in Palestine*, 19.

37 *Al-Anba*, October 1998, as cited in Boaz Ganor, "Hamas—The Islamic Resistance Movement in the Territories," Jerusalem Center for Public Affairs, *Survey of Arab Affairs*, no. 27 (February 2, 1992), http://www.jcpa.org/jl/saa27.htm.

38 Abu-Amr, *Islamic Fundamentalism in the West Bank and Gaza*, 14–15.

39 Ibid., 15.

40 Charbel, "The Khaled Mishaal Interview (2 of 7)."

41 Hamas document "al-Haqiqa wal-Wujud" [Truth and existence] (a semiofficial history of Hamas), 1990, part 1, p. 34, as cited in Mishal and Sela, *Palestinian Hamas*, 18.

42 "Subject: Presidential Decree/Sheikh Gamil Hamami," Report No. 10/4263-A/95, May 31, 1995, and Israeli intelligence report marked pages 0609–0614 of evidentiary material brought in *Stanley Boim et al. v. Quranic Literacy Institute et al.*, Civil No. 00 C 2905 (U.S. District Court, Northern District of Illinois, Eastern Division), June 5, 2002.

43 Hamas poster available from the Intelligence and Terrorism Information Center at the Center for Special Studies (C.S.S), Special Information Bulletin, *The Influence of the Legacy of Global Jihad on Hamas: Glorification of the Image and Islamic-Political Doctrines of Dr. 'Abdallah 'Azzam, a Palestinian from Silat al-Harithiya*, November 2004, "Appendix B (1): The Picture of 'Abdallah 'Azzam on a Hamas Poster," http://www.intelligence.org.il/eng/sib/11_04/legacy.htm#b. For Ammar quote, see Jessica Stern, *Terror in the Name of God: Why Religious Militants Kill* (New York: Harper Collins, 2003), 48.

44 Regarding Yassin's focus on dawa and number of mosques in the Gaza Strip, see Mishal and Sela, *Palestinian Hamas*, 19, 21. For Arab analyst view, see Khaled Hroub, *Hamas: Political Thought and Practice* (Washington, D.C.: Institute for Palestine Studies, 2000), 234. Regarding early Israeli support for Islamists, see Hatina, *Islam and Salvation in Palestine*, 19; Anat Kurz with Nahman Tal, "Hamas: Radical Islam in a National Struggle,"

Jaffee Center for Strategic Studies, Memorandum No. 48 (Tel Aviv University, July 1997), 12.

45 Stern, *Terror in the Name of God,* 41. Contrary to his claim that the focus at this time was purely social and political, not military, Palestinian author Khaled Hroub lists several "military cells organized by the Muslim Brotherhood," including: Yahya al-Ghuoul's Mujahideen of Mifraqa Group, Salah Shehadah's Group Number 44, and Mohammad Sharathah's Group Number 101, all of which conducted various attacks against Israeli interests from 1985 to 1987. See Hroub, *Hamas: Political Thought and Practice,* 35.

46 Shanab quote in Stern, *Terror in the Name of God,* 41. For founders of al-Jam'iya al-Islamiyah and al-Mujama, and regarding the Islamic University in Gaza, see Abu-Amr, *Islamic Fundamentalism in the West Bank and Gaza,* 16–17, 63, and Hatina, *Islam and Salvation in Palestine,* 19. For Mishal interview, see Charbel, "The Khaled Mishaal Interview (2 of 7)." According to Mishal, the experience of Hamas officials who studied at Islamic Universities in Egypt, including Abdul Aziz al-Rantissi, Ibrahim Makadma, Mahmoud al-Zahar, Mousa Abu Marzook, and Ismail Abu Shanab, led to the idea of establishing an Islamic University in Gaza.

47 Others include Islamic Jihad–al-Aqsa Battalions (*al-Jihad al-Islami–Kata'ib al-Aqsa*), established in Jordan in 1982 by followers of Sheikh As'ad Bayyud al-Tamimi; Islamic Jihad–The Temple (*al-Jihad al-Islami–Bait al-Maqdas*), a faction of the Fatah movement which emerged in the early 1980s; and the Islamic Jihad Squad (*Tanzim al-Jihad al-Islami*), an Islamist offshoot of the Palestinian Popular Liberation Forces (PPLF) started by Ahmad Muhanna in the 1980s. Hezbollah, Iran's primary terrorist proxy, is also known by the name Islamic Jihad Organization (IJO).

48 *United States v. Sami al Arian et al.,* superseding indictment, Case No. 8:03CR77T30 TBM, Middle District of Florida, Tampa Division, 2004.

49 MFA, "Operation for the Confiscation of Terror Funds—Background," February 26, 2004, http://www.mfa.gov.il/MFA/Terrorism-+Obstacle+to+Peace/Terrorism+and+ Islamic+Fundamentalism-/Security+forces+seize+terrorist+funds+-+Background .htm. See also *U.S. v. Sami al Arian et al.*

50 "The Big Fish That Got Away," *Jerusalem Post,* October 17, 1997.

51 "A Secret Iran-Arafat Connection Is Seen Fueling the Mideast Fire," *New York Times,* March 24, 2002.

52 For Salah recruitment by Jamal Said, see Judith Miller, *God Has Ninety-Nine Names: Reporting from a Militant Middle East* (New York: Simon & Schuster, 1996), 385. For information on the "Palestine Organization," see Affidavit of Nadav regarding the Interviews of Abu Ahmed [Mohammad Salah], notarized by Justice Stevens, Acting Consul General of the United States of America at Tel Aviv, Israel, on September 29, 1995, p. 6, included in evidentiary material brought in *Stanley Boim et al. v. Quranic Literacy Institute et al.*

53 "The Military Prosecutor vs. Mohammad Abdel Hamid Salah, passport number 024296248 from Chicago, detained since 25 January, 1993," August 12, 1993, marked pages B003194 through B003201 of evidentiary material brought in *Stanley Boim et al. v. Quranic Literacy Institute et al.*

54 Akram Harubi's statement to Israeli police, January 17, 1999, marked pages 1347–1359 of evidentiary material brought in *Stanley Boim et al. v. Quranic Literacy Institute et al.*

55 For Harubi's activities, see Akram Harubi's statement to Israeli police, January 17,

1999, marked pages 1347–1359 of evidentiary material brought in *Stanley Boim et al. v. Quranic Literacy Institute et al.* Regarding Philadelphia meeting, see Dale L. Watson, assistant director for counterterrorism, Federal Bureau of Investigation, memorandum to R. Richard Newcomb, director of the Office of Foreign Assets Control, U.S. Department of the Treasury, "Holy Land Foundation for Relief and Development, International Emergency Economic Powers Act, Action Memorandum," November 5, 2001.

56 Jerrold M. Post, Ehud Sprinzak, and Laurita M. Denny, "The Terrorists in Their Own Words: Interviews with 35 Incarcerated Middle Eastern Terrorists," *Journal of Terrorism and Political Violence* 15, no. 1 (2003): 171–184.

57 Charbel, "The Khaled Mishaal Interview (2 of 7)."

58 Regarding Hamas serving as a front to protect the Muslim Brotherhood, see Robert Satloff, "Islam in the Palestinian Uprising," *Orbis* 33, no. 3 (1989): 396. For Mishal quotes, see Charbel, "The Khaled Mishaal Interview (2 of 7)."

59 The Avalon Project at Yale Law School, "The Covenant of the Islamic Resistance Movement." For Zahar quotes, see Anne Barnard, "Hamas Hardens Campaign Rhetoric: Leaders Praise Jihad and Renew Calls to Fight Israel," *Boston Globe,* January 24, 2006. For comments by Hamas candidate, see "Hamas' PLC Hopeful: We'll Enact Islamic Laws if Elected MPs," *Daily News,* http://Palestine-info.co.uk/, January 23, 2006.

60 Regarding *Majd,* see Charbel, "The Khaled Mishaal Interview (2 of 7)"; Shanab quote from Stern, *Terror in the Name of God,* 41. Interestingly, in the wake of the 1993 Oslo peace accord it would be Hezbollah spiritual leader Sheikh Mohammad Fadlallah who would assure groups like Hamas that "shifting the emphasis from armed jihad to communal activity, as dictated by circumstances, would not mean halting the struggle against Israel but rather continuing it by other means." See Hatina, *Islam and Salvation in Palestine,* 137.

CHAPTER 2 TERROR AND THE HAMAS POLITICAL LEADERSHIP

1 Reuters, "Yassin Sees Israel 'Eliminated' Within 25 Years," May 27, 1998.

2 Yassin's passport cites his birth date as January 1, 1929. David Hirst, "Sheikh Ahmed Yassin," *The Guardian,* March 23, 2004; The American-Israeli Cooperative Enterprise, "Sheikh Ahmad Yassin," *Jewish Virtual Library,* http://www.jewishvirtuallibrary.org/jsource/biography/yassin.html; Palestine History, "Yassin, Sheikh Ahmad," *Palestinian Biography,* http://www.palestinehistory.com/palbio15.htm; and Ziad Abu-Amr, "Shaykh Ahmad Yassin and the Origins of Hamas," in R. Scott Appleby, ed., *Spokesmen for the Despised: Fundamentalist Leaders of the Middle East* (Chicago: University of Chicago Press, 1997), 226.

3 Hirst, "Sheikh Ahmed Yassin"; and Abu-Amr, "Shaykh Ahmad Yassin and the Origins of Hamas," 228.

4 Biographical material on Yassin is culled from Ilene R. Prusher and Ben Lynfield, "Killing of Yassin a Turning Point," *Christian Science Monitor,* March 23, 2004; Hirst, "Sheikh Ahmed Yassin"; Ziad Abu-Amr, *Islamic Fundamentalism in the West Bank and Gaza: Muslim Brotherhood and Islamic Jihad* (Bloomington: Indiana University Press, 1994), 9; Ravi Nessman, "Sheikh Ahmed Yassin, Founder of Radical Hamas Group, Is Killed in Israeli Airstrike," Associated Press, March 22, 2004; and Abu-Amr, "Shaykh Ahmad Yassin," 228.

5 Associated Press, "U.S. Says It's 'Deeply Troubled' by Yassin Killing, But White House

Doesn't Condemn Israel Outright," March 22, 2005, http://www.msnbc.msn.com/id/4579005.

6 For Mishal quote, see Ghassan Charbel, "The Khaled Mishaal Interview (2 of 7)," *Dar al Hayat*, December 15, 2003, http://english.daralhayat.com/Spec/12-2003/Article-2003 1215-7a215ab8-c0a8-01ed-0015-c5ece4bc1b17/story.html. Regarding Yassin establishing cells, see Shaul Mishal and Avraham Sela, *The Palestinian Hamas: Vision, Violence, and Coexistence* (New York: Columbia University Press, 2000), 19.

7 Israel Ministry of Foreign Affairs (MFA), "Ahmed Yassin, Leader of Hamas Terrorist Organization," *Terror Background*, March 22, 2004, http://www.mfa.gov.il/MFA/Terrorism-+Obstacle+to+Peace/Terror+Groups/Ahmed+Yassin.htm; and Abu-Amr, "Shaykh Ahmad Yassin and the Origins of Hamas," 229.

8 U.S. Department of the Treasury, Office of Public Affairs, "U.S. Designates Five Charities Funding Hamas and Six Senior Hamas Leaders as Terrorist Entities," Washington, D.C., August 22, 2003, http://www.ustreas.gov/press/releases/js672.htm.

9 Israel Government Press Office statement, "4 Hamas Terrorists Killed along with Sheikh Ahmed Yassin," March 22, 2004; Lamia Lahoud, "Taiba Terrorists Lead PA to Explosives in Gaza Preschool," *Jerusalem Post*, March 19, 2000; Saud Abu Ramadan, "Police Arrest Hamas Leader's Bodyguard," United Press International, March 5, 2000.

10 Dr. Reuven Ehrlich and Col. (ret.) Shalom Harrari, "Ties and Links between Supporters of Bin Laden and Palestinians," Israeli Defense Forces Spokesperson, November 19, 2001; Israeli indictment of Nabil Awqil, author's personal files; Matthew Gutman, "Tentacles of Terror," *Jerusalem Post*, December 12, 2002.

11 The Avalon Project at Yale Law School, "The Covenant of the Islamic Resistance Movement," *Hamas Covenant 1988*, http://www.yale.edu/lawweb/avalon/mideast/hamas.htm.

12 Palestinian Information Center, "Hamas Symbols and Leaders," website of the Islamic Resistance Movement, http://www.palestine-info.co.uk/hamas/leaders (accessed May 2005); "Profile: Hamas Leader Rantissi," *BBC News World Edition*, April 17, 2004, http://news.bbc.co.uk/2/hi/middle_east/2977816.stm.

13 Biographical information on al-Rantissi culled from Palestinian National Authority State Information Service International Press Center, "Background: Dr. Abdel Aziz Al Rantisi," April 18, 2004, http://www.ipc.gov.ps/ipc_e/ipc_e-1/e_News/news2004/2004_04/115.html. UN General Assembly, Forty-seventh session, *Deportations by Israel, the Occupying Power, of Palestinian Civilians from the Occupied Palestinian Territory, Including Jerusalem*, A/47/858, January 8, 1993, http://domino.un.org/UNISPAL.NSF/0/569560501dc3a92285256aef0069d338?OpenDocument; Government of Israel Report, "Subject: The Interception of Abd Al Aziz Rantissi, the Hamas Leader in the Gaza Strip and the Individual Who Outlined the Hamas' Terror Attack Policy and Served as an Inspiration for the Perception of Terror Attacks," April 20, 2004; U.S. Department of the Treasury, "U.S. Designates Five Charities Funding Hamas."

14 Israel defense spokesperson, "Background Information: Abdel al-Aziz Rantissi, Senior Figure of Hamas in Gaza, Responsible for Directing Many Terrorist Attacks, and Chief Opponent of Any Cease-Fire or Cessation of Terrorist Attacks Against Israel," attributed to Israeli Security Sources, October 6, 2003.

15 Multaqa Al-Bahrain, http://bahrainonline.org/showthread.php?p=15762#post15762 (accessed June 22, 2005).

16 BBC interview from Agence France Presse, "Radical Palestinian Group Hamas Vows

Imminent New Attacks," May 2, 2002; interview from Matthew Tostevin, "Hamas Official Says Suicide Attacks to Resume," *Reuters*, December 8, 2003.

17 Government of Israel Report, "Subject: The Interception of Abd Al Aziz Rantissi."

18 Nidal al-Mughrabi, "Hamas Says Strike at Israeli Leaders," *Reuters*, July 31, 2001; Jessica Stern, *Terror in the Name of God: Why Religious Militants Kill* (New York: Harper Collins, 2003), 56.

19 U.S. Department of the Treasury, "U.S. Designates Five Charities Funding Hamas."

20 International Policy Institute for Counter-Terrorism (ICT), "Hamas: Harakat al-Muqawamah al-Islamiyya," *Group Profile*, http://www.ict.org.il/inter_ter/orgdet.cfm?orgid=13#history.

21 "Indictment," *United States of America v. Holy Land Foundation for Relief and Development* (U.S. District Court for the Northern District of Texas Dallas Division), filed July 26, 2004; Dale L. Watson, assistant director for counterterrorism, Federal Bureau of Investigation, memorandum to R. Richard Newcomb, director of the Office of Foreign Assets Control, U.S. Department of the Treasury, "Holy Land Foundation for Relief and Development, International Emergency Economic Powers Act, Action Memorandum," November 5, 2001 (hereafter, Watson memo).

22 Mary Anne Weaver, "The Quandry," *New Yorker*, August 19, 1996; ICT, "Hamas: Harakat al-Muqawamah al-Islamiyya."

23 "Affidavit of Joseph Hummel" (State of New York, County of New York, Southern District of New York), September 20, 1995, marked pages 0663–0675 of evidentiary material brought in *Stanley Boim et al. v. Quranic Literacy Institute et al.*, Civil No. 00 C 2905 (U.S. District Court, Northern District of Illinois, Eastern Division.

24 Ibid.

25 Ibid.

26 See Watson memo.

27 Bassem Musa quotes from "Subject: Hamas/Bassem Musa's Letter to Abu Marzook," Israeli report dated September 18, 1995, marked pages S2348-S2355 in evidentiary material brought in *Stanley Boim et al. v. Quranic Literacy Institute et al.* Marzook quotes from IslamOnline, "Call in Q&A with Hamas Mousa Abu Marzouk," January 5, 2004, http://islamonline.net/livedialogue/english/Browse.asp?hGuestID=JL923X.

28 Regarding "Palestine Organization" and Salah quote, see "Affidavit of Nadav regarding the Interviews of Abu Ahmed [Mohammad Salah], notarized by Justice Stevens, acting consul general of the United States of America at Tel Aviv, Israel," on September 29, 1995, p. 6, included in evidentiary material brought in *Stanley Boim et al. v. Quranic Literacy Institute et al.* Israeli intelligence quote from Brigadier General Yaakov Amidror, head of Analysis and Assessment Division, "Hamas—Musa Muhammad Abu Marzook (Abu Omar)—An Expert Opinion," Analysis and Assessment Division of Israel Defense Forces Intelligence, September 20, 1995, p. 5.

29 "Affidavit of Nadav," *Stanley Boim et al. v. Quranic Literacy Institute et al.*

30 Quote of U.S. investigators from "Affidavit of Robert Wright" (State of Illinois, County of Cook), June 8, 1998, included in evidentiary material brought in *Stanley Boim et al. v. Quranic Literacy Institute et al.* Salah quote from "Affidavit of Nadav," *Stanley Boim et al. v. Quranic Literacy Institute et al.* Regarding Nusseibeh plot, see Brigadier General Yaakov Amidror, head of Analysis and Assessment Division, "Hamas—Musa Muhammad Abu Marzook (Abu Omar)."

31 Biographical material on Mishal culled from: Charbel, "The Khaled Mishaal Interview (1)," *Dar al Hayat;* Yehudit Barsky, "The New Leadership of Hamas: A Profile of Khalid al-Mish'al," American Jewish Committee, http://www.ajc.org/InTheMedia/PubTerrorism .asp?did=1199 (accessed May 25, 2005); Palestinian Information Center, "Hamas Symbols and Leaders" (accessed September 4, 2002); Agence France Presse, "Meshaal: Hamas Political Leader Seen as New Number One," April 18, 2004. Members of the Kuwaiti group include Khaled Mishal, Osama Hamdan, Mohammad Nazzal, and Ibrahim Ghawsah. The most senior members of the Gaza faction are Mousa Abu Marzook and Imad al-Alami.

32 Charbel, "The Khaled Mishaal Interview (2–4 of 7)," *Dar al Hayat;* Barsky, "New Leadership of Hamas."

33 Barsky, "New Leadership of Hamas."

34 U.S. Department of the Treasury, "U.S. Designates Five Charities Funding Hamas."

35 Randa Habib, "Jordan Arrests Top Hamas Leaders, Expels One to Iran," Agence France Presse, September 22, 1999; Jamal Halaby, "Detained Hamas Leaders Plead Not Guilty to Jordanian Charges," Associated Press, September 23, 1999; Associated Press, "Hamas Leaders Plead Not Guilty to Five More Charges," October 6, 1999.

36 Associated Press, "Hamas Leaders Plead Not Guilty to Five More Charges"; Jamal Halaby, "Jordan Issues Arrest Warrant for Four Top Hamas Leaders," Associated Press, August 31, 1999.

37 Author interview with Abdul-Elah al-Khatib, Amman, Jordan, November 10, 2004.

38 "Hamas Calls for Escalation of uprising," December 1, 2000; Reuters, "Hamas Designates New Leader," *Chicago Tribune,* April 19, 2004.

39 Regarding Sudan conference, see Mohammad Osman, "Radicals Call for Resolution Against PLO-Israel Accord," Associated Press, December 2, 1993. Regarding Mishal's 1999 meeting, see Zeina Karam, "Iranian President Meets Palestinian Opposition, Assad in Syria," Associated Press, May 14, 1999. Regarding Mishal's 2002 conference see William Samii, "Tehran, Washington, and Terror: No Agreement to Differ," *Middle East Review of International Affairs* 6, no. 3 (2002), http://meria.idc.ac.il/journal/2002/issue3/jv6n3a5.html.

40 "Khameini: 'Zionists Had Close Relations with Nazis,'" *Jerusalem Post,* April 25, 2001.

41 Regarding 1996 meeting in Iraq, see Agence France Presse, "Hamas says Baghdad backs Palestinian cause," December 15, 1996. Information about Mishal seeking closer ties to Iran from author interview with Israel expert on Hamas, Jerusalem, November 14, 2004.

42 Intelligence and Terrorism Information Center at the Center for Special Studies (C.S.S.) Special Information Bulletin, *Interpal, Part II,* "Appendix B (1): Information Disclosed by Jamal Muhammad Farah al-Tawil, Founder of Al-Islah Charitable Society in Ramallah-Al-Bireh, about the Circumstances Surrounding Its Founding by Hamas," Israel, December 2004, http://www.intelligence.org.il/eng/sib/12_04/images/dec15_04.pdf; C.S.S. Special Information Bulletin, *Interpal, Part I,* "Appendix B: Interpal Transfer of Contributions to the Designated Hamas-affiliated Al-Islah Charitable Society, both the Ramallah-Al-Bireh and Bethlehem Branches," December 2004, http://www.intelligence .org.il/eng/sib/12_04/interpal_app_b.htm.

43 C.S.S., *Interpal, Part II,* "Appendix B(1): Information Disclosed by Jamal Muhammad Farah al-Tawil."

44 C.S.S., *Interpal, Part I,* "Appendix B: Interpal Transfer of Contributions," and C.S.S.

Special Information Bulletin, *The Union of Good: An Umbrella Organization Comprised of More than 50 Islamic Charitable Funds and Foundations Worldwide,* February 2005, http://www.intelligence.org.il/eng/sib/2_05/funds.htm#contents, "Appendix D: The Transfer of Funds from the UG to the Hamas-Affiliated Ramallah-Al-Bireh Al-Islah Charitable Society."

45 Brigadier General Yaakov Amidror, head of Analysis and Assessment Division, "Hamas—Organizational Structure and Decision Making Procedure—An Expert Opinion," Analysis and Assessment Division of Israel Defense Forces Intelligence, September 20, 1995, p. 5.

46 For Palestinian report, see Israel Defense Forces, Military Intelligence, "Iran and Syria as Strategic Support for Palestinian Terrorism," September 2002, http://www.intelligence .org.il/eng (report based on the interrogations of arrested Palestinian terrorists and captured Palestinian Authority documents). Ammar quote from Stern, *Terror in the Name of God,* 48. Brigadier General Ammar made similar statements to the author in a July 1997 interview in Gaza.

47 Information on Hamas activities in Jordan culled from author interview with two Jordanian counterterrorism officials, Amman, Jordan, November 9, 2004; author interview with Jordanian intelligence official, Amman, Jordan, November 11, 2004; and Jamal Halaby, "King Pardons 25 Hamas Officials; Four Leaders Sent to Qatar," Associated Press, November 21, 1999. For Rawabdeh and "other Jordanian officials" quotes, see Nicole Brackman, "PeaceWatch #226: Clampdown on Hamas: King Abdullah Strikes Out on His Own," *PolicyWatch/PeaceWatch,* Washington Institute for Near East Policy, October 6, 1999, http://www.washingtoninstitute.org/templateC05.php?CID=1917.

48 U.S. Department of the Treasury, "U.S. Designates Five Charities Funding Hamas."

49 Regarding Canadian intelligence report, see Canadian Secret Intelligence Service (CSIS), "'Terrorist Group Profiler," June 2002, author's personal files. See also Stewart Bell, "Hamas May Have Chemical Weapons: CSIS Report Says Terror Group May Be Experimenting," *National Post* (Canada), December 10, 2003. For Israeli claims see "Ya'alon: Syria and Iran involved in Palestinian terror," *Jerusalem Post,* December 7, 2003.

50 For Straw quote in 2003, see Agence France Presse, "British FM Hopeful for EU Ban on Hamas," September 5, 2003. Regarding EU freezing Hamas assets, see Agence France Presse, "EU Reaches Consensus to Blacklist Hamas: French FM," June 6, 2003. For Solana quote, see Agence France Presse, "EU Could Reverse Stand on Hamas if It Cut Ties with Terror," September 7, 2003. For Straw quote in 2002, see Khaled Abu Toameh, "Straw Salutes Sharon's 'Courage,'" *Jerusalem Post,* June 8, 2005.

51 Adar Primor, "Yes, This Friend Is in Need," *Ha'aretz,* July 26, 2005.

52 Stern, *Terror in the Name of God,* 48.

53 Human Rights Watch, *Erased in a Moment: Suicide Bombing Attacks Against Israeli Civilians* (New York: Human Rights Watch, 2002), 63.

CHAPTER 3 ECONOMIC JIHAD: HOW HAMAS FINANCES TERROR

1 This issue is often described in academic discourse as the "political economy" of terrorism; Matthew Levitt, "The Political Economy of Middle East Terrorism," *Middle East Review of International Affairs* 6, no. 4 (December 2002).

2 Ed Johnson, "Cutting Off Terrorist Funding Essential, America Tells G-7 Meeting," Associated Press, February 5, 2005.

3 Oral statement by Louise Richardson, executive dean, Radcliffe Institute for Advanced Study, Harvard University, "Appearance for Hearing of U.S. Senate Committee on Banking, Housing and Urban Affairs," October 22, 2003, http://banking.senate.gov/_files/richrdsn.pdf.

4 For GAO report, see U.S. Senate, United States General Accounting Office, *Statement of Loren Yager and Richard Stana, Combating Terrorism: Federal Agencies Face Continuing Challenges in Addressing Terrorist Financing and Money Laundering, Testimony Before the Caucus on International Narcotics Control*, GAO-04-501T, March 4, 2004, http://www.gao.gov/new.items/d04501t.pdf.

5 For FBI Testimony, see U.S. House Committee on Financial Services, Subcommittee on Oversight and Investigations, *Testimony of John Pistole, Assistant Director, Counterterrorism, FBI*, "The Terrorist Financing Operations Section," September 24, 2003, http://www.fbi.gov/congress/congress03/pistole092403.htm. The United States estimates Hamas' annual budget to be approximately $50 million. Also in 2003 the *New York Times* ran a story estimating Hamas' annual budget at "about $10 million a year"; see Don Van Natta Jr. and Timothy L. O'Brien, "Flow of Saudis' Cash to Hamas Is Scrutinized," *New York Times*, September 17, 2003. In 2001 a story in the *Chicago Sun-Times* estimated Hamas' budget was $30 million a year; see Dave Newbart and Chris Fusco, "Millions of Dollars Go to Fund Terror Groups," *Chicago Sun-Times*, September 30, 2001. For estimate of $25 million to $30 million see Israel Ministry of Foreign Affairs (MFA), "Hamas' Use of Charitable Societies to Fund and Support Terror," *MFA Library 2003*, September 22, 2003, http://www.mfa.gov.il/MFA/MFAArchive/2000_2009/2003/9/Hamas-s%20use%20of%20charitable%20societies%20to%20fund%20and%20su. GID estimate from author interview with GID officials, Amman, Jordan, November 18, 2004. Shin Bet analysis from author interview with Shin Bet officials, Tel Aviv, November 11, 2004. See also Israeli intelligence estimates of Hamas' budget of between $70 million and $90 million culled from author interview with Israeli intelligence official, January 2004.

6 For the Salah Shehada interview, see Molly Moore and John Ward Anderson, "Suicide Bombers Change Mideast's Military Balance," *Washington Post*, August 18, 2002. Hezbollah estimate was given in an interrogation of Mountasar Abu Ghalyoun. While he is a member of Hezbollah, we can assume that the cost of terror operations has the same going rate in the Palestinian territories. This data and the data for Housein and Ghanem are available from the MFA, "Operation for the confiscation of terror funds— Background," *Terror Communiqués*, February 26, 2004, http://www.mfa.gov.il/MFA/Terrorism-+Obstacle+to+Peace/Terrorism+and+Islamic+Fundamentalism-/Security+forces+seize+terrorist+funds+-+Background.htm. For other estimates, see Serge Schmemann, "In the Arabs' Struggle Against Israel, There Are Many Players," *New York Times*, March 30, 2002; and "Why Suicide Bombing Is Now All the Rage," *Time*, April 15, 2002, 32–39.

7 "Al-Rantisi: University Operation One of 60 Operations That Hamas Has Planned to Carry Out against Israel," *Al-Sharq Al-Awsat*, August 2, 2002. See also Alia Shukri Hamzeh, "IAF Delivered 'Clear' Message to U.S. on Regional Policy—Mansour," *Jordan Times* (Amman), July 26, 2002.

8 For February 2002 document, see MFA, "Iran and Syria as Strategic Support for Palestinian Terrorism," *MFA Library, September 2002*, September 30, 2002, http://www.

intelligence.org.il/eng. Regarding obtaining intelligence, see Intelligence and Terrorism Information Center at the Center for Special Studies (C.S.S.), *A Captured Document Showing That in Bethlehem the Fatah (Under Its Various Names) and the PA Intelligence Apparatuses Maintain a Regime of Oppression Based on Intimidation, Extortion, Unwarranted Arrests and Abuse of the Local Christian Population,* http://www.intelligence .org.il/eng/var/fatah.htm.

9 MFA, "Mountasar Abu Ghalyoun: Operation for the Confiscation of Terror Funds—Background." Exchange rates from Bank of Israel, August 6, 2004, http://www.bank israel.gov.il.

10 C.S.S. Special Information Bulletin, *Interpal, Part I,* December 2004, http://www .intelligence.org.il/eng/sib/12_04/interpal.htm.

11 For transfer of $6.8 million, see "Selected Recipients of HLFRD Funds: Jan. 1997–Sept. 2000," declassified FBI table marked page 0732 of evidentiary material brought in *Stanley Boim et al. v. Quranic Literacy Institute et al.,* Civil No. 00 C 2905 (U.S. District Court, Northern District of Illinois, Eastern Division). According to Mohammad Anati, the head of the Holy Land Foundation office near Jerusalem, "office expenses are $2000 per month, including salaries but not including the rent." For the FBI's conclusion, see Dale L. Watson, assistant director for counterterrorism, Federal Bureau of Investigation, memorandum to R. Richard Newcomb, director of the Office of Foreign Assets Control, U.S. Department of the Treasury, "Holy Land Foundation for Relief and Development, International Emergency Economic Powers Act, Action Memorandum," November 5, 2001 (hereafter, Watson memo).

12 C.S.S. Special Information Bulletin, *Interpal, Part I,* "Appendix B: Interpal Transfer of Contributions to the Designated Hamas-Affiliated Al-Islah Charitable Society, Both the Ramallah-Al-Bireh and Bethlehem Branches—Another Test Case Examining Interpal's Connections with One of Hamas' Leading Institutions in the PA-Administered Territories," December 2004, http://www.intelligence.org.il/eng/sib/12_04/interpal_ app_b.htm; and C.S.S. Special Information Bulletin, *Interpal, Part III,* December 2004, http://www.intelligence.org.il/eng/sib/12_04/interpal_app_bc.htm. Data received in New Israeli Shekels (NIS) and converted into American dollars using the exchange rate of 4.08 NIS=1 US$; for conversion rate, see Central Intelligence Agency, "Exchange Rates," *World Factbook,* http://www.umsl.edu/services/govdocs/wofact2001/fields/exchange_ rates.html (accessed March 18, 2005).

13 Wages extrapolated from average daily wage of Palestinian workers in the territories and multiplied over a thirty-day period. From Palestinian Central Bureau of Statistics, Labour Force Survey (January–March 2005), Round (Q1/2005): Press Conference on the Labour Force Results (Ramallah: April 28, 2005), www.pcbs.org/press_r/Labor Q1_05E.pdf. Averages were calculated by averaging the distinct payments to specific individuals or families. Larger payments were made to groups of persons or families, but these had to be excluded as the number of families each payment was disbursed to was unknown. C.S.S. Special Information Bulletin, *Interpal, Part I,* "Appendix B."

14 C.S.S. Special Information Bulletin, *The Union of Good: An Umbrella Organization Comprised of More than 50 Islamic Charitable Funds and Foundations Worldwide,* "Appendix C: Transfer of Funds from the Union of Good Through Al Tadhmun to the Hamas-Affiliated Tulkarm Charity Committee," http://www.intelligence.org.il/eng/sib/ 2_05/funds_c.htm.

15 For Yassin estimate, see Lee Hockstader, "Palestinians Find Heroes in Hamas; Popularity Surges for Once-Marginal Sponsor of Suicide Bombings," *Washington Post*, August 11, 2001. For Israeli report, see MFA, "Hamas' Use of Charitable Societies to Fund and Support Terror."

16 Author interview with Israeli intelligence analyst, Jerusalem, Israel, June 2002.

17 Israeli government report marked "Report No.: 10/4374/95; Subject: The Holyland Foundation," June 5, 1995, included in evidentiary material presented in *Stanley Boim et al. v. Quranic Literacy Institute et al.*, Civil No. 00 C 2905 (U.S. District Court, Northern District of Illinois, Eastern Division), exhibit 45 in file marked "Holy Land Foundation for Relief and Development," stamped pages 0736–0743.

18 C.S.S. Special Information Bulletin, *Spotlight on a Hamas Dawah Institution in the West Bank: A File of Palestinian Preventive Security Documents Identified the Bethlehem Orphan Care Society as Hamas-affiliated*, January 2005, http://www.intelligence.org.il/eng/sib/1_05/dawah.htm.

19 "Subject: Hamas/Bassem Musa's Letter to Abu Marzook," Israeli report dated September 18, 1995, marked pages S2348-S2355, in evidentiary material brought in *Stanley Boim et al. v. Quranic Literacy Institute et al.*

20 "Subject: Hamas/Bassem Musa's Letter," in *Stanley Boim et al. v. Quranic Literacy Institute et al.*

21 Information on the Islamic Red Crescent from U.S. Senate Committee on Banking, Housing, and Urban Affairs, *Prepared Testimony of Jean-Charles Brisard, International Expert on Terrorism Financing Lead Investigator, 9/11 Lawsuit CEO, JCB Consulting International*, October 22, 2003, accessed through Federal News Service; Agence France Presse, "Saudi Pilot on FBI List Denies Terror Links," October 16, 2001, and U.S. Department of the Treasury, Office of Public Affairs, *Treasury Department Statement on the Designation of Wa'el Hamza Julidan*, September 6, 2002, http://www.treas.gov/press/releases/po3397.htm. For Taylor quote, see U.S. Department of State, International Information Programs, "State's Taylor Summarizes Annual Global Terrorism Report," *Washington File*, May 21, 2002, http://www.usembassy.it/file2002_05/alia/a2052103.htm. For Pakistan, see Timur Kuran, "Islam and Mammon: Book Excerpt," *The Milken Institute Review: A Journal of Economic Policy* (3rd Qtr. 2004): 76.

22 C.S.S. Special Information Bulletin, "The Speech Given by Hassan Nasrallah, Hezbollah Leader," *Jerusalem Day*, December 2003, http://www.intelligence.org.il/eng/bu/iran/jerusalem.htm.

23 Adnan Hussein Abu Nasser, *Palestine in the Speeches of the Ayatollah Khoeini (Arabic)*, The Syrian Ministry of Information (2000), 120, as cited in C.S.S. Special Information Bulletin, *Interpal, Part I*.

24 For Qardawi, see "The Muslim Brotherhood Movement in Support of Fighting American Forces in Iraq," Middle East Media Research Institute (MEMRI), Special Dispatch Series, No. 776, September 3, 2004, http://memri.org/bin/articles.cgi?Page=subjects&Area=middleeast&ID=SP77604. Amany Abdel-Moneim, "Online with the Sheikh," *Al Ahram Weekly*, no. 563, December 2001. For *Palestine Times*, see "Sheikh Yousuf al-Qaradawi: Hamas and the Islamic Jihad represent the glorious face of the Islamic Umma- Interview," *Palestine Times*, September 1999, http://www.ptimes.org/issue99/index0.htm. For Sheikh Omar Bakri Mohammad, see Douglas Davis, "UK Muslim

Cleric Faces Deportation for Calling on Followers to Join Al-Qaida," *Jerusalem Post*, January 19, 2005.

25 Center for Religious Freedom, Freedom House, "Saudi Publications On Hate Ideology Fill American Mosques," January 2005, http://freedomhouse.org/religion/publications/Saudi%20Report/FINAL%20FINAL.pdf.

26 The Middle East Media Research Institute (MEMRI), "Palestinian Authority and Iraqi Media on Iraqi Support of the Intifada," *Special Dispatch—Iraq/Jihad and Terrorism Studies*, no. 415, August 28, 2002, http://www.memri.org/bin/opener_latest.cgi?ID=SD41502 (accessed August 29, 2002).

27 "Selected Recipients of HLFRD Funds: Jan. 1997—Sept. 2000," declassified FBI table marked page 0732 of evidentiary material brought in *Stanley Boim et al. v. Quranic Literacy Institute et al.*; C.S.S., *Interpal, Part I*; and C.S.S. Special Information Bulletin, *Interpal, Part II*, December 2004, http://www.intelligence.org.il/eng/sib/12_04/images/dec15_04.pdf.

28 Damrah also served as an officer of Maktab al-Khidmat (MAK), also known as the Afghan Services Bureau or Alkifah Refugee Center. See *United States of America v. Fawaz Damrah* (U.S. District Court for the Northern District of Ohio, Eastern Division), 2004; and *United States of America v. al Arian et al.* (U.S. District Court for the Middle District of Florida, Tampa Division), 2005.

29 "Round Table Discussion About Jihad and the Intifada" held in Cleveland, Ohio, on April 7, 1991, transcript p. 13, in court documents from *United States of America v. Fawaz Damrah*.

30 For "O brothers" quote, see Residence, Box 9, Tape #12, Fundraiser, Beit Hanina Club, Cleveland, Ohio, 9/27/91, p. 3, in court documents from *United States of America v. Fawaz Damrah*. For quote on Zalloum, see "Round Table Discussion About Jihad and the Intifada."

31 Tape of 2nd Annual Conference of ICP, Chicago, Ill., December 22–25, 1989, Fourth Symposium: "Palestine, the Intifada and the Horizons of Islamic Resurgence," in court documents from *United States of America v. Fawaz Damrah*.

32 IDF spokesperson, "Hamas Is Conducting A Global Search for Financing for Terrorism Activities," November 29, 2002, www.imra.org.il.

33 Created August 18, 1998, this website was registered to IANA and al-Hussayen was the director, administrator, a webmaster, and an adviser to some of the site's other webmasters in creating, maintaining, and controlling the site's format and content. See *United States of America v. Sami Omar Al-Hussayen* (U.S. District Court for the District of Ohio), 2004.

34 C.S.S. Special Information Bulletin, *Spotlight on a Hamas Dawah Institution in the West Bank*.

35 Abd al-Rahman al-Rashed, "Follow the Money," *al-Sharq al-Awsat*, October 20, 2004, as translated in a C.S.S. Special Information Bulletin, *Financing of Terrorism: An (Exceptional) Article Printed in Al-Sharq Al-Awsat, an Arabic Newspaper Published in London (October 20, 2004), Concludes That Funds Donated for Charity Are Used for the Financing of Terrorism and Nurturing of Extremism*, November 2004, http://www.intelligence.org.il/eng/sib/12_04/financing.htm.

36 U.S. Senate Select Committee on Intelligence and U.S. House Permanent Select Com-

mittee on Intelligence, *Joint Inquiry into Intelligence Community Activities Before and After the Terrorist Attacks of September 11, 2001*, 107th Cong., 2d sess., S. Rept. 107-351, H. Rept. 107-792, 308–9, http://www.gpoaccess.gov/serialset/creports/911.html.

37 U.S. Senate Committee on Banking, Housing, and Urban Affairs, *Testimony of John Pistole, Assistant Director, Counterterrorism Division, FBI, "Identifying, Tracking and Dismantling the Financial Structure of Terrorist Organizations,"* September 25, 2003, http://www.fbi.gov/congress/congress03/pistole092503.htm.

38 "Subject: Hamas/Bassem Musa's Letter," in *Stanley Boim et al. v. Quranic Literacy Institute et al.* Currency unstated, likely in NIS or U.S. dollars.

39 First report from Israeli PowerPoint presentation based on the interrogation of Jamal Tawil, slide on "Financing the Terror Cells from 'Daawa' Funds," author's personal files; second report from Israel Defense Forces/Military Intelligence, "Iran and Syria as Strategic Support for Palestinian Terrorism."

40 Major [*Ra'id*] Khaled Abu Yaman to Palestinian General Security, General Intelligence, West Bank District Directorate, "The Ramallah-Al-Bireh Charity Committee," December 22, 2001, trans. and cited in C.S.S. Special Information Bulletin, *Interpal, Part II*, "Appendix A: Interpal Transfer of Contributions to the Designated Hamas-Affiliated Ramallah-al-Bireh Charity Committee: A Test Case to Examine the Connection Between Interpal and One of Hamas' Leading Institutions in the PA-Administered Territories," http://www.intelligence.org.il/eng/sib/12_04/interpal_app_a.htm. Jafar Sadaqah, "Palestinians Comment on US Freezing of Palestinian Companies' Assets," *al-Ayyam*, December 5, 2001, translated text available in *BBC Monitoring Middle East—Political, BBC Worldwide Monitoring*.

41 Jeff Breinholt, "Terrorist Financing: The Clean Money Cases: U.S-Based Fund-raising by NGOs and Charities," *United States Attorneys' Bulletin* 51, no. 4 (2003): 14.

42 For Wayne quote, see U.S. House Committee on Financial Services, *Testimony of E. Anthony Wayne, Assistant Secretary for Economic and Business Affairs, Department of State, "The Hamas Asset Freeze and Other Government Efforts to Stop Terrorist Financing,"* September 24, 2003, http://financialservices.house.gov/media/pdf/092403eaw.pdf. For Terrorism Financing Task Force, see Breinholt, "Terrorist Financing." For reference to "Islam Online website," see Israel Defense Forces Spokesperson's Unit, "Hamas-Related Associations Raising Funds throughout Europe, the US and the Arab World," http://www.idf.il/english/announcements/2002/july/Hamas.stm.

43 For Pistole quote, see U.S. House Committee on Financial Services, *Testimony of John Pistole, "The Terrorist Financing Operations Section."* For Hutchinson, see "U.S. Drug Ring Tied to Aid for Hezbollah," *New York Times*, September 3, 2002. For GAO report, see U.S. General Accounting Office (GAO), Report to Congressional Requesters, *Terrorist Financing: U.S. Agencies Should Systemically Assess Terrorists' Use of Alternative Financing Mechanisms*, Rept. GAO-04-163, November 2003, http://www.gao.gov/new .items/d04163.pdf.

44 Amir Buchbot, "Forgeries in the Service of Terror," *Ma'ariv*, August 14, 2002; John Mintz and Douglas Farah, "Small Scams Probed for Terror Ties; Muslim, Arab Stores Monitored as Part of Post–Sept. 11 Inquiry," *Washington Post*, August 12, 2002; Jon Swartz, "Terrorists' Use of Internet Spreads," *USA Today*, February 21, 2005.

45 For $20 million to $30 million estimate see Mintz and Farah, "Small Scams Probed for Terror Ties"; GAO report from U.S. GAO, *Terrorist Financing*. Regarding the DEA, see

U.S. Drug Enforcement Administration (DEA), "Drugs and Terrorism: A New Perspective," *Drug Intelligence Brief,* September 2002, http://www.usdoj.gov/dea/pubs/intel/02039/02039.html. For information on Ali Nizar see Mark S. Steinitz, "Middle East Terrorist Activity in Latin America," *Center for Strategic and International Studies: Policy Papers on the Americas* 14, Study 7 (2003). See also Jeffrey Goldberg, "In the Party of God: Hezbollah Sets Up Operations in South America and the United States," *New Yorker,* October 28, 2002.

46 Homeland Security, "Homeland Security Operations Morning Brief," January 11, 2005, http://cryptome.org/hsomb/hsomb.htm.

47 For U.S. investigations, see U.S. House Committee on Financial Services, *Testimony of John Pistole, "Identifying, Tracking and Dismantling the Financial Structure of Terrorist Organizations."* For U.S. Department of State, see U.S. House Committee on Financial Services, *Testimony of E. Anthony Wayne, "The Hamas Asset Freeze."* For U.S. Treasury Department information, see U.S. Department of the Treasury, Office of Public Affairs, "Treasury Designates Al-Aqsa International Foundation as Financier of Terror: Charity Linked to Funding of the Hamas Terrorist Organization," May 29, 2003, http://www.treas.gov/press/releases/js439.htm. For distribution of funds to martyrs including Hamdan, Mishal, and Marzook, see U.S. Department of the Treasury, Office of Public Affairs, "U.S. Designates Five Charities Funding Hamas and Six Senior Hamas Leaders as Terrorist Entities," August 22, 2003, http://www.ustreas.gov/press/releases/js672.htm. For Barghouti case, see Amos Harel, "Israel Does Little to Stop Money Flow to Terror; Shin Bet Sets Up New Unit," *Ha'aretz,* December 30, 2003; and MFA, "ISA and IDF Arrest Ramallah Area Hamas Cells," *Communiqués 2003,* December 23, 2003, http://www.mfa.gov.il/mfa/go.asp?MFAH0o3o0.

48 For FBI communication, see FBI Electronic Communication (EC) from Director FBI to FBI Jackson et al., "Subject: Abdelhaleem Hasan Ashar," February 8, 1993. Account name from FBI files, Copy of signature card for Suntrust Bank account number 16811688 in the name of "Abdelhaleem Hasan Ashqar for Al-Mojamaa al-Eslami—Gaza Strip." For FBI statement, see FBI Letterhead Memorandum (LHM), "Abdelhaleem Hasan Ashqar," November 27, 2001, 3.

49 For FBI memorandum including Ashqar, Rumahi, and Marzook's activities, see FBI LHM, "Abdelhaleem Hasan Ashqar," November 27, 2001, 4. For Rumahi's April 2002 trip see Israeli Police document, "Transcript of Interview with Mahmud Rumahi," trans. by the FBI, February 21, 1993 (included in FBI files).

50 For Rumahi's statement, see Israeli Police document, "Transcript of Interview with Mahmud Rumahi."

51 For FBI conclusions on HLFRD and SDT designation, see Watson memo. For weapons procurement and funding in the Tutange murder, see Affidavit of Israeli Police Officer Goel Nenti, Certified by Iriti Kohm, Director, Department of International Affairs, Ministry of Justice, State of Israel, September 27, 1995 (included in FBI files); For Bashirat bombing statements, see Israeli Police document recording Arouri's January 27, 1993, interview, "Subject: Transcriptions of the Police Interviews with Salah Arouri," marked pages S2268–S2286 of evidentiary material brought in *Stanley Boim et al. v. Quranic Literacy Institute et al.* For QLI decision and following actions, see Noreen S. Ahmed-Ullah, Kim Barker, Laurie Cohen, Stephen Franklin, and Sam Roe, "Struggle for the soul of Islam; Hard-liners won battle for Bridgeview mosque," *Chicago Tribune,*

February 8, 2004; and Deborah Horan and Laurie Cohen, "Bank closes mosque account," *Chicago Tribune*, March 11, 2005.

52 Israeli Police document, "Transcript of Interview with Sufian Abu Samara on 7th January, 1991," August 21, 1995 (included in FBI files). For Marzook's 1997 interview, see Roger Gaess, "Interview with Mousa Abu Marzook," *Middle East Policy* 5, no. 2 (1997): 113–128.

53 Regarding Sawalha's mosque trusteeship appointment, see Nick Fielding and Abul Taher, "Hamas link to London mosque," *The Times*, February 13, 2005. For all additional information on Sawalha, see *U.S. v. Marzook et al.* (U.S. District Court, Northern District of Illinois, Eastern Division), Special August 2003 Grand Jury, Second Superseding Indictment unsealed August 2004.

54 C.S.S., *Spotlight on a Hamas Dawah Institution in the West Bank.*

55 For Palestinian intelligence reports, see Major [*Ra'id*] Khaled Abu Yaman to Palestinian General Security, "The Ramallah-Al-Bireh Charity Committee"; Israeli intelligence official from author's e-mail correspondence with a former Israeli intelligence official, March 8, 2005. For Israeli HFLRD report, see Israeli Government, "Report No.: 10/4374/95," in *Stanley Boim et al. v. Quranic Literacy Institute et al.*

56 For Sarsour quote, see Israeli Police report, Interview of Jamil Sarsour, January 28, 1999, marked pages 1191–1195 of evidentiary material presented in *Stanley Boim et al. v. Quranic Literacy Institute et al.*

57 Interview of Jamil Sarsour in *Stanley Boim et al. v. Quranic Literacy Institute.*

58 For Peres quote, Shimon Peres, "Address to the Knesset by Prime Minister Peres on Hamas attacks in Jerusalem and Ashkelon," *Historical Documents 1995–1996*, Israel Ministry of Foreign Affairs, February 26, 1996, http://www.mfa.gov.il/MFA/Foreign%20Relations/Israels%20Foreign%20Relations%20since%201947/1995-1996/Address%20to%20the%20Knesset%20by%20Prime%20Minister%20Peres%20on.

CHAPTER 4 THE LOGISTICS OF TERROR: TACTICAL USES OF THE DAWA

1 General Security Service (GSS, since renamed Israel Security Agency, ISA), "Subject: Memo: Intelligence Estimate—Background on Search Missions for the Purpose of Preventing and Foiling a Bombing Attack," August 3, 1997.

2 GSS, "Subject: Memo: Intelligence Estimate."

3 GSS report from GSS, "Subject: Memo: Intelligence Estimate." Regarding the report on suicide bombing, see "Martyrdom and Murder," *The Economist*, January 8, 2004, http://www.economist.com/displaystory.cfm?story_id=2329785.

4 FBI summary of translated transcripts of Philadelphia meeting, marked "typed version of Bates 203–287," Entry for 10/2/93, Tape 6—Conference Room, p. 35, included in evidentiary material brought in deportation hearing for Abdel Haleem Ashqar in *U.S. v. Abdel Haleem Ashqar* (U.S. Immigration Court), Case No. A 75 422 626, 2003.

5 FBI summary, "typed version of Bates 203–287," Tape 7—Conference Room, p. 38–39, included in *U.S. v. Abdel Haleem Ashqar.*

6 Many Hamas members, including Sheikh Mohammad Siyam and Abdelhaleem al-Ashqar, worked for the Islamic University in Gaza (IUG) at one time or another. Among the wire transfers exceeding $10,000 that al-Ashqar sent to Gaza was a total of $13,300 to Siyam at IUG. Al-Ashqar also received $100,000 from IUG via the Arab Land Bank in Jordan (Undated summary document from Immigration and Natural-

ization Service (INS) files, "Ashqar Transactions Totaling $10,000 or more"). For al-Zakah Committees, see FBI summary, "typed version of Bates 203–287," Tape 7, p. 39, included in *U.S. v. Abdel Haleem Ashqar;* al-Ashqar transferred over $500,000 to The Association of Islamic Studies and Culture in Jerusalem alone (INS files, "Ashqar Transactions Totaling $10,000 or more").

7 Regarding Ramallah Islamic syndicate and Islamic Youth Association, see FBI summary, "typed version of Bates 203–287," Tape 7, p. 39. For Shabib's other classifications of Hamas organizations, see FBI summary, "typed version of Bates 203–287," Tape 9, p. 49; Shabib's Hamas designations also included in *U.S. v. Abdel Haleem Ashqar.*

8 Interestingly, al-Qaeda cells in Europe operated in a remarkably similar fashion, recruiting disaffected Muslim youth from neighborhood soccer teams, substance abuse programs, jails, and radical mosques. See, for example, Sebastian Rotella, "A Pool of Militants: Europe Holds Fertile Soil for Jihadis," *Los Angeles Times,* December 5, 2001. For State Department conclusions, see U.S. House Committee on Financial Services, *Testimony of E. Anthony Wayne, Assistant Secretary for Economic and Business Affairs, Department of State, "The Hamas Asset Freeze and Other Government Efforts to Stop Terrorist Financing,"* September 24, 2003, http://financialservices.house.gov/media/pdf/092403eaw.pdf.

9 Jerrold M. Post, Ehud Sprinzak, and Laurita M. Denny, "The Terrorists in Their Own Words: Interviews with 35 Incarcerated Middle Eastern Terrorists," *Journal of Terrorism and Political Violence* 15, no. 1 (2003): 171–184.

10 Regarding Saltana's acknowledgments relating to recruitment, see Dale L. Watson, assistant director for counterterrorism, Federal Bureau of Investigation, memorandum to R. Richard Newcomb, director of the Office of Foreign Assets Control, U.S. Department of the Treasury, "Holy Land Foundation for Relief and Development, International Emergency Economic Powers Act, Action Memorandum," November 5, 2001 (hereafter, Watson memo). In a May 2004 interview with the author in Tel Aviv, Israel Security Agency (Shin Bet) officials highlighted the scope and content of Hamas issues dealt with at the Jenin zakat committee. Said one official, "I wish I had one microphone at zakat meetings." For background on Saltana and Jarrar's Hamas actions, see Intelligence and Terrorism Information Center at the Center for Special Studies (C.S.S.) Special Information Bulletin, *The Union of Good: An Umbrella Organization Comprised of More than 50 Islamic Charitable Funds and Foundations Worldwide,* "Appendix D: The Transfer of Funds by Interpal to the Hamas-affiliated Jenin Charity Committee," http://www.intelligence.org.il/eng/sib/2_05/funds.htm; and specifically for Jarrar, see C.S.S. Special Information Bulletin, *IRFAN: A Hamas Front Organization Operating in Canada to Enlist Financial Support for Hamas Institutions in the Palestinian Authority-Administered Territories,* "Appendix C: IRFAN support of the Jenin Charitable Society, identified with Hamas," November 2004, http://www.intelligence.org.il/eng/sib/11_04/irfan.htm.

11 For the soccer team at Jihad Mosque, see Ian Fisher, "A Sudden, Violent End for a Promising Youth," *New York Times,* June 13, 2003. For other sports clubs, see Simon Wiesenthal Center Snider Social Action Institute Report, *Unmasking Hamas' Hydra of Terror,* August 2003, http://www.wiesenthal.com/atf/cf/%7BDFD2AAC1-2ADE-428A-9263-35234229D8D8%7D/hydraofterror.pdf. Regarding the soccer tournament in Beit Sahour region, see C.S.S. Special Information Bulletin, *Spotlight on a Hamas Dawah*

Institution in the West Bank: A File of Palestinian Preventive Security Documents Identified the Bethlehem Orphan Care Society as Hamas-Affiliated, "Appendix O: Palestinian Preventive Security report about Hamas in Bethlehem, mentioning the Bethlehem Orphan Care Society," January 2005, http://www.intelligence.org.il/eng/sib/1_05/dawah.htm.

12 Author interview with senior Israeli Military Intelligence official, Tel Aviv, May 16, 2004.

13 "Subject: Research Summary of the Charity Committee Heads in the Territories and their Ties with Hamas," Report No.: 10/4390/01, July 10, 2001, marked HLF exhibit 56, pages 0845–0854 of evidentiary material brought in *Stanley Boim et al. v. Quranic Literacy Institute et al.,* Civil No. 00 C 2905 (U.S. District Court, Northern District of Illinois, Eastern Division), June 5, 2002.

14 Jessica Stern, *Terror in the Name of God: Why Religious Militants Kill* (New York: Harper Collins, 2003), 50 and 51.

15 Israeli Police document recording Arouri's January 27, 1993, interview, "Subject: Transcriptions of the Police Interviews with Salah Arouri," marked pages S2268–S2286 of evidentiary material brought in *Stanley Boim et al. v. Quranic Literacy Institute et al.*

16 C.S.S. Special Information Bulletin, *Spotlight on a Hamas Dawah Institution in the West Bank.*

17 For Israeli analyst's conclusions, see C.S.S. Special Information Bulletin, *Interpal, Part I,* December 2004, http://www.intelligence.org.il/eng/sib/12_04/interpal.htm. Israeli intelligence official and tailor shop information from author interview with Israel Security Agency officials, Tel Aviv, May 13, 2004; IRA raids from Watson memo. For Nablus schoolteacher, see Mohammed Daragmeh, "After Israel's Warning, Militants Shave Off Beards, Ditch Cell Phones to Escape Intensified Manhunt," Associated Press, August 27, 2003.

18 *Susan Weinstein et al. v. The Islamic Republic of Iran et al.* (U.S. District Court for the District of Columbia), Civil Action No. 00–2601 (RCL), February 6, 2002.

19 Regarding Tahaina, see "Subject: The Charity Associations Who Received Funds from the HLF," Report No.: 10/6394/98, June 2, 1998, marked HLF exhibit 57, pages 0856–0863 of evidentiary material brought in *Stanley Boim et al. v. Quranic Literacy Institute et al.* For the identification of Hamas activists by other activists, see Israeli Police document, "Transcript of Interview with Mahmud Rumahi," trans. by the FBI, December 23, 1992 (included in FBI files), included in *U.S. v. Abdel Haleem Ashqar.*

20 Israeli Police document, "Transcript of Interview with Mahmud Rumahi," in *U.S. v. Abdel Haleem Ashqar.*

21 Regarding Rumahi characterization of Yusef, see Israeli Police document, "Transcript of Interview with Mahmud Rumahi." For Mishal's identification, see Ghassan Charbel, "The Khaled Mishaal Interview (2 of 7)," *Dar al Hayat,* December 15, 2003, http://english.daralhayat.com/Spec/12-2003/Article-20031215-7a215ab8-c0a8-01ed-0015-c5ece4bc1b17/story.html.

22 For Amr, see U.S. Department of the Treasury, Office of Public Affairs, "Treasury Designates Al-Aqsa International Foundation as Financier of Terror: Charity Linked to Funding of the Hamas Terrorist Organization," May 29, 2003, http://www.treas.gov/press/releases/js439.htm. For al-Ashqar, see Watson memo. Regarding Maghawri, see FBI Electronic Communication (EC) from FBI WFO (CT-1) to Director FBI, "Subject:

Mueen Shabib," March 28, 1994, included in *U.S. v. Abdel Haleem Ashqar*. For Shabib, see Watson memo.

23 For Shabib appointment, see Watson memo. For FBI statements, see FBI EC, "Subejct: Mueen Shabib," in *U.S. v. Abdel Haleem Ashqar*. For Shabib and Hamami, see Charbel, "The Khaled Mishaal Interview (2 of 7)." For FBI report, see FBI EC, "Subject: Mueen Shabib," in *U.S. v. Abdel Haleem Ashqar*.

24 Watson memo.

25 For statement by Hamas operatives, see "Hamas Relies on Jerusalem Cell for Logistics," *Middle East Newsline*, October 23, 2003. For Sarsour, see Laurie Cohen, "Target of Hamas Fundraising Probe Here Charged in Wisconsin," *Chicago Tribune*, January 7, 2003.

26 C.S.S. Special Information Bulletin, *An Important Step in the Struggle against the Financing of Terrorism from Europe: A German Court Upholds a Government Decision to Outlaw the German Office of the Al-Aqsa Charitable Foundation, Used by Hamas as a Front for Fundraising*, December 2004, http://www.intelligence.org.il/eng/sib/1_05/german.htm. Details on al-Sharouf in C.S.S. Special Information Bulletin, *Spotlight on a Hamas Dawah Institution in the West Bank*.

27 Regarding Palestinian Intelligence sources, see C.S.S. Special Information Bulletin, *Spotlight on a Hamas Dawah Institution in the West Bank*. The ten Hamas members identified in the Political Security Department intelligence report included Nasri Mousa Issa Abadah, Yusuf Said Assad al-Natshe, Khasr Yousuf Mohammad Juma, Ismail Oud Awida Abbiyat, Salah Yousuf Mohammad Jubran, Khalik Ali Rashed Dar Rashed, Shaban Mohammad Salem Abu al-Tin, Hussein Ahmad Hussine Mousa, Mohammad Naman Yusuf Qaraqi, and Ahmad Issa Mohammad Jawarish.

28 For information on the Orphan Care Society, see C.S.S. Special Information Bulletin, *Spotlight on a Hamas Dawah Institution in the West Bank*. For HLFRD donations, see "Selected Recipients of HLFRD Funds: Jan. 1997–Sept. 2000," declassified FBI table marked page 0732 of evidentiary material brought in *Stanley Boim et al. v. Quranic Literacy Institute et al.*

29 C.S.S. Special Information Bulletin, *Spotlight on a Hamas Dawah Institution in the West Bank*.

30 Ibid.

31 For Palestinian General Intelligence report, see Major [*Ra'id*] Khaled Abu Yaman to Palestinian General Security, General Intelligence, [West] Bank District Directorate, "The Ramallah-Al-Bireh Charity Committee," December 22, 2001, trans. and cited in C.S.S. Special Information Bulletin, *Interpal, Part II*, "Appendix A: Interpal Transfer of Contributions to the Designated Hamas-Affiliated Ramallah-al-Bireh Charity Committee: A Test Case to Examine the Connection Between Interpal and One of Hamas' Leading Institutions in the PA-Administered Territories," http://www.intelligence.org.il/eng/sib/12_04/interpal_app_a.htm. For committee expense report, see C.S.S. Special Information Bulletin, *Interpal, Part II*, "Appendix B5: Al-Islah Charitable Society, Ramallah-al-Bireh as Part of Hamas' Terrorism-Supporting Apparatus: The Society's Activity During November and December 2000."

32 C.S.S. Special Information Bulletin, *Interpal, Part II*, "Appendix A(2): The Ramallah-al-Bireh Charity and Contribution Committee." The activists listed in another Palestinian intelligence report were Husni Mohammad Abd al-Qadir Abu Awad (chairman);

Darwish al-Zaban (al Zien); Mohammad Omar Hamdan; Aql Rabia; Nabil Abd al-Hadi Mustafa Mansour; Muhtadi Mahmoud Ibrahim Muslih; and Mahmoud Ahmad Abd al-Rahman al-Rahmi.

33 Regarding the Hebron area sweep and the Junaydi arrest, see Wafa, "Palestinian Agency Reports Israeli Army Arrests, Raids in West Bank, Gaza," December 6, 2004, translated text available in *BBC Monitoring—Middle East—Political.* For Natsheh arrest, see *IPR Strategic Business Information Database,* "Head of Hamas in Hebron Arrested," September 1, 2002. For Natsheh referrals, see C.S.S. Special Information Bulletin, *Interpal, Part III,* "Appendix C(1): Information Obtained through the Interrogation of Abd al-Khaliq al-Natsheh, Head of the Islamic Charitable Society—Hebron, Regarding his Activity in the Ranks of Hamas," December 2004, http://www.intelligence.org.il/eng/sib/12_04/interpal_app_c.htm. For Adora and Karmey Tzur attacks, see IPR Strategic Business Information Database, "Head of Hamas in Hebron Arrested," September 1, 2002; Margot Dudkevitch, "West Bank Hamas commander arrested," *Jerusalem Post,* August 29, 2002.

34 Other senior Hamas activists who served as officers of the society include Mustafa Kamil Khalil Shawar, Nabil Nu'aym Esahq Natsheh, and Issa Khayri al-Jabari. See C.S.S. Special Information Bulletin, *Interpal, Part III,* "Appendix C: Transfer of Funds by Interpal to the Islamic Charitable Society—Hebron."

35 For al-Masri statement, see Agence France Presse, "Gaza Voters Elect Local Leaders for First Time in History," January 27, 2005. For PA intelligence report, see C.S.S. Special Information Bulletin, *Spotlight on a Hamas Dawah Institution in the West Bank.*

36 For U.S. government description and Citibank's response, see Judith Miller and Riva D. Atlas, "Citibank Weighs Ending Ties with an Arab Bank," *New York Times,* January 24, 2001. Regarding the Treasury Department, see U.S. Department of the Treasury, Office of Public Affairs, "Shutting Down the Terrorist Financial Network," December 4, 2001, http://www.treas.gov/press/releases/po841.htm?IMAGE.X=23\&IMAGE.Y=13.

37 For Israel and UNDP, see Benny Avni, "Despite Israeli Alerts, U.N. Transfers Thousands to Hamas Affiliates," *New York Sun,* January 28, 2005. For Hansen's statement, see *CBC News,* "Canada Looking at UN Agency over Palestinian Connection," October 4, 2004, http://www.cbc.ca/story/world/national/2004/10/03/unwra041003.html. Regarding terror uses of UNRWA, see Matthew Gutman, "IDF: 13 UN Employees Were Arrested in Past 4 Years for Terror Links," *Jerusalem Post,* October 5, 2004, http://www.jpost.com/servlet/Satellite?pagename=JPost/JPArticle/ShowFull&cid=1096959298553.

38 C.S.S. Special Information Paper, *The Terrorist Organizations In and Outside the PA Areas Exploit the Status of UNRWA Employees for Facilitating Terror Activities: Nahed Rashid Ahmed Attalah, a Senior UNRWA Employee in the Gaza Strip—A Case Study,* March 2003, http://www.intelligence.org.il/eng/bu/unrwa_b/ter.htm.

39 Transcript of "Suicide Bomber: The Planning of the Bloodiest Suicide Bombing Campaign in Israel's History," *60 Minutes,* CBS, October 5, 1997; MFA, "Details Released on Hamas Bombing Supporters," *MFA Library,* May 1996, May 9, 1996, http://www.mfa.gov.il/mfa/go.asp?MFAH0cbi0; *Susan Weinstein et al. v. The Islamic Republic of Iran et al.;* and *Leonard I. Eisenfeld et al. v. The Islamic Republic of Iran et al.* (U.S. District Court for the District of Columbia), Civil Action Number 98-1945 (RCL), 2000.

40 C.S.S., *Filasteen Almuslima: A Hamas Journal Published in London and Distributed to*

the Palestinian Authority Areas and Worldwide, http://www.intelligence.org.il/eng/bu/britain/journal.htm.

41 C.S.S. Special Information Bulletin, *The Union of Good.*

42 Israel Defense Forces (IDF) Background Report, "Details of the Operation Against the Hamas Terrorist Infrastructure in Ramallah," *Independent Media and Review Analysis (IMRA),* December 5, 2003, http://www.imra.org.il/story.php3?id=19071.

43 Daragmeh, "After Israel's Warning, Militants Shave Off Beards."

44 For the State Department's annual report, see U.S. Department of State, Office of the Coordinator for Counterterrorism, "Middle East Overview," *Patterns of Global Terrorism, 2000,* April 30, 2001, http://www.state.gov/s/ct/rls/pgtrpt/2000/2438.htm. For Rajoub's statement, see Amira Hass, "Hamas Store Explosives in Gaza Kindergarten," *Ha'aretz,* March 19, 2000.

45 Regarding the garbage truck plot, see MFA, "ISA and IDF Arrest Ramallah Area Hamas Cells," *Communiqués 2003,* December 23, 2003, http://www.mfa.gov.il/mfa/go.asp?MFAH0o3o0; and Amos Harel, "Hamas Plotted to Decapitate Its Victims," *Ha'aretz,* December 24, 2003. For head of al-Islah, see C.S.S. Special Information Bulletin, *Interpal, Part II,* "Appendix B1," December 2004, http://www.intelligence.org.il/eng/sib/12_04/images/dec15_04.pdf. For Zivad cell, see IMRA, "Hamas terrorist network based in Jenin disabled," March 2, 2005.

46 For the Islamic Charity Society in Hebron, see "Subject: The Charity Associations Who Received Funds from the HLF," in *Stanley Boim et al. v. Quranic Literacy Institute et al.* For Gaza cell and libraries, see Israeli Police document, "Transcript of Interview with Sufian Abu Samara on 14th January, 1991," August 21, 1995 (included in FBI files).

47 For radical sermon videotapes, see Yosi Elgazi, "Cassettes Calling for Terrorist Acts Against Israelis Disseminated in Triangle," *Ha'aretz,* February 27, 2000. For the Tulkarm charity committee, see C.S.S. Special Information Bulletin, *The Union of Good,* "Appendix C." For West Bank library projects in Hebron and Bethlehem, see Watson Memo; C.S.S. Special Information Bulletin, *Spotlight on a Hamas Dawah Institution in the West Bank.* Regarding the Ramallah library, see C.S.S. Special Information Bulletin, *Interpal, Part II.* For the Jenin library, see C.S.S. Special Information Bulletin, *The Union of Good,* "Appendix B7."

48 Author interview with Col. (ret.) Yoni Fighel, former Israeli Military Governor in Jenin, Tel Aviv, June 23, 2004.

49 For al-Razi hospital, see C.S.S. Special Information Bulletin, *The Union of Good.* The hospital is identical to the al-Razi hospital cited by the FBI as being affiliated with Hamas; see Watson memo. For Amjad confession, see MFA, "Terrorists Misuse of Medical Services to Further Terrorist Activity," *MFA Library, August 2002,* August 26, 2002, http://www.israel-mfa.gov.il/mfa/go.asp?MFAH0md20. For FBI report, see Watson memo.

50 For FBI records, see "Selected Recipients of HLFRD Funds," in *Stanley Boim et al. v. Quranic Literacy Institute et al.* For Mahlalati, see "Subject: The Charity Associations Who Received Funds from the HLF," in *Stanley Boim et al. v. Quranic Literacy Institute et al.* For Nahsha, see "Subject: Muhammad Othman Abd Al-Rahman Anati—HLF," Report No. 10/319/98, January 19, 1998, Marked page 1263 of evidentiary material brought in *Stanley Boim et al. v. Quranic Literacy Institute et al.,* marked Holy Land Foundation for Relief and Development, deposition exhibit 26.

51 For Nidal and Nimr, see MFA, "The Use of Ambulances and Medical Material for Terror—Background Information," MFA Library, December 2003, December 22, 2003, http://www.mfa.gov.il/mfa/go.asp?MFAH0o3b0. For Nidal, see also "Subject: Muhammad Othman Abd Al-Rahman Anati—HLF," in *Stanley Boim et al. v. Quranic Literacy Institute et al.*, Holy Land Foundation, deposition exhibit 26.

52 Ziad Abu-Amr, *Islamic Fundamentalism in the West Bank and Gaza: Muslim Brotherhood and Islamic Jihad* (Bloomington: Indiana University Press, 1994), 15 and 77. For Palestinian intelligence, see C.S.S. Special Information Bulletin, *Comité de Bienfaisance et de Secours aux Palestiniens (CBSP): A French Hamas-Affiliated Fund Which Provides Financial Support for Hamas Institutions in the PA-Administered Territories,* "Part A: Background Information About Hamas's Terrorism-Funding Apparatus and Its Civilian Infrastructure (*da'wah*)," March 2005, http://www.intelligence.org.il/eng/sib/4_05/cbsp_e.htm#contents.

53 For Palestinian intelligence report, see C.S.S. Special Information Bulletin, *Spotlight on a Hamas Dawah Institution in the West Bank.* For al-Ein mosque, see C.S.S. Special Information Bulletin, *Mosques in the Palestinian Authority-Administered Territories and on the Temple Mount Are Centers for Inflammatory Anti-American Incitement,* November 2003, http://www.intelligence.org.il/eng/sib/mpa_11_03/mosques.htm. For Salah and Arouri, see Israeli Police document, "Subject: Transcriptions of the Police Interviews with Salah Arouri," in *Stanley Boim et al. v. Quranic Literacy Institute et al.*

54 C.S.S. Special Information Bulletin, *Spotlight on a Hamas Dawah Institution in the West Bank.*

55 Israeli Police document, "Subject: Transcriptions of the Police Interviews with Salah Arouri," in *Stanley Boim et al. v. Quranic Literacy Institute et al.*

56 Congressional Research Service (CRS), "Hamas: The Organizations, Goals and Tactics of a Militant Palestinian Organization," October 14, 1993. See also C.S.S. Special Information Bulletin, *Mosques in the Palestinian Authority-Administered Territories.*

57 C.S.S. Special Information Bulletin, *Spotlight on a Hamas Dawah Institution in the West Bank.*

58 Note that al-Tadoman featured prominently on Muin Shabib's list of "our," i.e., Hamas, institutions. For Bitawi statement, see Dan Perry, "Four Killed In Tel Aviv Cafe Blast; Hamas Claims Responsibility," Associated Press, March 21, 1997; and C.S.S. Special Information Bulletin, *The Union of Good.*

59 C.S.S. Special Information Bulletin, *The Union of Good.*

60 Ibid.

61 Regarding the al-Tadoman Charitable Society, see Itmar Marcus, "'Ask for Death!': The Indoctrination of Palestinian Children to Seek Death for Allah-Shahada," *Palestine Media Watch,* www.pmw.org.il. For the Association of Religious Clerics, see IDF spokesman, "Hamas—The Islamic Resistance Movement," *Israel Foreign Ministry—Information Division,* January 1993, www.fas.org/irp/world/para/docs/930100.htm; and Margot Dudkevitch, "Israeli Killed by Terrorist in Bethlehem," *Jerusalem Post,* February 12, 2003. For Harmas, see "Subject: The Charity Associations Who Received Funds from the HLF," in *Stanley Boim et al. v. Quranic Literacy Institute et al.* For Bitawi, see "Senior Palestinian Authority Religious Judge Condones Homicide Bombings," October 3, 2002, *Arab-Jewish News,* www.nclci.org/news/arab-jewish.htm. "Po-

litical Arrest . . . What for?" *Palestinian Human Rights Monitor* 4, no. 3, www.phrmg .org/monitor2000/jun2000-political.htm; and Marcus, "'Ask for Death!'"

62 For Bitawi interviews, see Marcus, "'Ask for Death!'"; and William B. Helmreich, "No Sense Negotiating with Terrorists," *Newsday,* June 30, 2004, A40. For Bitawi's crowd address, see Agence France Presse, "Thousands of Demonstrators Urge Bomb Attacks Against Israel," April 3, 1998. For Yassin rally, see Islam Online, "'Sad Friday' Rallies Against Yassin Assassination," www.islamonline.net/English/News/2004-03/26/article 06.shtml.

63 Watson memo.

64 In a sign of the importance of this charity to the organization, Hamas leader Khaled Mishal identified Hashem Natshe as one of the "next generation" of Hamas leaders. See Charbel, "The Khaled Mishaal Interview (2 of 7)."

65 Khaled Mishal identified Hamed Bitawi as one of the "next generation" of Hamas leaders. See Charbel, "The Khaled Mishaal Interview (2 of 7)."

CHAPTER 5 TEACHING TERROR: HOW THE DAWA RADICALIZES PALESTINIAN SOCIETY

1 Sabah El-Said, "Between Pragmatism and Ideology: The Muslim Brotherhood in Jordan, 1989–1994," Policy Papers, Number 29 (Washington, D.C.: Washington Institute for Near East Policy, 1995), 8.

2 Shaul Kimhi and Shmuel Even, "Who Are the Palestinian Suicide Terrorists?" *Strategic Assessment* 6, no. 2 (Jaffe Center for Strategic Studies), Tel Aviv University, September 2003.

3 *Isra* and *Mi'raj* refer to Palestine as the land from which the Prophet Mohammad left on his night journey from Jerusalem to heaven; *Rabat* is the Islamic name for peripheral areas where Muslims served as guards of the border areas of the Muslim nation. See Intelligence and Terrorism Information Center at the Center for Special Studies (C.S.S.) Special Information Bulletin, *IRFAN: A Hamas Front Organization Operating in Canada to Enlist Financial Support for Hamas Institutions in the Palestinian Authority-Administered Territories,* "Appendix D(1): Hosni Hassan Khawajah, Head of the Tulkarm Charitable Society and Hamas Activist Thanks the Jerusalem Fund (IRFAN's Predecessor) for Its Financial Support. The letter of thanks emphasizes importance of the political-Islamic aspect of the support, which will increase Palestinian motivation to fight against Israel," November 2004, http://www.intelligence.org.il/eng/sib/11_04/ irfan.htm.

4 For FBI assessment, see Dale L. Watson, assistant director for counterterrorism, Federal Bureau of Investigation, memorandum to R. Richard Newcomb, director of the Office of Foreign Assets Control, U.S. Department of the Treasury, "Holy Land Foundation for Relief and Development, International Emergency Economic Powers Act, Action Memorandum," November 5, 2001 (hereafter, Watson memo); U.S. Department of the Treasury, Office of Public Affairs, "U.S. Designates Five Charities Funding Hamas and Six Senior Hamas Leaders as Terrorist Entities," August 22, 2003, http:// www.ustreas.gov/press/releases/js672.htm. Regarding Marzook, see Roger Gaess, "Interview with Mousa Abu Marzook," *Middle East Policy* 10, no. 2 (1997): 113–128. For quote by Palestinian mother of ten, see Jamie Tarabay, "Islamic Militants Gain Influence," Associated Press, March 2, 2001.

5   For Abu Hein, see P. W. Singer, "Terrorists Must Be Denied Child Recruits," *Financial Times*, January 20, 2005. For Shehadah, see Israel Ministry of Foreign Affairs (MFA), "The Exploitation of Children for Terrorist Purposes—Jan 2003," *MFA Library, January 2003*, January 15, 2003, http://www.mfa.gov.il/mfa/mfaarchive/2000_2009/2003/1/the+exploitation+of+children+for+terrorist+purpose.htm.

6   Doha Al-Jazirah Satellite Channel Television in Arabic, "Al-Jazirah Shows Video of Eretz Operation Perpetrator Reading Her Will—VIDEO," GMP20040114000152, 1307 GMT, January 14, 2004, Foreign Broadcast Information Service (FBIS).

7   Alex Fishman, "How Hamas Turned Adulteress Into Suicide Bomber," *Yediot Ahronot*, January 18, 2004, http://www.imra.org.il/story.php3?id=19474 (English).

8   Interview by Lisa Ling, "Female Suicide Bombers: Dying to Kill," *National Geographic Explorer*, 2004. For Sheikh Mohammad, see Mark Huband, "Radical Muslims Turn to Words of War: Tensions Between Older and Younger Followers of Islam Have Complicated Attempts to Reduce the Rise in Extreme Attitudes since the Attacks of September 11 2001," *Financial Times*, January 20, 2005.

9   Amira Hass, "The Youngest Palestinian Under Arrest," *Ha'aretz*, October 24, 2003.

10 Kimhi and Even, "Who Are the Palestinian Suicide Terrorists?"

11 For Israel Security Agency report, see Israel Security Agency (Shin Bet), "2004 Terrorism Data," *GSS Announcements*, Prime Minister's Office, Government of Israel, January 4, 2005, http://www.pmo.gov.il/PMOENG/COMMUNICATION/SPOKESMAN/GSS/GSS060105.HTM. For Israeli raid in Qalqilya and Shin Bet assessment, see MFA, "Exploitation of Children for Terrorist Purposes."

12 Interview by Lisa Ling, "Female Suicide Bombers."

13 For Israeli intelligence, see Israel Security Agency, "2004 Terrorism Data." For the April 2005 discovery by Israeli authorities, see Margot Dudkevitch, "Soldiers Foil Attempt to Smuggle Bullets in Gaza," *Jerusalem Post*, February 2, 2005; Efrat Weiss, "Palestinian Girl Hides Gun in Underwear," *Yediot Ahronot*, April 14, 2005, www.ynetnews.com/articles/0,7340,L-3072677,00.html (English).

14 Brian Handwerk, "Female Suicide Bombers: Dying to Kill," *National Geographic Explorer*, December 13, 2004, http://news.nationalgeographic.com/news/2004/12/1213_041213_tv_suicide_bombers.html.

15 Interview by Lisa Ling, "Female Suicide Bombers."

16 Regarding the Hamas charter, see the Avalon Project at Yale Law School, Article 12 in "The Covenant of the Islamic Resistance Movement," *Hamas Covenant 1988*, http://www.yale.edu/lawweb/avalon/mideast/hamas.htm. For Sheikh Yusef, see "We Don't Need Women Suicide Bombers—Hamas Spiritual Leader," *Jordan Times*, February 3, 2002. For Abu-Zuhry, see Kevin Peraino and Joanna Chen, "Flexing Their Muscles," *Newsweek Online*, May 10, 2005.

17 Spokesperson for the Israel Defense Ministry (IDF), Government of Israel, "The Involvement of Female Palestinians in Terror," http://www.idf.il/newsite/english/0218-5.stm.

18 David Rohde, "Grief Turns to Pride for the Family of a Woman Who Helped Set an Awful Precedent," *New York Times*, April 13, 2002. For the interview with Ayat's parents, see interview by Lisa Ling, "Female Suicide Bombers."

19 For Mishal historical framework, see Ghassan Charbel, "The Khaled Mishaal Interview (2 of 7)," *Dar al Hayat*, December 15, 2003, http://english.daralhayat.com/Spec/12-

2003/Article-20031215-7a215ab8-c0a8-01ed-0015-c5ece4bc1b17/story.html. For Israeli police investigations, see *Ma'ariv*, "Arab Groups Suspected of Transferring Money
to Hamas," March 1, 1996, 2, in FBIS-NES-96-042, March 1, 1996, 23. For the phenomenon relating to Israeli-Arab communities, see IDF Radio, "MK Says Local Arab
Councils Transferring Funds to Hamas," March 6, 1996, in FBIS-NES-96-045, 47. For
information on Aghbariyah's detention, see Qol Yisrael Radio, "Arab Deputy Mayor
Detained for Transferring Funds to Hamas," March 7, 1996, in FBIS-NES-96-046, 55.

20 C.S.S. Special Information Bulletin, *Spotlight on a Hamas Dawah Institution in the West
Bank: A File of Palestinian Preventive Security Documents Identified the Bethlehem Or-
phan Care Society as Hamas-Affiliated*, "Appendix A: Intelligence Report Dealing with
Funds Raised by Hamas Activists in Israel with the Aid of Sheikh Ra'ed Salah for the
Bethlehem Orphan Care Society and the Hamas Movement in Bethlehem," January
2005, http://www.intelligence.org.il/eng/sib/1_05/dawah.htm.

21 For the State Department, see U.S. House Committee on Financial Services, *Testimony
of E. Anthony Wayne, Assistant Secretary for Economic and Business Affairs, Department
of State, "The Hamas Asset Freeze and Other Government Efforts to Stop Terrorist Financing*," September 24, 2003, http://financialservices.house.gov/media/pdf/092403
eaw.pdf. For June 2000 PA report, see Amos Harel, "'The PA Steals from Me, Hams
Takes Care of Me,'" *Ha'aretz*, June 27, 2002. For 1993 Philadelphia meeting, see FBI
Electronic Communication (EC) from FBI WFO (CT-1) to Director FBI, "Subject:
Mueen Shabib," March 28, 1994, included in *U.S. v. Abdel Haleem Ashqar* (U.S. Immigration Court), Case No. A 75 422 626, 2003.

22 C.S.S. Special Information Bulletin, *The Union of Good: An Umbrella Organization
Comprised of More than 50 Islamic Charitable Funds and Foundations Worldwide*, February 2005, "Appendix B: The Transfer of Funds by the Union of Good to the Hamas-
Affiliated Jenin Charity Committee," http://www.intelligence.org.il/eng/sib/2_05/funds_
b.htm.

23 For Palestinian analysts, see Nidal al-Mughrabi, "Analysis: Hamas Plays Key Role in
Palestinian Uprising," Reuters, August 1, 2001. Regarding Nazir Madi, see Peraino and
Chen, "Flexing Their Muscles."

24 Despite the PA's concern that Hamas penetrated the PA Ministry of Education, in at
least one instance Yasser Arafat sent a personal condolence letter to the family of Omar
Mansur al-Hadiri, a Hamas suicide bombing planner responsible for such attacks as
the March 2002 "Passover Massacre" at the Park Hotel. Arafat's letter, uncovered in a
raid of the Tulkarm office of the Islamic Jihad–associated al-Ihsan Charitable Society,
offered his "warmest and most sincere sympathy" and cited Koranic verses praising
suicide attacks. See C.S.S. Special Information Bulletin, *Yasser Arafat Encourages and
Legitimizes Suicide Bombing Attacks Against Israel: Religious Islamic Terminology Encouraging the Attacks Was Found in a Condolence Telegram Arafat Sent to the Family of
a Hamas Military Operative in 2001*, November 2003, "Appendix A: The Condolence
Telegram Sent by Yasser Arafat to the al-Hadiri Clan in Tulkarm and Which Was
Found Among the Documents of al-Ihsan Charitable Society," http://www.intelligence
.org.il/eng/bu/arafat/ar_12_03.htm. For Hamas and Islamic Jihad bribes from Palestinian General and Preventative Intelligence, see C.S.S. Special Information Bulletin, *A
Captured Document Showing That in Bethlehem the Fatah (Under Its Various Names)
and the PA Intelligence Apparatuses Maintain a Regime of Oppression Based on Intimi-*

dation, Extortion, Unwarranted Arrests and Abuse of the Local Christian Population,
http://www.intelligence.org.il/eng/var/fatah.htm.

25 Asylum Affidavit of Ms. J. (Office of the Immigration Judge, Executive Office for Immigration Review, State of New York), December 2003 (at the request of her attorney,
the author agreed to withhold the identity of Ms. J.), author's personal files.

26 Asylum Affidavit of Ms. J., author's personal files. For Palestinian intelligence report,
see C.S.S. Special Information Bulletin, *Hamas Penetration into the PA Ministry of Education and Its Growing Influence over Palestinian Youth,* http://www.intelligence.org
.il/eng/bu/Hamas/education.htm.

27 C.S.S. Special Information Bulletin, *Interpal, Part III,* "Appendix B(10): Al-Islah Charitable Society, Bethlehem Branch, Stresses the Importance of Opening Centers for
Qur'an Memorization as a Means of Combating 'Negative (i.e., Permissive) Environment' Created Primarily by the Christians in the Bethlehem District," December 2004,
http://www.intelligence.org.il/eng/sib/12_04/interpal_app_bc.htm.

28 C.S.S. Special Information Bulletin, *A Captured Document.*

29 Harel, "PA Steals from Me."

30 "Subject: Muhammad Othman Abd Al-Rahman Anati—HLF," Report No. 10/319/98,
January 19, 1998, Marked page 1263 of evidentiary material brought in *Stanley Boim
et al. v. Quranic Literacy Institute et al.,* Civil No. 00 C 2905 (U.S. District Court, Northern District of Illinois, Eastern Division), June 5, 2002, marked Holy Land Foundation
for Relief and Development, deposition exhibit 26.

31 "Selected Recipients of HLFRD Funds: Jan. 1997—Sept. 2000," declassified FBI table
marked page 0732 of evidentiary material brought in *Stanley Boim et al. v. Quranic Literacy Institute et al.*

32 C.S.S. Special Information Bulletin, *"Charity" and Palestinian Terrorism—Spotlight on
the Hamas-Run Islamic Al-Tadhamun "Charitable Society" in Nablus: A Case Study of
the Workings of the Palestinian Terrorism Support-System Infrastructure and the Organizations Abroad Which Finance It,* February 2005, http://www.intelligence.org.il/eng/
sib/3_05/charity_2.htm.

33 For the Islamic Charitable Society in Hebron, see C.S.S. Special Information Bulletin,
Interpal, Part III, "Appendix B(5–6): Two Documents Dealing With the Transfer of
$33,800 by Interpal to Al-Islah Charitable Society, Ramallah-al-Bireh." Information on
other Hamas companies from author interview with Israeli official responsible for military administration of the West Bank, Tel Aviv, June 18, 2002.

34 For the Jebaliya refugee camp, see Gavin Rabinowitz and Ravi Nessman, "Jebaliya
Refugee Camp's History as Militant Haven Inspires Caution by Israeli Army," Associated Press, October 6, 2004. For "unsuspecting" popular support, see MFA, "The Financial Sources of the Hamas Terror Organization," *MFA Library, July 2003,* July 30,
2003, http://www.israel-mfa.gov.il/mfa/go.asp?MFAH0nmu0. Regarding Yassin, see
Catherine Hours, "Charity and Bombings: Hamas Gains Ground with Desperate
Palestinians," Agence France Presse, August 15, 2001. Information on Nablus area from
author interview, Tel Aviv, June 18, 2002.

35 Regarding monthly handouts, see Lee Hockstader, "Palestinians Find Heroes in
Hamas; Popularity Surges for Once-Marginal Sponsor of Suicide Bombings," *Wash-
ington Post,* August 11, 2001. For al-Islah Charitable Society report, see C.S.S. Special
Information Bulletin, *The Union of Good,* "Appendix D: The Transfer of Funds from

the Union of Good to the Hamas-Affiliated Ramallah-al-Bireh al-Islah Charitable Society." For the FBI, see Watson memo.

36 Jerrold M. Post, Ehud Sprinzak, and Laurita M. Denny, "The Terrorists in Their Own Words: Interviews with 35 Incarcerated Middle Eastern Terrorists," *Journal of Terrorism and Political Violence* 15, no. 1 (2003): 171–184.

37 Watson memo.

38 C.S.S. Special Information Bulletin, *Spotlight on a Hamas Dawah Institution in the West Bank,* "Appendix F: A Report Dealing with the Distribution of 'Offerings' [Portions of Meat] to Hamas Members in the Bethlehem Area for Eid al-Adha (the Feast of the Sacrifice)."

39 MFA, "Hamas's Use of Charitable Societies to Fund and Support Terror," *MFA Library, September 2003,* September 22, 2003, http://www.israel-mfa.gov.il/mfa/go.asp?MFAH 0nt70. For Tulkarm charity committee, see C.S.S. Special Information Bulletin, *IRFAN,* "Appendix D(2): IRFAN transfer of funds for food to the Tulkarm Charitable Society."

40 Examples include the family of Yasser Hajaj, "a Hamas activist serving a life sentence for placing an explosive charge on a Tel Aviv beach on July 28, 1990, killing a Jewish tourist from Canada"; the brother of Raid Zakarana, a Hamas terrorist who committed suicide in Aula in April 1994; and the family of Suleyman Idan, killed during a car bomb attack in Beit-El in October 1993. See Watson memo.

41 Israeli government report marked "Report No.: 10/4374/95; Subject: The Holyland Foundation," June 5, 1995, included in evidentiary material presented in *Stanley Boim et al. v. Quranic Literacy Institute et al.,* Exhibit 45 in file marked Holy Land Foundation for Relief and Development and stamped pages 0736–0743.

42 Israeli government report marked "Report No.: 10/4374/95; Subject: The Holyland Foundation," *Stanley Boim et al. v. Quranic Literacy Institute et al.*

43 C.S.S. Special Information Bulletin, *The Union of Good.*

44 Colin L. Powell, interview by Tony Snow, *Fox News Sunday,* Fox News Channel, June 30, 2002, http://usembassy.state.gov/tokyo/wwwhse1499.html.

45 Though Hamas-affiliated schools, student groups, and universities can hardly be described as "secular," we use the term here to distinguish these institutions from the mosque proper.

46 One of the original and largest Hamas charitable organizations, the Islamic Society is headed by Dr. Ahmad Bahar, who has described terrorism as "Hamas' heroic attacks," and has publicly espoused the belief that "the resistance is the only way to pressure the Jews." See Khaled Abu Toameh, "Hamas: Gaza Pullout Is Victory for Intifada," *Jerusalem Post,* March 24, 2005. For graduations, see C.S.S. "Subject: Education for Hatred and Terrorism—The Graduation Ceremony of Children from 'Islamic Association' Network Kindergartens Supported by Saudi Money," *Saudi Money Transfers to the Hamas and to Extremist Groups Identified with It,* http://www.intelligence.org.il/eng/bu/saudi/ap_c.htm. For Shubaka statement, see Watson memo.

47 For "instruction cards" and other "educational materials," see C.S.S. Special Information Bulletin, *Incitement to Terror and Hatred: Extremist Islamic Messages Encouraging Hatred, Violence and Terror against Israel Are Inculcated into High School Students in Bethlehem and Other Parts of the Palestinian Authority–Administered Territories by the Hamas Civilian Infrastructure (the da'wah),* "Appendix A: The Student Instruction Card: A Tool for Indoctrinating the Students to Become Shaheeds for the Sake of Allah,

to Identify with Hamas 'Martyrs' and to Encourage Future Recruits into the Ranks of the Suicide Bombers," June 2003, http://www.intelligence.org.il/eng/var/h_sch/hs_inc.htm. According to Palestinian sources, Issa Khalil Shawkah was a known member of Hamas who was killed on July 14, 1997, when a bomb he was assembling for a future Hamas bombing exploded in his hands. Bethlehem area police chief Col. Kamal al-Sheikh reported that Shawkah's death prompted Palestinian police to arrest and question some of Shawkah's friends and relatives. In the weeks following his death, further investigation led to the discovery of a large cache of explosives in an apartment in the town of Beit Sahour outside of Bethlehem used by Hamas as an explosives laboratory. According to Palestinian police, the stash in the apartment included nine explosive devices, plus Jewish prayer shawls, skull caps, wigs, and Israeli uniforms for use by Hamas terrorists seeking to blend into Israeli society on route to carrying out an attack. Col. Al-Sheikh stated that TNT, hydrogen, chemicals, acids, timers, and watches were also found in the apartment—all standard materials used by Hamas explosives experts to prepare improvised explosive devices (IEDs, or homemade bombs). For information on Shawkah, see "Israeli Army, Arabs Clash after West Bank Funeral," *Orlando Sentinel,* July 17, 1997; "Palestinians Bury Hamas Militant," *Sun-Sentinel,* July 17, 1997; "Bethlehem bomb factory points to Hamas," *The Australian,* July 23, 1997; "Clinton May Decide on Separate Talks with Netanyahu, Arafat," *Mideast Mirror* 11, no. 139, July 21, 1997. Quotes on Hamas cards from C.S.S. Special Information Bulletin, *Incitement to Terror and Hatred,* "Appendix B: Postcards in Memory of Issa Khalil Shawkah, Hamas Terrorist." For "The Martyrs," see Neil MacFarquhar, "Portrait of a Suicide Bomber: Devout, Apolitical and Angry," *New York Times,* March 18, 1996.

48 C.S.S. Special Information Bulletin, *The Union of Good,* "Appendix B(6): The Transfer of Funds by the Union of Good to the Hamas-Affiliated Jenin Charity Committee."

49 For al-Aqsa Intifada martyrs summer camp, see MFA, "The Exploitation of Children for Terrorist Purposes." For al Mashoukhi, see Khaled Abu Toameh, "Gaza Kids Undergoing Military Training at Summer Camps," *Jerusalem Post,* July 13, 2004.

50 MFA, "Participation of Children and Teenagers in Terrorist Activity During the Al Aqsa Intifada," *MFA Library, January 2003,* http://www.mfa.gov.il/mfa/go.asp?MFA H0n100.

51 C.S.S. Special Information Bulletin, *The Union of Good,* "Appendix B(6)."

52 For the Union of Good, see C.S.S. Special Information Bulletin, *The Union of Good,* "Appendix B(6)." For the Jenin charity committee, see "Selected Recipients of HLFRD Funds: Jan. 1997–Sept. 2000," *Stanley Boim et al. v. Quranic Literacy Institute et al.* For Koran centers, see C.S.S. Special Information Bulletin, *Interpal, Part II,* December 2004, http://www.intelligence.org.il/eng/sib/12_04/images/dec15_04.pdf. For the Women's League, see C.S.S. Special Information Bulletin, *Spotlight on a Hamas Dawah Institution in the West Bank,* "Appendix J: Report About Activities Organized by the Women's Hope League, a Branch of the Bethlehem Orphan Care Society, Including the Participation of Female Students Belonging to Hamas."

53 Tarabay, "Islamic Militants Gain Influence"; MFA, "The Exploitation of Children for Terrorist Purposes."

54 For class schedule, see C.S.S. Special Information Bulletin, *The Martyrdom and Suicide Culture in Palestinian Universities—al-Najah University in Nablus as a Case Study,* May 2003, http://www.intelligence.org.il/eng/bu/sib_mb/university.htm. For school sup-

plies, see C.S.S. Special Information Bulletin, *The Suicide Bombers and Martyr Culture at al-Najah University in Nablus: At the Beginning of the 2004–2005 School Year the Youth Movements Affiliated with the Various Palestinian Terrorist Organizations Distributed "Propaganda and Indoctrination Kits" to New Students*, October 2004, http://www.intelligence.org.il/eng/sib/11_04/najah.htm. For student elections, see Khaled Abu Toameh, "Hamas Wins Student Election Race on Israeli Bodycount Ticket," *Jerusalem Post*, December 11, 2003.

55 International Policy Institute for Counter-Terrorism (ICT), "Nablus' al-Najah University, Breeding Ground of Suicide Bombers," August 26, 2002, http://www.ict.org.il.

56 Jean Luc Renaudie, "As Deadline Nears, Israel and Palestinian Mull Clinton Peace Plan," Agence France Presse, December 26, 2000.

57 Agence France Presse, "Hamas Announces Death of Own Militant in Netanya Suicide Attack," January 9, 2001.

58 Agence France Presse, "Hamas Claims Responsibility for School Bus Bomb Attack," April 30, 2001.

59 Agence France Presse, "Hamas Claims West Bank Suicide Bombing Which Injured Two Police Officers," November 8, 2001.

60 David Rudge, "Terror Attack in Emmanuel Kills 10. Arafat Orders Hamas, Islamic Jihad Offices Closed," *Jerusalem Post*, December 13, 2001.

61 Joel Greenberg, "Portrait of an Angry Young Arab Woman," *New York Times*, March 1, 2001.

62 Joel Greenberg, "Mideast Turmoil: The Village," *New York Times*, June 30, 2002.

63 For Kutla Islamiya, see C.S.S. Special Information Bulletin, *Suicide Bombers and Martyr Culture at al-Najah University in Nablus*.

64 For Islamic Association of al-Bira, see C.S.S. Special Information Bulletin, *Israeli Security Forces Seize Palestinian Terrorist Assets Held in Banks Across the West Bank*, February 2004, http://www.intelligence.org.il/eng/c_t/ris_4_04.htm. For Mishal see Charbel, "The Khaled Mishaal Interview (2 of 7)."

64 Author interview with Col. (ret.) Yoni Fighel, former Israeli military governor in Jenin, Tel Aviv, June 23, 2004.

65 For al-Najah's 2004 student council, see C.S.S. Special Information Bulletin, *Suicide Bombers and Martyr Culture at al-Najah University in Nablus*. For Adwan, see ICT, "Nablus 'al-Najah University: Breeding Ground of Suicide Bombers," August 26, 2002, http://www.ict.org.il/articles/articledet.cfm?articleid=445.

66 For "greenhouse," see ICT, "Nablus 'al-Najah University." For Israeli July 2004 exposures, see C.S.S. Special Information Bulletin, *Suicide Bombers and Martyr Culture at al-Najah University in Nablus*.

67 C.S.S. Special Information Bulletin, *Anti-Israeli Incitement in the Palestinian Authority Since the Election of Abu Mazen (Update Number 1)*, February 21, 2005, http://www.intelligence.org.il/eng/sib/3_05/incite.htm.

68 "Subject: Muhammad Othman Abd Al-Rahman Anati—HLF," *Stanley Boim et al. v. Quranic Literacy Institute et al.*

69 C.S.S. Special Information Bulletin, *Martyrdom and Suicide Culture in Palestinian Universities*. Song lyrics were found on the official website of the Islamic Bloc of al-Najah University, http://www.khayma.com/islamic_block/ (accessed December 2004). As of March 2005, the website has been shut down, with the message: "Al-Kutla al-Islamiyah

at al-Najah University announces that our website has been stopped because of attacks from Zionist-American. We will be back, if God wills, with our new website, stay tuned."

70 Khaled Abu Toameh, "Hamas Calls for More Suicide Bombings," *Jerusalem Post*, January 10, 2005.

71 For Islamic Bloc recreation, see ICT, "Nablus 'al-Najah University." For details on the attack see Greg Myre, "Suicide Bombing in Jerusalem Pizza Restaurant Kills 15, Including American Woman," Associated Press, August 9, 2001; "Ticking Bomb's Terrorist Captured; Suicide Bomber's Family Praise 'Martyrdom,'" *Jerusalem Post*, August 12, 2001; MFA, "Suicide Bombing at the Sbarro Pizzeria in Jerusalem," MFA Library, October 2000, August 9, 2001, http://www.mfa.gov.il/MFA/MFAArchive/2000_2009/2000/10/Suicide%20bombing%20at%20the%20Sbarro%20pizzeria%20in%20Jerusale.

72 ICT, "Nablus' al-Najah University."

73 http://www.khayma.com/islamic_block (accessed December 2004).

74 Rudge, "Terror Attack in Emmanuel Kills 10."

75 This video was found on the official website of the Islamic Bloc of al-Najah University, http://www.khayma.com/islamic_block/ (accessed December 2004).

76 ICT, "Nablus' al-Najah University"; and "U.S. Gives Israel Green Light to Suffocate the Palestinians," *Palestine News*, http://www.palestinetimes.net/issue128/news.html.

77 C.S.S. Special Information Bulletin, *Martyrdom and Suicide Culture in Palestinian Universities.*

78 Tarabay, "Islamic Militants Gain Influence." Confirming the reporter's suspicions, the Islamic Charitable Society in Hebron received $1,156,386 in funding from the Holy Land Foundation in the period between January 1997 and September 2000. See "Selected Recipients of HLFRD Funds: Jan. 1997—Sept. 2000," *Stanley Boim et al. v. Quranic Literacy Institute et al.*

79 For January 10, 2003, speech see C.S.S. Special Information Bulletin, *Mosques in the Palestinian Authority-Administered Territories and on the Temple Mount Are Centers for Inflammatory anti-American Incitement,* "Appendix A: Anti-American Sermons Delivered in Gazan Mosques," November 2003, http://www.intelligence.org.il/eng/sib/mpa_11_03/mosques.htm. For "the resurrection . . . ," see Itamar Marcus and Barbara Crook, "PA Academic on PA TV: Killing of Jews Is Mandatory," *Palestinian Media Watch Bulletin*, http://www.pmw.org.il/Latest%20bulletins%20new.htm#manda. For January 7, 2005, see "Recent Anti-American Sermons from Palestinian Authority Mosques," *Special Dispatch—PA/U.S. & the Middle East*, No. 844, The Middle East Media Research Institute (MEMRI), January 11, 2005, http://memri.org/bin/articles.cgi?Page=archives&Area=sd&ID=SP84405.

80 Regarding al-Qaeda training camps in Afghanistan, see the Israeli indictment of Nabil Awqil, author's personal files; Matthew Gutman, "Tentacles of Terror," *Jerusalem Post*, December 12, 2002. For sermons, see C.S.S. Special Information Bulletin, *Mosques in the Palestinian Authority-Administered Territories and on the Temple Mount,* "Appendix A." For PA's reaction, see Nidal al-Mughrabi, "Senior Palestinian Slams Cleric for Anti-Semitism," Reuters, May 18, 2005. Excerpt from Wafa, "Prime Minister Chairs Cabinet's Weekly Meeting in Hebron; Israeli Aggression Flagrant Violation of Pacification Efforts and Sharm al-Shaykh Understandings; Quartet Committee, International Community Should Intervene to Stop Israel's Tampering with Region's Destiny," *Gaza*,

May 18, 2005, translated text available in *BBC Monitoring—Middle East—Political*, May 19, 2005.

81 For Abu-Snina, see C.S.S. Special Information Bulletin, *Anti-Israeli Incitement*. For ISA press release, see Government of Israel, Prime Minister's Office, "Israeli Arab Suspected of Collecting Intelligence for Hamas," *GSS Announcements*, August 4, 2004, http://www.pmo.gov.il/PMOEng/Communication/Spokesman/gss/shabackeng040804.html.

82 C.S.S. Special Information Bulletin, *Mosques in the Palestinian Authority- Administered Territories Are Used as Platforms for Provoking Anti-Israel and Anti-American Hatred, and as Hothouses for Training Terrorists: al-'Ein Mosqu in al Bireh as a Case Study*, November 2003, http://www.intelligence.org.il/eng/sib/mpa_11_03/alein_12_03.htm; and C.S.S. Special Information Bulletin, *Mosques in the Palestinian Authority-Administered Territories and on the Temple Mount.*

83 "Subject: Muhammad Othman Abd Al-Rahman Anati—HLF," *Stanley Boim et al. v. Quranic Literacy Institute et al.* For Atrash, see "Subject: The Charity Associations Who Received Funds from the HLF," Report No. 10/6394/98, June 2, 1998, marked HLF exhibit 57, pages 0856–0863 of evidentiary material brought in *Stanley Boim et al. v. Quranic Literacy Institute et al.*

84 Khaled Abu Toameh, "Hamas 'Wonder Boy' Wows Gaza Worshipers," *Jerusalem Post*, May 19, 2005.

85 Majeda El-Batsh, "Parents Fear Their Children Could Take on Suicide Missions," Agence France Presse, July 8, 2003.

86 MacFarquhar, "Portrait of a Suicide Bomber." For mother's account, see Asylum Affidavit of Ms. J, author's personal files.

87 Alfonso Chardy, "Parents Try to Keep Kids from Becoming Suicide Bombers," Knight Ridder, May 24, 2002.

88 Kimhi and Even, "Who Are the Palestinian Suicide Terrorists?"

89 Singer, "Terrorists Must Be Denied Child Recruits."

90 C.S.S. Special Information Bulletin, *Interpal, Part II*, December 2004, http://www.intelligence.org.il/eng/sib/12_04/images/dec15_04.pdf.

91 Author interview with Col. (ret.) Yoni Fighel, former Israeli military governor in Jenin, Tel Aviv, June 23, 2004.

92 "Affidavit of Joseph Hummel" (State of New York, County of New York, Southern District of New York), September 20, 1995, marked pages 0663–0675 of evidentiary material brought in *Stanley Boim et al. v. Quranic Literacy Institute et al.* For al-Qadi designation, see U.S. Department of State, "U.S. Designation of Terrorist Organizations," December 7, 2001.

93 Arnon Regular, "Leading Hamas Preacher Warns of Clash with Islamic Jihad," *Ha'aretz*, December 15, 2004. For Hamas charter, see the Avalon Project, "The Covenant of the Islamic Resistance Movement." Information on singing troupe from author interview with Israeli officials, Tel Aviv, November 18, 2004.

94 Regular, "Leading Hamas Preacher Warns of Clash." For al-Aqsa television, see "Hamas Launches TV Channel," *Asharq al-Awsat*, January 1, 2006; and Craig S. Smith, "Gaza Journal; Warm and Fuzzy TV, Brought to You by Hamas," *New York Times*, January 18, 2006.

95 C.S.S., *Report on the Hamas organ Filisteen Almuslima (Muslim Palestine) Is Directed from Damascus, Printed in Beirut and Distributed Worldwide from London, England*, http://www.intelligence.org.il/eng/bu/britain/sib2_10_03.htm.

96 C.S.S. Special Information Bulletin, *Interpal, Part III,* "Appendix C: Transfer of Funds by Interpal to the Islamic Charitable Society."

97 C.S.S. Special Information Bulletin, *Educating Children for Hatred and Terrorism: Encouragement for Suicide Bombing Attacks and Hatred for Israel and the Jews Spread via the Internet on Hamas' Online Children's Magazine (al-Fateh),* December 2004, http://www.intelligence.org.il/eng/sib/11_04/edu.htm.

98 Tarek Hamid's videotaped living will is available at http://terroristmedia.com/nukem/modules.php?name=Downloads&d_op=getit&lid=150.

99 C .S. S. Special Information Bulletin, *Profile of the Palestinian Islamic Jihad, Perpetrator of a Suicide Bombing Attack in Tel Aviv,* February 25, 2005, February 2005, http://www.intelligence.org.il/eng/sib/3_05/pji.htm.

100 C.S.S. Special Information Bulletin, *Marketing Terrorism: Hamas Exploitation of the Eastern European Internet Infrastructure to Operate Its Sites,* December 2004, http://www.intelligence.org.il/eng/sib/1_05/m_t.htm.

CHAPTER 6 FOREIGN FUNDING OF HAMAS

1 Intelligence and Terrorism Information Center at the Center for Special Studies (C.S.S.) Special Information Bulletin, "Appendix A(12): Who Subsidizes the Hamas-Run Ramallah-al-Bireh Charity Committee?" *Interpal, Part II,* December 2004, http://www.intelligence.org.il/eng/sib/12_04/interpal_app_a.htm.

2 C.S.S. Special Information Bulletin, *Interpal, Part I Synopsis,* December 2004, http://www.intelligence.org.il/eng/sib/12_04/interpal.htm.

3 Think tank report from Ahmad Rashad, "The Truth About Hamas," *Middle East Information Center,* June 7, 2003, http://www.middleeastinfo.net/article2822.html. Rashad is a research associate with the United Association for Studies and Research (UASR) and is also affiliated with the Islamic Association for Palestine (IAP), both of which U.S. authorities have tied to Hamas. U.S. government analysis culled from U.S. Department of the Treasury, Office of Public Affairs, "U.S. Designates Five Charities Funding Hamas and Six Senior Hamas Leaders as Terrorist Entities," August 22, 2003, http://www.ustreas.gov/press/releases/js672.htm.

4 1996 report from CIA document in author's personal files. The untitled document is referenced in Glenn Simpson, "Officials Had Information Many Years Before 9/11 Attacks, Report Indicates," *Wall Street Journal,* May 9, 2003. Regarding western intelligence services, see Agence France Presse, "Riyadh Aids Islamic Extremists via Non-Governmental Group: Report," June 30, 1996.

5 For the United Arab Emirates Friendship Association, PCC, and IICO, see index of documents seized by IDF forces in Operation Defensive Shield, April 2003, author's personal files. Regarding al-Mounasara Fund, see C.S.S. Special Information Bulletin, *Interpal, Part I—Synopsis,* "Part 4: Islamic 'Charity Funds and Foundations' in Europe and the Middle East Which Support Hamas, Designated Hamas-Affiliated Organizations," December 2004, http://www.intelligence.org.il/eng/sib/12_04/interpal.htm. For IICO, also see Mark Huband, "Bankrolling bin Laden," *Financial Times,* November 29, 2002. The Fund for the Care of Families is headed by Abu al-Abd; this organization is described as "a body established by the Hamas leadership so as to regulate the transfer of money to the families of Hamas casualties and prisoners." This fund was in direct contact with Hamas operatives in the West Bank and sent Hamas

funds through a Hamas-controlled charity committee in Ramallah. See Israel Ministry of Foreign Affairs (MFA), "Iran and Syria as Strategic Support for Palestinian Terrorism," September 30, 2002, http://www.israel-mfa.gov.il/mfa/mfaarchive/2000_2009/2002/9/iran+and+syria+as+strategic+support+for+palestinia.htm.

6 For Marzook, see Roger Gaess, "Interview with Mousa Abu Marzook," *Middle East Policy* 5, no. 2 (1997): 113–128. Regarding Inforcom and HLFRD, see Dale L. Watson, assistant director for counterterrorism, Federal Bureau of Investigation, memorandum to R. Richard Newcomb, director of the Office of Foreign Assets Control, U.S. Department of the Treasury, "Holy Land Foundation for Relief and Development, International Emergency Economic Powers Act, Action Memorandum," November 5, 2001 (hereafter, Watson memo). For Elashi, see Yaakov Amidror, "Hamas—Musa Muhammad Abu Marzook (Abu Omar)—An Expert Opinion," *Analysis and Assessment Division of Israel Defense Forces Intelligence,* September 20, 1995, 6, included in evidentiary material brought in deportation hearing for Abdel Haleem Ashqar in *U.S. v. Abdel Haleem Ashqar* (U.S. Immigration Court), Case No. A 75 422 626, 2003. Infocom was exporting computer technology and providing ISP services for Libya and Syria in violation of U.S. export control law, was serving as the ISP for other U.S.-based terrorist front organizations such as the al-Qaeda associated Global Relief Foundation (GRF) and Benevolence International Foundation (BIF), and had received funds from and sent funds to Abu Marzook, a Specially Designated Terrorist with whom business is prohibited by law. For Elashi's brothers, see *United States of America vs. Bayan Elashi et al.,* CR No., 3:02-CR052-R (U.S. District Court for the Northern District of Texas, Dallas Division), December 17, 2002.

7 For Richardson mosque, see Steve McGonigle, "Aid Push Made for 5 Tied to Hamas—Backers Seek to Raise $500,000 for Muslim Brothers' Legal Team," *Dallas Morning News,* February 15, 2003. For document found in December 2003 see "Saudi Publications on Hate Ideology Fill American Mosques," *Center for Religious Freedom, Freedom House,* January 2005, http://freedomhouse.org/religion/publications/Saudi%20Report/FINAL%20FINAL.pdf.

8 Watson memo. For Treasury report, see U.S. Department of the Treasury, General Accounting Office, "Report to Congressional Requesters, Report # GAO-04-163, Terrorist Financing: U.S. Agencies Should Systemically Assess Terrorists' Use of Alternative Financing Mechanisms," November 2003, http://www.gao.gov/new.items/d04163.pdf.

9 Watson memo.

10 Watson memo. Though Ashqar had not been to the West Bank since 1989 and was under house arrest in northern Virginia—and wearing an electronic ankle bracelet—at the time of the elections, Ashqar placed advertisements in Arab newspapers announcing that "they restricted my movement but they couldn't suffocate my voice." See Matthew Barakat, "Candidate Seeks Palestinian Presidency While Under House Arrest," Associated Press, January 6, 2005.

11 FBI Electronic Communication (EC) from SAC, Philadelphia to Director, FBI, October 27, 1993 (subject line was censored out before declassification).

12 Not only does the FBI note that Hanooti raised millions of dollars for Hamas, but former U.S. Attorney Mary Jo White acknowledged he was named as an unindicted co-conspirator in the 1993 World Trade Center bombing and a subsequent plot to bomb New York City landmarks. See Watson memo and Brendan Lyons, "Imam Retains

Local Support," *Times Union*, July 14, 2002; also see Watson memo for "Samah" and "the Movement" references.

13 FBI summary of translated transcripts of Philadelphia meeting, Marked "typed version of Bates 203–287," Entry for 10/5/93, 3–4, included in *U.S. v. Abdel Haleem Ashqar*. In another sign of their global jihadist worldview, one participant also cautioned that charitable organizations would have to be convinced "not to divert [their] attention to trivial activities, such as Bosnia and Somalia" for fear donors would get the impression "that there is no more need in Palestine" in the wake of the Oslo Accords (Tape 6—Conference Room, 36).

14 FBI summary of translated transcripts of Philadelphia meeting, Marked "typed version of Bates 203–287," Entry for 10/5/93, 9–11, Tape 12—Conference Room, 51, Tape 6—Conference Room, 37, included in *U.S. v. Abdel Haleem Ashqar*.

15 FBI summary of translated transcripts of Philadelphia meeting, Marked "typed version of Bates 203–287," Entry for 10/2/93, Tape 9—Conference Room, 48, included in *U.S. v. Abdel Haleem Ashqar*.

16 Meir Litvak, "The Islamization of Palestinian Identity: The Case of Hamas," The Moshe Dayan Center for Middle Eastern Studies, Tel Aviv University, http://www.dayan.org/d&a-Hamas-litvak.htm.

17 Jaber Deposition, (04/09/03), 12–17, 222–225; Ahmad Deposition 38–39 and Israeli intelligence report marked pages 0609–0614 of evidentiary material brought in *Stanley Boim et al. v. Quranic Literacy Institute et al.*, Civil No. 00 C 2905 (U.S. District Court, Northern District of Illinois, Eastern Division), June 5, 2002. For Mishal, see Ghassan Charbel, "The Khaled Mishaal Interview (2 of 7)," *Dar al Hayat*, December 15, 2003, http://english.daralhayat.com/Spec/12-2003/Article-20031215-7a215ab8-c0a8-01ed-0015-c5ece4bc1b17/story.html. Damiri Dep., Ex. 2 included in *Stanley Boim et al. v. Quranic Literacy Institute et al.* For IAP and Philadelphia meeting, see Watson memo; also see Jaber Dep., Ex. 25.

18 For Hamas communiqué, see Ahmad Dep., Ex. 12, included in *Stanley Boim et al. v. Quranic Literacy Institute et al.* For Occupied Land Fund, see Ahmad Dep., Ex. 11, included in *Boim et al. v. Quranic Literacy Institute et al.* For conventions and conferences, see 1988, 1989, 1992, and 1993 IAP convention tapes, Bates Nos. BO 02666-67; BO 02676-77, included in *Boim et al. v. Quranic Literacy Institute et al.* For Siyam in Kansas City, see Matthew Levitt, *Boim et al. v. Quranic Literacy Institute et al.*, "Appendix A: Hamas Members Affiliated With Defendants." For rallies for jailed Hamas members, see Jaber Dep., Exs. 22, 24, 26, *Boim et al. v. Quaranic Literacy Institute et al.*

19 Regarding Filisteen al-Muslima, see C.S.S., *The Hamas Organ Filisteen Almuslima (Muslim Palestine) Is Directed from Damascus, Printed in Beirut and Distributed Worldwide from London, England*, http://www.intelligence.org.il/eng/bu/britain/sib2 10_03.htm. The July 4, 1993, edition of the IAP publication *Muslim World Monitor* features a form for renewing or initiating IAP membership. The form includes options for "Basic Membership," "Family Membership," "Donations," and for subscriptions to the IAP publications *Muslim World Monitor* and al-Zaitonah and to Falasteen Almuslimah; included in *Stanley Boim et al. v. Quranic Literacy Institute et al.* For December 1989 communiqué, see "Communiqué issued by the Information Office of the Islamic Association for Palestine in North America, the Intifada's Third Year," marked 1370229–1, included in *Boim et al. v. Quranic Literacy Institute et al.* For February 1989

communiqué, see "A Call for Continuation with Jihad to Raise the Word of Allah," Communiqué No. 36, Islamic Association for Palestine, marked exhibit 12 of Ahmad deposition, included in *Stanley Boim et al. v. Quranic Literacy Institute et al.*

20 For IAP's primary function, see Abu Baker Dep., Ex. 19; Abu Baker Dep., 64-66, 125-127, *Stanley Boim et al. v. Quranic Literacy Institute et al.* For IAP's solicitations from HLFRD, see "Annual Ramadan Fundraising Program Agreement," American Muslim Society (AMS)/Islamic Association for Palestine (IAP) & Holy Land Foundation for Relief and Development (HLFRD), marked deposition exhibit 19, IAP 00072, included in *Boim et al. v. Quranic Literacy Institute et al.;* Ahmad Dep., Exs. 7, 10-11; Jaber Dep., Ex. 21; Abu Baker Dep., Exs. 13, 18 included in *Boim et al. v. Quranic Literacy Institute et al.* For 1996 FBI report, see Watson memo.

21 The Council on American-Islamic Relations, "Muslim Charity Suspends Activity Over Government Actions," January 19, 2005, http://www.kinderusa.org/donorletter.htm.

22 On Mohmed and Abdelkarim, see David Koenig, "Muslim Charity Trying to Reverse Shutdown," Associated Press, September 6, 2002. The U.S. Treasury Department noted that after being designated a terrorist organization in March 2002, the Bosnian branch of the al-Haramain Islamic Foundation "reconstituted itself and continued operations under the name 'Vazir.'" In another case, Treasury also noted that the Indonesian branch of al-Haramain also attempted to operate under an assumed name, "Yayasan Al-Manahil-Indonesia", U.S. Department of the Treasury, Office of Public Affairs, "Treasury Announces Joint Action with Saudi Arabia Against Four Branches of Al-Haramain in the Fight Against Terrorist Financing," Document number JS-1108, January 22, 2004, http://www.treas.gov/press/releases/js1108.htm. Similarly, the al-Rashid Trust was designated a terrorist group by the United States on September 23, 2001, and by the U.N. 1267 Sanctions Committee on October 6, 2001. U.S. intelligence indicates that, as of mid-March 2002, al-Akhtar Trust was conducting all activities of the former al-Rashid Trust; U.S. Department of the Treasury, Office of Public Affairs, "U.S. Designates al-Akhtar Trust Pakistani Based Charity Is Suspected of Raising Money for Terrorists in Iraq," Document number JS-899, October 14, 2003, http://www.treas.gov/press/releases/js899.htm. In the Philippines, IIRO was renamed the Islamic Mercy Foundation and continued Moro Islamic Liberation Front activities under that title; Zachary Abuza, "Funding Terrorism in Southeast Asia: The Financial Network of Al-Qaeda and Jemaah Islamiyah," *National Bureau of Asian Research* 14, no. 5 (2003).

23 Anayat Durrani, "Humanitarianism Under Attack." *Al-Ahram Weekly On-Line,* no. 588, May 5–June 30, 2002.

24 For CAIR description, see Council on American-Islamic Relations website at http://www.cair-net.org/asp/aboutcair.asp. Regarding Awad, see Stephen F. Hayes, "Uncle Sam's Makeover; The State Department's Answer to Osama bin Laden Is to 'Redefine America,'" *Weekly Standard,* June 3, 2002. For Royer, see Mary Beth Sheridan, Caryle Murphy, and Jerry Markon, "Va. 'Jihad' Suspects: 11 Men, Two Views; U.S. Sees Conspiracy; They Proclaim Piety," *Washington Post,* August 8, 2003, A01. For Khafagi, see Bill Morlin, "Egyptian with UI Ties Held in Probe," *Spokesman Review,* March 14, 2003, A1.

25 For Alamoudi's comments at 2000 rally, see Nedra Pickler, "Bonior's Refusal to Return Donation from Muslim Becomes Campaign Issue in Mich. Governor's Race," Associated Press, January 9, 2002. For Alamoudi's conference attendance, see Minaret of Freedom Institute, "Imad-Ad-Dean Ahmad's Address to the First Conference on Jeru-

salem," January 29, 2001, http://www.minaret.org/beirutconference.htm. For ICE, see Declaration in Support of Detention, *USA v. Abdurahman Muhammad Alamoudi et al.*, Case no. 03-1009M (U.S. District Court, Eastern District of Virginia, Alexandria Division), September 30, 2003; *United States of America v. Abdurahman Muhammad Alamoudi et al.*, CR no. 03-513-A (U.S. District Court, the Eastern District of Virginia, Alexandria Division), October 22, 2003.

26 For Alamoudi's plea agreement, see *United States of America v. Abdurahman M. Alamoudi*, CR no. 03-513-A, (U.S. District Court, Eastern District of Virginia, Alexandria Division), July 29, 2004. For Treasury Department, see U.S. Department of the Treasury, Office of Public Affairs, "U.S. Treasury Designates Two Individuals with Ties to al-Qaida, UBL Former BIF Leader and al-Qaida Associate Named Under E.O. 13224," December 21, 2004, http://www.treas.gov/press/releases/js2164.htm; and U.S Department of the Treasury, "Treasury Designates MIRA for Support to Al-Qaida," July 14, 2005, http://www.treas.gov/press/releases/js2632.htm.

27 *United States of America v. Sami Omar al-Hussayen*, Superseding Indictment, (U.S. District Court for the District of Idaho), January 9, 2004.

28 Language specialist el-Touni, FBI Translation of Session ID: mtgb_19931002_5, Saturday 93-10-02, Washington Field Office, April 24, 2001, 3, included in *Stanley Boim et al v. Quranic Literacy Institute et al.*

29 Regarding al-Aqsa worldwide operations, see C.S.S. Special Information Bulletin, *An Important Step in the Struggle Against the Financing of Terrorism from Europe: A German Court Upholds a Government Decision to Outlaw the German Office of the al-Aqsa Charitable Foundation*, December 2004, http://www.intelligence.org.il/eng/sib/1_05/german.htm. Statement by Britain's Treasury Ministry from "Britain Freezes Assets of Charity with Suspected Terror Links," Agence France Press, May 29, 2003. For Canadian intelligence report, see Canadian Secret Intelligence Service (CSIS), "Terrorist Group Profiler," June 2002, author's personal files; see also Stewart Bell, "Hamas May Have Chemical Weapons: CSIS Report Says Terror Group May Be Experimenting," *National Post* (Canada), December 10, 2003. Al-Aqsa's contributions to Hamas were well known among Hamas activists. In a telephone conversation recorded by the FBI, Ashqar and then–Hamas representative to Yemen Mohammad Siyam make mention of Ali Muqbil (a.k.a. Abu Hamza), commenting "he's (in charge of) charity work at the office." According to the U.S. Treasury Department, "Ali Muqbil, the General Manager of the al-Aqsa Foundation in Yemen and a Hamas official, transferred funds on al-Muayad's orders to Hamas, Islamic Jihad or other Palestinian organizations assisting 'Palestinian fighters'"; FBI translation of March 13, 1994, telephone call between Sheikh Siam, Abdelhaleem Ashqar, and Unknown male, Session ID 94-2_19940313 _000000, LS Geergis, Washington Field Office, May 6, 2001, included in *Boim et al. v. Quaranic Literacy Institute et al.*; and U.S. Department of the Treasury, Office of Public Affairs, "Treasury Designates al-Aqsa International Foundation as Financier of Terror Charity Linked to Funding of the Hamas Terrorist Organization," May 29, 2003, http://www.treas.gov/press/releases/js439.htm.

30 For Moayad and FBI informant, see *USA vs. Mohammed Ali Hasan Al-Moayad*, M-03-0016 Affidavit in Support of Arrest Warrant (U.S. District Court, Eastern District of New York), January 5, 2003. For Palestinian intelligence document, innocuous donations, and al-Islah Charitable Society, see C.S.S. Special Information Bulletin, *An Im-*

portant Step in the Struggle against the Financing of Terrorism from Europe. For seized documents, see index of documents seized by IDF forces in Operation Defensive Shield, April 2003, author's personal files.

31 C.S.S. Special Information Bulletin, *An Important Step in the Struggle against the Financing of Terrorism from Europe.*

32 Ibid.

33 For al-Aqsa in the Netherlands, see MFA, "Hamas's Use of Charitable Societies to Fund and Support Terror," September 22, 2003, http://www.israel-mfa.gov.il/mfa/go.asp? MFAH0nt70. For EU and Nova TV actions, see C.S.S. Special Information Bulletin, *Interpal, Part I.*

34 MFA, "Hamas's Use of Charitable Societies to Fund and Support Terror."

35 C.S.S. Special Information Bulletin, *An Important Step in the Struggle against the Financing of Terrorism from Europe.*

36 "Treasury Designates Al-Aqsa International Foundation as Financier of Terror: Charity Linked to Funding of the Hamas Terrorist Organization," U.S. Department of the Treasury, Office of Public Affairs, http://www.treas.gov/press/releases/js439.htm.

37 "UK Government: Charity Watchdog Closes Inquiry into Interpal," *M2 Presswire* Coventry, September 24, 2003, 1 (accessed from Proquest).; C.S.S. Special Information Bulletin, *Interpal, Part I;* e-mail correspondence found in the offices of the Hebron Islamic Charitable Society bear the clearinghouse function. The charity received an e-mail from Interpal advising it that while the charity should rely on a report issued by the al-Aqsa Charitable Foundation in Holland it should contact Interpal, not al-Aqsa, "for any inquiries or information requests." See C.S.S. Special Information Bulletin, *An Important Step in the Struggle against the Financing of Terrorism from Europe.*

38 For Treasury Department designations, see U.S. Department of the Treasury, "U.S. Designates Five Charities Funding Hamas and Six Senior Hamas Leaders as Terrorist Entities." For Australian designations, see Associated Press, "Australia Lists Six Hamas Leaders as Terrorists and Freezes Charity Assets," November 21, 2003. For Canada, see CSIS, "Terrorist Group Profiler"; Bell, "Hamas May Have Chemical Weapons." For telephone intercepts, see Gideon Maron and Yuval Karni, "The Secret Intercepts of Shaykh Salah," *Yediot Ahronot,* August 29, 2003 (Hebrew).

39 The listed beneficiaries were the al-Islah Charitable Society in Ramallah and al-Bireh; the al-Ram Zakat Committee in Jerusalem; the al-Salah Charitable Association in Gaza; the al-Dheisha Refugee Camp Zakat Committee in Bethlehem; the Islamic Charitable Society in Hebron; the Jenin Zakat Committee; the Mercy Association for Children in Gaza; the Orphans and Needy Welfare Society in Jericho; the Qalqilya Society for the Disabled; the Ramallah Zakat Committee; the Social Charitable Society in Rafah; and the Tularm Zakat Committee. See C.S.S. Special Information Bulletin, *Interpal, Part I.*

40 For U.S. Treasury designation, see U.S. Department of the Treasury, "US Designates Five Charities Funding Hamas and Six Senior Hamas Leaders as Terrorists." For the U.K. Charity Commission, see Charity Commission for England and Wales, "Palestinians Relief and Development Fund, Registered Charity No. 1040094 (Interpal)," http://www.charitycommission.gov.uk/investigations/inquiryreports/interpal.asp.

41 C.S.S. Special Information Bulletin, *Interpal, Part I.*

42 Ibid. For Tawil, see C.S.S. Special Information Bulletin, *Israeli Security Forces Seize*

Palestinian Terrorist Assets Held in Banks Across the West Bank, February 25, 2004, http://www.intelligence.org.il/eng/c_t/ris_4_04.htm.

43 C.S.S. Special Information Bulletin, *Interpal, Part III,* "Appendix B (5–6). Two documents dealing with the transfer of $33,800 by Interpal to Al-Islah Charitable Society, Ramallah-Al-Bireh," December 2004, http://www.intelligence.org.il/eng/sib/12_04/interpal_app_bc.htm. For Palestinian intelligence report, see C.S.S. Special Information Bulletin, *Spotlight on a Hamas Dawah Institution in the West Bank: A File of Palestinian Preventive Security Documents Identified the Bethlehem Orphan Care Society as Hamas-Affiliated,* January 2005, http://www.intelligence.org.il/eng/sib/1_05/dawah.htm.

44 *USA v. Mohammed Ali Hasan Al-Moayad,* M-03-0016 Affidavit in Support of Arrest Warrant, U.S. District Court, Eastern District of New York), January 5, 2003. For informant, see Transcript videotaped meeting, January 9, 2003, starting approximately 10:55am, CD: Rm6231, Government Exhibit T-5, *USA v. Mohammed Ali Hasan Al-Moayad et al.* (U.S. District Court, Eastern District of New York), February 2005.

45 French government, "French Position on Hamas," 2004 author's personal files. For documents highlighted by Israeli authorities, see "Israel Accuses French Charity of Helping Hamas," Agence France Press, March 6, 2005. For Canadian Secret Intelligence Service, see CSIS, "Terrorist Group Profiler." Bell, "Hamas May Have Chemical Weapons."

46 C.S.S. Special Information Bulletin, *Interpal, Part I.* For Israeli prohibition of the Union of Good, see C.S.S. Special Information Bulletin, *The Union of Good: An Umbrella Organization Comprised of More than 50 Islamic Charitable Funds and Foundations Worldwide,* February 2005, http://www.intelligence.org.il/eng/sib/2_05/funds.htm.

47 Transcript videotaped meeting, January 9, 2003, starting approximately 10:55am, CD: Rm6231, Government Exhibit T-5, *USA v. Mohammed Ali Hasan Al-Moayad et al.* (U.S. District Court, Eastern District of New York), February 2005.

48 For the Union of Good's fundraiser, see C.S.S. Special Information Bulletin, *An Important Step in the Struggle against the Financing of Terrorism from Europe;* C.S.S. Special Information Bulletin, *The Union of Good.*

49 In a letter to the committee written on Interpal letterhead that outlines funding commitments is the "Supported by Muslim Aid, Union for Good—UK." Similarly, a "Transfer of Funds Advice/Receipt Form" on Interpal letterhead documents the transfer of over 14,000 British pounds to the Ramallah Zakat Committee and lists the donor organization as "Muslim Aid—Union for Good—UK." See C.S.S. Special Information Bulletin, *Interpal, Part II.* For "the blind Sheikh," see Leslie Miller, "Official: Cat Stevens on Watch List Because of Possible Tie to Terrorists," Associated Press, September 22, 2004. For Yusef Islam's denied entrance, see Associated Press, "Cat Stevens Denies Support for Islamic Terrorists," July 14, 2000.

50 For the Union of Good's donations, see C.S.S. Special Information Bulletin, *Interpal, Part I.* For the al-Tadhoman, see C.S.S. Special Information Bulletin, *The Union of Good.*

51 C.S.S. Special Information Bulletin, *The Union of Good.* For al-Zindani, see U.S. Department of the Treasury, Office of Public Affairs, "United States Designates bin Laden Loyalist," February 24, 2004, http://www.treas.gov/press/releases/js1190.htm.

52 For U.S. actions against Salah and QLI, see Paul Salopek, "Saudi Businessman Denies Terrorist Ties," *Chicago Tribune,* October 14, 2001. For charges against Sarsour, see

"Hiding in Plain Sight: College Instructor on Federal List of Suspected Terrorists," *ABC News,* June 5, 2003, http://abcnews.go.com/sections/wnt/US/wnt_watchlist030605 .html; and U.S. Department of Justice, United States Attorney, Eastern District of Wisconsin, "News Summary," January 22, 2003, http://www.usdoj.gov/tax/usaopress/ 2003/pr012203_sarsour_ind.pdf. For Sarsour's sentence in Israeli jail, see Laurie Cohen and Kin Barker, "Target Hamas Fundraising Probe Here Charged in Wisconsin," *Chicago Tribune,* January 7, 2003. For items found on Sarsour during his arrest, see Associated Press, "Wisconsin Man Arrested for Aiding Hamas," December 28, 2002. For Sarsour's brother, see Tom Kertschur, "Charity or Terrorism? Milwaukee Businessman Jailed for Giving Money to Hamas," *Milwaukee Journal Sentinel,* October 28, 2001, http://www.jsonline.com/news/metro/oct01/Hamas29102801a.asp.

53   For Ghosheh see Ahmad Rashad, "The Truth About Hamas," *Middle East Information Center,* June 7, 2003, http://www.middleeastinfo.net/article2822.html. For U.S. designations, see The White House, "Fact Sheet on Shutting Down the Terrorist Financial Network," December 4, 2001, http://www.whitehouse.gov/news/releases/2001/12/200 11204-11.html.

54   For "Hamas Heights," see David Kaplan, "Hamas Heights," *U.S. News and World Report Online,* January 9, 2004, http://www.usnews.com/usnews/issue/040119/whispers/19 whisplead.htm. For Marzook and Mostan, see *USA v. Soliman S. Biheiri,* Case no. 03-365-A, Redacted Sentencing Declaration (U.S. District Court for the Eastern District of Virginia, Alexandria Division), December 10, 2003.

55   *United States of America vs. Bayan Elashi et al.,* CR No. 3:02-CR052-R, Superseding indictment (U.S. District Court for the Northern District of Texas, Dallas Division), December 17, 2002. In the Infocom case, Elashi was convicted of three counts of conspiracy, one count of money laundering, and two counts of making false statements about shipments, and has also been indicted for ties to Hamas leader Mousa Abu Marzook. According to a flow chart presented at the Infocom trial, Ghassan Elashi was in charge of Infocom's business contacts while his brothers handled the company's bank accounts, shipping, Internet operations, and sales. Through Infocom, the brothers illegally sold computer hardware and services to Libya (via Italy and Malta) and Syria. See Government Exhibits 32B, 32C, 32D, and 32E.

56   For the al-Raji family, see Guido Olimpio, "Palestinian Sources—Saudis Increasing Funding to Hamas," FBIS document ID#FTS19970513001208, Milan Corriere della Sera, February 27, 1997. For Zakarna and Nasarallah, see C.S.S. Special Information Bulletin, *The Union of Good.*

57   For Gurule's trip to Europe, see Douglas Farah, "U.S. Pinpoints Top Al-Qaeda Financiers, Treasury Official Heads to Europe to Seek Help in Freezing Backers' Assets," *Washington Post,* October 18, 2002. For Gurule's statement to his European counterparts, see U.S. Department of the Treasury, Office of Public Affairs, *Testimony of Jimmy Gurulé, Under Secretary for Enforcement, U.S. Department of the Treasury, Before the U.S. Senate Judiciary Committee,* November 20, 2002, http://www.ustreas.gov/press/releases/po3635.htm.

58   "Al-Rantisi: University Operation One of 60 Operations That Hamas Has Planned to Carry Out Against Israel," *Al-Sharq Al-Awsat,* August 2, 2002; see also Alia Shukri Hamzeh, "IAF Delivered 'Clear' Message to U.S. on Regional Policy—Mansour," *Jordan Times,* July 26, 2002.

59 For Canadian intelligence report, see CSIS, "Terrorist Group Profiler"; Bell, "Hamas May Have Chemical Weapons." For conclusion by U.S. officials, see Mark S. Steinitz, "Middle East Terrorist Activity in Latin America," *Policy Papers on the Americas* 14, Study 7, Center for Strategic and International Studies, July 2003.

60 Rohan Gunaratna, *Inside Al-Qaeda: Global Network of Terror* (New York: Columbia University Press, 2002), 61. For Spanish investigators, see Central Trial Court No. 5 (Spanish National High Court), CASE 35/2002, Don Baltasar Garzon Real, Magistrado Juez del Juzgado Central de Instrucción, July 19, 2002.

61 Gunaratna, *Inside Al-Qaeda,* 114.

62 For U.S. designation of al-Taqwa, see U.S. Department of the Treasury, Office of Public Affairs, "Statement of John B. Taylor," November 7, 2001, http://www.treas.gov/press/releases/po771.htm. For European intelligence services, see Gunaratna, *Inside Al-Qaeda,* 69; U.S. Treasury Department monies were confirmed in conversations the author held with European intelligence officials in September 2003. See U.S. Department of the Treasury, House Financial Subcommittee Oversight and Investigations, *Testimony of Juan C. Zarate, Deputy Assistant Secretary, Terrorism and Violent Crime,* February 12, 2002; and Lucy Komisar, "Shareholders in the Bank of Terror?" Salon .com, March 15, 2002; and Mark Hosenball, "Terror's Cash Flow," *Newsweek,* March 25, 2002.

63 Simpson, "The U.S. Provides Details of Terror-Financing Web Defunct Investment Firm in New Jersey Is the Hub; Suspect to Stay in Custody," *Wall Street Journal,* September 15, 2003.

64 Money collected for needy Palestinian women and children is not always spent as the donor intends it to be. In the case of the Muslim Woman Society, part of the Islamic Concern Project, "only $5,7750, or about 3 percent of the $178,858 that passed through the account between 1990 and 1995 went to children." Thousands of dollars were also used to pay credit card bills and other personal items. Some of the money even went to salaries for members of Palestinian Islamic Jihad who were working in the United States. See Michael Fechter, "Collected 'Charity' Went Elsewhere, FBI Agent Testifies at al-Arian Trial," September 2, 2005. Regarding documents on charity committees, see index of documents seized by IDF forces in Operation Defensive Shield, April 2003, author's personal files.

65 For Tulkarm charity committee, see Israel Defense Forces, "Documents Captured by the IDF: Large Sums of Money Transferred by Saudi Arabia to the Palestinians Are Used for Financing Terror Organizations (Particularly the Hamas) and Terrorist Activities (Including Suicide Attacks inside Israel)," May 3, 2002, www.idf.il/saudi_arabia/site/english/main_index.stm. For al-Rajhi Banking, see Dore Gold, "Saudi Arabia's Dubious Denials of Involvement in International Terrorism," *Jerusalem Viewpoints* 504, October 1, 2003, http://www.jcpa.org/jl/vp504.htm.

66 For Saudi texts, see Gold, "Saudi Arabia's Dubious Denials." For 1999 Palestinian report, see C.S.S. Special Information Bulletin, *Spotlight on a Hamas Dawah Institution in the West Bank.* For 2002 and WAMY, see Matthew Levitt, "Combating Terrorist Financing, Despite the Saudis," *PolicyWatch* 673, November 1, 2002, http://www.washington institute.org/watch/Policywatch/policywatch2002/673.htm.

67 C.S.S. Special Information Bulletin, *Saudi Money Transfers to the Hamas and to Extremist Groups Identified With It,* http://www.intelligence.org.il/eng/bu/saudi/saudi.htm.

CHAPTER 7 **STATE SUPPORT FOR HAMAS**

1 Ahmad Rashad, "The Truth About Hamas," *Middle East Information Center,* June 7, 2003, http://www.middleeastinfo.net/article2822.html.

2 The CIA description generates little controversy in the developed world. According to British Prime Minister Tony Blair, Iran "certainly does sponsor terrorism. There is no doubt about that at all." See Associated Press, "Blair Says Iran Must Not Hinder Peace in Middle East," February 8, 2005. Palestinian scholar Ziad Abu-Amr concurs, noting that "Iran also provides logistical support to Hamas and military training to its members." See Ziad Abu-Amr, *Islamic Fundamentalism in the West Bank and Gaza: Muslim Brotherhood and Islamic Jihad* (Bloomington: Indiana University Press, 1994), 88; and according to Canadian intelligence, "Hamas has training camps in Iran, Lebanon, and Sudan. Hamas camps in Lebanon are said to be under Iranian supervision." See Canadian Secret Intelligence Service (CSIS), "Terrorist Group Profiler," June 2002, author's personal files. See also Stewart Bell, "Hamas May Have Chemical Weapons: CSIS Report Says Terror Group May Be Experimenting," *National Post,* December 10, 2003.

3 For Israeli estimates, see Israel Foreign Ministry (MFA), "The Financial Sources of the Hamas Terror Organization," July 30, 2003, http://www.israel-mfa.gov.il/mfa/go.asp?MFAH0nmu0. For Canadian Secret Intelligence Service, see CSIS, "Terrorist Group Profiler." See also Bell, "Hamas May Have Chemical Weapons." For Palestinian sources, see Abu-Amr, *Islamic Fundamentalism in the West Bank and Gaza,* 88. See *Diana Campuzano et al. v. The Islamic Republic of Iran* (U.S. District Court, District of Columbia), Civil Action No.: 00-2328 (RMU), January 2003. See Testimony of Patrick Clawson and Reuven Paz in *Susan Weinstein et al. v. The Islamic Republic of Iran et al.* (U.S. District Court, District of Columbia), Civil Action No. 00-2601 (RCL), February 6, 2002. Some estimates are much higher. According to court documents in the case of *Leonard Eisenfeld et al. v. The Islamic Republic of Iran et al.,* "Hamas acknowledges support from Iran in the amount of $15,000,000 per month, funds which support both terrorism and a broad range of welfare activities as part of its program. See *Leonard Eisenfeld et al. v. The Islamic Republic of Iran et al.* (U.S. District Court, District of Columbia), Civil Action No. 98-1945 (RCL), 2000.

4 In this regard, Iran operates much like the financiers of al-Qaeda-affiliated terrorist organizations. For example, "in an effort to solidify the support of key financial backers sponsoring attacks," Musin al-Fadhli, an operative tied to al-Qaeda associate and Iraqi insurgent Abu Musab al-Zarqawi, "requested that tapes be made shoring evidence of successful attacks in Iraq." See U.S. Department of the Treasury, Office of Public Affairs, "Treasury Takes Action to Stem Financing of Iraqi Insurgency," February 15, 2005, http://www.treasury.gov/press/releases/js2252.htm. See *Susan Weinstein et al. v. The Islamic Republic of Iran et al.* (U.S. District Court, District of Columbia), Civil Action No. 00-2601 (RCL), February 6, 2002. For Khamene'i Shallah meeting, see Ali Nouri Zadeh, "Islamic Jihad, Hamas, and the Palestinian Authority Meet in Iran," *al-Sharq al-Awsat,* June 8, 2002. For U.S. officials and Tehran's incentive system, see Douglas Frantz and James Risen, "A Secret Iran-Arafat Connection Is Seen Fueling the Mideast Fire," *New York Times,* March 24, 2002.

5 Zeev Schiff, "Iran and Hezbollah Trying to Undermine Renewed Peace Efforts," *Ha'aretz,* May 12, 2004.

6 Author interview with Israel expert on Hamas, Jerusalem, November 14, 2004.

7 Intelligence and Terrorism Information Center at the Center for Special Studies (C.S.S.), Special Information Paper, *Iran as a State Sponsoring and Operating Terror,* "Chapter 3: Iranian Aid to Palestinian Terror," April 2003, http://www.intelligence.org.il/eng/bu/iran/chapt_c.htm. For Jordanian prime minister's assessment, see author interview with Abdel-Elah Al-Khatib, Amman, Jordan, November 10, 2004. For Fatah official's assessment, see author interview with Hatem Abd al-Qader, East Jerusalem, Israel, November 17, 2004.

8 For May 2000 meeting, see C.S.S. Special Information Paper, *Iran as a State Sponsoring and Operating Terror,* "Chapter 3: Iranian Aid to Palestinian Terror." For Palestinian intelligence document, see C.S.S. Special Information Paper, *Iran and Syria as Strategic Support for Palestinian Terrorism (Based on the Interrogations of Arrested Palestinian Terrorists and Captured Palestinian Authority Documents),* "Appendix D: Translation of Captured Document," August 2002, http://www.intelligence.org.il/eng/bu/aug/aug9.doc. For conclusions by U.S. courts, see *Diana Campuzano et al. v. The Islamic Republic of Iran* (U.S. District Court, District of Columbia), Civil Action No. 00-2328 (RMU), January 2003.

9 For Bush and Abdullah II's meeting on February 1, 2002, see Daniel Sobelman, "Jordan Uncovers Iranian Plan to Initiate Attacks on Israel," *Ha'aretz,* February 5, 2002. For House International Relations Committee hearing, see U.S. House of Representatives, *The President's International Affairs Budget Request for FY 2003: Hearing before the Committee on International Relations, House of Representatives,* 107th Cong., 2nd sess., February 6, 2002, http://commdocs.house.gov/committees/intlrel/hfa77532.000/hfa77532_0f.htm. For Jordanian diplomat's assessment, see author interview with Ali al-Ayed, Jordanian Foreign Ministry, Amman, Jordan, November 10, 2004.

10 For Solana description see, Sharon Sadeh, "EU Says Karine-A Affair Changed Mideast Conflict," *Ha'aretz,* February 7, 2002. A "senior U.S. official" confirmed then–Israeli defense minister Binyamin Ben-Eliezer's contention regarding Mughiyeh's role, see Nora Boustany, "Yugoslavia's Search for Truth," *Washington Post,* February 13, 2002. See also Matthew Lee, "Top Israeli Security Official Calls Palestinian Arms Ship Probe 'Absurd,'" Agence France Presse, January 10, 2002.

11 For U.S. officials' conclusions, see author interviews with U.S. officials, Washington D.C., February 2002. For DIA report, see Bill Gertz, "Intelligence Agency Highlights Threat of Anti-American Terror in Tajikistan," *Washington Times,* December 9, 1997. For 1998 plan, see Paul Quinn-Judge, "Stalking Satan: As Their Leader Offers Friendship, Iran's Revolutionary Guards Keep a Menacing Watch over Their Backyard," *Time,* March 30, 1998.

12 C.S.S. Special Information Paper, *Iran and Syria as Strategic Support for Palestinian Terrorism,* "Appendix D: Translation of Captured Document."

13 For Hezbollah and PFLP-GC maritime smuggling efforts, see ibid. For the Abu Hassan fishing vessel, see Greg Myre, "Israel Says Explosives Expert Was on Fishing Boat It Seized," *New York Times,* May 22, 2003.

14 Transcript of "Suicide Bomber: The Planning of the Bloodiest Suicide Bombing Campaign in Israel's History," *60 Minutes,* CBS, October 5, 1997.

15 For camps directed by Tamazar reported in August 2002, see "Iran Establishes Rocket Training Centers in Lebanon," *Middle East Newsline,* August 8, 2002. For IRGC train-

ing program and "underwater" operations, see Nicholas Blanford, "Report Claims Iran Running Beka'a Training Camp," *Daily Star,* August 13, 2002 (this article also appeared in Arabic in the Beirut daily An Nahar). The Beka'a Valley terrorist training program was apparently the result of a secret meeting in the Tehran suburb of Darjah on June 1, 2002. The meeting occurred just in advance of the previously mentioned two-day conference convened in Tehran (June 1–2) in support of the Palestinian intifada. For IRGC's Qods Force, see Sean O'Neill, "Terror Training 'Run by Hardline Mullahs,'" *Daily Telegraph,* August 12, 2002.

16 Parisa Hafezi, "Iranian Hardliners Register as Suicide Bombers," Reuters, April 21, 2005. For Khomeini sanctions all attacks, see Reuters, "Iran Hard-liners Mark 1983 Attack on U.S. Marines," December 2, 2004.

17 C.S.S. Special Information Bulletin, *Iraqi Support for and Encouragement of Palestinian Terrorism (Part 1),* August 2002, http://www.intelligence.org.il/eng/bu/iraq/iraq_f_a .htm#ES.

18 For July 18, 2002, ceremony, see C.S.S. Special Information Bulletin, *Iraqi Support for and Encouragement of Palestinian Terrorism (Part 1).* For letter addressed to ALF, see C.S.S Special Information Bulletin, *"Charity" and Palestinian Terrorism—Spotlight on the Hamas-Run Islamic Al-Tadhamun "Charitable Society" in Nablus: A Case Study of the Workings of the Palestinian Terrorism Support-System Infrastructure and the Organizations Abroad Which Finance It,* "Appendix H: External sources of funding for Al-Tadhamun's terrorist-supporting apparatus: Transfer of funds from Saddam Hussein's Iraq through the Arab Liberation Front (Jabhat al-Tahrir al-'Arabiyyah) (2001)," February 2005, http://www.intelligence.org.il/eng/sib/3_05/charity_2h.htm.

19 For ALF account, see C.S.S. Special Information Bulletin, *Iraqi Support for and Encouragement of Palestinian Terrorism (Part 1).* For al-Rantissi quote, see "PA Allows Pro-Iraq Rallies," *Middle East Newsline,* January 13, 2003. For Saddam Hussein, see Middle East Media Research Institute (MEMRI), "Palestinian Authority and Iraqi Media on Iraqi Support of the Intifada," *Special Dispatch—Iraq/Jihad and Terrorism Studies,* no. 415, August 28, 2002, http://www.memri.org/bin/opener_latest.cgi? ID=SD41502.

20 For House International Relations Committee hearings, see "Reminder: Saddam Used Oil-for-Food $$ for Suicide Bombers (Chart of Payments)," *The Counterterrorism Blog,* January 24, 2005, http://counterterror.typepad.com/the_counterterrorism_blog. For Ambassador Yaseen, see "Oil-for-Food Money Went to Palestinian Bombers' Families," *Front Page Magazine,* November 18, 2004, http://www.frontpagemag.com/Articles /ReadArticle.asp?ID=16008.

21 U.S. Department of State, Office of the Coordinator for Counterterrorism, "Country Reports on Terrorism—Chapter 6: Terrorist Groups," April 27, 2005, http://www .state.gov/s/ct/rls/45394.htm. For DFLP official, see Issam Hamza, "Syrian Defense Chief Meets PLO Guerrilla Leader," Reuters, May 21, 2001.

22 Zeev Schiff, "Sources Say Syria Pushing Hamas to Renew Attacks," *Ha'aretz,* May 20, 2002.

23 Amos Harel, "Shin Bet Arrests More Than Twenty Hamas Activists," *Canadian Jewish News,* October 4, 2001. For training the recruits received, see Dr. Reuven Ehrlich, "State-Sponsored Terrorism: Terrorism as a Preferred Instrument of Syrian Policy," October 2001, http://www.ci-ce-ct.com/article/showquestion.asp?faq=3&fldAuto=1379.

24 C.S.S. Special Information Paper, *Iran and Syria as Strategic Support for Palestinian Terrorism.*

25 Ibid.

26 Ibid.

27 Ravi Nessman, "Hamas Recruit Says He Was Trained in Syria," Associated Press, March 29, 2005.

28 For 2005 Arab press reports, see "Syria Taxes Employees to Help Insurgents," *Middle East News Line,* January 28, 2005. For Scott McClellan, see "White House Presses Syria to Expel Terror Groups," Agence France Presse, March 2, 2005. For April 2005 and Syria, see Amos Harel, "IDF: Hezbollah Not Pressing Palestinians to Carry out Attacks," *Ha'aretz,* April 6, 2005.

29 U.S. Department of State, "Patterns of Global Terrorism—2003," June 29, 2004. For Hamas website, see HAMASonline, "Sudan says Hamas, Islamic Jihad are freedom fighters," October 24, 2003, http://www.hamasonline.com/index.php?itemid=51.

30 Jerrold M. Post and Ehud Sprinzak, "Terror's Aftermath," *Los Angeles Times,* July 7, 2002. For Salamah and military training, see "Suicide Bomber," *60 Minutes,* CBS.

31 For al-Khalifa's statement, see Agence France Presse, "HAMAS Given Office, Land in Sudan," June 2, 1998. For "al-Aqsa for Media" public relations office in Khartoum, see "Sudan Says Hamas, Islamic Jihad Are Freedom Fighters," *HAMASonline,* October 24, 2003, http://www.hamasonline.org/nucleus/plugins/print/print.php?itemid=51; Associated Press, "Sudan Snubs Powell, Says Hamas, Jihad 'Freedom Fighters,'" October 23, 2003. The former Hamas representative to Khartoum, Jamal Issa, was reassigned to head the group's representation office in Yemen in the fall of 2003. See Reuters, "Hamas Official Denies Group Has Quit Sudan," November 16, 2003.

32 For Treasury Department designation, see Associated Press, "Treasury accuses Islamic relief agency of aiding terrorists," October 13, 2004. For Olajuwon's contributions see Matt Kelley, "AP Exclusive: Former NBA Star's Mosque Donated Money to Alleged Terror Fronts, Records Show," Associated Press, February 10, 2005. For Dhanab, see C.S.S. Special Information Bulletin, *The Union of Good: An Umbrella Organization Comprised of More than 50 Islamic Charitable Funds and Foundations Worldwide,* February 2005, http://www.intelligence.org.il/eng/sib/2_05/img/feb22_05.pdf.

33 For forty-five-day "jihad camps" see Kim Murphy, "Khartoum at Crossroads," *World Report,* July 27, 1993. For Israeli military intelligence report, see C.S.S. Special Information Paper, *Iran and Syria as Strategic Support for Palestinian Terrorism.* Indeed a Canadian intelligence report dated June 2002 confirms that Sudan is one of the countries where Hamas maintains training camps. See CSIS, "Terrorist Group Profiler." See also Bell, "Hamas May Have Chemical Weapons." For Israeli intelligence officials, see author interview with Israeli intelligence official, Herzliya, Israel, November 17, 2004. For statement on Hamas in Jordan, see Roger Gaess, "Interview with Mousa Abu Marzook," *Middle East Policy* 5, no. 2 (1997): 113–128. See also regarding Hamas in Sudan Amos Harel, "Hamas Trains Bomb Experts in Sudan," *Ha'aretz,* September 19, 2002. For conversations with the FBI, see FBI telephone intercept of March 13, 1994, conversation between Abdelhaleem Ashqar, Mohammad Siyam, and Jamil Hamami, marked "Typed Version of Bates 530–543," included in FBI documents included in *U.S. v. Abdel Haleem Ashqar.*

34 For December 21, 2004, attack, see "Saudi Student Carried out Suicide Bombing of US

Base in Mosul: Report," Agence France Press, January 3, 2005. For HRI, see Untitled CIA document, author's personal files; the document is referenced in Glenn Simpson, "Officials Had Information Many Years Before 9/11 Attacks, Report Indicates," *Wall Street Journal,* May 9, 2003. For Mishal-Yassin meeting, see Ghassan Charbel, "The Khaled Mishaal Interview (1)," *Dar al Hayat,* December 5, 2003, http://english.daral hayat.com/Spec/12-2003/Article-20031205-4343f65c-c0a8-01ed-0012-e4cdc62232f8/story.html.

35 U.S. Department of State, "Patterns of Global Terrorism—2000," April 30, 2001. For Tripoli protest, see Agence France Presse, "Thousands Demonstrate in Libya after Is-raeli Killing of Hamas Leader," March 23, 2004.

36 According to the State Department, Libya has been known to use couriers to transport money to terrorist organizations. Usually the transfer would occur in a third country. See U.S. Department of State, "Patterns of Global Terrorism—2000"; *United States v. Abdurham M. Alamoudi* (U.S. District Court Eastern District of Virginia Criminal Complaint), September 30, 2003.

37 *United States v. Abdurham M. Alamoudi* (U.S. District Court Eastern District of Virginia Criminal Complaint), September 30, 2003. See also Associated Press, "Israel Closes Down to [sic] Charitable Groups Over Links to Militants," December 3, 1996.

38 For Marzooks' investment, see Scott Gold, "Quiet End to Muslim Brothers' Trial," *Los Angeles Times,* July 2, 2004. For UASR see Timothy Dwyer and Jerry Markon, "Imam Not Allowed to Attend Va. Meeting," *Washington Post,* March 27, 2004. For Israeli in-telligence officials, see author interview with Israeli intelligence official, Herzliya, Is-rael, November 17, 2004.

39 For U.S. official, see U.S. Department of the Treasury, Office of Public Affairs, *Written Testimony of David D. Aufhauser, General Counsel, Before the House Financial Services Committee Subcommittee on Oversight and Investigations,* September 24, 2003, http://www.treas.gov/press/releases/js758.htm. For Israeli intelligence analysts assessment of Hamas budget coming from the Gulf, see author interview with Israeli intelligence an-alyst, Jerusalem, Israel, June 2002. For 2003 information on Saudi aid to Hamas' dawa, see Israel Ministry of Foreign Affairs (MFA), "The Financial Sources of the Hamas Terror Organization," July 30, 2003, http://www.israel-mfa.gov.il/mfa/go.asp?MFAH0 nmu0.

40 Anthony H. Cordesman and Nawaf Obaid, "Saudi Counter Terrorism Efforts: The Changing Paramilitary and Domestic Security Apparatus," CSIS, May 26, 2005, http://www.csis.org/burke/saudi21/050202_SaudiCounterterrorism.pdf

41 For Palestinian sources, see Abu-Amr, *Islamic Fundamentalism in the West Bank and Gaza,* 88. For Italian press reports sources, see Guido Olimpio, "Palestinian Sources—Saudis Increasing Funding to Hamas," *Milan Corriere della Sera,* February 27, 1997. For U.S. officials and testimony, see U.S. House Committee on Financial Services, *The Hamas Asset Freeze and Other Government Efforts to Stop Terrorist Funding,* September 24, 2003, http://commdocs.house.gov/committees/bank/hba92334.000/hba92334_0 .HTM. For "Accounts 98," see Reuters, "US Berates Europe for Ambiguous Stand on Hamas," November 27, 2002.

42 For Hamas recruits at Mecca during Hajj, see Anna Robinowitz, "Terror at the Hajj," *Washington Institute for Near East Policy,* March 3, 2004. The first of the Hamas cell ar-rested in Galilee in 2003 was Khadir Shalatah, who was recruited and given prelimi-

nary training in Mecca, with plans for further training in Jordan. The second, Amin Hassan, was recruited by the same operative in 2001. The other two members of the cell, Rami Hiadrah and Malek Zuabi, had joined Hamas as students in Jordanian universities and later met with Hamas operatives during the Hajj. See Margot Dudkevitch, "Shin Bet Nabs Israeli-Arab Hamas Cell," *Jerusalem Post*, November 13, 2003. For Rizek arrest, see Arieh O'Sullivan and Edgar Lefkovits, "Hizbullah Member, Other Palestinians Arrested by Security Forces," *Jerusalem Post*, October 8, 2001. For the cousins' arrest, see Dudkevitch, "Three Israeli Arabs Held in Terrorist Plot," *Jerusalem Post*, April 4, 2003.

43 CSIS, "Terrorist Group Profiler." See also Bell, "Hamas May Have Chemical Weapons." For Israeli intelligence analysts, see author interview with Israeli intelligence analyst, Jerusalem, Israel, June 2002.

44 For Orphan Care Society, see C.S.S. Special Information Bulletin, *Spotlight on a Hamas Dawah Institution in the West Bank: A File of Palestinian Preventive Security Documents Identified the Bethlehem Orphan Care Society as Hamas-affiliated*, January 2005, http://www.intelligence.org.il/eng/sib/1_05/dawah.htm. For Abbas and Saudi authorities, see C.S.S. Special Information Bulletin, *Large Sums of Money Transferred by Saudi Arabia to the Palestinians Are Used for Financing Terror Organizations (Particularly the Hamas) and Terrorist Activities (Including Suicide Attacks Inside Israel)*, "Appendix E: Arafat: Where Did the Saudi Aid Money Go? (Transferred to Hamas . . .)," http://www.intelligence.org.il/eng/bu/saudi/sa_mappe.htm.

45 For Palestinian Preventative Security Apparatus, see C.S.S., *Large Sums of Money*, "Appendix E." For the Saudi Committee for the Support of the Al-Aqsa Intifada see C.S.S. Special Information Bulletin, *Interpal, Part I—Synopsis*, "Appendix B," December 2004, http://www.intelligence.org.il/eng/sib/12_04/interpal_app_b.htm. For sworn declaration by chief banking officer, see *Philip Litle et al. v. Arab Bank, PLC* (U.S. District Court, Eastern District of New York), First Amended Complaint, 2005. For the Saudi Committee's website, see Scott Peterson, "Saudis Channel Anger into Charity," *Christian Science Monitor*, May 30, 2002. For the Committee and the Union of Good, see C.S.S. Special Information Bulletin, *"Charity" and Palestinian Terrorism—Spotlight on the Hamas-run Islamic Al-Tadhamun "Charitable Society" in Nablus*, "Appendix G: External Sources of Funding for Al-Tadhamun's Terrorist-Supporting Infrastructure," February 2005, http://www.intelligence.org.il/eng/sib/3_05/charity_2g.htm.

46 C.S.S. Special Information Bulletin, *"Charity" and Palestinian Terrorism*, "Appendix G."

47 For the World Assembly of Muslim Youth, see Matthew Levitt, "Charity Begins in Riyadh," *Weekly Standard*, February 2, 2004, http://www.washingtoninstitute.org/templateC06.php?CID=462. For Bush's statement, see The White House, "President Bush Meets with President Mubarak of Egypt," June 3, 2003, http://www.whitehouse.gov/news/releases/2003/06/20030603-1.html. For al-Jubeir, see Saudi-American Forum, "Adel Al-Jubeir, Advisor to Crown Prince Abdullah Briefing to the Press," June 12, 2003, http://www.saudi-american-forum.org/Library/SAF_Library_26b.htm.

48 Anthony H. Cordesman and Nawaf Obaid, "Saudi Counter Terrorism Efforts: The Changing Paramilitary and Domestic Security Apparatus," CSIS, February 9, 2006.

49 For the Council on Foreign Relations 2004 report, see Council on Foreign Relations, "Update on the Global Campaign Against Terrorist Financing: Second Report of an In-

dependent Task Force on Terrorist Financing Sponsored by the Council on Foreign Relations," June 15, 2004, http://www.cfr.org/pdf/Revised_Terrorist_Financing.pdf. For al-Rahsed, see Abd al-Rahman al-Rashed, "Follow the Money," C.S.S.Special Information Bulletin, *Financing of Terrorism: An (Exceptional) Article Printed in Al-Sharq Al-Awsat, an Arabic Newspaper Published in London (October 20, 2004) Concludes That Funds Donated for Charity Are Used for the Financing of Terrorism and Nurturing of Extremism,* November 2004, http://www.intelligence.org.il/eng/sib/12_04/financing.htm. For former senior U.S. official, see author interview with Dennis Lormell, former chief of the FBI's Terror Financing Operations Section, Washington, D.C., April 27, 2004. For Israeli 2004 report, see C.S.S. Special Information Bulletin, *IRFAN: A Hamas Front Organization Operating in Canada to Enlist Financial Support for Hamas Institutions in the Palestinian Authority-Administered Territories,* November 2004, http://www.intelligence .org.il/eng/sib/11_04/irfan.htm. For FIU, see U.S. Department of the Treasury, Office of Public Affairs, *Testimony of Stuart Levey, Under Secretary Office of Terrorism and Financial Intelligence, U.S. Department of the Treasury, before the House Financial Services Subcommittee on Oversight and Investigations and the House International Relations Subcommittee on International Terrorism and Nonproliferation,* May 4, 2005, http://www .treas.gov/press/releases/js2427.htm.

50 "Bipartisan Coalition of 22 Legislators Push Bill to Sanction Saudis," *U.S. Fed News,* April 25, 2005.

51 Independent Media Reviw Analysis (IMRA), "ISA and Israel Police Arrest Senior Hamas Terrorist," September 27, 2005, http://www.imra.org.il/story.php3?id=27007.

52 For Siyam and Sayid, see Transcript videotaped meeting, January 9, 2003, starting approximately 10:55am, CD: Rm6231, Government Exhibit T-5, *USA v. Mohammed Ali Hasan Al-Moayad et al.* (U.S. District Court, Eastern District of New York), February 2005. For Yemen's position on Hamas, see Al-Jazeera TV, "Yemeni President on Intifadah, Arab Relations, USS Cole, Internal Affairs," *BBC Monitoring Middle East— Political, BBC Worldwide Monitoring,* September 6, 2001. For Salih and Hamas delegation, see Republic of Yemen Radio, "Yemeni president receives Hamas delegation," *BBC Monitoring Middle East—Political BBC Worldwide Monitoring,* May 4, 2002. For Mishal and Salih, see Charbel, "Part 7 of Interview with Khaled Mishaal," *al-Hayat,* December 10, 2003, 15, Foreign Broadcast Information Service, included in evidentiary material presented in *Stanley Boim et al. v. Quranic Literacy Institute et al.* No. 00 C 2905 (Northern District of Illinois, Eastern Division), December 2004.

53 For the Islah party, see *Yemen Observer,* "Yemen: Party Urges Training Fighters to Help Palestinians," *BBC Monitoring Middle East—Political, BBC Worldwide Monitoring,* April 20, 2002. For the party's rallies, see *Yemen Times,* "Yemen: Islah Party Leader Expresses Concern Over Foreign Troops," *BBC Monitoring Middle East—Political, BBC Worldwide Monitoring,* October 8, 2001. For Sheikh Yassin demonstration, see Agence France Presse, "Yemen Denounces Israeli 'State Terrorism,' Students Call for Holy War," March 22, 2004. For April 2002 demonstration, see Yemen Observer, "Yemen: Party Urges Training Fighters to Help Palestinians."

54 For Israeli military intelligence, see C.S.S. Special Information Bulletin, *Iran and Syria as Strategic Support for Palestinian Terrorism.* For press reports citing Yemeni and Western intelligence and al-Ammar's marriage, see John F. Burns, "Yemen Links to bin

Laden Gnaw at F.B.I. in Cole Inquiry," *New York Times,* November 26, 2000. For primer on al-Ammar, see Intelligence Newsletter, "Ali Saleh Mohsen al-Ahmar (Yemen)," *Who's Who?* no. 238, April 7, 1994.

55 Transcript videotaped meeting, January 10, 2003, starting approximately 7:29pm, Government Exhibit T-12, *USA v. Mohammed Ali Hasan Al-Moayad et al.* (U.S. District Court, Eastern District of New York), February 2005.

56 For the January 2005 attack, see Associated Press, "Yemen Ruling Party Office Attacked by Gunmen; 2 Injured," January 13, 2005. For Treasury Department fact sheet, see U.S. Department of the Treasury, Office of Public Affairs, "United States Designates bin Laden Loyalist," February 24, 2004, http://www.treas.gov/press/releases/js1190.htm. For Moayad at the Frankfurt meetings, see Transcript videotaped meeting, January 8, 2003, starting approximately 11am, CD: Rm6231 #2 18-78, Government Exhibit T-4, *USA v. Mohammed Ali Hasan Al-Moayad et al.* (U.S. District Court, Eastern District of New York), February 2005.

57 For three-day rally in 1995, see court transcript of *USA v. Mohammed Ali Hasan Al-Moayad et al.* (U.S. District Court, Eastern District of New York), February 2005, 2228–2230. For the "group wedding," see Kati Cornell Smith, "Groomed for Terror at Sheikh's 'Wedding,'" *New York Post,* February 24, 2005.

58 Transcript of "The Group Wedding Video," included in evidentiary material in *USA v. Mohammed Ali Hasan Al-Moayad et al.* (U.S. District Court, Eastern District of New York), February 2005; a copy of the video is in the author's personal collection.

59 Transcript videotaped meeting, January 9, 2003, starting approximately 10:55am, CD: Rm6231, Government Exhibit T-5, *USA v. Mohammed Ali Hasan Al-Moayad et al.* (U.S. District Court, Eastern District of New York), February 2005.

60 Transcript videotaped meeting, January 9, 2003, starting approximately 10:55am, CD: Rm6231, Government Exhibit T-5, *USA v. Mohammed Ali Hasan Al-Moayad et al.* (U.S. District Court, Eastern District of New York), February 2005.

61 Agence France Presse, "Qatar Offered to Take in Four Deported Hamas Leaders," November 21, 1999.

62 Charbel, "The Khaled Mishaal Interview (1)."

63 For Mishal and security in Qatar, see Charbel, "The Khaled Mishaal Interview (1)." For financial support, see U.S. Department of State, "Patterns of Global Terrorism—2003," April 2004.

64 U.S. Department of State, "Patterns of Global Terrorism—2003." For Canadian intelligence, see CSIS, "Terrorist Group Profiler," June 2002, author's personal files. See also Bell, "Hamas May Have Chemical Weapons"; Nicholas Blanford, "Report Claims Iran Running Bekaa Training Camp," *Beirut Daily Star,* August 13, 2002.

65 For "legal resistance groups" and for Central Bank request, see U.S. Department of State, "Patterns of Global Terrorism—2003." For special investigations commission, see "Sponsoring Terrorism: U.S. Department of State," *Middle East Quarterly* 11, no. 2 (Spring 2004).

66 Dudkevitch, "IDF May Pull Out of Jenin, Nablus by Sunday," *Jerusalem Post,* April 18, 2002; and "I.D.F. Activities in the West Bank Last Night and the Arrest of the Head of Hamas in Ramallah and the Commander of the City's Military Brigade," http://www .idf.il/english/announcements/2002/april/16.stm. For Tawil interrogation, see C.S.S. Special Information Bulletin, *Iran and Syria as Strategic Support for Palestinian Terror-*

ism. For U.S. Department of the Treasury, Office of Public Affairs, "U.S. Designates Five Charities Funding Hamas and Six Senior Hamas Leaders as Terrorist Entities," August 22, 2003, http://www.ustreas.gov/press/releases/js672.htm. For Ein al-Hilweh refugee camp, see "Palestinians in Lebanon Cheer News of Rishon Bombing," *Jerusalem Post,* May 9, 2002. For clashes between Hamas and Fatah supporters, see *Al-Sharq Al-Awsat,* "Tense Situation Between Hamas and Fatah in Lebanon After Fifth Ein al-Hilweh Bombing," August 7, 2002; Jonathan Schanzer, *Al-Qaeda's Armies: The Middle East Affiliate Groups and the Next Generation of Terror* (New York: Specialist Press International and the Washington Institute for Near East Policy, 2004).

67 For Hamdan's statement, see Al-Mustaqbal, "Hamas Official Comments on 'Resistance,' Palestinian Dialogue, Other Issues," *BBC Monitoring Middle East,* October 1, 2004. For Park Hotel bombing statement, see Jason Keyser, "Holiday Bombing Kills 19 Israelis," Associated Press, March 27, 2002. For U.S. government and Hamdan see Department of the Treasury, Office of Public Affairs, "U.S. Designates Five Charities Funding Hamas and Six Senior Hamas Leaders as Terrorist Entities," August 22, 2003, http://www.ustreas.gov/press/releases/js672.htm.

CHAPTER 8 WILL HAMAS TARGET THE WEST?

1 Rantissi threat from "Hamas leader al-Rantisi declares 'battle is open,'" Al-Jazeera TV, March 22, 2004, translated text available in *BBC Monitoring Middle East—Political.* For travel advisory, see U.S. Department of State, "Travel Warning: Israel, the West Bank and Gaza," March 23, 2004. Regarding Rantissi's funeral, see Molly Moore and John Ward Anderson, "Hamas Chief Mourned by Thousands in Gaza," *Washington Post,* April 19, 2004, http://www.washingtonpost.com/wp-dyn/articles/A21798-2004 Apr18.html. For Mishal reaction, see Albert Aji, "Damascus-Based Hamas Leader Blames America for Rantisi's Killing," Associated Press, April 18, 2004.

2 For 2001 Hamas statement, see Gregory Katz, "Hamas Defies Arafat, Pledges More Attacks: Americans Added as Targets as Group Plans to Avenge More Deaths," *Dallas Morning News,* December 18, 2001. For 2002 chat room discussion, see "The Hamas Website Provides a Platform for Surfers Who Support the Murder of American Citizens," *Israel Defense Forces Spokesperson's Unit,* June 26, 2002, www.idf.il/english/announcements/2002/june/forum_hamas.stm.

3 Mishal quote from Khaled Abu Toameh, "Rantisi: Hamas Won't Hit US," *Jerusalem Post,* March 25, 2004. Rantissi and Zahar quotes from Lara Sukhtian, "Hamas Leaders Say Militants Are Not Targeting United States," Associated Press, March 25, 2004.

4 For Rantissi threat, see Associated Press, "New Hamas Chief: Bush Is 'Enemy of God,'" March 28, 2004. Rantissi's retreat statement from Agence France Presse, "Despite Rantissi Pledge Not to Target Americans, US Still Sees Hamas as Threat," March 25, 2004. For comments on space shuttle Columbia and Iraq, see Israel Ministry of Foreign Affairs (MFA), "Press Release Communicated by Israeli Security Sources," April 18, 2004, http://www.mfa.gov.il/MFA/Terrorism+Obstacle+to+Peace/Terror+Groups/ Abdel+Aziz+Rantisi.htm. Regarding Hamas radio station, see Intelligence and Terrorism Information Center at the Center for Special Studies (C.S.S.) Special Information Bulletin, *Incitement on Local Radio Stations: Sawt al-Aqsa, a Hamas Radio Station Operating from the Gaza Strip, Broadcasted a Sermon Calling upon the Terrorist Organizations to Unite in order to Resume the Violent Confrontation with Israel (the Intifada),*

and Lashing Out Against the US and the UK, July 17, 2005, http://www.intelligence
.org.il/eng/sib/7_05/al_quds_b.htm. For pamphlets see C.S.S. Special Information
Bulletin, *Hamas Identifies with and Supports Chechen and International Islamic Terrorism on CDs Found in the Palestinian Authority–Administered Territories,* September
2004, http://www.intelligence.org.il/eng/sib/9_04/chechnya.htm. Protest slogans from
Israel Ministry of Defense, "PA Allows Pro-Iraq Rallies," January 13, 2003.

5 For Rantissi statement, see Albert Aji, "Damascus-Based Hamas Leader Blames Amer-
ica for Rantisi's Killing," Associated Press, April 18, 2004. For Marzook statement, see
Khaled Abu Toameh, "Hamas Urges Israel's Beduins Not to Serve in IDF," *Jerusalem
Post,* December 16, 2004. For Qassam Brigades statement, see Toameh, "Hamas Split
Over Exporting Terror Campaign," *Jerusalem Post,* September 26, 2004.

6 For Nazzal statement, see Agence France Presse, "Hamas Official Denies Decision to
Strike Israel Abroad," September 26, 2004. Regarding Hamas/Islamic Jihad joint man-
ifest, see "Hamas and Islamic Jihad: We Will Continue Suicide Bombings," *Ha'aretz,*
December 17, 2001. Regarding *Time* magazine, see Johanna McGeary, "Radicals on the
Rise: Militant Islamic Group Hamas Enjoys a Boost in Popularity as It Goes about Its
Business of Slaughtering Israelis," *Time,* December 17, 2001. On August 17, 2002, Is-
raeli authorities broke up the Hamas cell responsible for this and other bombings.
Under interrogation, Mohammad Odeh (who placed the bomb at the university and
then detonated it remotely) indicated that his intent was not to target Americans but
to avoid injuring Arabs—a strange assertion given the university's large Israeli Arab
population. See Serge Schmemann, "Hamas Members Held in Recent Bombings," *New
York Times,* August 22, 2002. Regarding U.S. officials' calculations, see author interviews with U.S. officials, Washington, D.C., August 1, 2002.

7 Regarding FBI conclusions, see Eli Lake, "Hamas Agents Lurking in US, FBI Warns.
Fears Rantisi's Vow to Attack May Awaken Operatives Here," *New York Sun,* April 29,
2004. For Hamas statement, see Agence France Presse, "Hamas Threatens 'Strike'
Against US Interests," February 11, 1997.

8 Regarding Akal's emigration to Canada, see "[Corrected] Hamas-Trained Terrorist,
Canadian National, Arrested by ISA," *Independent Media Review Analysis (IMRA),* De-
cember 8, 2003, http://imra.org.il/story.php3?id=19094. See also Stewart Bell, "Envoy
Faces Censure for Hamas Revelation," *National Post,* December 6, 2003.

9 Bell, "Envoy Faces Censure for Hamas Revelation."

10 Regarding Akal's training and tasking by Wahabe, see IMRA, "[Corrected] Hamas-
trained terrorist, Canadian National, arrested by ISA." Regarding Israeli authorities, see
Bell, "Arrest 'Prevented Terror Attack': Rebutting Ottawa's Skepticism, Israel Alleges
Akkal Was Bound for New York to Kill Jews," *National Post* (Canada), December 9,
2003. Israeli Embassy in Ottawa's statement from Jeff Sallot, "Canadian Is Hamas As-
sassin, Israel Says," *Globe and Mail,* December 5, 2003.

11 IMRA, "[Corrected] Hamas-Trained Terrorist, Canadian National, Arrested by ISA."

12 For series of events at Mike's Place on April 30, 2003, see *The Queen v. Parveen Akther
Sharif et al.* (Central Criminal Court), United Kingdom, Amended Opening Note,
April 15, 2004. According to a report commissioned by the Danish Ministry of Justice,
authorities have documented other cases where European converts to Islam went to
Damascus to study—as Hanif and Sharif did—but "were inserted into regular strong-
holds of Hamas and the Muslim Brotherhood." See Michael Taarnby, "Recruitment of

Islamist Terrorists in Europe: Trends and Perspectives," Danish Ministry of Justice, January 14, 2005, http://www.jm.dk/image.asp?page=image&objno=73027. Government lawyers stated to the court in the course of their prosecution of several of the bombers' family members who knew of the pending attacks but did nothing to stop them in *The Queen v. Parveen Akther Sharif et al.* For the bombers' living will, see Ian MacKinnon, "British Suicide Bombers Boast About Killings," *The Times,* March 9, 2004.

13 Regarding the British authorities see *The Queen v. Parveen Akther Sharif et al.* (Central Criminal Court), United Kingdom, Amended Opening Note, April 15, 2004. Hamas' statement from Donald Macintyre, "The Bombers From Britain: Shortly Before Their Suicide Mission, These Men Proclaim on Video: 'It Is an Honour to Kill,'" *The Independent,* March 9, 2004.

14 U.S. Senate Banking Committee, *Testimony of Richard A. Clarke,* October 22, 2003, http://www.senate.gov/~banking/_files/clarke.pdf. For the FBI report, see Federal Bureau of Investigation, "Terrorism in the United States: 30 Years of Terrorism, A Special Retrospective Edition," FBI Publication #0308, Counterterrorism Threat Assessment and Warning Unit, Counterterrorism Division, 1999.

15 Central Intelligence Agency, *Worldwide Threat—Converging Dangers in a Post–9/11 World: Testimony of Director of Central Intelligence George J. Tenet before the Senate Select Committee on Intelligence,* February 6, 2002, www.cia.gov/cia/public_affairs/speeches/dci_speech_02062002.html. For internal FBI review, see Lake, "Hamas Agents Luring in U.S., FBI Warns."

16 Untitled CIA document, author's personal files; the document is referenced in Glenn Simpson, "Officials Had Information Many Years Before 9/11 Attacks, Report Indicates," *Wall Street Journal,* May 9, 2003. Interestingly, in 2002 the Islamic Community in Bosnia and Herzegovina, Office of Rasu-L-Ulama, donated $50,000 to a Hamas charity in the West Bank. See C.S.S. Special Information Bulletin, *The Union of Good: An Umbrella Organization Comprised of More than 50 Islamic Charitable Funds and Foundations Worldwide,* February 2005, http://www.intelligence.org.il/eng/sib/2_05/funds.htm.

17 For the CIA report, see Untitled CIA document, author's personal files; the document is referenced in Simpson, "Officials Had Information Many Years Before 9/11 Attacks, Report Indicates." For subsequent investigations see U.S. Senate Committee on Banking, Housing, and Urban Affairs, Subcommittee on International Trade and Finance, *Testimony of Matthew A. Levitt,* August 1, 2002, http://www.washingtoninstitute.org/media/levitt/levitt080102.htm. U.S. Department of the Treasury, Office of Public Affairs, *Written Testimony of David Aufhauser, Testimony before the Senate Committee on Banking, Housing and Urban Affairs, United States Senate,* September 25, 2003, http://www.treas.gov/press/releases/js760.htm. For U.S. officials' warning, see Brian Murphy and Mike Casey, "Saudi Charity in Tsunami Region Raises Concerns About Spreading Islamic Extremism," Associated Press, February 6, 2005. Regarding the CIA's documentation, see MFA, "The Financial Sources of the Hamas Terror Organization," July 30, 2003, http://www.israel-mfa.gov.il/mfa/go.asp?MFAH0nmu0. For Khalifa and his U.S. fundraising tour, see Rohan Gunaratna, *Inside Al Qaeda: Global Network of Terror* (New York: Columbia University Press, 2002), 114. Regarding Khalifa and relations with IIRO employees in the Philippines, see ibid., 145.

18 For Hamas delegation's participation in 1995 Islamic People's Congress, see Jessica

Stern, *Terror in the Name of God: Why Religious Militants Kill* (New York: Harper Collins, 2003), 253. Regarding the leader of a jihadist organization in Pakistan, see ibid., 211.

19 For Romanian intelligence, see Radu Tudor, "Terrorism in Romania (II)—The Terrorist Organizations Muslim Brothers and Hamas Have Dozens of Members in This Country," *Bucharest Ziua,* February 12, 2002. For Romanian security official quote, see author interview with Romanian security official, Washington, D.C., July 2004.

20 *U.S. v. Marzook et al.* (U.S. District Court, Northern District of Illinois, Eastern Division), Special August 2003 Grand Jury, Second Superseding Indictment unsealed August 2004. Regarding Dahman, see Associated Press, "Spaniard Suspected of Designing Kassam," May 25, 2005.

21 FBI conclusions culled from U.S. Senate, *"Current and Projected National Security Threats to the United States,"* Hearing Before the Select Committee on Intelligence of the United States Senate, February 6, 2002 (see response number 3 to "Questions for the Record" on page 339 of GPO print edition). For FBI summary transcript of the Philadelphia meeting, see "Tape 16—Conference Room, Date 10/2/93," marked page 1459 of evidentiary material presented in *Stanley Boim et al. v. Quranic Literacy Institute et al.* Civil No. 00 C 2905 (U.S. District Court, Northern District of Illinois, Eastern Division).

22 *U.S. v. Marzook et al.* (U.S. District Court, Northern District of Illinois, Eastern Division), Special August 2003 Grand Jury, Second Superseding Indictment unsealed August 2004.

23 John Mintz, "Palestinian-Born Man Deported to Jordan: Technician Accused of Immigration Fraud: Lawyer Fears Torture in Amman," *Washington Post,* January 30, 2001. See also Human Rights Watch, "Chapter VII: Conditions of Detention," in *Presumption of Guilt: Human Rights Abuses of Post–September 11 Detainees,* 14, no. 4, August 2002.

24 U.S. Department of the Treasury, Office of Public Affairs, "Shutting Down the Terrorist Financial Network," December 4, 2001, http://www.treas.gov/press/releases/po841 .htm?IMAGE.X=23\&IMAGE.Y=13.

25 *Joyce and Stanley Boim v. Quranic Literacy Institute and the Holy Land Foundation for Relief and Development* (U.S. Court of Appeals, Northern District of Illinois, Eastern Division), http://caselaw.lp.findlaw.com/scripts/getcase.pl?court=7th&navby=case& no=011969&exact=1.

26 U.S. Department of the Treasury, Office of Public Affairs, "US Designates Five Charities Funding Hamas and Six Senior Hamas Leaders as Terrorist Entities," August 22, 2003, http://www.treas.gov/press/releases/js672.htm.

27 Eric Lichtblau, "5 Tied to Islamic Charity Held; US Said Group Funded Hamas," *New York Times,* July 28, 2004.

28 Ted Bridis, "Senior Hamas Leader, 2 Others Indicted on Racketeering Charges," Associated Press, August 20, 2004.

29 Associated Press, "Mosque Founder Accused of Aiding Hamas Ordered to Leave U.S.," February 8, 2005. H. G. Reza, "Man Tied to Charity Stays in Jail; Buena Park Resident Was a Fundraiser for Holy Land Foundation, the Focus of an FBI Probe," *Los Angeles Times,* December 3, 2004. John M. Broder, "Judge Orders Islamic Fund-Raiser Deported," *New York Times,* February 9, 2005.

30 For public statements by an Israeli official, see IMRA, "[Corrected] Hamas-Trained Terrorist, Canadian National, Arrested by ISA." For Akal's family links to Hamas, see author interview with Israeli official, Tel Aviv, May 13, 2004. For remarks by an Israeli senior intelligence official, see author interview with senior Israeli intelligence official, Tel Aviv, May 16, 2004.

31 Officials conclusions regarding "local initiative" from author interview with group of Israeli analysts, Herzliya, November 17, 2004. For Akal plot and its association to Deif, see author interview with Israeli analysts, Tel Aviv, May 13, 2004. For officials' conclusions regarding unilateral contingency, see author interview with group of Israeli analysts, Tel Aviv, November 16, 2004. In the case of the attack on Mike's Place, the bar attacked by two Muslim Britons, Israeli intelligence experts concluded the suicide bombing was a cooperative "outside-inside" operation, planned and facilitated by operatives outside the West Bank but acting on the "local initiative" and logistical support of operatives in the Gaza Strip where the suicide bombers spent some time prior to their attack; author interview with group of Israeli analysts, Herzliya, November 17, 2004.

32 U.S. Department of State, "Travel Warning, United States Department of State, Bureau of Consular Affairs, Washington, D.C.," November 26, 2004, http://travel.state.gov/travel/Israel_warning.html. For senior Palestinian security official, see James Bennet, "Isolated and Angry, Gaza Battles Itself, Too," *New York Times,* July 16, 2004.

33 For Siyam, see "Subject: Presidential Decree/Sheikh Mouhamad Siam," Report No.: 10/4344-A/95, May 31, 1995, marked pages 0625–0629 of evidentiary material brought in *Stanley Boim et al. v. Quranic Literacy Institute et al.,* Civil No. 00 C 2905 (U.S. District Court, Northern District of Illinois, Eastern Division). For Rantissi's article, see P. David Hornik, "The Other Elections," *American Spectator,* February 1, 2005, http://www.spectator.org/dsp_article.asp?art_id=7709. For Rantissi and the Iraq war, see MFA, "Press Release Communicated by Israeli Security Sources."

34 For plan to seize Japanese embassy, see Samar Assad, "Court: Hamas Plotted to Seize Foreign Embassy in Israel," Associated Press, March 5, 1998. For Dichter, see Agence France Presse, "Israel Says It Foiled Plot to Strike Tourists in Egypt's Sinai," September 19, 2004. For Antwerp, see Agence France Presse, "Antwerp Muslim Leader Under Fire for Hinting at Hamas Attack," April 6, 2004.

35 Israel Defense Forces Spokesperson's Unit, "Diab Shawachi Charged with the Murder of Two International TIPH Inspectors," November 23, 2002.

36 Author interview with senior Israeli security official, Washington, D.C., February 18, 2005.

37 For the mourner at Khalil's funeral, see Associated Press, "Palestinians Bury Hamas Leader in Syria," September 27, 2004. For analyst's conclusions, see author interview with Israeli intelligence analysts, Tel Aviv, November 16, 2004.

38 Author interview with senior Israeli security official, Washington, D.C., February 18, 2005.

39 Author interview with Israeli intelligence analysts, Tel Aviv, November 16, 2004.

40 Author interview with senior Israeli security official, Washington, D.C., February 18, 2005.

41 For Rantissi claim, see Lara Sukhtian, "Suicide Bomber Blows Himself Up on Jerusalem Bus, at Least 20 Dead," Associated Press, August 19, 2003. For Israeli police identi-

fication of bomber, see James Bennet, "Bombing Kills 18 and Hurts Scores On Jerusalem Bus," *New York Times*, August 19, 2003. For videotape of the bomber, see Joel Greenberg, "Blasts Rock Iraq, Israel," *Chicago Tribune*, August 20, 2003.

42 MFA, "Hamas Terrorist Network Based in Jenin Disabled," March 2, 2005, http://www.mfa.gov.il/MFA/Terrorism-+Obstacle+to+Peace/Terrorism+and+Islamic+Fundamentalism-/Hamas%20terrorist%20network%20based%20in%20Jenin%20disabled%202-Mar-2005.

43 For Juma comment, see John Ward Anderson, "7 Arrested in Tel Aviv Bombing," *Washington Post*, February 27, 2005. For Mishal's statement, see Associated Press, "Hamas Leader: Some in Group Won't Sign No-Attack Pledge," February 3, 2004.

44 For State Department description, see U.S. Department of State, Office of the Coordinator for Counterterrorism "Patterns of Global Terrorism—2003: Middle East Overview," April 29, 2004, http://www.state.gov/s/ct/rls/pgtrpt/2003/31638.htm. U.S. Department of State, Office of the Historian, Bureau of Public Affairs, "Significant Terrorist Incidents, 1961–2003: A Brief Chronology," http://www.state.gov/r/pa/ho/pubs/fs/5902.htm. For Haron statement, see "Faction Listens to Arafat Only When He Says What It Wants to Hear," *Sydney Morning Herald*, August 7, 2004. For Israeli report, see IMRA, "Hamas Doublespeak," September 27, 2005.

45 Lake, "Hamas Agents Lurking in U.S., FBI Warns."

46 M. E. Bowman, "Some-Time, Part-Time and One-Time Terrorism," *Intelligencer: Journal of U.S. Intelligence Studies* (Winter/Spring 2003): 13–18.

47 For the "Charter of Honour," see Agence France Presse, "Palestinian Planned to Murder As Many 'Zionists' as Possible," February 25, 1997. For events of the July 1997 arrest, see Dan Barry, "Bombs in Brooklyn, the Overview: Police Break Up Suspected Bomb Plot in Brooklyn," *New York Times*, August 1, 1997. For report and correction on Mezer and Khalil's ties to Hamas, see Richard Pyle, "Source: Suspects in Foiled Attack on NYC Subways Linked to Hamas," Associated Press, August 1, 1997. See also Pyle, "Suspects Tied to Group that Terror-Bombed Jerusalem," Associated Press, August 1, 1997. For note denouncing U.S. support of Israel, see Pyle, "Jury Convicts One Palestinian, Acquits Second in Subway Bomb Plot," Associated Press, July 23, 1998.

48 For Elmerhebi's note, see Gary Dimmock, "Firebombing at Jewish School Linked to Killing of Hamas Chief: Imported Mideast Hatred Hits Montreal School," *Ottawa Citizen*, April 6, 2004. For U.S. law enforcement officials, see U.S. Department of Justice, Office of U.S. Attorney, "Chicago Man Arrested in Alleged Plot to Bomb Dirksen U.S. Courthouse in Chicago," August 5, 2004.

49 U.S. Senate Select Committee on Intelligence, *Testimony of Robert S. Mueller III, Director of the Federal Bureau of Investigation*, February 16, 2005.

50 For the National Security Council memorandum, see Richard A. Clarke, "Memorandum for Condoleezza Rice," January 25, 2001, http://www2.gwu.edu/~nsarchiv/NSAEBB/NSAEBB147/clarke%20memo.pdf. See Matthew Levitt, "Combating Terrorist Financing: Where the War on Terror Intersects the 'Road Map,'" *Jerusalem Issue Brief*, August 14, 2003, http://www.washingtoninstitute.org/templateC06.php?CID=481. For Israeli deportation, see Amos Harel and Baruch Kra, "Israel Deports Palestinian-American Aid Worker for al-Qaeda Links," *Ha'aretz*, December 5, 2002.

51 National Commission on Terrorist Attacks Upon the United States, *The 9/11 Commis-*

sion Report: Final Report of the National Commission on Terrorist Attacks Upon the United States, http://www.9-11commission.gov/report/index.htm.

52 For Goba/ Derwish meeting, see trial transcript of *USA vs. Mohammed Ali Hasan Al-Moayad et al.* (U.S. District Court, Eastern District of New York), February 2005, 2164. For Derwish's arrangements and information on Bouyeri, see Robert S. Leikin, "Europe's Angry Muslims," *Foreign Affairs* (July/August, 2005). For 2005 Iraqi security forces investigation see "5 Held in Baghdad Bombing That Killed 17," *Los Angeles Times,* May 14, 2005.

53 U.S. Senate, *Testimony of Robert S. Mueller, III,* February 16, 2005.

54 Site Institute, "Affidavit in Support of Search Affidavit" (U.S. District Court, Eastern District of Virginia, Alexandria Division), August 20, 2004.

55 Dr. Reuven Ehrlich and Col. (res) Shalom Harrari, "Ties and Links Between Supporters of Bin Laden and Palestinians," November 19, 2001. Israeli indictment of Awqil, author's personal files. See also Reuters, "Israel Charges Palestinian with al Qaeda link," September 8, 2005.

56 Author interview with Israeli analysts, Herzliya, Israel, November 17, 2004.

57 David Makovsky, "The Wrong Lesson from Gaza," *Baltimore Sun,* August 26, 2005.

58 Ahmad Rashad, "Martyr in a Wheelchair? The Life and Death of Sheikh Ahmed Yassin," *Palestine Chronicle,* July 22, 2004, http://www.palestinechronicle.com/.

CHAPTER 9 DISPLACING THE HAMAS DAWA

1 See Martha Crenshaw, "How Terrorism Declines," *Terrorism and Political Violence* 3, 1 (1991).

2 See Jeffrey Ross and Ted Gurr, "Why Terrorism Subsides," *Comparative Politics* 21, 4 (1989).

3 ICG April 2003 report from International Crisis Group, "Islamic Social Welfare Activism in the Occupied Palestinian Territories: A Legitimate Target?" *Middle East Report,* no. 13 (2003), http://www.intl-crisis-group.org/projects/showreport.cfm?reportid =933. For the *Washington Post* column, see Michael Getler, "The Language of Terrorism," *Washington Post,* September 21, 2003. For a rebuttal of this column, see U.S. Senate Committee on Banking, Housing, and Urban Affairs, *Testimony of Matthew Levitt, "Untangling the Terror Web: The Need for a Strategic Understanding of the Crossover Between International Terrorist Groups to Successfully Prosecute the War on Terror,"* October 22, 2003, http://www.washingtoninstitute.org/media/levitt/levitt102203.htm. For the *Boston Globe* column, see Christine Chinlund, "The Ombudsman; Who Should Wear The 'Terrorist' Label?" *Boston Globe,* September 8, 2003.

4 Regarding the NSC's policy coordinating committee on terrorism, see Reuters, "US Berates Europe for Ambiguous Stand on Hamas," November 27, 2002. Zahar quote from "Hamas Leader Defends Military Wing's Plan to Keep Weapons after Israeli Pullout," Al-Jazeera, translated text available in *BBC Monitoring Middle East—Political, BBC Worldwide Monitoring,* August 28, 2005.

5 For the State Department, see U.S. House Committee on Financial Services, *Testimony of E. Anthony Wayne, Assistant Secretary for Economic and Business Affairs, Department of State, "The Hamas Asset Freeze and Other Government Efforts to Stop Terrorist Financing,"* September 24, 2003, http://financialservices.house.gov/media/pdf/092403

eaw.pdf. For the Treasury Department, see U.S. House Financial Services Committee, Subcommittee on Oversight and Investigations, *Testimony of David Aufhauser, General Counsel, United States Department of the Treasury,* September 24, 2003.

6 David Aufhauser quote from Reuters, "US Berates Europe for Ambiguous Stand on Hamas," November 27, 2002. For Bush quote, see The White House, "President Bush, European Leaders Act to Fight Global Terror," June 25, 2003, http://www.whitehouse .gov/news/releases/2003/06/20030625-12.html. Treasury official quote from U.S. House Committee on Financial Services, *Testimony of E. Anthony Wayne, "The Hamas Asset Freeze."*

7 For "widows and orphans rallies," see Adel Zaanoun, "Gazans Protest Freeze on Accounts of Islamic Charities," Agence France Press, November 10, 2003. As noted above, Saudi Arabia openly funded the al-Salah Society, through which Hamas military commander Jamal Tawil laundered money received from Hamas political leaders in Syria and Lebanon and funded Qassam Brigade cells in the West Bank. For reporter quote on al-Salah, see "Hamas Rising from the Ashes," *The Economist,* November 1, 2003. For Hamad attack, see Arnon Regular, "Qureia Government Ponders Future of Freeze on Hamas Charity Funds," *Ha'aretz,* November 23, 2003. Abu Shanab quote from Roger Gaess, "Interview: with Ismail Abu Shanab," *Middle East Policy* 6, no. 1 (1998).

8 European Commission, Directorate-General Justice, Freedom and Security, "Draft Recommendations to Member States Regarding a Code of Conduct for Non-Profit Organizations to Promote Transparency and Accountability Best Practices," July 22, 2005, http://www.europa.eu.int/comm/justice_home/news/consulting_public/code_conduct_ npo/draft_recommendations_en.pdf. Information regarding EU officials culled from author interview with European Union officials, Brussels, Belgium, July 12, 2005.

9 This is particularly true given the rampant corruption of the PA. The same weekend of these pro-Hamas rallies, the BBC ran a story documenting the PA's funding of the al-Aqsa Martyrs Brigades while CBS's *60 Minutes* aired a segment on the personal fortune Arafat has amassed at the expense of the Palestinian people. See "Palestinian Authority Funds Go to Militants," *BBC,* November 7, 2003, http://news.bbc.co.uk/2/hi/ middle_east/3243071.stm; and "Arafat's Billions," *60 Minutes,* CBS, November 9, 2003, http://www.cbsnews.com/stories/2003/11/07/60minutes/main582487.shtml. It is assumed that there is a willingness on the part of the PA to put an end to the rampant corruption for which senior PA officials are infamously renowned, or at least an ability on the part of regulators to engineer sufficient transparency to prevent corruption. It also assumes the PA cease its rampant incitement against Israel. See, for example, Intelligence and Terrorism Information Center at the Center for Special Studies (C.S.S.) Special Information Bulletin, *Expressions of Incitement and Hatred Against Israel in the Palestinian Authority,* August 2003, http://www.intelligence.org.il/eng/bu/sib_au/aug .htm. Unfortunately, even at the height of Israeli-Palestinian security coordination in the mid-1990s, West Bank security chief Jibril Rajoub said, "I don't agree with the Israelis that we should fight Hamas. We will fight the phenomenon of violence," but not Hamas per se. See Jeffrey Goldberg, "From Peace Process to Police Process," *New York Times Magazine,* September 14, 1997. Regarding a third-party international intervention force, see Robert B. Satloff, ed., *International Military Intervention: A Detour on the Road to Israeli-Palestinian Peace* (Washington D.C.: Washington Institute, 2003).

10 The World Bank Group, "West Bank and Gaza Update: World Bank Report on Impact of

Intifada," April–June 2003, http://lnweb18.worldbank.org/mna/mena.nsf/Attachments/
Update+May+2003+English/$File/may+lay-en-Blue03.pdf.

11 Patrick Clawson, "Double or Nothing: The G8's Unhelpful Generosity," *New Republic Online,* July 19, 2005, http://www.washingtoninstitute.org/templateC06.php?CID=849.

12 The World Bank Group, "West Bank and Gaza Update."

13 For USAID pledge, see Associated Press, "Palestinians Refuse Aid Because of Anti-Terrorism Pledge," January 5, 2004. Regarding the NGO Network encouragement to protest, see "Palestinians Reject USAID Policy," *Jerusalem Times,* January 8, 2004; For Asfour, see Palestinian National Authority State Information Services, "Asfour: USAID Extorts Palestinian NGO's Political Reasons," January 14, 2004, http://www.ipc.gov .ps/ipc_e/ipc_e-1/e_News/news2004/2004_01/050.html.

14 See, for example, Matthew Levitt, "*PolicyWatch* Accounting and Accountability: Defining Donor Requirements for Palestinian Reform," Washington Institute for Near East Policy, July 18, 2002, http://www.washingtoninstitute.org/templateC05.php?CID=1516.

15 For $20 million donation, see Glenn Kessler, "U.S. Plans to Provide Direct Aid to Palestinians; Policy Shift Aims to Bolster Abbas and Counter Hamas," *Washington Post,* July 9, 2003. Regarding the prevention of outside auditors into the building see Josh Meyer, "Western Donors Weigh Billions for Palestinians," *Los Angeles Times,* March 1, 2005.

16 Unemployment in the West Bank in the first quarter of 2005 was 22.6 percent while unemployment in the Gaza Strip was 33.8 percent (both figures are according to ILO standards). See World Bank Group, "West Bank and Gaza Update," June 2005, http://siteresources.worldbank.org/INTWESTBANKGAZA/Newspercent20andpercent 20Events/20585353/UpdateJune05-EN.pdf.

17 Israeli intelligence estimates of Hamas' budget from author interview with Israeli intelligence official, January 2004. For U.S. estimates see U.S. House of Representatives, Committee on Financial Services, Subcommittee on Oversight and Investigations, *Testimony of John Pistole, Assistant Director, Counterterrorism, FBI, "The Terrorist Financing Operations Section,"* September 24, 2003, http://www.fbi.gov/congress/congress 03/pistole092403.htm. For June 2005 World Food Programme report and UNDP figures, see World Food Programme, "WFP Executive Board Visit to the Occupied Palestinian Territory: Other Business Agenda Item 14," June 6–10, 2005, http://documents .wfp.org/stellent/groups/public/documents/eb/wfp065855.pdf. For UNRWA's cash budget see UNRWA, "Finances," http://www.un.org/unrwa/finances/index.html. Regarding UNICEF summer camps, see "UNICEF Supports Child-Friendly Summer Camps," June 20, 2004, http://www.unicef.org/media/media_22370.html.

18 For European aid in 2003, see European Commission Technical Assistance Office for the West Bank and Gaza Strip, "Aid to Palestinians in 2003: EU Assistance to Palestinians in 2003," http://www.delwbg.cec.eu.int/en/cooperatio_development/aid2003.htm. European Commission Technical Assistance Office for the West Bank and Gaza Strip, "Aid to the Palestinians in 2004," http://www.delwbg.cec.eu.int/en/cooperatio_development/ aid2004.htm. For European aid in 2004, see European Commission Technical Assistance Office for the West Bank and Gaza Strip, "Aid to the Palestinians in 2004," http://www.delwbg.cec.eu.int/en/cooperatio_development/aid2004.htm. For European aid in 2005, see European Union, "European Commission to Support the Palestinians with €280 Million in 2005," http://europa.eu.int/rapid/pressReleasesAction.do?reference =IP/05/1159&format=HTML&aged=0&language=EN&guiLanguage=en. For bilat-

eral contributions, see European Commission Technical Assistance Office for the West Bank and Gaza Strip, "What We Do and How We Work," http://www.delwbg.cec.eu.int/en/about_us/role.htm. See also "Hamas Faces European aid Threat," *BBC News,* January 29, 2006.

19 Regarding the Palestinian budget, see World Bank, "Twenty-Seven Months—Intifada, Closures and Palestinian Economic Crisis: An Assessment," May 2003, http://lnweb 18.worldbank.org/mna/mena.nsf/Attachments/27+Months+of+Intifada,+Closures/ $File/27+months+Intifada,+Closures . . . An+Assessment.pdf. Regarding U.S. officials and unsupervised handouts, see Patrick Clawson, "The G8's Unhelpful Generosity. Double or Nothing," *New Republic Online,* July 19, 2005. Regarding the 2004 poverty level see World Bank, "World Bank Report: Palestinian Economy Remains Stagnant After Four Years of Intifada," November 22, 2004, http://web.worldbank.org/WBSITE/EXTERNAL/NEWS/0,,contentMDK:20285216~isCURL:Y~menuPK:34463~pagePK:64003015~piPK:64003012~theSitePK:4607,00.html.

20 For UNRWA's reported deficit, see The World Bank, "Twenty-Seven Months." There are important lessons international aid organizations could learn by studying how Hamas gets such tremendous bang for relatively little buck. For example, a study conducted in the late 1990s found that more than 275,000 Palestinians in the West Bank and Gaza Strip receive aid from Islamic social institutions, but that number is believed to have increased substantially since 2001 as a result of the second Intifada. See International Crisis Group, "Islamic Social Welfare Activism in the Occupied Palestinian Territories: A Legitimate Target?" Arafat quote from author interview with Peter Gubser via e-mail, January 2004. Hamas openly boasts of the widespread support it regularly receives among Palestinian UNRWA employees, especially in Gaza. See Roger Gaess, "Interview with Mousa Abu Marzook," *Middle East Policy* 5, no. 2 (1997): 113–128.

21 FBI summary of translated transcripts of Philadelphia meeting, Marked "typed version of Bates 203–287," Entry for 10/2/93, Tape 9—Conference Room, 48, included in evidentiary material brought in deportation hearing for Abdel Haleem Ashqar in *U.S. v. Abdel Haleem Ashqar* (U.S. Immigration Court), Case No. A 75 422 626, 2003.

22 Solana quote from "Solana Urges Hamas to Disarm," *Middle East Online,* July, 12, 2005. Chirac statement from Adar Primor, "Yes, This Friend Is in Need," *Ha'aretz,* July 26, 2005.

23 Regarding Abu Etzev, see Independent Media Review Analysis (IMRA), "ISA and Israel Police Arrest Senior Hamas Terrorist," September 27, 2005, http://www.imra.org.il/story.php3?id=27007. Akel quote from John Ward Anderson, "Palestinians Say Israel Targets Militant Candidates," *Washington Post,* December 12, 2004. Regarding Hamas candidates, see Zvi Barel, "Hamas on a Role," *Ha'aretz,* June 8, 2004.

24 See David Makovsky, "*Peacewatch,* Are All Politics Local? A Look at Palestinian Municipal Election Results," Washington Institute for Near East Policy, December 28, 2004, http://www.washingtoninstitute.org/templateC05.php?CID=2224. Anderson, "Hamas Won Power in West Bank Vote; Local Elections May Prove to Be Harbinger," *Washington Post,* January 6, 2005. For 2006 election results, see Central Elections Commission—Palestine, "The CEC announces the final results of the second PLC elections," January 29, 2006, http://www.elections.ps/template.aspx?id=291.

25 Khaled Abu Toameh, "Hamas PLC Bid: Against Oslo Accords," *Jerusalem Post,* March 20, 2005.

26 C.S.S., *The Hamas Perceived the Dialogue with the Palestinian Authority Which Was*

Held in Egypt as a Means to Tighten its Relations with Egypt and Deepen the PA's Support for Hamas Terrorist Activities, http://www.intelligence.org.il/eng/bu/hamas/hamas.htm.

27 Regarding post–al-Rantissi splits and Sheikh Rian, see Regular, "Leaderless Hamas Squabbles Over Tactics in Gaza," *Ha'aretz,* October 4, 2004; and James Bennet, "The Interregnum," *New York Times Sunday Magazine,* March 13, 2005.

28 Author interview with Israeli expert on Hamas, Jerusalem, November 14, 2004.

29 Ehud Ya'ari, "After the Palestinian Elections," *Jerusalem Issue Brief* 14, no. 15 (2005), http://www.jcpa.org/brief/brief004-15.htm.

30 For Abbas statement, see Regular, "Martyrs' Brigades Call on Abbas to Counter Hamas Inroads," *Ha'aretz,* February 20, 2005. Regarding Kurd, see Scott Wilson, "Israeli Pullout Creates Political Opportunity," *Washington Post,* September 5, 2005.

31 Israel expert quote from Zohar Palti, "*PeaceWatch,* Advancing Palestinian Society by Weakening Hamas," The Washington Institute for Near East Policy, January 21, 2004, http://www.washingtoninstitute.org/templateC05.php?CID=2132. American expert quote from Makovsky, "Gaza: Moving Forward by Pulling Back," *Foreign Affairs* 84, no. 3 (2005).

32 The World Bank trust fund was called The Public Financial Management Reform Trust Fund. See Philip Pullella, "World Bank Offers Trust Fund for Palestinian Aid," Reuters, December 10, 2003. Regarding pledges by Arab countries, see World Bank Group, "Fifteen Months—Intifada. Closures and Palestinian Economic Crisis: An Assessment," http://lnweb18.worldbank.org/mna/mena.nsf/Countries/West+Bank/67FB14AF1F5 4168785256B85003C5F07?OpenDocument.

33 Regarding the IMF report, see *Jewish Virtual Library,* "IMF Report on the Economy in the Palestinian Authority," September 20, 2003, http://www.us-israel.org/jsource/arabs/imfreport.html. Regarding the 2004 PLC session, see Maher Abukhater, "Ranking Officials Implicated in Embezzlement," *Jerusalem Times,* January 8, 2004.

34 European Anti-Fraud Office, OLAF Press Release, "OLAF Investigation Concerning Allegations of Misuse of EU Budgetary Support to the Palestinian Authority," February 5, 2003, http://europa.eu.int/comm/anti_fraud/press_room/pr/2003/2003_03_en. html. Regarding the European Parliament, see Regular, "Donor Support for PA Is Waning," *Ha'aretz,* December 11, 2003. For from Britain's international development minister, see Sharmila Devi and Harvey Morris, "Empty Coffers," *Financial Times,* November 25, 2003.

35 James Sterngold, "Expert Says Palestinians Don't Need Financial Aid," *San Francisco Chronicle,* September 4, 2005.

36 Interview with American scholar, Washington, D.C., April 11, 2005.

37 See Levitt, "Hezbollah: A Case of Global Reach," September 8, 2003; and Levitt, "Hezbollah: Financing Terror through Criminal Enterprise," May 25, 2005.

38 Author interview with Israel intelligence officials, Tel Aviv, November 18, 2004.

39 Craig S. Smith, "Gaza Journal; Warm and Fuzzy TV; Brought to You by Hamas," *New York Times,* January 18, 2006.

40 Chris McGreal, "New-Look Hamas Spends £100,000 on an Image Makeover," *The Guardian,* January 20, 2006.

41 *Palestine-info,* "Mishaal: Hamas Ready to Unite Weapons Under One National Liberation Army," *Daily News,* January 24, 2006.

42 See comments of Ibrahim Madeiras as cited in C.S.S. Special Information Bulletin,

Anti-Israeli Incitement by the Palestinian Authority Since the Election of Abu Mazen, February 8, 2005, http://www.intelligence.org.il/eng/sib/2_05/abu_mazen.htm. For quote from Qassam Brigades leader, see Sahker El Oun, "Palestinian Armed Factions Capitalize on Truce to Regroup," Agence France Presse, March 22, 2005. "Dawn of Victory" from Toameh, "Hamas Divulges Names of Commanders," *Jerusalem Post*, September 3, 2005, http://www.alqassam.ws/fajr-alentisar.htm. Deif statement from Associated Press, "Top Hamas Fugitive Deif Appears in Video," August 27, 2005. Regarding Hamas tactics, see Barel, "Hamas, Inside and Out," *Ha'aretz*, August 26, 2005.

43 Regarding the Philadelphia meeting, see FBI summary of translated transcripts of Philadelphia meeting, Marked "typed version of Bates 203–287," Entry for 10/5/93, 10–11, included in evidentiary material brought in deportation hearing for Abdel Haleem Ashqar. Senior U.S. official quote from Arieh O'Sullivan, "U.S.: Syria Still Enabling Terror Funding," *Jerusalem Post*, February 15, 2005. For Zahar quotes on "playing in all fields" and not changing its covenant, see Reuters, "Hamas Says Will Stick to Resistance, Keep Weapons," January 25, 2006. For quote on entering legislative council, see Anne Barnard, "Hamas Hardens Campaign Rhetoric: Leaders Praise Jihad and Renew Calls to Fight Israel," *Boston Globe*, January 24, 2006. For Blair quote, see "We Will Not Talk to a Terrorist Hamas, Says Blair," *Times Online*, January 23, 2006. For Rice quote, see Reuters, "Rice Says US Has Problems Dealing with Hamas," January 23, 2006.

INDEX